OUR TIME HAS COME

OUR TIME HAS COME

━━━━◦◦◦◦◦━━━━

HOW INDIA IS MAKING ITS PLACE IN THE WORLD

ALYSSA AYRES

A Council on Foreign Relations Book

OXFORD
UNIVERSITY PRESS

OXFORD
UNIVERSITY PRESS

Oxford University Press is a department of the University of Oxford. It furthers
the University's objective of excellence in research, scholarship, and education
by publishing worldwide. Oxford is a registered trade mark of Oxford University
Press in the UK and certain other countries.

Published in the United States of America by Oxford University Press
198 Madison Avenue, New York, NY 10016, United States of America.

CIP data is on file at the Library of Congress
ISBN 978–0–19–049452–0

1 3 5 7 9 8 6 4 2

Printed by Edwards Brothers Malloy, United States of America

The Council on Foreign Relations (CFR) is an independent, nonpartisan membership organization, think tank, and publisher dedicated to being a resource for its members, government officials, business executives, journalists, educators and students, civic and religious leaders, and other interested citizens in order to help them better understand the world and the foreign policy choices facing the United States and other countries. Founded in 1921, CFR carries out its mission by maintaining a diverse membership, with special programs to promote interest and develop expertise in the next generation of foreign policy leaders; convening meetings at its headquarters in New York and in Washington, DC, and other cities where senior government officials, members of Congress, global leaders, and prominent thinkers come together with CFR members to discuss and debate major international issues; supporting a Studies Program that fosters independent research, enabling CFR scholars to produce articles, reports, and books and hold roundtables that analyze foreign policy issues and make concrete policy recommendations; publishing *Foreign Affairs*, the preeminent journal on international affairs and U.S. foreign policy; sponsoring Independent Task Forces that produce reports with both findings and policy prescriptions on the most important foreign policy topics; and providing up-to-date information and analysis about world events and American foreign policy on its website, www.cfr.org.

The Council on Foreign Relations takes no institutional positions on policy issues and has no affiliation with the U.S. government. All views expressed in its publications and on its website are the sole responsibility of the author or authors.

CONTENTS

List of Figures and Tables   ix
Acronyms and Terms   xi

PART ONE: Looking Back
Prologue   3

1. Introduction   11
2. India and the World   37
3. Opening to the World   67

PART TWO: Transition
4. Seeking India's Rightful Place   95
5. A Cautious Power   125

PART THREE: Looking Ahead
6. India's Changing Global Role   163
7. A Changing Economic Future?   183

8. How the United States Should Work with a Rising India   207

Epilogue   243

Acknowledgements   247
Notes   251
Bibliographic Note   289
Bibliography   291
Index   323

LIST OF FIGURES AND TABLES

Figures

3.1 Overseas Trade of India (2300 BC–800 AD)   71
5.1 A trader with mock chains around his wrists and a gag tied around his mouth attends a protest in New Delhi, September 27, 2012   144
7.1 Ambassador cars outside the Ministry of Finance, 2009   184
8.1 What Americans Feel about India   214

Tables

1.1 IMF Staff Estimates: Ten Largest Global Economies, GDP (PPP), 2015 and 2016   12
1.2 India and China Population Growth, 2015 to 2050, in billions   13
1.3 Ten Largest Global Economies, GDP (PPP) Share of World Total, %   29
4.1 H-1B Petitions Approved by Country of Birth (% of all beneficiaries)   115
7.1 Automobile Domestic Sales Trends   197
8.1 Leading Destinations of U.S. Study-Abroad Students, 2014–2015   236
8.2 Enrollments of Selected Foreign Languages in U.S. Higher Education, 2013   237

8.3   Foreign Language and Area Studies Funding, by World Area
      in FY 2015   238
8.4   National Resource Centers Funding by World Area
      in FY 2015   239

ACRONYMS AND TERMS

AAP — Aam Aadmi Party ("Common Man" Party)
AIIB — Asian Infrastructure Investment Bank
APEC — Asia-Pacific Economic Cooperation forum
ASEAN — Association of Southeast Asian Nations
BCCI — Board of Control for Cricket in India
BIMSTEC — Bay of Bengal Initiative for Multisectoral Technical and Economic Cooperation
BJP — Bharatiya Janata Party ("Indian Peoples' Party")
BRICS — Brazil-Russia-India-China-South Africa
CFR — Council on Foreign Relations
CICA — Conference on Interaction and Confidence-Building Measures in Asia
CII — Confederation of Indian Industry
CPI — Communist Party of India
CPI(M) — Communist Party of India (Marxist)
CTA — Central Tibetan Administration
DHS — U.S. Department of Homeland Security
DMK — Dravida Munnetra Kazhagam, a Tamil Nadu-based party

EAS	East Asia Summit
ECI	Election Commission of India
FCRA	Foreign Contribution Regulation Act, 2010
FDI	Foreign Direct Investment
FICCI	Federation of Indian Chambers of Commerce and Industry
FTA	free trade agreement
GATS	General Agreement on Trade in Services
GDP	Gross Domestic Product
GST	Goods and Services Tax
G4	Group of Four (Brazil, Germany, India, and Japan)
G6	Group of Six (France, Germany, Italy, Japan, United Kingdom, United States)
G7	Group of Seven (Canada, France, Germany, Italy, Japan, United Kingdom, United States)
G8	Group of Eight (Canada, France, Germany, Italy, Japan, Russia, United Kingdom, United States)
G20	Group of Twenty (Argentina, Australia, Brazil, Canada, China, France, Germany, India, Indonesia, Italy, Japan, Mexico, Russia, Saudi Arabia, South Africa, South Korea, Turkey, United Kingdom, United States, and the European Union)
HRW	Human Rights Watch
IBEF	India Brand Equity Foundation
IBSA	India, Brazil, and South Africa
ICC	International Cricket Council
ICCR	Indian Council for Cultural Relations
IEA	International Energy Agency
IFES	International Foundation for Electoral Systems
IIIDEM	India International Institute of Democracy and Election Management
ILO	International Labour Organization
IMF	International Monetary Fund
IONS	Indian Ocean Naval Symposium
IORA	Indian Ocean Rim Association
IPL	Indian Premier League
IT	Information Technology

ITECH	Indian Technical and Economic Cooperation Program
LEMOA	Logistics Exchange Memorandum of Agreement
Lok Sabha	India's lower house of parliament, the "house of the people"
NAM	Non-Aligned Movement
NASSCOM	National Association of Software and Services Companies
NATO	North Atlantic Treaty Organization
NDA	National Democratic Alliance
NDB	New Development Bank, the "BRICS Bank"
NETAP	National Employability Through Apprenticeship Program
NGO	nongovernmental organization
NITI Aayog	National Institution for Transforming India Aayog (replaced the Planning Commission)
NSA	National Security Advisor
NSDC	National Skill Development Corporation
NSG	Nuclear Suppliers Group
OECD	Organisation for Economic Co-operation and Development
PPP	Purchasing Power Parity
Rajya Sabha	India's upper house of parliament, the "council of states"
RCEP	Regional Comprehensive Economic Partnership
RSS	Rashtriya Swayamsevak Sangh
SAARC	South Asian Association for Regional Cooperation
SCO	Shanghai Cooperation Organization
TPP	Trans-Pacific Partnership
UN	United Nations
UNCTAD	United Nations Conference on Trade and Development
UNDEF	United Nations Democracy Fund
UNDP	United Nations Development Program
UNHRC	UN Human Rights Council
UPA	United Progressive Alliance
USCIRF	U.S. Commission on International Religious Freedom
WEF	World Economic Forum

OUR TIME HAS COME

PART ONE
Looking Back

Prologue

WHEN I FIRST SET foot in New Delhi for a semester abroad program in September 1990, India seemed very far away, not just in distance but in mind. Crinkly aerograms took two weeks to reach home, and long-distance "trunk calls" needed advance booking. India made the news in America mainly when catastrophe struck—whether the toxic gas leak in Bhopal, Hindu-Muslim riots, or the insurgency in Kashmir. More often than not, American media depicted India as a land of saints and beggars, a place defined by an admixture of faith, deprivation, and no small measure of chaos. Few American companies had stakes in India, as the reforms that ended its economic isolation were yet to begin. Although New Delhi and Washington shared the bedrock values of democracy and pluralism, that never was enough to overcome chronic estrangement from each other. Formally nonaligned, in practice social-ist India tilted heavily toward the undemocratic Soviet Union.

None of those concerns was on my mind when I began my semester abroad, eager to experience one of the world's great civilizations. But nothing prepared me for the crises roiling the country. That September began India's autumn of discontent. The coalition government headed by then Prime Minister V. P. Singh was sinking in a bitter political fight over affirmative action. The prime minister had announced his plan to implement "reservations," or quotas, in government and in public uni-versities for people from historically low-caste backgrounds as a means of righting centuries of discrimination. The social earthquake about to follow would take his government down.

Barely a few weeks after my arrival in Delhi, a student set himself on fire to protest the reservations policy. Others copied him in the days to follow. All told, some seventy students self-immolated against affirmative action. Cities, including the capital, shut down for days to prevent violence from spiraling out of control. My enduring memory of that month will always be images of bodies ablaze—I had never seen this form of protest before, and could not understand it. The student protests created an opening for the Bharatiya Janata Party (BJP) to withdraw its support for the coalition government and launch a movement to build a temple at an historic site it said had been taken from Hindus by Muslims more than four hundred years earlier. By November, the government had collapsed. Another short-lived coalition followed.

I had expected that semester abroad to consist of a lot of classroom as well as experiential learning. I had not adequately appreciated the extent to which history would unfold before me. Here was an India wrestling publicly, and violently, with questions of caste, faith, and history, and how to create more equal opportunities for its citizens. That September was a turning point for India's trajectory on caste and social discrimination, and the reservations policy implemented then remains in place to this day. Meanwhile, the BJP, which began its drive to power with the movement to build a temple to the Hindu god Ram, now leads the national government.

I didn't know it at the time, but my own long passage to India, both personal and professional, had already begun. Against my parents' advice—they worried that my pursuit of India studies would never lead to a job—I returned to spend the following summer in India just as the country found itself amid new turmoil. Former prime minister and Congress party president Rajiv Gandhi had just been assassinated on the campaign trail by a member of the Tamil Tigers, a Sri Lankan terrorist group. After an unexpected leader, P. V. Narasimha Rao, emerged from internal party politicking, Congress formed the next coalition government. In June, Rao was sworn in as prime minister just in time for India's economic crisis. India's currency reserves were dwindling, and in May 1991 the government resorted to airlifting crates of gold bars to Switzerland as collateral for a loan.[1] But the collateral didn't last very long, and by June India was staring at default. Driven in part by International Monetary Fund (IMF) bailout requirements, India— under the new Rao government, with finance minister Dr. Manmohan

Singh at his side—began wide-ranging economic reforms. The Rao government moved to open the economy by devaluing the rupee, ending much of the licensing regime that stifled business, and finally allowing the beginnings of foreign investment in some sectors.

India's 1991 opening to the world would be an historic turning point. The beginning of liberalization would, over the next fifteen years, propel the country's rapid growth and its rise as an international economic force. Notably, these 1991 reforms took place in an atmosphere of crisis, and were done under duress. As important, they remain incomplete.

But the crises of the early 1990s now seem a lifetime ago. The India of more recent years is a vastly different place, and it interacts with the world in very different ways. If the India of the nineties was a place that attracted the spiritually hungry, more adventurous tourists, and committed academics, today it is just as likely to draw investors seeking deals and Fortune 500 CEOs looking to grow their company's bottom line. The pre-liberalization marketplace of deprivation—an academic adviser suggested back in 1990 that I should bring plastic placemats as gifts for people—has become a consumer land of plenty. The nondescript youth hostel I stayed in during the fall of 1990 now houses India's preeminent software industry association, the National Association of Software and Services Companies (NASSCOM), whose members have seen their exports explode from $100 million in 1990 to around $100 billion by 2015.[2] Lured by India's large and growing middle class, major U.S. companies all have an India strategy and some of them have tens of thousands of employees based there. Lately I've been hearing more and more about the new adventurous Americans—some of Indian descent, some not—interested in heading to India to found start-ups. It's another world.

This growing sense of ambition and possibility, an optimism about India's global importance, contrasts sharply with the past. Bitter political fights still unfold, but no one worries these days about chronic government instability as they did in the 1990s. Governments last their full term. And the social change that has accompanied increased urbanization and a communications revolution has shaped the country's dreams for itself and its children. India's two most recent prime ministers have come from backgrounds not of privilege, but of sheer grit: former Prime Minister Manmohan Singh—once Rao's finance minister—studied by candlelight as a child before scholarships to Cambridge and Oxford launched his career as an economist, then he became a trusted political appointee, and eventually made it to the top. And Prime Minister Narendra Modi has traversed a path from hawking tea on rail platforms to state-level leadership and then all the way to the prime minister's office. The message is that drive can take individuals to wherever they want to go, infusing Indians with new visions for what they can do. That same ambition is pushing the country to envision a larger role for itself on the world stage.

India is now on track to become the world's third-largest economy at market exchange rates over the next fifteen years. Using another measure—purchasing power parity (PPP), which accounts for price differences across countries—India became the world's third-largest economy in 2011, surpassing Japan.[3] As annual economic growth soared from 4 to more than 8 percent in the mid-2000s, crossing 10 percent by 2010, more than one hundred sixty million people moved out of abject poverty in the period from 2004-5 to 2011-2, according to World Bank figures.[4] Economic progress has moved India from a minor player on the international stage to a major one. Its politics are covered by the mainstream media in the United States—although not as much as they should be— and major Indian news makes the U.S. headlines. The country's increased visibility has made Indian culture more familiar to Americans, yoga is ubiquitous, and even Bollywood needs no further introduction.

Economic growth has changed individual lives in India, and the rise of new opportunities—as well as resulting social changes—has been well chronicled. India's role as an emerging power and increasingly consequential actor on the world stage has happened in a less obvious and less discussed fashion. In a world of low growth in the developed markets, India's large population and comparatively high economic growth rates have made it a crucial place to be for global companies, likely for decades to come. Within global institutions, as a vocal World Trade Organization (WTO) member, an emerging-market leader in the Group of Twenty (G20), and a critical player in global climate talks, India now plays a greater and more visible leadership role than it did, say, during the days in which the handful of Group of Seven (G7) countries could expect to set the global economic agenda.

But New Delhi continues to chafe at its exclusion from a permanent seat in the UN Security Council, and still feels that the World Bank and International Monetary Fund should better reflect the changing clout and interests of emerging markets. Even while pressing for reform of these twentieth-century global organizations to account for India's rising global voice, New Delhi has asserted at the same time its commitment to new multilateral groupings like the Brazil-Russia-India-China-South Africa (BRICS) cohort and the Shanghai Cooperation Organization (SCO).

It's time to get used to the fact that while India still struggles at home with poverty and a plethora of social issues—and likely will continue to for the forseeable future—it is less and less reticent about its global ambitions. In other words, while many of the internal cleavages that have preoccupied India for decades remain unresolved—in that sense, a status quo—at the same time, the country has embarked upon a larger role for itself internationally. It is India's more confident quest for global prominence that forms the subject of this book.

Former foreign secretary and former Indian ambassador to China and the United States Nirupama Rao described this as a sensibility, a consciousness within India that "India has not got its due on the world stage" despite its size, its democracy, and its accomplishments.[5] Senior politician Baijayant "Jay" Panda, a member of the Biju Janata Dal party and a longtime chair of the India-U.S. Forum of Parliamentarians, added another layer to that description: "I see India as a *re-emerging* great power." In his view, India's previous foreign policy of diffidence is being gradually supplanted, as a result of India's opening to the world, by a larger sense of landscape and responsibility.[6]

That sense of destiny, as the following pages explore, appears focused first and foremost on attaining recognition for India as one among the world's powers. The pursuit of recognition—status—has a corollary desire: larger roles for India in global institutions such as the UN Security Council. While India is not a revisionist power seeking to overturn the global liberal order, New Delhi does seek for the institutions of global governance to accommodate it with greater voice and the heightened status many feel has been unfairly denied. In the arena of trade and global commerce, India's stock has risen quickly, and it would be hard to find a major corporation without deep stakes in India. But the geopolitical world has been slower to adjust.

What New Delhi seeks to do on the world stage as a global power remains a work in progress. India has largely refrained, apart from crises in its own neighborhood, from taking major positions on unfolding peace and security matters that preoccupy the transatlantic diplomatic agenda. But a new focus on attaining primacy in the Indian Ocean, and a declared willingness to serve as a "net provider of regional security," suggests an expanding sense of responsibility for itself in the security sphere, such as providing humanitarian assistance beyond its own citizens in distress, and an emerging new program of security assistance to Indian Ocean countries and Vietnam. India is beginning to position itself in different ways, too, shedding the oppositional stance so characteristic of the Non-Aligned Movement and forging strong partnerships with many Western liberal democracies, the United States included. In recent months, India stood firm on its commitments made under the Paris Agreement, stepping up as a global climate leader just as the United States took a step back. At the same time, its ties with Russia remain deep, and its self-identification as a prominent voice of the global South remains strong.

Despite India's emergence as a top-ten world economy, its self-perception as a developing country remains ineradicable, and its stances in international trade matters reflect this view. As Fareed Zakaria has observed, the world has new powerhouse economies now—China, and now India—which have grown large in the aggregate even while remaining comparatively poor.[7] China's economic heft has given it the throw-weight to push what it wants either through inducements or assertiveness in a growing number of places around the world. India, by contrast, still lacks the deep pockets that have made Beijing a consequential sovereign investor, and it cannot necessarily determine global outcomes on its own. (Although these days, it's harder and harder for any country to single-handedly shape global decisions.) In many contexts, India shies away from or remains ambivalent about pushing its own views, often preferring to remain quiet or offer carefully crafted positions designed not to offend. In this sense, India treads carefully—cautiously—where others might employ a more vocal approach.

That said, while India remains some distance behind China, the days of being seen solely as a careening overcrowded land of poverty are long gone. India's transition includes a self-belief that India's ascent to power on the world stage is deserved, and unfolding now. In a 2015 speech delivered in Kuala Lumpur, Prime Minister Modi conveyed an assuredness about India's moment: "Now, it is India's turn. And we know that our time has come." His conviction about both time and India's place echoed those of his predecessor Manmohan Singh eight years earlier: "I am confident that our time has come. India is all set to regain its due place in the comity of nations."[8]

Despite the hurdles India still has left to clear, India has already become a consequential global actor. As it continues to shed its past diffidence it will realize its ambitions as a global power, likely in its own more cautious way, in the decades to come in a way that was unimaginable twenty-five years back. This book is about that process as Indian citizens make their country's place in the world.

I

Introduction

A FIRM CONSENSUS DOES not yet exist about whether India is a global power. But it is getting there. As longtime diplomat and former Under Secretary of State for Political Affairs Nicholas Burns explained to me, "If you survey 195 countries in the UN system, and you ask, 'What are the countries that have global interests, and have the capacity to act globally?', it's a handful of countries. . . . India by virtue of its geography, its history, and now its strategic interests, is increasingly being taken in a global direction as opposed to just thinking of itself as a regional power."[1] Many Americans do not yet realize the economic and strategic capacity India has already put in place, because it still faces daunting developmental needs, and because India remains on the outside of some of the routine institutions the United States and the West turn towards to manage global interaction. But India is steadily increasing its global involvement, with the ambition to be one among the major global powers.

Over the past decade, India has broken into the ranks of the world's largest economies. Its economic growth has positioned the country favorably in boardrooms, and thereby increased its clout in global capitals. With growing means to invest in its defense, India has embarked on one of the world's largest military modernization efforts, and has declared its ambition to become an Indian Ocean power. Its new national maritime security strategy proclaims the twenty-first century the "Century of the Seas," a "key enabler in [India's] global resurgence."[2] Indian leaders make no bones about their dissatisfaction with institutions of global governance that do not include it, and seek recognition as a global power along with a larger voice in global governance.

As with China, the fate of the Indian economy plays the starring role in its global transformation. Economic and demographic indicators have begun to swing in India's direction. In 1990, prior to India's balance-of-payments crisis and the onset of its major economic reforms in 1991, India was the twelfth-largest economy in the world at market exchange rates, using International Monetary Fund data. By 2010, India had broken into the top ten, at number nine. By 2015, India had reached number seven, surpassing Italy, Brazil, and Canada, and hovering just below the United Kingdom and France (Table 1.1).[3] U.S. government projections place India as the world's third-largest economy at market exchange rates—surpassing Japan—by 2029.[4]

India's economy has come back from a dip during the 2011 to 2014 period, and during 2015 it grew at 7.6 percent, which thanks to China's slowdown that year made India the fastest-growing major economy in the world. For most of 2016, the International Monetary Fund (IMF) projected that India would maintain this growth rate for the year.[5]

TABLE 1.1 International Monetary Fund (IMF) Data: Ten Largest Global Economies, GDP (current prices), 2015 and 2016 data in USD billions

Rank	Country	2015	2016
I	United States	18,037	18,569
2	China	11,226	11,218
3	Japan	4,382	4,939
4	Germany	3,365	3,467*
5	United Kingdom	2,863	2,629
6	France	2,420	2,463
7	India	2,088	2,256
8	Italy	1,825	1,851
9	Brazil*	1,801	1,799
10	Canada	1,553	1,529

Source: IMF World Economic Outlook Database, April 2017. An asterisk indicates an IMF staff projection.

However, the November 2016 demonetization, or the sudden removal from circulation of old 500- and 1000-rupee currency notes, resulted in a drop in India's growth rate, causing the IMF to revise its 2016 forecast to 6.6 percent. (The IMF expects the Indian economy to recover from the temporary demonetization effect, getting back up to 7.7 percent by 2018.)[6] India's National Institution for Transforming India Aayog (NITI Aayog) has charted a path for the country's economy to reach $10 trillion (again, at market exchange rates) by 2032, along with steps required to attain the 10 percent growth rates to get there.[7] While nothing is guaranteed, of course, the idea that a $10 trillion economy was within grasp would have been unimaginable even fifteen years ago.

India has 1.3 billion people, and the United Nations estimates that it will overtake China as the most populous country in the world by 2022 (Table 1.2).[8] India's youthful demographic profile means that it will be the youngest major country in the world by then, with a median age of twenty-eight.[9] The workforce-age population, meaning those between the ages of fifteen and sixty-four, will continue to grow until 2050.[10] This creates what experts call the demographic dividend: a large working-age population supporting relatively few retired people. By contrast, Japan, Western Europe, and even China will be much older countries.

India's middle class has just begun to feel its consumer power, and a variety of estimates put its size at anywhere from 30 million to nearly 270 million today—depending on whether the middle class means a threshold individual income of $10 per day, or Rs. 340,000 annually for an entire household. A 2007 McKinsey report estimated that the middle class, defined as a band with annual disposable household income ranging from $4,380 to $21,890 (in 2000 dollars), could balloon to nearly 600 million by 2025.[11] Whatever the threshold, the Indian

TABLE 1.2 India and China Population Growth, 2015 to 2050, billions

	2015	2020	2025	2030	2035	2040	2045	2050
India	1.311	1.389	1.462	1.528	1.585	1.634	1.674	1.705
China	1.376	1.403	1.415	1.416	1.408	1.395	1.375	1.348

Source: United Nations Department of Economic and Social Affairs, Population Division, *World Population Prospects: The 2015 Revision*.

middle class will expand dramatically in the years to come. This will make India a sought-after market given its size and anticipated growth, especially compared with the low-growth economies throughout much of the developed markets. It's no wonder that brands like Maruti Suzuki, Hero Honda, Samsung, and LG—all targeting middle-class consumers—are growing fast in India. Meanwhile, despite its low per capita income level, India's top three e-commerce platforms do more business now than its top ten retailers offline.[12]

India fields the world's third-largest military, with a force strength of nearly 1.4 million on active duty, and 1.15 million reservists.[13] For 2016–2017, its defense budget was a little over $52 billion, and it plans to spend $100 billion over the next decade on its extensive military modernization.[14] With its more comfortable economic position, India has been the world's largest importer of military equipment for the last five years, and its procurements from American companies have gone from essentially zero to more than $15 billion over the past decade.[15] According to the Stockholm International Peace Research Institute, India became the world's fifth largest military spender in 2016, ahead of France and the United Kingdom. The International Institute for Strategic Studies pegged India's military budget as the sixth largest in the world in 2016, ahead of Japan and France and only slightly behind the United Kingdom. Either way, India is clearly moving up. It has begun a process of defense indigenization so it can develop its own advanced defense technologies.[16]

In some ways India already boasts an advanced technological base. Its space program sent a probe to the moon in 2008, and has another in the works. In 2014, Indian space scientists successfully placed a vehicle in orbit around Mars—at a fraction of the cost of NASA's Mars Rover, and less than the budget for the Hollywood film *Gravity*. When the vehicle entered the Mars orbit, a photograph taken from the Bangalore mission control room showed scientists embracing each other with joy—women, draped in saris with jasmine flowers pinned to their hair. The image went viral globally on social media. As Canadian scientist Catherine Mavriplis tweeted, "When was the last time you saw women scientists celebrate a space mission?"[17]

But many of India's vulnerabilities persist: despite its economic growth over the past two decades, India remains home to the largest number of the world's poor. This is often how the world still stereotypes India, even in the face of its many other accomplishments. A recent World Bank research paper explained the persistence of India as the home of the world's poor against the progress India has made in poverty reduction as one essentially of the country's scale.[18] Growth has lifted some 162 million people out of extreme poverty during 2004–2005 to 2011–2012, from an estimated 430.3 million in 2004 to 268 million in 2011. Still, 21.9 percent of the population, or around 262 million people, continue to live below the World Bank benchmark for extreme poverty of $1.90 per day.[19] With its per capita income of around $1,700, India ranks in the bottom third globally. With such a large and youthful population, India needs to create one million jobs per month to absorb new entrants to the workforce. The country's global successes in information technology (IT) and related services also hid a weakness: a relatively smaller manufacturing sector unable to provide at scale the good entry-level jobs that pulled much of East Asia out of poverty.

Despite over a decade of high-level alarm about India's infrastructure needs, Indian cities still strain at the seams to handle the ever-growing influx of new urbanites. McKinsey put it best: India needs to build the equivalent of "a new Chicago every year" just to accommodate its urban boom.[20] Beyond the cities, many rural areas still lack basic electrical grid connectivity. The grid that exists needs urgent upgrades to prevent another blackout like the one in 2012 that left nearly 700 million in the dark—the largest electrical power failure in history.[21] And despite decades of rural development programs, half of Indian village homes do not have toilets. Still, that's an improvement over the 60 percent of rural homes without toilets as recently as 2012, and reflects the massive toilet-building undertaking launched first by the previous Congress-led government, then given a higher profile brand identity as the "Swachh Bharat" ("Clean India") sanitation initiative promoted by Modi as a personal priority.[22]

On top of this list of concerns, India's famously diverse population still struggles to achieve social inclusion and end discrimination, whether of gender, caste, religion, or even region. In an increasingly prominent puzzle, and a challenge to gross domestic product (GDP) growth, female labor-force participation rates have dropped in the last decade, according to International Labour Organization figures.

From about 37 percent in 2005, the female participation rate dropped to 29 percent in 2010. This puts India at the tail end of 131 countries for which comparative data were compiled. IMF Managing Director Christine Lagarde has publicly urged "urgent remedies" for this unexpected development.[23] (Remedies would bring economic benefits: McKinsey Global Institute has assessed that increasing female labor force participation to parity with the "best-in-region" levels could add as much as $700 billion to India's GDP by the year 2025.)[24]

What's more, rising per capita incomes have not ended caste and religious strife in India. No one worries anymore about "fissiparous tendencies"—a keyword for mid-twentieth-century anxieties about the Indian nation-state holding itself together—but that does not mean protests, occasional violence, and deep divisions have ended. India's big political debate over the role of religion in defining the nation remains: Will it continue to cleave to Nehruvian secularism or will the majority faith, Hinduism, play an ever-larger role in the public sphere? Events during the first half of 2017, such as the appointment of a monk widely described as a "Hindu nationalist firebrand" as chief minister of India's largest state (Uttar Pradesh) following a landslide BJP victory, indicate a more pronounced turn toward religious nationalism from the party's heavy emphasis on economic growth and good governance during the first three years of the Modi government. Indeed, I do not expect this debate to be resolved anytime soon—just as, in the United States, we still struggle with the long-standing fissures of race, gender, class, and region. The social issues that rose to the fore in the 2016 U.S. presidential election serve as a reminder that developed economies have not overcome numerous social divides despite reaching higher income levels.

India also sits within a tough neighborhood. Its historically difficult relationship with Pakistan goes back to the partition of British India in 1947, a territorial division that separated one country formed on the basis of religion (Pakistan and Islam) from another constitutionally committed to secularism (India).[25] Four wars and seventy years later, ties remain fraught. Even as New Delhi has managed to overcome differences on its eastern border with Bangladesh—which, until its 1971 secession, was East Pakistan—relations with Pakistan remain impervious to civilians' efforts to improve them. I use the word "civilians" purposely, for each recent attempt by Indian and Pakistani elected leaders to improve ties has been followed shortly by terrorist attacks on India traced back to groups operating from Pakistan. Pakistan has failed to uphold its most basic obligation to prevent terror, and that is a larger conundrum discussed in later pages. While Pakistan's malignancies cannot curtail India's global ambitions, the chronic threat of terrorism from Pakistan leading to a worst-case scenario of nuclear war, combined with the lost potential for region-wide economic activity, all stand as drags on India's greater potential. I am sympathetic to New Delhi's concerns on this front.

All these limits on India at times seem daunting. Even as India rises on the world stage, it does so while still remaining comparatively poor, aware of its domestic development needs, and with the conflict threat of Pakistan hovering in its side-view mirror. The developed West is unaccustomed to thinking of a place that still has much to overcome as a major global power. This presents, as with the case of China, unique challenges for the world. It also presents challenges for India, as the country pursues its ambitions of a larger global role, while battling its domestic vulnerabilities at the same time.

Dr. C. Raja Mohan, director of Carnegie India, has served twice on India's external National Security Advisory Board. He has been a prolific observer of the development of Indian power, whether from his perch as a journalist or from within Indian think tanks and universities, for decades. During a long discussion over tea in his office, he framed India's rise to become a major power as already underway, pointing first to the size of the Indian economy. Combined with that growing might, Raja Mohan pointed out that India is now among the world's largest defense spenders, "edging past Germany, England, France" and the third-largest armed force in size. In his view:

> If you take the classic indicators of hard power, it's absolutely clear that India's aggregate indicators make it a power. . . . That does not mean we don't have problems of the past, because we are still only a $2,000 per capita economy. So the domestic discourse remains one of a third world developing country, but the aggregate capabilities externally demand that we respond like a major power in the international system.[26]

To put it bluntly, as Raja Mohan did, "We're going to be powerful in an aggregate sense before we are individually rich." I believe he is correct, and anticipate that India will be a major power long before fully overcoming many of its domestic challenges.

"India has begun to get its due on the international stage," said Prime Minister Narendra Modi to a crowd in his new home constituency, Varanasi, in early November 2014.[27] Mr. Modi, the first Indian leader in thirty years to win a single-party majority in national elections, told the gathering that the world's newfound respect for India—countries "looking at us with deference or as an equal"—resulted from the strength of his mandate.

This was not entirely true. Modi's immediate predecessor, the Oxford-trained economist Dr. Manmohan Singh of the Indian National Congress party, was feted around the world for his sober economic stewardship—until his administration sank into corruption scandals in its second term and economic growth collapsed by half. Before Singh, there was the poet-politician Atal Bihari Vajpayee of Modi's own party, the BJP. Vajpayee authorized India's 1998 nuclear tests, ending ambiguity about India's nuclear capabilities. He forced the world to view India in a new light, and his government advanced economic reforms with wide-ranging effect.

But Modi was on to something. While India had indeed integrated itself more tightly with the global economy, and had boosted its visibility in global economic and political forums, domestic turmoil seemed to put India on "pause" during the second term of the Congress-led United Progressive Alliance government (UPA), from 2009 to 2014. India had been on an upward economic growth trajectory, crossing 10 percent in 2010, but as the government's political problems mounted and it lost its earlier momentum, the Indian body politic appeared to turn its energies inward. Difficult domestic quandaries like high-profile corruption cases, a string of shocking gang rapes, and interminable coalition disputes slowed decision making and stoked public anger.

India, the world's largest democracy, is a living laboratory for politics. From its early commitment at independence in 1947 to universal adult franchise—at a low income level, and indeed a low literacy rate at the time—Indian democracy has defied the naysayers, as Brown University political scientist Ashutosh Varshney has observed.[28] Its politics have also become ever-more complex. The difference between American and Indian political gridlock is like the difference between a square drawn on a piece of paper and a Rubik's cube.

Was India always so complicated? Yes, in terms of geographical, linguistic, and religious diversity, but not in terms of national politics. For decades after independence, the Indian National Congress—the party of Mahatma Gandhi and Jawaharlal Nehru that led India to freedom from the British—dominated national politics, and concentrated political and economic power in New Delhi. For many years, Congress also dominated state politics. As late as 1966, nearly two decades after independence, Congress had lost an election in only one major state: Kerala in the south. The party adopted a state-planning-led approach to the economy, and cast itself as the secular umbrella under which India's many religions would flourish. This policy of inclusion was especially important in the years after independence, which freed Indians from the colonial yoke but also created the trauma of Partition. Despite the vivisection of the former British India into Muslim-majority Pakistan and Hindu-majority but secular India, Congress leaders explicitly crafted a national ideology that was ecumenical in nature, designed to refute the idea that religion formed the ineluctable and irradicable basis for a nation-state.

Over the decades, however, local politics and deeper political participation threw up a plethora of new political parties, many of which became increasingly powerful, if not dominant, within their states. Beginning in 1967, the year Congress lost six states in state-level elections, Congress slowly became a less dominant force within the states as newer "single-state" parties, to use scholar John Echeverri-Gent's term, won support by taking up regional and caste-based issues. With a slight lag, Congress dominance also began to shrink at the national level. After the 1984 election, in which Rajiv Gandhi's Congress won a staggering three-fourths majority in parliament, no party achieved even a simple majority until 2014, the year of Modi's election. In practical terms, from 1989 forward, the act of forming a national government required cobbling together complex coalitions, at times including upward of twenty parties.[29]

As the influence of Congress slowly shrank, and single-state parties became more prominent, a new party slowly began to extend its national reach. The Bharatiya Janata Party, or BJP, was founded in 1980 as the new avatar of the Jan Sangh, a Hindu-nationalist party founded after Partition. An increasingly powerful political force, the BJP describes itself as "the party with a difference." One of those differences has been a political structure not reliant on an individual family for leadership, as the Congress party has done. Another of those differences has been a stronger emphasis on shifting India toward economic liberalization, and away from cronyism and corruption. The third, and most socially divisive, has been the party's focus on defining India as culturally Hindu: "It has no doubt about Hindu identity and culture being the mainstay of the Indian nation and of Indian society," as the BJP's own short history puts it.[30]

The BJP is the political party within a "family" of organizations called the Sangh Parivar that all have a relationship of some kind with the Rashtriya Swayamsevak Sangh ("National Volunteers' Association), or RSS. Founded in 1925, the RSS has a mission to "bring to life the all-round glory and greatness of our Hindu Rashtra [nation]," and believes that India "must stand before the world as a self-confident, resurgent, and mighty nation," as its website explains. The nationalism of the RSS explicitly prioritizes Hinduism. At three points in Indian history—after the 1948 assassination of Mahatma Gandhi, during Indira Gandhi's 1975 to 1977 suspension of democracy, and after the 1992 destruction of the Babri mosque in Ayodhya (the sixteenth-century mosque believed to have been built on the site of the Hindu god Ram's birthplace)—the RSS was banned due to concerns about its role spurring religious violence.

The RSS and the BJP believe that under the guise of secularism the Congress party has for decades created policies to appease religious minorities, policies that have not treated all Indians as equal citizens, and worse, have subordinated the Hindu majority's interests. During the rise of the BJP to national prominence in the 1990s, the party's language and attention focused on emotional religious issues such as building the temple to Lord Ram in Ayodhya. That focus receded during the 2014 national election campaign, in which an emphasis on economic growth, good governance, and anti-corruption became calling cards for the party, broadening its appeal to people who prioritized economic reform and governance. At the time of this writing, and as noted above, the BJP appears to be tilting back toward a more overt focus on religion, with concerns such as cow protection and the Ram temple at Ayodhya once more rising to the fore.

Modi, the party's charismatic and overwhelmingly popular prime minister, remains a controversial figure for some Indians. In 2002, shortly after he became chief minister of the western state of Gujarat, Hindu-Muslim riots in the state claimed about one thousand lives, the majority of them Muslim. While a member of Modi's state-level cabinet was convicted for her role in the riots, legal proceedings concerning Modi's responsibility stretched out over more than a decade, finally ending in December 2013 due to insufficient evidence. Modi had also thrown himself into economic development initiatives over the years—over time, peace had returned to the state—and became known as a particularly able administrator for his ability to attract investment with business-friendly policies and a corruption-free environment.

But religious tensions have not disappeared, and they remain among the country's major social cleavages. In 2012, doctored photos of allegedly anti-Muslim violence circulated via text messages abetted conflict between Muslims and an ethnic group from India's northeast, leading to an exodus of some three hundred thousand northeasterners from Indian cities. Hindu-Muslim riots in Uttar Pradesh during 2013 killed fifty and displaced forty thousand people. I cite these cases to illustrate that religious conflict has taken place in states led by parties other than the BJP.

Following the election of the Modi government, concerns about religious intolerance began to preoccupy the Indian press in late 2014. During 2015, the provocations of Hindu extremists led to some alarming instances of mob violence in the name of religion, most frighteningly, attacks on Muslims for the mere suspicion of cow smuggling or cow slaughter—a great sin for those who see the cow as a sacred being. (In perhaps the most tragic of several cases, a mob beat a man to death in Uttar Pradesh.) The emergence of small groups of thuggish vigilantes beating non-Muslim low-caste workers who handled cow carcasses marked another ugly turn during 2016. During 2017, more active "cow protection" vigilante groups responsible for violent attacks and even murders in some Indian states appeared to escalate their activities. These actions have increased religious tensions.

Although Modi was quick to publicly disavow anti-Muslim comments from more extremist supporters during the 2014 national election, as prime minister he has been accused of waiting too long to speak out publicly against this violence, hesitant to alienate a large support base. Indian media and the political opposition have pursued these issues vigorously. While religious conflict is unlikely to end in India, the institutions of democracy, the press, the judiciary, and of course India's constitution all act as checks and balances within the Indian system.

Religion is arguably the most important fissure within India, and one that will continue to play out as a central point of contention for the coming years. Many in India who worry about the effects of majoritarianism have voiced concerns about whether a single-party majority rule by the BJP, which emphasizes India's Hindu rather than syncretic civilizational past, will spell the end of the country's secular liberalism. These are serious questions of national identity, and they will not all disappear overnight. But India's domestic challenges do not necessarily constrain the country from carving out a larger role for itself globally. Some challenges have a much more direct effect on India's interaction with the world than others. For this reason, the pages contained here focus on the domestic matters that weigh most heavily on how the country acts internationally.

India's democracy acts as the constant national check. In India, little advantage accrues to political incumbents—in fact, analysts routinely discuss the "anti-incumbency factor" shaping Indian voting behavior. From its onetime national dominance, Congress has become a much smaller party on the national stage, and over the past two decades, the BJP has become India's second major national party, forming one of two political cores around which national coalition governments form. The BJP and the Congress both have the ability to win elections at the state level in many states, but the powerful hold of single-state parties like those in Andhra, Bihar, Jammu and Kashmir, Maharashtra, Orissa, Punjab, Tamil Nadu, and Telengana ensures that both national parties must work with single-state parties in order to accomplish their national as well as state-level agendas. Between them the two major national parties on their own currently control just fifteen of thirty-one states and union territories. The BJP has extended its national reach across India, and by March 2017 held power on its own in ten states and with coalition allies could count on another seven. It shows how India's national parties need to work with regional parties, and there are many. The Election Commission of India recognizes seven national parties, a bountiful fifty-three state parties, and, in the world of India's unrecognized but registered parties, more than 1,700 separate parties.[31]

As if the political landscape wasn't blessed with enough actors, India is home to a very activist judiciary—complete with a special provision that allows nearly any citizen to file lawsuits in the public interest regardless of the filer's direct standing on the subject. India's judiciary has become active over the past twenty years as an environmental steward, for example, ordering vehicle conversions to natural gas, halting mining activity, and proscribing cricket in the state of Maharashtra due to a drought. In recent years, the politically nonpartisan judiciary has issued orders focused on morality and social order, such as a command to stand for the national anthem in movie theaters, and a prohibition on alcohol served within 500 meters of highways. As might be expected, a new conversation has begun in India about judicial overreach.

More recently, activists and journalists have expressed concerns about the shrinking space for freedom of expression and civil society in a more nationalistic India. Traditionally, India's vigorous press has thrived, playing a vocal oversight role, and has increasingly held governments, business, the police, and individual wrongdoers to account. An active, organized civil society speaks out to register dissent, and the media amplifies the debates.

With this level of complexity, it's no wonder that India often finds it difficult to advance contentious economic reforms or make a major strategic policy shift. Governments have to constantly juggle the demands of so many different parties, not to mention the threat of public interest litigation and the ever-watchful eye of the inquisitive press. Compared to the 1990s, when a big policy change like implementing affirmative action reservations for subordinate castes could literally bring down the government, things are a lot less volatile, but the absence of volatility has not meant smooth or easy governance.

This explains why when Modi told the Varanasi crowd that the last three decades in India threw up "fractured verdicts," he linked it to the country's profile in the world. Or as he put it, "The political instability that ensued was reflected in the world's attitude towards India." He continued: "Today, whenever the leader of a foreign country meets Modi he does not see only Modi the PM. He sees the huge support of 1.25 billion countrymen that helped me reach where I am."

Well, that was 2014. Three years into the Modi government, it had become clear that even a simple majority in India's lower house of parliament—without a majority in the indirectly elected upper house—would not be enough to push through some long-standing "second generation" reform issues requiring legislation. Tough reforms like those on India's restrictive labor laws and overly complex land acquisition laws kept falling prey to parliamentary gridlock. As in any multiparty, pluralist democracy, many competing opinions about how best to fulfill the nation's needs jostle for attention. Sometimes opposition parties choose to obstruct legislation simply because they do not want the government to succeed. To that end, the long-awaited passage in August 2016 of India's goods and services tax (GST), requiring a constitutional amendment, marked an important step in structural reform.

First mooted by the Congress-led UPA government—as an idea in 2005, then as a bill in 2011—the GST bill failed to pass and lapsed with the conclusion of the lower house of parliament in mid-2014. The new BJP-led government introduced its version of a GST bill in December 2014, six months into its new government, and was unable to secure sufficient support for it until the summer of 2016. After nearly two years of efforts to shepherd the amendment to passage, it finally received a unanimous vote of approval in both of India's houses of parliament, and was approved by the required 50 percent of Indian state-level assemblies in under one month. The GST amendment showed that significant reforms can move, including with the higher parliamentary threshold required for a constitutional amendment. But the GST's tough incubation period also reflected the painstaking political work the government undertook to convince all parties across the entire country to vote for it.

Colloquially called the "democracy tax," India's politics preclude the country from acting as quickly as an authoritarian state like China.[32] It all goes to show that India's democracy—even without a coalition government—creates a condition of caution when it comes to change. But I have not met a single person in India who would trade the country's often shambolic politics for a faster-moving authoritarian system.

INDIA'S AMBITIONS

Looking back at two early American analyses of Indian thinking on its place in the world—Stephen P. Cohen and Richard Park's 1978 volume, *India: Emergent Power?*, and George Tanham's essay "Indian Strategic Thought" from 1992—it is remarkable to see the continuity in some of India's ambitions. Cohen and Park remarked upon the gap between studies of world politics that viewed India as a "middle power" compared with India's self-regard: "Criticism from outsiders has not deflected India from its recognition of itself as a major nation that has achieved great power status."[33] Tanham noted that India sought to: "Approach world-power status by developing nuclear and missile capabilities, a blue-water navy, and a military-industrial complex, all obvious characteristics of the superpowers; yet recognition as a great world nation (rather than as a superpower) was the paramount goal."[34] Then, as now, the desire for *recognition* and an elevation in its global rank—status—has played a powerful role in Indian ambitions. But as important, attention to economic growth as the foundation for building national capabilities has become a cornerstone of contemporary Indian goals.

Tanham's observation about the desire for recognition as a great world nation bears further comment. To be clear, India's goal does not appear to be a rise to power to supplant others, but rather, and specifically, to at last be one among many in a world order explicitly seen as multipolar. The multipolar view is so ingrained as to require little comment within India, and spans the strategic thinking of both major parties. In this view, India should take "its rightful place in the comity of nations," as former Prime Minister Manmohan Singh put it in a favored phrase when defending the U.S.-India nuclear deal before a raucous Indian parliament during a July 2008 confidence vote.[35] The desire to grow its economy, industrialize further, gain space to develop its defenses, protect its territory and its citizens, and in tandem carve out formal membership and leadership in the most important global institutions—the ability to shape the global order—mark India's long-standing strategic aims.

In the early 2000s, when India's IT industry was growing rapidly and the country's middle class was poised for a boom, Goldman Sachs published its "Dreaming with BRICs" report. Suddenly, global interest in India perked up. The Bush administration placed a high priority on expanding ties with India, and indeed in helping India rise as a global power. This period of heady optimism appeared to crystallize in the 2008 passage of a civil-nuclear agreement between India and the United States. The agreement, which freed India from sanctions imposed after it tested nuclear weapons in 1974 and 1998, seemed to portend a trans-formative, even decisive, moment for India on the world stage.

The global financial crisis of 2008 raised the G20's profile as a more relevant consultative mechanism than the narrower Group of Eight (G8). Prime Minister Manmohan Singh's prominent participation in G20 deliberations—he was one of the few trained economists among his peers—moved India toward the center of global discussions. But as the Singh government slid toward policy paralysis and unpopularity, a new and more cautious conversation about India's own ambitions in the world began to form, almost as if to clip ideas of global power that had ridden the coattails of faster economic growth. India's domes-tic needs and the country's inward focus in many ways kept it from meeting its own goals on the world stage. Veteran political journalist Shekhar Gupta put it this way: "India overestimates its stature in the world . . . and yet ends up under-delivering."[36]

There is now, in India, a very active analytical as well as prescrip-tive discussion about what India's ambitions in the world should be. These conversations span academia to politics to media. In the mid-2000s, scholar Sunil Khilnani proposed that India could be described as a "bridging power," linking the developed and developing world. Others began to ask questions about the nature of India's global role.[37] Former foreign secretary and former prime ministerial special envoy Shyam Saran wrote that India's hesitance to take positions on conten-tious global issues was the result of its relative external power having outstripped its internal well-being, leading to a situation of being a "premature power."[38]

One of India's most esteemed historians, Ramachandra Guha, explicitly challenged the notion that India was on a path toward becoming a superpower, and argued bracingly that India would not head in that direction, and moreover *should* not.[39] Guha listed seven domestic vulnerabilities facing India, including rising inequality, Hindu majoritarianism, and environmental degradation. He argued that India ought not to compare its position with others in the world, but rather measure itself against its own ideals, the norms of India's unique founding ideology of inclusivity for all.[40]

Two scholars of India based outside the country, Amitabh Mattoo, at the time in Australia, and Deepa Ollapally in the United States, came to separate but similar conclusions about India's path to power. Mattoo saw in India's rise a trajectory toward becoming a superpower, but one marked with an "awkwardness" due to the country's deprivations, and even a reluctance with which it approached its rise.[41] Ollapally similarly identified an inherent ambivalence about power itself, linked to the complexities of India's own identity as a state.[42]

Almost echoing this sentiment at the Munich Security Conference in 2013, the then national security advisor Shivshankar Menon, who served previously as India's foreign secretary and ambassador to China, referred to India's ambitions as "modest" and domestically focused.[43] When I went to visit him in his Delhi home, after his time as NSA, he expanded further on his concerns about the question of India's rising power. He noted that public attention had not yet tackled the issue of what type of power India would become; the debate had revolved around, "When are we going to be a superpower? Why are we not a superpower? Why isn't the world recognizing us as a superpower?" instead of the path down which Indian power should head.[44]

Congress party member Jairam Ramesh—a four-time former minister (commerce, power, environment, and rural development) and longtime economic strategist within the party—had a reflective take on Indian ambitions for its rise and its expectations from the world:

Indian global policy still is predicated on the belief that India has rights, and no responsibilities. That the world owes us something because of our size, because of our market, because of our history, because of our obvious talent. . . . That as a rising global power we are not yet used to the fact that the world will demand certain patterns of behavior on our part which is in tune with the new position that we occupy.[45]

At the other end of the political spectrum, leading conservative writer Swapan Dasgupta, recently inducted after a lifetime in letters into the Rajya Sabha (India's upper house of parliament), told me over coffee in his study that the "desire to play a bigger role globally is now a bipartisan consensus." His concern, however, lies in the lack of planning to connect that desire, that sense of "providence, India's manifest destiny" as he put it, with the policy steps necessary to take the country to global power.[46] But the ambition, in his view, was already an accepted fact.

I also paid a visit to someone uniquely and deeply involved with BJP and RSS thinking, Ram Madhav—a general secretary of the BJP, former spokesman of and lifelong worker in the RSS—to get his sense of what the party envisioned for India's role in the world:

> The party and the government see the rise of India in this century as inevitable in a way. . . . But when I say that it's an ambition to rise as a global power, I'm not talking about in the sense of any military power, any hegemonic power, anything like that. I'm essentially talking about India rising as a strong economic and democratic country in the world. In that sense India has all the right credentials.[47]

The domestic challenges India faces will not be overcome overnight, and it has many, spanning the entire range from infrastructure and economic reform to education, skills training and job creation, to managing the country's great diversity, all the way to a stronger defense and national security capacity. But despite the ups and downs of recent years, India has done comparatively well for itself and for its citizens, and that has helped boost its relative prospects at a time of great turmoil in the world.

The slowdown of China's growth—albeit at a much higher level of per capita income than India's—has sent ripples throughout the deeply interconnected global economy. The Asian Development Bank forecasts slowing growth for China, dropping from 6.7 percent in 2016 to 6.5 percent in 2017 and down to 6.2 percent in 2018.[48] Problems in Brazil have caused its economy to shrink, as has Russia's, increasing India's relative weight as a result. India is not hitting its desired growth targets, but it is growing fast and it is increasing its share of global GDP quickly compared with other economies.

Looking at the comparative IMF data over the decades illustrates precisely what this means. In PPP terms, India accounted for a little more than 3 percent of the world's GDP in 1985. India's rising share illustrates the global pattern of emerging markets becoming an increasingly larger part of the world economy as they grow. By 2015, India's share had more than doubled to 7 percent (Table 1.3).

If the economy continues to grow fast, as IMF projections indicate, India will hasten its emergence as a central global economic force. IMF staff estimates for future economic growth suggest that the Indian economy has a good chance of growing to become 8.4 percent of global GDP by 2020. India will still lag China and the United States, although not by as much. But the opportunity for further economic

TABLE 1.3 Ten Largest Global Economies, GDP (PPP) Share of World Total (%)

2015 rank	Country	1985	1990	1995	2000	2005	2010	2015*	2020*
1	China	3.4	4.1	5.9	7.4	9.8	13.9	17.1	19.6
2	United States	22.6	22.0	20.1	20.6	19.3	16.8	15.7	14.7
3	India	3.3	3.6	3.7	4.2	4.8	6.0	7.0	8.4
4	Japan	8.5	8.9	7.8	6.8	6.0	5.0	4.5	3.9
5	Germany	6.2	6.0	5.3	4.9	4.1	3.7	3.4	3.1
6	Russia	n/a	n/a	3.6	3.3	3.7	3.6	3.3	2.9
7	Indonesia	1.6	1.9	2.2	1.9	2.0	2.2	2.5	2.7
8	Brazil	4.0	3.7	3.4	3.2	3.0	3.1	2.8	2.4
9	United Kingdom	3.8	3.7	3.2	3.1	3.0	2.5	2.4	2.2
10	France	4.2	4.1	3.5	3.4	3.0	2.6	2.3	2.1

*IMF staff estimates; author rounded to one decimal point.
Source: International Monetary Fund World Economic Outlook Database, April 2017.

growth in India's future is perhaps unique in the world: in the words of the Council on Foreign Relations Independent Task Force Report, for which I was honored to serve as project director, "it has the potential over the next two to three decades to follow China on the path to becoming another $10 trillion economy."[49] No other country in the world presents similar potential scale.

Looking comparatively, India's share of global GDP (PPP) now resembles that of Japan of 1995 or China of 2000, and the rate of growth relative to other countries affects India's contribution to global growth. As India's *Economic Survey 2015–2016* details, the country's contribution to global growth ticked up from an average 8.3 percent during 2000–2007, to 14.4 percent in 2014. At a time of slowing growth around the world, especially in larger developed economies, India's contribution to global growth exceeded that of the United States, a much larger economy, during 2013 and 2014.[50] This plays out in India's attractiveness as a global business destination: In June 2016, a survey of global CEOs conducted by the consultancy KPMG found that India had moved up five notches to become the number one country where CEOs envisioned the greatest growth opportunities over the next three years.[51] Add to that the strategic capacity India is slowly putting into place through its military modernization, and the outcome of a more powerful Indian nation long before its citizens are individually rich appears an apt description. India will have challenges at home, even as it becomes much more important to the world at the same time.

OUR TIME HAS COME

India's recent heated debate over how far its national ambitions should reach coincided with the country's economic upswing followed by its inward turn during 2009 to 2014, the UPA's second term. It was as if the early 2000 speculations about India's rise gave way to an intellectual correction, a sensibility that some felt too much was left undone on the national domestic agenda to shift gears to a more active international strategy. But interestingly, decades ago when the Indian economy faced far greater challenges, Indian leaders held ambitions for their country to play a major international role—as a global mediator, as a model of democratic virtue, and as a beacon of independence against world superpower dominance.

In the first flush of independence, Nehru confidently wrote to the chief ministers of India's states in 1951, "In spite of our desire to remain aloof of international entanglements, a certain leadership is thrust upon India in pursuing the policy we have adopted which has a large appeal to considerable numbers of people abroad, more especially in Asia."[52]

In fact, as the doyen of South Asian studies in the United States Stephen P. Cohen wrote back in 1978, refuting American stereotypes of Indian ambitions: "It may come as a surprise . . . to realize that military defense, aspirations for regional and global influence, leadership in the building of a new international economic order, and the gradual curtailment of superpower dominance over world affairs have been central policies of the Government of India since its founding in 1947."[53] Prime Minister Vajpayee told parliament, following the nuclear tests of 1998, that the country should "work together toward our shared objective in ensuring that as we move toward a new millennium, India will take its rightful place in the international community."[54]

And even though its second term led to a slump, the UPA government, to its credit, sought to enhance India's stature in the world, particularly through Manmohan Singh's pursuit of the civil-nuclear agreement with the United States. His speech before parliament defending the agreement in 2007 concluded with an appeal that "It is another step in our journey to regain our due place in global councils." During his years as prime minister, Dr. Singh from time to time spoke publicly about India's future and its "rightful place in the world."[55]

That ambient recent discomfort about *whether* India would rise on the global stage has begun to dissipate. The BJP government's focus on its external relations, coupled with cautious but resolute steps toward economic reform, has boosted India's economic growth, brought in foreign investment, and raised India's visibility as a country that wants to play a greater role in shaping the world. In a nutshell, India is now setting its sights more plainly on power.

Modi makes no bones about this. In September 2015, at a Silicon Valley stadium brimming with nearly twenty thousand Indian Americans, Modi spoke about the twenty-first century belonging to India. He credited them with putting India on the global map: "you—the billion-plus compatriots who resolved and dreamed that now India will no longer remain behind. . . . The whole world, that until yesterday saw India at the margins, today sees India as the focal point."[56]

Modi's more overt approach follows directly from the BJP's preferred foreign policy and national security worldview. As scholar Chris Ogden has elucidated in great detail, the "BJP's core norms of assertiveness, pragmatic engagement, and making India a global power . . . enabled the NDA to add substance to policies that had often been only embryonic prior to their arrival in power."[57] As important, just as Ogden observes with respect to the previous NDA government led by Vajpayee (1998 to 2004), the policy shifts are not major changes in direction but a sort of "gear shift," an acceleration. This is particularly the case in terms of new energy devoted to economic statecraft as foreign policy, but also seen in the accelerated efforts to strengthen ties with all the world powers, while also building a special relationship with the United States as a country that can uniquely play a role in India's global rise.

A government unambiguously staking a claim to global leadership signals India's ambitions to the world. It's welcomed in the business world, where the size of India's market and its demographics, especially with growth slowing elsewhere, now stand out. Anand Mahindra, chairman and managing director of the global conglomerate Mahindra and Mahindra, views this as an historic shift. "It's about time there were any expectations at all. Because expectations for India had vanished. The last time I remember somebody articulating a very coherent vision for India was at independence."[58]

In a wide-ranging discussion at her airy, light-filled office on Kasturba Gandhi Marg in New Delhi, leading businesswoman Shobhana Bhartia, the Hindustan Times group chairperson and editorial director—who served a term in India's upper house of parliament during the UPA years—sounded equally bullish: "I don't think anyone can deny the fact that India is already a global power, when you're sitting on such a large population, and a great demographic dividend, with bulk of our population, over 70 percent, being under the age of thirty-five. It's a great market and it cannot be ignored. And it's also strategically positioned."[59]

For a foreign visitor, the more globally ambitious mood in India is palpable. Recent public opinion data reaffirm this shift—Indian citizens overwhelmingly approve of the direction their country is heading on the world stage. While the combative Indian press sometimes criticizes the prime minister for spending too much time abroad, and not enough time tending to India's many problems at home, public opinion data tell a different story. Several polls show widespread support for Modi—especially among the youth demographic—and clearly show that Indian citizens approve of his international initiatives. It appears likely that, barring an unforeseen setback, a more ambitious, globally engaged India is here to stay.

The Pew Research Center has carried out public opinion surveys in India since 2002, with larger and nationally representative samples since 2013. Its recent surveys have included favorability ratings of leading politicians. In the first major survey carried out after the BJP government's election, Pew found that record high numbers declared their confidence in Modi's leadership in 2015: 87 percent of Indians surveyed held a favorable opinion. The youth demographic felt even more strongly: those between the ages of eighteen to twenty-nine held either a "very" or "somewhat" favorable view of him, for a total of 91 percent favorability—the highest marks of any demographic.[60] That high degree of favorability carried over to 2016, with a small dip down to a still-high 81 percent. In 2016 the percentage of respondents surveyed who were "satisfied" with the way things were going in their country had ticked up to 65 percent, from 56 percent in 2015.[61] A Gallup World Poll in India found 63 percent approval for Modi's job performance, a contrast to the 27 percent who approved of former prime minister Manmohan Singh in 2013. (Singh had a 50 percent approval rating in 2012.) Gallup also found that 58 percent of Muslims approve of Modi's job performance.[62]

In addition, the 2015 data showed an increased number of respondents viewing their country with more respect in the world: 39 percent said "India is as respected as it should be," up from 27 percent who held that view in 2013. But 57 percent believe "India should be more respected around the world."[63] We see here again the ambition to be on that global map rather than at the margins, just as Modi described in his San Jose speech, animating Indian public opinion today. Some of these numbers are surely ephemeral, but at the very least they suggest one incontrovertible fact: Indians seek respect on the world stage and approve of a leader who they feel can help them gain it.

I thought I might be able to gain some additional insights into public sentiment by asking India's leading television news anchor, someone whose style seems to have captured the public mood. So I went to visit Arnab Goswami, at the time editor-in-chief of Times Now, at his bustling Kamala Mills studio in Mumbai. Until his late 2016 departure from Times Now to set up his own channel, Republic TV, Goswami ran the most argumentative, most-watched nightly English news program on Indian television today, *The Newshour*. The program commanded nearly 76 percent market share for English news in his time slot, according to one metric.[64] One television historian described him as tapping into "the middle-class impatience" in the country, although he thinks that description isn't quite complete.[65] Still, his brash and prosecutorial style, taking on governments, uncovering scandals, and staking out a nationalistic, tough line on Pakistan, has moved nightly news miles away from the more soft-spoken approach of two decades back, and in that sense offers a new kind of national presentation. Vice News described his program as "Fox News on steroids."[66]

In person, he's reflective and Oxbridge thoughtful, and had much to say about the ambitious mood in India. Based on feedback he had received about his former program, with a viewership that Goswami said came as much from small towns in India as from its six major metros, he believed that Indian citizens want to "see their country in the top league of the top five nations in the world, one of the strongest military powers in the world, on par with China, with an economy that competes with and even exceeds that of China. With democratic institutions that are far stronger and far more resilient than China's. And with a strong presence across the world in various arenas from technology to media."

"So I think Indians believe our time has come. I am among those Indians who believe our time has come, and I think that ten years from now, we will see a far more confident India."[67]

I think he is right about this ambition. A more confident India, better able to shape its environment through the power of its market and its growing strategic resources, is unfurling bigger global visions for its security role across the Indian Ocean and Asia Pacific, and is pressing ever harder for institutions of global governance to reform and include it commensurate with the size of its population and economy. It will still struggle with many domestic challenges, but it wants to be recognized as one of a handful of global powers in a multipolar world. Between the opinion data pointing to a broader public sensibility favoring a larger presence in the world, support from Indian business that increasingly seeks a larger global footprint for itself, and the fact that many of the Modi government foreign policy initiatives have pressed the accelerator pedal on policies of earlier governments, we can see the prospects of a more active, globally oriented India for the forseeable future. Of course, India's ability to credibly maintain this more active posture does rest upon a trajectory of economic growth. Major economic shocks to the system could—as has occurred in the United States—pull citizens to press their elected leaders for a more predominantly inward focus. But for the time being, I'm betting that the desire for global leadership rests on a broadly felt foundation, and is likely to continue.

2

India and the World

HOW HAS INDIA SEEN its place in the world, and how have these ideas shaped its ambitions? Despite Indian knowledge traditions spanning millennia, many of India's own historical, scientific, and strategic traditions feature meagerly if at all in the global disciplines outside India. Part of this relates to the artificial academic separation of Indian history, philosophy, and religion from studies of contemporary India's international relations, as if the former have no connection to the present. Part of this can be attributed to the still-limited offerings on India in U.S. colleges and universities, compared with those on China, let alone on Europe. This knowledge gap has practical consequences. Increasingly, Indians are drawing from their past to define themselves using Indian terms—and inattention to India's ways of thinking about its past and its major debates can make it harder to perceive how the country's leaders and policymakers conceptualize their country and its global role.

A few years ago, well before the election of the Narendra Modi government, I began to notice in India a quiet but growing interest in bringing Indian knowledge traditions to bear on contemporary questions. At first this phenomenon struck me as limited to foreign policy, particularly a renewed scholarly interest in India's premier text of statecraft, the *Arthashastra* of the fourth century BCE. But once focused on this question, I saw the great popularity of a new category of business writing, drawing from ancient statecraft as well as epic literature to answer questions of leadership today. Titles such as *Corporate Chanakya* or *Chanakya's 7 Secrets of Leadership* crowd Indian bookstores. Writers, scholars, and policy practitioners mine India's history, including the ancient epic *Mahabharata*, for negotiating tactics in trade and in diplomacy.

I asked one of India's most distinguished diplomats, Shyam Saran, a former foreign secretary and former head of the National Security Advisory Board, what he made of this desire to address current questions with the help of India's civilizational past. Ambassador Saran pointed out that the new focus on ancient texts like the *Arthashastra* remains limited to a still small elite: "It would be great if there was a more visible Indian theory of statecraft: Hindu, Buddhist, Jain ways of looking at the state," he said. But just because this approach is not widespread does not mean it is insignificant. For one, in India, as in many countries, foreign policy formulation tends to be an elite preserve. As Saran reflected further upon Indian cosmology and statecraft, he noted that "how India looks at the world is related to how it looks at the universe."[1]

In its most elemental depiction, Hindu cosmology—reflected similarly in the philosophies of Buddhism and Jainism—sees the universe as a series of seven concentric oceans. A sacred mountain, Mount Meru, looms up to the heavens at the center, with the continent of man, a "lotus-shaped island" called Jambudvipa, to the south. India, or Bhārata in ancient texts, lies on one of the southern petals of the island of Jambudvipa. Surrounding the larger continent of Jambudvipa lie six ever-widening concentric rings of oceans and islands.[2] Distinguished Harvard scholar of religion Diana Eck has written that "India's imaginative world map does not place India directly in the center of the world, as did Anaximander when he drew the first world map with Greece in the center, or the medieval cartographers when they placed Jerusalem and the Holy Land in the center. Rather, Bhārata is but one of the petal continents." She goes on to observe, "Far from the usual cosmological ethnocentrism in which one's own world is described as civilized while the surrounding lands, vaguely known, are thought to be less so, even barbarian, the Indian visionaries who described the world actually idealized the other petals of the world, the lands beyond."[3]

Contrast that depiction with the Chinese idea of the "Middle Kingdom," in which China itself occupies the center of the universe, and the external world one of barbarians. For Saran, this Indian sense of cosmology may not operate consciously all the time, but the difference between Asia's two giants is nonetheless striking: "India is not looking at itself at the center of the universe, but at the margin, aspiring to get to the center." The metaphor applies very well to Indian international ambitions today.

Without suggesting that current Indian beliefs derive solely from inherited culture, nor suggesting the absence of material interests, and certainly without suggesting that culture remains unchanged over time, I believe several Indian ideas, lesser-discussed outside India, help shape India's approach to its international interactions. A better appreciation of these influences clarifies India's complex internal debates about its global role and its involvement on the world stage—and provides a sense of how India differs from other powers in this matter.

LESSONS OF THE PAST FOR THE PRESENT

Realist India: The Arthashastra and Indigenous Knowledge Traditions

India boasts of expansive literary and scientific traditions going back two millennia, which include self-contained theories of nearly everything, including: astronomy, ethics, economics, mathematics, medicine, linguistics, philosophy, and statecraft. In the West, however, knowledge of these Indian traditions remains limited and they are hardly taught beyond a handful of research universities—and even there, to only a handful of students. In recent years, correlated with China's global rise, the Chinese strategist Sun Tzu (544–496 BCE) has become better known in the West, with his *Art of War* increasingly appearing in American university courses. But mention of the aforementioned late-fourth century BCE text, the *Arthashastra*, for the most part still draws blank stares outside India.[4]

The *Arthashastra* presented theories of statecraft, international relations, and economic management lessons designed for an empire that stretched northwest from today's Afghanistan, east to the Bay of Bengal, and south to the plains of the Deccan. Just as Machiavelli, the great Italian political strategist of the late fifteenth and early sixteenth century, has come to serve as a shorthand for craftiness and political maneuvering, so too does "Chanakya" connote a deftness and political acumen. The German sociologist Max Weber, in his famous "Politics as a Vocation" lecture, nodded at the "radical Machiavellianism" of Chanakya's *Arthashastra*.[5] Chanakya is a daily presence in contemporary India, even a reference point in popular culture: India's state-run television channel, Doordarshan, sponsored a forty-seven-part series about the top-knotted sage in the early 1990s that aired for an entire year. New Delhi's diplomatic enclave, Chanakyapuri, laid out in the 1950s, bears his name. Myriad writers invoke "Chanakya" or "Kautilya" to signal topics of diplomacy, strategy, and statecraft.

The *Arthashastra* itself is a how-to manual for a king, covering war and strategy, economics, the role of the king, and methods of state administration.[6] The text offers prescriptions across a range of topics in statecraft. The most important for thinking about foreign policy is its framework for organizing international relations, or the state's relations with its neighbors and beyond. The *mandala* theory, the best-known tenet of the text, broadly envisions the world as a series of concentric rings, and presumes that a state's immediate neighbors would be natural enemies, but the immediate neighbor of an enemy could be an ally. In other words, the enemy of my enemy is my friend. This saying, often attributed in the West to an unspecified "Arab proverb," more appropriately derives from the *Arthashastra*.[7] The text also emphasizes the importance of economics, or maintaining the state treasury, and offers prescriptions on the military, the practice of foreign policy, and the use of intelligence gathering.[8] (In general, Chanakya was a huge fan of spycraft, including of the king's own subjects—what Roger Boesche describes as "Kautilya's Spy State.")[9]

Among Indian scholars, interest in the *Arthashastra* is hard to miss. A few years ago during the UPA government, India's Institute for Defence and Strategic Analyses (IDSA), a premier think tank, created the "Ancient Indigenous Historical Knowledge" initiative—rather unusual for an institution funded by India's defense ministry, and a security-focused institution best known for its advocacy for nuclear weapons capability. IDSA's publications from this initiative have centered on the *Arthashastra* as a source of lessons on economic and strategic statecraft relevant for today.[10] Titles include "Kautilya's *Arthashastra*: Restoring Its Rightful Place in the Field of International Relations,"

"Statecraft and Intelligence Analysis in the Kautilya-Arthashastra," and "Using Temple Gold for Shoring Up the Economy: Learning from Kautilya's *Arthashastra*." In late 2016, HarperCollins India published a volume intended to articulate a new national security strategy for a country that generally does not declare or publish them. Its title? *The New Arthashastra: A Security Strategy for India.*

In the business world, a whole cottage industry has sprung up of management books interpreting the lessons Chanakya offers for leadership challenges in today's India—blending the weighty history of Indian knowledge traditions passed down over millennia with Stephen Covey–style "*7 Habits*" pragmatism. These books are ubiquitous in English-language bookstores in India; many display several such titles. In a more scholarly vein, Penguin Books India has launched, under the stewardship of best-selling writer and former Procter & Gamble India CEO Gurcharan Das, a new book series that explores the history of Indian business. Initial titles cover the *Arthashastra,* the East India Company, the history of South Indian trade, and money in ancient India.[11]

India is also witnessing renewed interest in its literary epic traditions and their application to contemporary life. Indian terms for viewing the world and its challenges are beginning to supplement Western theories that form the core of global disciplines. In *The Difficulty of Being Good,* Gurcharan Das drew upon the *Mahabharata* to develop an ethics for the present day, one inspired by Indian thought on *dharma.* A 2014 study by Amrita and Aruna Narlikar draws from the *Mahabharata* specific examples useful for bargaining, such as the importance of honor and face, the use of coalitions, the moral "high horse," and the tactic of going it alone when required.[12] A younger scholar, Deep K. Datta-Ray, published an in-depth study arguing for an understanding of Indian diplomacy through indigenous terms—against Eurocentrism— highlighting the reference point that the Indian epic *Mahabharata* provides for Indian thinking about diplomacy.[13] For Datta-Ray, the ethics of modern Indian thinking, and therefore Indian diplomacy, have their roots in the *Mahabharata.*

The Mumbai-based bestselling writer Devdutt Pattanaik has written more than thirty popular adult and children's books bringing lessons from the Indian epics to contemporary readers—in addition to his corporate life as a highly sought-after counselor to India's leading companies, like Reliance and the Future Group. For a time, he served as the Future Group "chief belief officer." When I spoke with him about his work, he observed that the present interest in India's literary past, its "lore of the land" as he put it, represents a larger global trend of turning inward in a search for identity. Devdutt noted that many of his readers are in their twenties and thirties, the generation born after liberalization, so a demographic more global in its upbringing and less steeped in traditional lore than his had been. Hence the interest in Indian traditions and their meaning for life.[14]

Devdutt pulls one common thread through some of his recent titles: the application of Indian epics to corporate disciplines. As he put it in *Business Sutra,* "The truth of the East is always studied in Western terms, rarely has the truth of the West been studied in Eastern terms. If it has, it has been dismissed as exotic, even quaint."[15] Though trained as a physician, Devdutt has found great success through bringing Eastern terms to the "Western" fields of business and management. His titles include *An Indian Approach to Wealth: The Success Sutra; Business Sutra: A Very Indian Approach to Management;* and *The Leadership Sutra: An Indian Approach to Power.* To offer one example from his *Business Sutra,* Devdutt links the belief in reincarnation common to Hinduism, Buddhism, and Jainism as a perspective "comfortable with the absence of binary logic, where there are no fixed goals, continuously changing plans . . . a reliance on resourcefulness that gives way to contextual, non-replicable improvisations."[16] That his particular blend of insights has become so popular attests to the felt desire in India to show the relevance of Indian traditions to trade and commerce. (Anecdotally, it has struck me that the new rise to market prominence of an ayurvedic brand of noodles, soaps, and supplements, Patanjali ([a consumer products company launched by the omnipresent television yogi Baba Ramdev]), represents the same urge to indigenize consumer goods. Baba Ramdev's proclamation that the brand will soon produce "swadeshi" jeans is a case in point.)

The push to mine India's past for lessons applicable to today's strategic and economic realities represents a strong and growing Indian sensibility: Indian thinkers increasingly want to see their own representations of their country's approach to the world. Some of this impulse naturally can be seen as a reaction to India's colonial past, and the still-present resentment of subordination under the British so ably chronicled by Manjari Chatterjee Miller in her book *Wronged by Empire*.[17] But the desire for self-definition extends well beyond just wanting to right the wrongs of a colonial era that ended nearly seventy years ago. It now incorporates a desire to highlight—or even resuscitate—Indian terms and concepts and showcase their relevance for larger global disciplines and debates.

In some cases, Indian concepts may not differ so greatly from those in the West, such as the bargaining strategies of coalition building, or going it alone, elucidated by the Narlikars. But having an Indian definition for these approaches rooted in India's own past appears to be the goal. (I distinguish this understandable impulse, a patriotic desire for the country's own traditions to be on par with those of the West, from the exclusionary nationalism of some fringe groups that make extravagant claims for India's past. Within India, there is some concern that more extreme Hindu nationalists seek, especially in higher education, to replace the scholarly consensus with historically unsupported assertions about India's golden era. This debate, like similar debates in other countries, will likely continue.) It's a quiet but important shift, and signals a country not only ready to describe its rise in its own words, but also determined to see those words appreciated and accepted by the rest of the world.

Self-Reliant India: Gandhi, Swaraj, and Swadeshi

Mohandas K. (Mahatma) Gandhi has been celebrated worldwide for his nonviolent civil disobedience, a moral inspiration to freedom struggles across the globe. Yet one of his most important legacies lives on in India in the concept of *swaraj* ("swa" + "raj," self-rule). The idea of self-rule and its relative, *swadeshi*, or self-reliance, energized the Indian independence movement through its emphasis on resistance to colonial exploitation, and its romanticization of self-sufficient village life.[18] Today, the principle of self-reliance still percolates through Indian political debates. The universe of its connotations extends capaciously outward, to incorporate ideas about the economy, negotiations, strategy, and India's positioning in the world.

Gandhi's political tract *Hind Swaraj*, first published in Gujarati in 1909, built its case for independence through a "dialogue" of an editor (Gandhi) with his questioning reader. The tract was an argument focused on careful moral principles of rights and justice. It was a call for deeper spiritual awakening of the individual. It was a cry for nonviolent civil disobedience. And it was a critique of Western civilization. In 1910 Gandhi would translate the tract himself into English as *Indian Home Rule*.[19]

The idea of Indian home rule was first and foremost a political struggle for sovereignty. As Ananya Vajpeyi has shown, it was also a search for Indian self-identity, or "the self's sovereignty."[20] At the same time, it contained a strong commitment to economic nationalism, a way of fighting back against British economic control. In the economic realm, self-rule converged with ideas about self-reliance and self-sufficiency, very much interlinked in a way that reflected India's experience with the interconnections of colonization and trade, for the British Raj began with the East India Company's commercial ventures. For India's founding fathers, trade and exploitation went together.

The independence movement created symbols that resonate even today, keeping the idea of self-reliance active. Take the spinning wheel and *khadi*, or hand-spun cloth. Gandhi called for Indians to reclaim textile production and its profits for themselves by rejecting fabrics woven in Britain from Indian cotton, and then exported back to India at higher prices. He urged Indians to produce their own cloth beginning with the thread itself, and he elevated traditional hand-spinning of cotton thread to a daily meditative practice. That Indian politicians today continue the tradition of wearing hand-spun *khadi* fabrics illustrates the nationalist appeal this fabric retains—a presentation of self that symbolically rejects the West, showcases Indian tradition, and most of all highlights national economic pride.[21] In 2016, Indian media reported that Delhi's sleek and modern airport planned to acquire and prominently display the world's largest wooden spinning wheel, a four-ton wheel carved of teak, to "showcase India's symbol of nonviolence to the world." Its association with self-reliance suggests a quiet irony for it to be one of the first sights likely to greet many visiting foreign investors.[22]

Gandhi's Salt March of 1930, the most famous example of his philosophy of nonviolent civil disobedience, derived its power from an argument of economic self-reliance: in its simplest formulation, Indians would no longer pay foreigners for that which they could, and should, make themselves from their own natural resources. Under British rule, the government monopolized salt production. Colonial authorities prohibited Indians from producing their own salt, and also taxed this staple. In protest, Gandhi launched a 240-mile march from Ahmedabad to Dandi on the western coast, where, upon reaching the shore, he picked up a fist of salt and through that act "produced" his own: "With this salt I am shaking the foundations of the [British] empire."[23] The act would motivate many thousands to similar nonviolent protest, and would echo around the world, later inspiring the civil disobedience movement led by Martin Luther King Jr. in the United States.

While Gandhi rejected Western modernization and idealized the Indian village way of life as central to national identity, Jawaharlal Nehru saw industrialization as a force to power the Indian economy. Their differences over this point notwithstanding, both saw economic self-reliance as a central goal and a requirement for Indian prosperity. Nehru's preference for Fabian socialism led to newly independent India's adopting an import-substitution model, a commitment to promote state enterprises in heavy industry, and an economy cut off, for all intents and purposes, from easy commerce with the outside world. The belief in self-reliance has had follow-on effects, which the next chapter explores in greater depth, among them decades of economic autarky under socialist planning; a sense that commerce was inherently exploitative rather than a tool that can empower; and a specific suspicion of foreign capital as a Trojan Horse of domination to be resisted.

Those ideas continue to affect current debates about globalization, particularly in the way Indians talk about global trade and India's international economic policy. Many of India's own businesses became global conglomerates during the 2000s, but even as the Indian economy benefited from the gradual economic liberalization begun in 1991, suspicion of commerce and especially foreign capital has remained a consistent feature of domestic conversation. While the United States has witnessed a rising protectionist sensibility, particularly acute during the 2016 presidential election, it is starting from a position of much greater openness to begin with, whereas the Indian economy has not yet opened as much as its Asian peers.

These twentieth-century ideas continue to shape Indian foreign policy, although they are fraying at the edges today more than ever before. An instinctive bent toward self-reliance is perfectly understandable as an anti-colonial strategy, but as an economic principle it sits uncomfortably with the globalization of today's India—particularly with an India actively pursuing its own interests around the world.

Nonaligned India: Nehru and Autonomy in International Relations

From 1947 until his death of a heart attack in 1964, India's first prime minister, Jawaharlal Nehru, served longer than any other. His expansive vision, and the duration of his tenure, forged the country's early institutions. Nehru saw India as a global leader due to its moral force, its inspiration to other post-colonial countries, and its role as an alternative to the emerging Cold War blocs in geopolitics. The practices he set in place for Indian diplomacy and its approach to the world had an outsized influence on the country's foreign policy in the decades to follow.

Nehru left Indian foreign policy with a unique philosophical legacy: nonalignment. In a sense the principle resembles *swaraj* in its focus on protecting India's independence of choice—indeed, Nehru would describe it as such in his 1963 *Foreign Affairs* essay: "Essentially, 'nonalignment' is freedom of action which is a part of independence."[24] The concept of nonalignment and its principles have been seen, in India, as part of India's contribution to the global order. It was an approach Nehru elaborated upon in his very first year as prime minister. In India's first year of independence, as Nehru wrote in one of his fortnightly letters to the chief ministers of every state, India would pursue "a policy of not aligning with any power group but of being friends with all countries as far as possible. I am convinced that there is no other possible policy for us either in the present or in the foreseeable future."[25]

A few years later, with India's independent foreign policy approach established, Nehru sought to mediate in the Korean War—a role he saw India particularly suited for as an independent moral voice, even if the rest of the world was agnostic at best or did not buy into this view. Nonalignment with any bloc, in Nehru's view, had propelled India to a position of trust and influence in the world. Over time, the world has forgotten this history, but it remains part of living memory in India.

Nehru's own words of May 1953 provide a helpful lens onto how he viewed the success of his external strategy, so I will quote at length:

> The turn that international events have taken has brought India more into the picture and cast a heavy responsibility on her. The independent policy that we have pursued and our constant attempts to remain friendly with all countries have borne fruit. The Great Powers look upon us with respect and realize that what we say will be listened to by many. Hence, they have to listen to it also. We remain the principle link between these rival blocs. The fact of our political and economic stability and the earnest attempt that we are making to better our conditions by the Five Year Plan and other methods has also impressed the world. The result, no doubt, is pleasing to us, but it is also disturbing, because of the additional responsibility cast upon us. In the Korean deadlock, attempts are made on both sides to utilize India's services to help to resolve it.[26]

In the quest to establish a global alternative voice for neutrality, Nehru played a leading role in the Bandung Afro-Asian Conference in 1955, a gathering of twenty-nine Asian and African countries in the Indonesian hill station of Bandung. The gathering would result in a declaration of ten "principles of international peace and cooperation," including a core set of five principles, or "panchsheel" ("panchan" means five in Sanskrit) that had been agreed upon the previous year between India and China. The core *panchsheel* principles emphasized "respect for each other's territorial integrity and sovereignty; non-aggression; non-interference; equality and mutual benefit; and peaceful co-existence."[27]

These principles, codified at Bandung, would later be adopted by the Non-Aligned Movement (NAM), which held its first summit in Belgrade in 1961. As with Bandung, Nehru played an important role from the start in shaping NAM. While NAM had an additional focus on supporting decolonization and the self-determination of peoples, the core principles of respect for sovereignty and noninterference were central to NAM's commitments—especially as members sought, at least in theory if not always in practice, to counter perceived interference from the West and the Communist blocs, especially in the forms of the North Atlantic Treaty Organization (NATO) and

Warsaw Pact alliances. These ideas diffused throughout the developing world. The Organization of the African Union adopted similar principles in 1961, carried over to the successor African Union in 2002. (Although by 2004 the African Union replaced "noninterference" with "non-indifference" in response to conflict on the continent and the development of the "right to protect" norm within the United Nations.)[28]

The principles espoused by NAM have continued to shape current Indian foreign policy strongly. Idealizing policy independence and antipathy toward alliances (indeed, the purpose of NAM was to bandwagon for greater strength against the major alliances of the Cold War), generations of Indian strategic thinkers saw alliance obligations as unacceptable constraints on Indian freedom of action. After all, entering an alliance would likely mean narrowing the range of options available to future Indian policymakers. This idealized principle of sovereignty often led to India's viewing international agreements with heightened suspicion rather than as opportunities to enhance Indian power and boost economic development.

The end of the Cold War did not end nonalignment in India. However, the vocabulary and form attached to the idea underwent a mutation. Nonalignment's successor, "strategic autonomy," has its roots in Nehru's vision, though the terminology has adapted to a changed geopolitical landscape. In a post–Cold War world, strategic autonomy offers a theory of preserving maximum options for India's international decisions. In his second term, Manmohan Singh gravitated toward strategic autonomy. At least for now, the Modi government, as subsequent chapters explore in greater depth, has done away with this terminology. In 2016, Modi also became the first Indian prime minister to skip attending the NAM summit entirely. However, in their deliberations over various international agreements, Indian officials continue to explain their positions on trade in terms of "sovereign rights." They portray the country's multiplicity of partners as part of an Indic tradition of treating the world as a family. In substance, if not always in form, India continues to prioritize a desire to prevent commitments from constraining future choices over taking a stand that would explicitly define a future path. The spirit of nonalignment may be diminished, but it is certainly not dead.

Emissary to the World: Swami Vivekananda and Indian Soft Power

The Midway Plaisance on the South Side of Chicago—about a thousand acres of wide boulevards and lush green lawn—bisects the University of Chicago's campus. Designed in 1871 by the firm Olmsted and Vaux, best known for planning New York's Central Park, the Midway was originally meant to be a linked series of lagoons. Today it houses ice rinks in the winter, and playing fields the rest of the year.[29] During my years at the University of Chicago, each time I passed the Midway I would imagine it filled with the exhibitions it housed as the site of the 1893 World's Columbian Exposition, also known as the Chicago World's Fair, a kind of coming-out party for a city on the cusp of global prominence. The Fair drew more than twenty million visitors from all over the world to marvel at its Beaux Arts buildings, giant Ferris wheel, and life-size replicas of Christopher Columbus's ships. It also included an unprecedented event: the first World's Parliament of Religions, which ran from September 11 to September 27 at the Art Institute of Chicago.

India's Swami Vivekananda made his American debut at the parliament, and single-handedly created a new popular appreciation in the United States for the teachings of Hinduism. Eyewitness notes from his inaugural address describe the "peal of applause that lasted for several minutes" after Vivekananda merely opened his remarks by addressing the "Sisters and Brothers of America."[30] His speeches and comments over a series of days during the parliament presented his views of Hinduism as a capacious religion, one in consonance with nature and of which "the whole force . . . is directed to the great central truth in every religion, to evolve a god out of man." He offered that if "there is ever to be a universal religion, it must be one which will hold no location in place or time; which will be infinite like the God it will preach, whose sun shines upon the followers of Krishna or Christ, saints or sinners alike, which will not be in the Brahmin or Buddhist, Christian or Mohammedan, but the sum total of all of these."[31] He rebutted negative perceptions of "idolatry" and polytheism, and spoke of Hinduism's search for unity as a preoccupation similar to science.

Vivekananda's remarks struck a chord not only with his audience, but with Americans more generally. He spent months in Chicago after the parliament, speaking to the "ladies' fortnightly club," to community groups in Evanston, and at churches, all to wide acclaim. Coverage of his Evanston lectures, for example, referred to his "magnetic presence" and "brilliant oratory," and declared that his "stay in Chicago has been a continual ovation."[32]

So popular was Vivekananda that he ended up staying on in the United States (punctuated with a trip to London) for several years, delivering talks about India, Hinduism, Hindu ethics, and Buddhism—in venues ranging from private homes to music halls, churches to universities.[33] He traveled throughout the American Midwest (Minneapolis, St. Louis, Des Moines, Detroit), the South (Memphis), and the East (Washington, Baltimore, New York, Boston, Northampton). In May 1894, Vivekananda spoke to about fifty members of the "mysterious" social group known as the V Club in New York about vegetarianism and virtue. The next day he spoke in the home of a Miss Phillips at 19 West 38th Street. In Boston, he addressed the Harvard Religious Union in Sever Hall, a "singularly impressive" performance, according to the *Crimson.* His lessons appealed to a group of feminists in Boston, who began—under Vivekananda's tutelage—practicing yoga. In October 1894 he delivered lectures on reincarnation (one titled "KARMAX!") and "Gods of All Nations" in a two-night engagement at Metzerott Music Hall in Washington, DC.[34] He founded a Vedanta Society in New York in 1894, and one in San Francisco in 1900. The societies created institutional spaces for Americans to further study Vivekananda's teachings, and exist to this day.

Vivekananda's American peregrinations presented a confident Hinduism to his rapt listeners—a picture quite different from that back home where British colonial authorities often saw Hindu practices as inferior to their own and targets for reformation and modernization. In addition, Vivekananda's ability to bridge religious divides—particularly for the many Christians he encountered during his American travels— through a depiction of Hindu philosophical goals as rational and scientific, gave his audiences scope to feel that there were lessons from Indian traditions that could benefit the West.[35] In other words, Vivekananda presented a Hinduism that seemed a lot less exotic and a lot more similar to their own faith than many of his listeners had anticipated. He was a messenger for what Indian spiritual teachings could offer the world, and in many ways a precursor to many who would follow in his footsteps.

Vivekananda was certainly not the first nor only Indian to travel as an "ambassador-at-large" for Indian civilization. In centuries past, Buddhist pilgrims had spread across Southeast and East Asia, and helped the faith take root outside the land of its Indian birth. South Indian traders' interaction with the Indonesian archipelago as early as the first century CE suggests a route through which Hindu practices spread throughout Sumatra, Java, and Bali. In the twentieth century, the writer-artist-educationist Rabindranath Tagore became a prominent public figure after he received the 1913 Nobel Prize for literature, the first Asian to receive the honor. His travels in Europe, and indeed in Japan, highlighted modern Indian literature in a new way to a new audience. Today many Indians see each of these as examples of the power of India's unique civilizational appeal. But in the 1890s, a historical moment when India's faith in its own practices had been battered by the colonial encounter, the rock star status Americans accorded to Vivekananda, a Hindu swami garbed in saffron robes, turned the tables and still sets him apart in Indian history.

Within India, Vivekananda and his teachings represented a process of Hindu reform, but he has come to symbolize over and above all a source of pride in what India could send to the world beyond its borders—as a way to advance its own interests. This is because Vivekananda's American venture came about after a revelation of his life's purpose experienced while meditating on a "rock island" (now a memorial) at the southernmost tip of India, Kanyakumari. As his biographer Swami Nikhilananda wrote, "there flashed before his mind the new continent of America, a land of optimism, great wealth, and unstinted generosity. He saw America as a country of unlimited opportunities, where people's minds were free from the encumbrance of castes or classes. He would give the receptive Americans the ancient wisdom of India and bring back to his motherland, in exchange, the knowledge of science and technology. If he succeeded in his mission to America, he would not only enhance India's prestige in the Occident, but create a new confidence among his own people."[36]

That goal sounds similar in many ways to some of Modi's globetrotting pitches. Indeed, in a tribute letter written in 2012, then chief minister of Gujarat Narendra Modi wrote that Vivekananda visualized India's pre-ordained destiny of taking on the mantle of the world's leadership. . . . At Kanyakumari Swamiji realized India's purpose—its message of spirituality, its mission to teach human beings the science of life—a destiny of wearing the crown of world leader. He spent his entire life in spreading this message.[37]

So today, Vivekananda serves as an icon for Indian global involvement, and above all as an emissary to the world for the cultural and religious traditions of India. Vivekananda signals an expectation that India has something uniquely valuable to contribute to the world outside its borders, and that the world would naturally seek to advance Indian traditions once they learn more about them. In short, Indian soft power to advance Indian interests. Undoubtedly this is particularly pronounced under a prime minister who views the Hindu monk as a personal hero.

IDEAS, POLITICS, AND INFLUENCES

Ideas do not exist in a vacuum, and India has an exceptionally lively (indeed, contentious) political landscape. India's democracy contains such diversity, with numerous national and even more numerous state-level parties, that every major question before the country attracts significant—often highly partisan—deliberation. But India's political complexity, like other complicated polities, does not map neatly onto terms like "left wing" or "right wing," despite the fact that journalists often use these terms as a shorthand. The terms are unhelpful because they assume divisions among beliefs that simply do not map onto political parties in the same way in India as they do in the West. Historically, much of the Indian right has held ideas about economics and trade that would belong firmly to the left in the United States, United Kingdom, or Australia. For that reason, it is worth contextualizing how respect for Indian wisdom, belief in self-reliance, a tradition of non-alignment, and pride in Indic culture shape beliefs and, through them, policy positions in Indian political parties. At least for a Western reader, this is not intuitive.

India's two major national parties, the ruling Bharatiya Janata Party and the Indian National Congress, play the most important roles in national decisions. As discussed earlier, the dominance of Congress through most of independent India's history has given the party an outsized influence on Indian strategic thinking, foreign policy development, and approaches to international economic policy. But its influence has been shrinking slowly over time. Since the 1990s, the BJP has grown dramatically. It has led national governments in coalition twice, and since 2014 has commanded a rare single-party majority of its own. As important, all across India the rise of state-level parties with their own specific and highly local interests has chipped away at the ability of any single party to fully dominate the country. The more inward-looking preoccupations of state-level parties mean that they generally have less to say about India's role in the world—unless an international issue directly influences their state. This happens most often with questions of economic policy, and with border states such as Punjab, Assam, West Bengal, and Tamil Nadu.

Indigenous Indian Knowledge

It may seem natural to draw direct lines of influence from Gandhi and Nehru—the Congress party's giants—to today's Congress, and from Chanakya and the nineteenth-century spiritual ambassador Swami Vivekananda to today's BJP, which prizes Hinduism and ancient Indian glory. This interpretation would be incomplete, however. While today's Congress indeed sees itself as protecting the ideational heritage of its early leaders, and today's BJP invokes India's premodern civilizational heritage far more often, a simplistic binary belies the multidimensional influences on current foreign policy debates. In practice, when it comes to ideas both major parties at times draw from the same well.

Take Indian indigenous knowledge traditions. The BJP, given its emphasis on Hindu tradition, has a pronounced inclination to advocate the revival of India's greatness through its civilizational accomplishments dating to the premodern era (i.e., accomplishments before the coming of Islam or Europeans). Indeed, during its previous term leading the central government (1998–2004), the BJP took steps to boost Indian traditions, such as its systems of medicine (especially ayurveda) and the study of Sanskrit.

But the BJP has no monopoly on ancient India as a reference point. Nehru famously read the *Arthashastra* while in prison prior to India's independence, and expounded upon it in his *Discovery of India.* More recently, the Indian press often referred to the late Congress party leader and tenth prime minister of India P. V. Narasimha Rao as a "modern-day Chanakya" for his role ushering in India's politically difficult economic reforms in 1991. To offer just two additional examples, Congress party political strategist, former minister, and public intellectual Jairam Ramesh penned a column for years titled "Kautilya," signaling his intellectual inspiration. And Shivshankar Menon, Manmohan Singh's second-term national security advisor, gave a landmark speech on the importance of the text.[38] These examples do not even begin to indicate the widespread invocation of the top-knotted sage by Congress politicians.

For this reason, the *Arthashastra* and the philosophical realism it represents should be seen as an influence that occupies a special intellectual place in India across political divides. The *Arthashastra*'s well-known principle of strategic thought, the conceptualization of the world and one's region into *mandalas*, or concentric circles defining friends and enemies, has no partisan limitations. A younger scholar, Dhruva Jaishankar, recently speculated that the structure of India's foreign ministry draws upon the mandala theory.[39] Another common principle from the text, self-interest, may not be admired widely but may either underlie the growth of realism in strategic thinking—as opposed to a moral approach to India's international relations—or indeed serve as an indigenous justification for realist approaches. We should see these ideas as available and utilized across parties in their influence.

The Importance of Self-Reliance

The realm of economics shows most acutely how spectrums of right and left, or even conservative and liberal, do not mean the same thing in India as they do in the West. If in the West, left and right connote ideas about the appropriate role of the state in the economy—call it "big government" versus "small government" for short—this simply does not hold in India. And indeed, though a BJP-leaning constituency for reform has sprung up over the past two decades, for the most part the term "right wing" in India carries more the connotation of Hindu nationalism, rather than libertarianism or a belief in free markets.

A long history of state planning, expansive regulations across virtually every sector, deep government involvement in the economy, and a belief in the power of state-owned enterprises to propel economic growth combines with long-standing views on the necessity of large welfare programs to assist the poor. While this orientation has evolved over time in a more market-friendly direction, this evolution has been slow. One of the bedrock beliefs that centers Indian economic thinking can be linked not only to Fabian socialism, so influential on Nehru and the first decades of independent India, but also to Gandhi's most perduring principle of self-rule, which marries political sovereignty with economic nationalism.

The Gandhian ideals of home rule, self-rule, and self-reliance continue to affect what Indian citizens and their leaders see as sources of national strength and ability to resist pressure from outside powers. And here, hardly any party in India is untouched by Gandhian thought. Gandhi's theory of self-rule and self-reliance has overwhelmingly affected the way India pursued economic development, and indeed continues to appeal to wings within both the Congress and BJP—even when sections within these parties seek to move the country in other directions. Both major parties contain economic liberalizers, seeking to integrate India with the world, but by the same token both contain factions that prefer to see India advance through policies that embody the notion of self-reliance. Independent India's only genuinely market-oriented party, the Swatantra Party, flowered briefly in the 1960s before the charismatic Indira Gandhi drowned it in a wave of electorally popular statism.

Today, ambivalence about deep-rooted economic changes marks both major parties. A Congress-led government ushered in economic reforms in 1991 by scrapping industrial licensing and opening India's economy to the world after decades of autarky. But it was also a Congress-led government that fiercely resisted further opening India to global trade, leading to the collapse of the 2008 Doha Round negotiations. A Congress-led government created domestic welfare policies on food stockpiling (self-reliance for food security) so enormous in scale that they affected the country's negotiations in the World Trade Organization. Similarly, a BJP-led government took dramatic economic reform steps from 1998 to 2004, including opening up new sectors of the economy such as telecoms and insurance to foreign investment. But the BJP too balked at allowing foreigners to fully own businesses in India, capping their share at 26 percent in insurance and 49 percent in telecom services, to offer two examples of earlier arbitrary limits.

After ten years of tepid progress under Congress, the BJP is currently seen as the more reform-minded national party. Yet many of its supporters believe strongly that economic strength comes only through self-reliance. Organizations in the broader Sangh Parivar "family" of affiliated Hindu groups explicitly reaffirm this belief. Indeed, the Swadeshi Jagran Manch ("Self-Reliance Awakening Forum"), an RSS-affiliated outfit distinct from but generally supportive of the BJP, advocates economic self-reliance—in their view, this represents a rejection of foreign economic collaboration, at home or abroad. Its magazine, *Swadeshi*, calls itself the "voice of self-reliance." The organization generally opposes liberalization of foreign investment rules, and argues that "for total economic freedom it is necessary to make swadeshi a way of life." They urge awareness of "ongoing economic imperialism."[40] Similarly, BJP-affiliated organizations like the Bharatiya Mazdoor Sangh ("Indian Workers Union") often lead protests against easing socialist-era labor laws to allow easier hiring and firing, or the introduction of genetically modified crops.

At the other end of the political spectrum, communism remains alive in India, although its presence has been dwindling and its influence now stands at its lowest point ever. Not surprisingly, India's communists map most easily onto the traditional Western divide between left and right. As one would expect, they support statist approaches to economic development, and that means keeping the Indian economy insulated from foreign involvement. (Though at the state level in West Bengal, communist Chief Minister Buddhadeb Bhattacharjee, in power from 2000 to 2011, took a more open view of foreign direct investment, or FDI.) At the national level, India's communists routinely oppose efforts to raise FDI caps, and have urged India to boycott the WTO. These economic *swaraj*-ists find common ground from time to time with some of India's state-level parties. The state-level parties typically say little about India and the world, given their generally narrow domestic concerns. Nonetheless their stance can at times matter enormously.

Take, for example, the fate of the U.S.-India civil-nuclear deal initi-ated and negotiated under the first term of India's Congress-led UPA government (2004 to 2009). A "Left Front" of communist parties sup-ported this coalition from outside, which meant backing it in parlia-ment without formally joining the government and accepting a share of ministerial power. The Left Front withdrew its support to the coalition over the civil-nuclear deal, believing it would subject India to "external pressure" from the United States.[41] Ultimately the government won a confidence vote in July 2008, a nail-biter of an event, marked by charges of money changing hands, and eventually dependent on support from a large caste-based north Indian party lacking any particularly well-formulated views on foreign policy or India's growing closeness with the United States.[42]

Given the widespread conviction that self-reliance holds the key to national strength, it's no wonder that India's approach to economic reforms, no matter the party in power, remains one that advances in small steps rather than giant strides. This orientation has resulted in a kaleidoscope of policies across sectors of the economy reflecting hard-fought policy battles. One sector may allow foreigners to own only 26 percent of a company, another may demand that manage-ment control remain with Indian nationals, and another may remain fully closed. With a gift for understatement, noted economist Montek Singh Ahluwalia, vice chairman of the Planning Commission under the Congress-led UPA government, characterized economic reform in India as "gradualism."[43] Arvind Subramanian, chief economic advisor to the finance minister in the Modi government, uses the term "creative incrementalism."

As described earlier, despite the rapid growth of the Indian economy, Indian leaders continue to project the developing country face rather than the major economy aspect in global forums. In effect this means that domestic economic decisions often conflict with India's interna-tional ambitions. For instance, one way to think about an emphasis on self-reliance rather than global linkages is that India has missed out on becoming part of the global manufacturing supply chains that have gen-erated so much prosperity in East Asia. Here the heritage of Gandhian thinking has its most lasting effects, often dominating decisions that might otherwise have turned on Chanakyan realism and self-interest.

In addition to the anticolonial inheritance of *swaraj* that prizes resistance to the foreign, a heated debate rages in India on the role of economic growth and the market in eliminating poverty. It is impossible to discuss economic growth without discussing integration with the global economy. But in India, the suspicion of foreign involvement is not the only hurdle. In most of the world, the importance of growth in eliminating poverty is a settled matter. In India, some people argue that economic growth itself should not be the primary policy focus for lifting hundreds of millions out of poverty—the scale India requires for its seven hundred million individuals living below $3.10 a day.[44] At times this heated national debate devolves into caricature, with pro-growth proponents accused by their detractors of not caring about the poor. The divisions over growth are best captured by the 2013 public dispute between the preeminent economists Jagdish Bhagwati and Amartya Sen (both long settled in the United States, but retaining deep personal and professional involvement with India).

It would be hard to imagine a debate between two of the world's top economists becoming the subject of prime-time news in the United States, but that's exactly what happened in India in the run-up to the 2014 national elections. Bhagwati's book *Why Growth Matters*, written with another esteemed Columbia University economist, Arvind Panagariya, advocated further liberalization of the economy and an enhanced role for the private sector as the growth-led path out of poverty. The same year *An Uncertain Glory,* a book coauthored by Sen with Jean Drèze, a Belgian-origin economist now a citizen of India, advocated greater public investment in social services such as health and education as the preconditions necessary for poverty eradication.[45] In effect, Bhagwati and Panagariya want India to focus on growing its economic pie so there is more revenue available to redistribute. Sen and Drèze doubt that growth itself is a magic bullet.

The very fact that this debate exists at all appears puzzling to people familiar with the East Asian–style emphasis on growth. But in India everything is hotly contested.[46] As it happened, this debate split neatly along partisan lines: Congress emphasizes a Sen-based approach, and Drèze served on the UPA government's National Advisory Council. The BJP has sought advice from Bhagwati, and Panagariya now serves as a cabinet minister–ranked member of the Modi government, leading the National Institution for Transforming India Aayog—the successor to the Planning Commission.

Autonomy, Sovereignty, and Nonalignment

Gandhi's preeminence in the freedom struggle notwithstanding, Nehru's overarching influence has probably been more important in terms of shaping independent India's trajectory. His long tenure as India's first prime minister as well as its foreign minister (he kept the portfolio) left a decisive imprint on how India approaches the world. While Gandhi and Nehru stood for dramatically different economic models—the former harked back to an idealized pre-industrial past while the latter dreamed of rapid industrialization—nonetheless, Nehru effectively reinforced the idea of self-reliance with his emphasis on a planned economy walled off from global trade. In addition, Nehru's specific imprimatur can clearly be seen in Indian foreign policy, and in how Indian citizens see their place in the world and the choices before them.

Given the Congress party's reverence for Nehru, and that his descendants continue to lead it, one might expect Nehruvian ideas to live on most prominently within Congress. This remains broadly the case. Congress-led governments have displayed acute sensitivity to balancing their country's international ties with the great powers, and have been wary of falling too deeply into Washington's embrace. But by the same token, former Congress prime minister Manmohan Singh cast his lot with the United States in 2005 by embarking upon the civil-nuclear agreement, and went to the mat—almost losing that razor-thin confidence vote in parliament—to see it through.

Nonetheless, old habits of thought die hard. In Singh's second term, the UPA government cooperated in an effort to redefine nonalignment for the post–Cold War world, resulting in a publication titled *Non-Alignment 2.0* in 2012.[47] Though officially an undertaking of a think tank, New Delhi's Centre for Policy Research, the report described deliberations "in the presence" of members of the then national security advisor Shivshankar Menon and his staff, suggesting at the minimum a modicum of support from the government. I was serving in the State Department when this tract emerged, and recall my surprise at the revival and recasting of a concept we in the United States thought had "lost its meaning" with the end of the Cold War, as former Secretary of State Condoleezza Rice put it in a 2007 speech. The *Wall Street Journal* put it less diplomatically in a story titled "Non-Alignment Rises from Dustbin of History."[48]

In contrast to the Congress, the BJP has been more comfortable seeking a stronger relationship with the United States without fear that doing so would make it subservient. Prime Minister Vajpayee's BJP government helmed the historic opening with the United States in 2000 marked by President Bill Clinton's five-day visit to India. Vajpayee espoused a vision for closer ties with Washington, which he had articulated a year and a half before President Clinton's pathbreaking visit.

Vajpayee charted out this vision of rapprochement between India and the United States in a speech at the Asia Society in New York in September 1998, just a few months after nuclear tests by India had put the relationship in deep freeze. I had the privilege of witnessing that speech firsthand, since I had just begun working at the Asia Society, and was able to offer a *namaste* to the prime minister as he made his way through the receiving line. Vajpayee's warmth contrasted with India's historic standoff-ishness toward the United States. "India and the United States are natural allies in the quest for a better future for the world in the 21st century,"[49] he declared, a sentiment that would be echoed subsequently by leaders on both sides. Vajpayee likely did not intend to imply the pursuit of a military alliance—that would have been too sharp a departure from the script of Indian diplomacy—but as a term of art, "natural allies" broke new ground in framing the idea of partnership between India and the United States.

Years later, we can see the imprint of Vajpayee's approach in the Modi government—a willingness to pursue stronger ties with the United States without concern that it will look "too close" to the world's super-power. This does not mean, however, that Indian concerns about protecting itself from excessive U.S. influence have ended. India—across all parties—never wants to be any country's "junior partner," as C. Raja Mohan so aptly puts it. The new BJP government may be warmer to Washington than its predecessor, but that does not mean New Delhi has inched any closer to being a formal part of a U.S.-led alliance structure.

India has moved away from nonalignment between two competing blocs to an approach that emphasizes crafting numerous agreements with multiple countries it views as helpful to its rise. This has led to a series of declaratory "strategic partnerships" with the world's major powers—the United States, Russia, Japan, France, Germany, the United Kingdom, and Australia. A "vision" for a future strategic partnership with China was declared in 2013. But it's not just major powers that get to partner India strategically. At last count, New Delhi has also declared strategic partnerships with Afghanistan, Brazil, Indonesia, Kazakhstan, Malaysia, Mongolia, Nigeria, Saudi Arabia, Singapore, South Africa, South Korea, Tajikistan, United Arab Emirates, Uzbekistan, Vietnam, and with the Association of Southeast Asian Nations, the European Union, and all of Africa.[50]

While India has moved a great distance from its earlier hortatory nonalignment, it's hard not to wonder if the proliferation of strategic partnerships might well accomplish a similar goal of balancing all international relationships without having to make choices among them. Former U.S. ambassador to India Robert D. Blackwill, my colleague at the Council on Foreign Relations, referred to this transition as a "multi-aligned" foreign policy.[51]

Notably, in its first three years the Modi government has not emphasized the terms "strategic autonomy" or "nonalignment." Those terms carry Nehruvian baggage that the BJP sees itself as shedding. But the distinct preference for seeing India's global position advanced through independence remains. For Nehru that vision meant "being friends with all countries as far as possible."[52] For the Modi government, the "world is a family," as depicted by the Sanskrit proverb *vasudhaiva kutumbakam*. Indeed, the BJP's election manifesto of 2014 asserted: "Instead of being led by big power interests, we will engage proactively on our own with countries in the neighbourhood and beyond."[53] The orientation and terminology differ from the past, but the core preference remains an important starting point that helps determine just how far India will likely stray from its foundational ideas.

In one additional way, Nehru's influence continues to shape Indian policy decisions. The NAM legacy of nonintervention remains a cornerstone for Indian decision-making on foreign policy. This is why India tends to steer clear of resolutions that single out a particular country in bodies like the UN Human Rights Council. To India, such efforts usually suggest unacceptable meddling with another country's sovereignty. And although India is consistently among the world's largest annual contributors of troops to UN peacekeeping operations, it seeks the UN imprimatur for deployment rather than joining a NATO-plus or other coalition-of-the-willing elsewhere, seeing anything not blessed by the United Nations as lacking international legitimacy. These preferences have held regardless of the party leading the central government.

At the same time, as many observers of Indian foreign policy have noted, India can be quite forceful when it comes to the domestic politics of its smaller neighbors. India may steer clear of comment on Iraq and the rise of the self-proclaimed Islamic State, but it will press firmly on Nepal, Bangladesh, Sri Lanka, Bhutan, and Maldives, where it sees its security interests affected. Here, the noninterventionism of nonalignment gives way to a clear Chanakyan realism within India's own neighborhood. And again, all parties have displayed this preference equally.

Presenting Indian Values Abroad

Swami Vivekananda and what he represents—an India proud of and actively spreading its Hindu cultural and spiritual traditions abroad—would be expected to appeal more to the BJP than to the Congress. Former prime minister Vajpayee invoked Vivekananda as an icon; Modi has taken this further, paying lavish public tribute to the monk and highlighting him as a source of personal inspiration. In 2012, then chief minister Modi went on a highly visible month-long trek across Gujarat to carry Vivekananda's "message to the youth of the state" in advance of his 150th birth anniversary.[54] As prime minister, Modi has brought fresh international visibility to Vivekananda's legacy, such his unveiling of a Vivekananda statue during a 2015 visit to Malaysia. And as I discuss in greater detail in Chapter 4, BJP-led governments also tend to invest more time and attention on using Indian traditions such as yoga as a tool of soft power.

But as with other influences on Indian encounters with the world, such a dichotomy would be too simplistic. As prime minister, Nehru too noted the influence of Vivekananda on Indian thought, including his lessons for India's current troubles. In a 1964 contribution to *Prabudha Bharata*, Nehru interpreted Vivekananda's call for India to "stand fearless," to include the need for India to confront its weakness and strengthen itself after China's attack on the Indian border in 1962. Here, for Nehru, Vivekananda's spiritual teachings provided a lesson in statecraft.[55] Under Indira Gandhi, the Indian government declared Vivekananda's birthday "National Youth Day," and it has remained a day of national observation for every government since.

In a more institutionalized way, India uses cultural diplomacy to project soft power and showcase its traditions to the world. Regardless of who controls the government, India's diplomatic missions highlight its artistic, religious, and cultural riches. You might find kuchipudi dancers performing in Jakarta, Baul singers in Moscow, and Rajasthani folk paintings on display in Paris. This is because in 1950, freedom fighter and then Indian minister of education, Maulana Azad, led the government's creation of a body specifically charged with furthering the role of culture in India's relations abroad: the Indian Council for Cultural Relations (ICCR). This institution counts the foreign secretary of India as its ex-officio vice president, and is seen as the "cultural arm" of the Ministry of External Affairs. It draws from the external affairs, culture, and education ministries for numerous governing board members, and also includes board leadership from members of parliament and Indian universities.[56] The composition ensures nonpartisan continuity through the participation of so many serving civil servants, but also makes room for elected politicians to play a role in its governance.

ICCR carries out academic as well as more purely cultural activities: it sponsors scholarships for foreign students to study in India; it supports dozens of chairs for Indian studies and Hindi teaching in foreign universities; it convenes conferences on subjects of Indian cultural traditions; it sends Indian artists to perform around the world; and it sponsors Indian Cultural Centers abroad, from the expected (London and Moscow) to the farther-flung (Paramaribo and Suva). Indian Cultural Centers to date number thirty-six. This is more than many countries might have, but not even one-tenth of the reportedly nearly five hundred Confucius Institutes sponsored by the Chinese government around the world. Still, India's efforts to make its civilizational traditions more familiar to non-Indians are growing. In addition to the 140 ICCR chairs operational in such universities as Fudan, McGill, and University of the West Indies (with sixty-nine of these focused on teaching Hindi), the Indian government has made strategic endowments to create permanent chairs focused on India, and has some three dozen proposals for renewal chairs or new chairs around the world.[57] The Vivekananda Visiting Professorship established by India's Ministry of Culture at the University of Chicago in 2012, with a ceremony that featured India's then finance minister (later president), Pranab Mukherjee, marks one such example.

As another way to connect with countries—in a very Vivekanandan manner—at times India has used its Buddhist heritage as a civilizational bridge. Buddhist tourism has for long brought visitors from Japan, China, and other East Asian countries to the Indian cities of Sarnath and Bodh Gaya, important places in the life of the Buddha. In 2012, when Indian ties with Sri Lanka were at a low point over Sri Lankan inaction on allegations of rights abuses at the end of the country's civil war, the Indian Ministry of Culture sponsored a journey to Sri Lanka of several important Buddhist relics, the bones of the Buddha himself. India's relationships with countries that have large Buddhist populations, like Sri Lanka, Myanmar, and much of East Asia, draw upon different influences than New Delhi shows to the West, leveraging culture in an approach that has endured across governments.[58]

What appeals to the Vivekananda tradition do not fully answer, however, is what role these values—Indian values—should play in India's international efforts. While India makes use of its civilizational heritage, its cultural traditions, its religious diversity, and its scholarly traditions as facets of itself it would like the world to know more about, these have been soft pushes dependent upon interest already generated elsewhere. It's also the case that Indian leaders have historically seen the success of their country's democracy—its scale and the fact that the Indian experiment overcame the odds—as one of its great moral strengths in the world, its source of soft power. India's successful management of its extreme diversity has been its soft power calling card, and has underwritten the country's ability to stand as an example for others. Should India's own internal challenges worsen, or should a more exclusionary religious nationalism impinge upon the country's ability to successfully uphold its diversity as a model, that form of soft power appeal might diminish.

Secondly, would a more robust approach informed by Vivekananda's active and highly personalized diplomacy mean an India more involved in the internal developments of other countries? It's worth recalling the final lines of Vajpayee's 1998 "natural allies" speech to suggest one possible vision for an India using its soft power more actively in the world. Vajpayee quoted a poem written by Vivekananda, "To the Fourth of July," written to celebrate the American Independence Day. It closes with these lines:

> Till men and women, with uplifted head,
> Behold their shackles broken, and
> Know, in springing joy, their life renewed!

India's vision of itself as a moral power and a model for the developing world depends on an idea that others will seek out what Indian civilization has to offer. But it is possible to imagine that over time, a stronger and more powerful India will view its spiritual and cultural traditions as those destined to support freedom more actively for others in need.

THE ROAD AHEAD

The sources of influence on Indian thinking about its place in the world affect everything from trade to the pursuit of foreign investment, to questions of sovereignty and involvement abroad, all the way to how India presents itself and its soft power to the external world. Some of the influences bear more heavily on the Congress than the BJP, and vice versa, but all are reflected in the way both national parties have led governments, and will likely continue to do so regardless of the party in power.

As India gains greater power on the world stage—more visibility, a louder voice, a greater ability to shape outcomes, and the seat it long desires in major institutions—do Indians see their country as a global leader, or a careful and reserved presence on the global stage? The answer, somewhat paradoxically, is both. India sees itself as a great civilization with much to offer the world; at the same time, it often seeks to "remain aloof" of world entanglements. This dichotomy highlights the ambivalence with which Indians envision their country's role on the global stage. The Modi government has begun a process of changing how India presents itself and relates to the world, with a focus on transitioning from a "balancing power" to a "leading power," but that will take time, and it will continue to be inflected by the strands of influence that have long shaped India's encounters with the world, even as those influences interact with other, more material compulsions. The next chapter examines in greater detail how that process is unfolding in the economic domain, where change is perhaps most rapid.

3

Opening to the World

IN JUNE 2010, LARRY SUMMERS—then a member of President Obama's cabinet as director of the National Economic Council—delivered the keynote address at the U.S.-India Business Council's annual dinner. Speakers at these dinners often tick through a laundry list of recent accomplishments in bilateral ties, a necessary task but one that does not usually make for a scintillating speech. In a provocative departure from the usual format, Summers instead proposed to all of us in the room— I was there on behalf of the Washington strategic advisory McLarty Associates—that we project ourselves into the future, and imagine how we might evaluate our present.

When we look back three hundred years from now, said Summers, the defining story of our era will be neither the end of the Cold War nor the struggle between the West and the Islamic world. Instead, in the grand sweep of history, he proposed that the most important development of our time would be the rise of the developing world—of India, China, and other emerging countries. He observed that 40 percent of the world's population having experienced an increase in living standards of some thirty- to one hundred-fold in an individual lifespan was an "event that ranks only with the Renaissance and the Industrial Revolution." Moreover:

> India will look at a nation that has the world's largest labor force, that has by a wide margin one of its three largest economies, that has over a billion people in middle-class living standards, that can look back

at a period in which tremendous economic energy was unleashed—first with the reforms of the 1990s and the first decade of the twentieth century that saw a profound opening-up of trade and investment to the rest of the world, that saw the beginning of movement from a presumption of prohibition to a presumption of permission.[1]

From a vantage point in 2040, said Summers, people will look back and recognize that India was "the first developing country to embrace on a major scale the knowledge economy," and one that made great strides in renewable energy. By 2040, the Washington Consensus and Beijing Consensus will have become "interesting historical ideas," but a *Mumbai* Consensus of people-centered growth may well have eclipsed both.

Now, whether a "Mumbai Consensus" will in fact become conventional wisdom on how to organize a country's political economy is hard to predict. But the India of the coming generation will affect the world far more profoundly than the India of the late twentieth century. The central factor in this transformation is economic. While India's dismantling of old barriers remains incomplete, the past fifteen years have already propelled the country from the margins of global commerce toward the edges of the center—like the *jambudvipa* of Hindu cosmology. India is shaking off its socialist past and making its way—ever on its own terms—into the front ranks of the global economy.

Though India has come a long way from its 1991 economic opening, the reform agenda remains largely incomplete. No national consensus exists on the role of markets and how open the Indian economy should be to the world, and virtually every reform step requires Indians to renegotiate their own beliefs and biases about commerce. Unlike in the United States, where a president could proudly state that "the chief business of the American people is business," until relatively recently enthusiasm for business in India was more limited—a byproduct of the powerful ideas that spurred the Indian independence movement.[2]

Each step in India's halting process of reform shows still-powerful resistance to opening the economy further to both market forces and global capital, even in a period in which Indian businesses and their global expansion has converted the Indian government—ironically—into an advocate for opening markets abroad. There is no other issue that so powerfully determines the role that India will play on the global stage, yet one that to this day remains the subject of at times paralyzing political differences. India's ambivalence about openness explains why its reform process has been fitful, and indeed why "reform by stealth" became a well-known descriptive term. It also explains why the reform-minded Modi government has had to muster up its craftiest political skills to accomplish the major reform steps it has already accomplished.

INDIA'S GLOBAL TRADING PAST

Americans with a passing acquaintance with India know the broad contours of its twentieth-century economic history. They have an idea that India had been closed to the world previously, and that its once-socialist economy has more recently embarked upon market-based reforms. While this is largely correct, and captures some of the difficulties in doing business in India, it also oversimplifies a much more nuanced economic history in which an inherent contradiction hovers in the background. On the one hand, mistrust of the market remains high, leading to a reform process often criticized for its leisurely pace. At the same time, many Indian thinkers—across political parties—nurture a sense of pride that in its more glorious past India played a larger and globally significant role in the world, including in trade.

The invocation of Indian cultural influence, especially across Southeast Asia, rests upon an earlier history of India as a trading nation. Indeed, in the premodern world, India was a source of significant global trade; trade helped disseminate Indian influences, including Hinduism, Buddhism, and the Sanskrit language to what is today's Afghanistan, and through much of Southeast Asia.[3]

In 2011, the opening of a long-sealed vault of the Sri Padmanabhaswamy temple in the southern state of Kerala unearthed an estimated $20 billion trove of treasures and currency from centuries past and places distant. As Gurcharan Das explains, the vault turned out to hold "a vast store of gold coins of the Roman Empire, from almost 2,000 years ago; Venetian gold ducats of the 14th and 15th centuries . . . Portuguese currency from its days of glory in the 16th century; 17th century coins of the Dutch East India Company; Napoleon's gold coins from the early 19th century" and other valuables.[4] Das describes the trade surplus ancient India ran with ancient Rome; Roman senators "complained that their women used too many Indian spices and luxuries," in ongoing exchange for the Roman empire's gold. Pliny the Elder, in his *Natural History*, remarked upon the seemingly insatiable demand in ancient Rome for Indian goods, measured by the more than "fifty million sesterces of our empire's wealth" sent annually to India in exchange for the latter's luxuries.[5] (This observation became transformed, likely via amateur translations by British colonial officers, into the notion that Pliny had called India "the sink of the world's gold," although Pliny never used such a phrase.)[6]

This map of India's overseas trade from 2300 BCE to 800 CE—published in 1970, at the height of economic autarky—suggests how Indians continued to value their country's historic commercial power even through the worst days of the socialist planned economy (Figure 3.1).[7]

Coincidentally, the map was prepared for a volume celebrating India's "contributions to the world" published by the Vivekananda Rock Memorial Committee, a living monument to the monk's visit to the southernmost tip of India in 1892, during which he found his calling "to arouse the nation from its dismal slumber of a thousand years of slavery and rediscover its past glory."[8]

Across party lines, politicians cite this once-glorious commercial footprint across the Indian Ocean and the Asia Pacific as evidence of India's great past and inherent potential. In his 2011 address to the Ethiopian parliament, former prime minister Manmohan Singh noted that Indian merchants had crossed the Indian Ocean to trade with eastern Africa, flocking "to the ancient port of Adulis, trading silk and spices for gold and ivory."[9] Similarly, the BJP's election platform of 2014 invoked the broad reach of ancient Indian trade as a feature that had earned the country global recognition—and should be reclaimed:

> From the Vedas to Upanishads and Gautam [the Buddha] and Mahavira [the 24th Jain Tirthankara] and then to Kautilya and Chandra Gupta and down up to the eighteenth century, India was respected for its flourishing economy, trade, commerce and culture. It had an international outreach from Korea to Arabia, from Bamiyan to Borobudur and beyond. Before the advent of Britishers, Indian goods were internationally recognized for their quality and

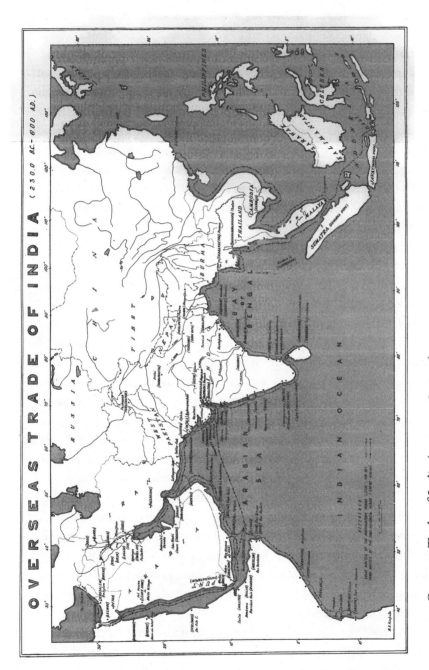

FIGURE 3.1 Overseas Trade of India (2300 BC–800 AD)

Source: Chandra, ed., *India's Contribution to World Thought and Culture*. Used with permission.

craftsmanship. India had a much bigger role and presence in industry and manufacturing than any nation in Europe or Asia.[10]

British colonization disrupted this interconnection with the world. To
fully appreciate India's persistent suspicion of foreign capital, it helps to
recall that the colonization of India by the British began commercially,
with the East India Company.[11] The early British presence in India,
known as the "Company Raj" period, was a period in which control
was exercised not by a foreign government, but instead by the East
India Company itself. From its seventeenth-century origins as a company with a British royal charter to trade with India, to its eighteenth-
and nineteenth-century expansion into administration and governance
in India, the East India Company history illustrates an era and a form
of sovereignty driven by British commercial interests. In 1784 the India
Act put the East India Company under British government control,
but it would not be until 1858 that the British government formally
assumed authority over the Indian territories it controlled.[12]

As Congress party politician Shashi Tharoor put it in his debate
speech at the Oxford Union in 2015, in which he called for British
reparations to India, "At the beginning of the 18th century, India's
share of the world economy was 23 percent, as large as all of Europe
put together. By the time the British departed India, it had dropped
to less than 4 percent. . . . By the end of the 19th century, India was
Britain's biggest cash-cow, the world's biggest purchaser of British
exports."[13] This is the context that Indian thinkers have in mind when
they reflect on India's economic role in the world, nursing the loss of
an earlier greatness that the West plundered. Memories of the East
India Company remain just below the surface even today. Take the
response to Facebook's Free Basics effort in 2016 to provide limited
free Internet access in India. Indian regulators ultimately quashed the
idea as incompatible with net neutrality, but as importantly, one of the
most widely cited criticisms called it "imperialism and the East India
Company all over again."[14]

The Gandhian emphasis on *swaraj*—self-rule—and its close relative
self-reliance delivered India its independence, and represented resistance to the exploitation of the West. But it was Nehru the determined
modernizer, not Gandhi the traditionalist, who determined the path

India's economy would take. Early leaders of independent India wanted to rebuild the domestic economy, but mostly viewed trade as synonymous with the colonial project that had subjugated their nation. To prevent a return to weakness, and to make up lost ground, the state would take on a robust role; state-owned firms would control the so-called "commanding heights" of the economy, in a term borrowed from Lenin that Nehru used to describe the government's role in organizing a mixed economy.[15]

At the time this was not an unusual strategy for the newly decolonized countries of Asia and Africa. In the 1950s, many countries around the world adopted socialist planning. Nehru believed that his economic choices would swiftly deliver the developmental miracle the country greatly needed. In 1948, Nehru was "generally speaking . . . committed to the nationalization of key industries" but settled for limited state ownership given resource limitations. He envisioned a future in which, "as industrialization proceeds, the State ownership of industry will also rapidly increase."[16] Iron, steel, and power would be the "foundations of all industrial progress."[17] Inspired by the apparent success of the Soviet Union, a central planning commission would roll out a series of five-year plans and formulate strategies to deliver the envisioned industrial progress.

Shortly after independence, the dominant Congress party moved to codify socialism as India's goal. India's lower house of parliament passed a resolution in December 1954 that declared "that the pattern of society . . . should be socialistic."[18] In January 1955, the Congress party reached a consensus during their annual meeting, held that year in Avadi outside today's Chennai, that declared commitment to "a socialistic pattern of society."[19] To this day people look back at the Avadi Resolution as a definitive moment in Indian economic history.

Writing to his chief ministers in late 1956, Nehru referred to the adoption of the goal of socialism as a process that had not been sudden, but rather "a natural development of our thinking and our national movement." He saw socialism as a protection against the "enormous power" of big monopolies emerging in industrialized capitalist economies, and wrote that the main goal of the Avadi Resolution was "idealistic considerations and a desire to raise the under-privileged and to eliminate . . . the big differences between various classes and groups in the country."[20] India's second Five-Year Plan outlined the country's new approach of a "socialist pattern of society" in which the government would take "main responsibility" for developing heavy industries, oil, coal, and atomic energy.[21]

Despite the best of intentions—and Nehru's words illustrate, above all, a desire to deliver a better future for his country—in practice the pursuit of a closed, planned economy coupled with licensing requirements for matters like materials imports, production quotas, sales quotas, you name it, burdened the nominally private sector. With the government in control of the "commanding heights," private industry had to seek permissions for almost everything, beholden to the whims of government bureaucrats for even the most elementary questions of output and pricing. The state controlled key heavy industries such as arms, iron and steel, casting and forging, mining, rail and air transportation, shipbuilding, telephones, and electricity. Over the years, the state would also seek progressive involvement in industries like antibiotics, fertilizer, chemical pulp, and road transport.[22]

Following Nehru's death in 1964, he was succeeded briefly by Lal Bahadur Shastri, a Congress leader from the northern state of Uttar Pradesh. When Shastri died suddenly, in 1966, Nehru's daughter Indira Gandhi stepped up to the prime ministership. In the view of many economists and economic historians, it was Indira Gandhi who significantly intensified economic controls. As Columbia University's Arvind Panagariya observes, the period of 1965–1981 resulted in "extra regulations applicable to large enterprises . . . severe restrictions on foreign investment . . . further tightening of the licensing regime; the small-scale industries reservation; and the nationalization of banks, insurance firms, and the coal and oil industries."[23] In addition to the nationalization of several industries, constraints placed on the size of firms made it impossible for Indian private companies to grow larger. This vision did not allow India's private sector to compete globally.

At the same time, though not mostly directed at economic matters, the Indira Gandhi years popularized a new vocabulary for thinking about threats to India: the "foreign hand." Mrs. Gandhi used the term to indicate shadowy outside forces she believed were acting against India's interests—with the United States a frequent "target of concern," as the late Paul Kreisberg put it. Suffice it to say that India's fear of foreign capital and fear of the foreign hand went together.[24]

Given this backdrop, economic growth was limited in the early decades after independence. According to Panagariya, from 1951 to 1965 the Indian economy grew at an average of 4.1 percent; from 1965 to 1981, at only 3.2 percent.[25] Economist Raj Krishna coined the derisive term "Hindu rate of growth" to describe this chronic underperformance. Though it was Indira Gandhi who was responsible for the tightening of the licensing system and other forms of state control, the path she took was the one that had been set out by Nehru. The commonly used term "Nehruvian Socialism" has come to specify the Indian approach to economic management during these years.[26]

Indira Gandhi's son Rajiv, a former airline pilot, succeeded her as prime minister after her assassination in 1984 by her Sikh bodyguards. He put in place minor reforms, such as loosening licensing requirements and liberalizing trade at the margins in order to promote exports. Gandhi dreamed of India improving its technology and becoming "modern," and was known for his focus on telecommunications reforms and computerization. Growth ticked up during his term in office (1984–1989). But after Gandhi's defeat in 1989—in large part due to corruption allegations involving a Swedish arms manufacturer, Bofors—India entered a period of chaotic national politics.[27]

Two shaky coalition governments followed in the space of eighteen months. They spent their energies managing the fallout from political and social national crises. The first of these, a motley coalition of "peoples'" parties supported from the outside by both communists and the BJP in a grand alliance against Congress, fell apart in less than a year. A caretaker regime followed, best remembered for presiding over a dramatic foreign reserves crisis in the spring of 1991. India's foreign currency reserves dipped dangerously low, enough to fund only two weeks of imports. That was the iconic moment of India's sale of twenty tons of gold to the Union Bank of Switzerland.[28] When a Congress-led coalition government came into office in June 1991, they inherited an economy on the ropes.

The Narasimha Rao government, with Dr. Manmohan Singh as finance minister, began its tenure facing the real possibility of economic collapse. By late June 1991, India faced a $72 billion foreign debt burden, with only $1.1 billion in hard-currency reserves. The new government used gold reserves to buy time in July, sending four further tranches, altogether about 47 tons of gold, abroad to the Bank of England as collateral for loans that totaled around $400 million.[29] The gold sales were highly controversial at the time, a subject of parliamentary discussion and nightly news coverage, in which the political debate centered on notions of "national humiliation," "honor," and the "pain" of hocking the nation's gold outside the country.[30] For the apocryphal "sink of the world's gold," a society that values the precious metal as a visible symbol of wealth, pawning the nation's treasure in distress represented the decisive failure of the goal of self-reliance.

Gold sales would mark only the beginning of the sweeping changes ushered in by India's balance-of-payments crisis. The Rao government sought support from the International Monetary Fund and began a difficult process of dismantling many long-standing economic controls. In a nationally televised nighttime address on Indian state-run television, Doordarshan, Prime Minister Rao told the nation that there were no "soft options" remaining, and that India would need to "open the door" to foreign investment, make it easier to do business, and ease industrial policy.[31] Then finance minister Singh compared India with South Korea, saying that "we have fallen way behind while South Korea has emerged as an economic giant."[32]

The prospect of reforms carried out under duress led to an outpouring of sentiments about autonomy and sovereignty that echo even today. Ashis Nandy, a leading political scientist, told the *New York Times* that "this will be seen as a kind of interference with India's autonomy." The then general secretary of the Communist party of India said to the *Times*, "Is the IMF imposing its economic sovereignty over India, that's what we want to know."[33] But the Rao government moved forward with vast reforms to save the country from default. They believed, rightly, that India had no other choice.

As the summer of 1991 unfolded, the Rao government took dramatic steps: sensitive industries like arms, atomic energy, and mining would remain in the public sector, but they abolished the long-standing licensing regime for all but a subsection of "specified" industries such as petroleum, aerospace and defense, and hazardous chemicals, among others. A country once synonymous with autarky suddenly began to welcome foreign investment by allowing foreigners to invest up to 51 percent equity in such "high priority" industries as steel casting and forging, electrical equipment, and engineering production, among others.[34] The government decided to promote foreign technology agreements; announced a review of public sector policy that would open the door to private competition and disinvestment; and scrapped limits on the size of "dominant" companies, regulations that had artificially dwarfed private industry.

Revisiting the July 1991 statement on industrial policy that detailed these changes is a reminder of how extensively, and how abruptly, Rao and Singh, in the span of a single day, opened the Indian economy.[35] Not only did they avert collapse, but the economy rebounded. Growth rates ticked up to around 6 percent. Although academic debate exists concerning whether the 1991 reforms were the singular catalyst for India's increased rates of economic growth, they certainly went much further than anything before to dismantle the policies that had stifled the Indian economy. The dismantling of trade barriers marked India's economic reentry to the world, and of the world to India. Forty-four years after independence, India had chosen a new path.

After the Rao government completed its term in 1996, India experienced another period of short-lived coalition governments. The 1998 election of the National Democratic Alliance (NDA), led by the BJP, brought a government with a more economically conservative, market-oriented philosophy to power. In its six years in office, the NDA championed India's second round of structural reforms, including in, as Panagariya describes, "international trade, foreign investment, insurance, telecommunications, electricity, roads, privatization, and education."[36] Panagariya's analysis shows that India's higher growth rates of up to 8 percent generated a few years later "must be attributed largely to these reforms."

The world took notice. During this time, with the statesmanlike Vajpayee at the helm as prime minister, India became sharply more visible as an emerging market. In those years I was working at the Asia Society in New York, where our policy and business programs regularly featured political and corporate speakers from India, increasingly to packed rooms eager to hear more about new opportunities there. In addition to hosting Indian Prime Minister Vajpayee, who broached the idea of a stronger U.S.-India relationship as "natural allies" to everyone's surprise, the Asia Society hosted a growing agenda of India programs. When the then chief minister of Andhra Pradesh, N. Chandrababu Naidu, presented what amounted to his "roadshow" seeking investment in his state in September 1998, he clicked through a PowerPoint presentation about technology, looking more like a businessman making a pitch to investors than an old-style politician fearful of foreign capital.

A year later, we hosted Indian Internet entrepreneur Ajit Balakrishnan, whose Rediff.com had just started a U.S. edition and was on the verge of an IPO that would raise $55 million in its NASDAQ debut.[37] That same year, the director general of the Confederation of Indian Industry (CII) at the time, Tarun Das, presented his vision of how India could get to sustained 10 percent growth with further reforms. The hall was packed and the ambition was palpable. A decade earlier, sustained growth above 5 percent seemed unimaginable, and U.S. corporate interest in India was minuscule. India was on the brink of an entirely new phase in its interaction with the world.[38]

When Goldman Sachs published its "Dreaming with BRICs" report in the fall of 2003, projecting that the emerging markets of Brazil, Russia, India, and China could surpass the Group of Six (G6) economies by 2050, international interest in India picked up further.[39] Around the same time, Indian business houses began to develop a much more active international profile; IT companies like Infosys made headlines with major international contracts, and Bharti Airtel attracted more than $1 billion in foreign investment. That same year, India's Ministry of Commerce and Industry formed a partnership trust with CII to focus on telling India's story abroad: the India Brand Equity Foundation (IBEF). In its own words, the IBEF sought to create "international awareness of the Made in India label in markets overseas and to facilitate dissemination of knowledge of Indian products and services."[40] In the span of a few years, India's businesses and bureaucrats had gone from confrontation to collaboration.

Despite their reformist agenda and plaudits from global investors, in May 2004—to the surprise of most political observers—the BJP-led government lost the national elections. This defeat against the backdrop of an election campaign touting prosperity ("India Shining") had serious consequences for India's economy. It seemed to lead the incoming

Congress-led coalition government, known as the United Progressive Alliance, to press the brakes on reforms, in part to satisfy their coalition partners, a group of communist and socialist parties known as the Left Front. This created an unexpected irony: Finance Minister Manmohan Singh, who famously opened India to the world in 1991, ended up leading a government that slowed the pace of reforms.

THE TELECOM AND TELEVISION REVOLUTION

The story of India's opening would not be complete without a brief mention of the changes that transformed the country's media and communications environment, and directly plugged India into the rest of the world. These changes are hardly unique to India—the telecom revolution is one of the great clichés of globalization—but the scale and speed of India's metamorphosis remains breathtaking.

From today's kaleidoscopic perspective, recalling the drabness of the not-so-distant past can be difficult. In the India I first visited as a college student, families had to apply for a landline connection and wait in some cases for many years for their turn. International "trunk" calls for those even with phones had to be booked in advance; it could take hours for an operator at the state-owned telecom firm to call you back. Line quality was so bad that a conversation often resembled a shouting match.

Prior to 1991, India had just one television channel, the government-run Doordarshan (which means "far-away vision," a calque of "television" using Sanskritic roots instead of Greek and Latin). Deregulation gave birth to India's telecommunications revolution—foreshadowed by Rajiv Gandhi's interest in the sector in the 1980s, but dramatically taking off only in the late 1990s and 2000s. The telecom revolution—going from 52 million mobile subscribers to more than one billion in a little more than a decade—was matched by an explosion of television and print media, including in local languages all across the country.[41] The latter has been closely linked with economic liberalization, especially so due to advertising's part in the creation of market-based media. By 2015, that single plain government television station had been joined by hundreds of channels in two dozen–plus languages. As television historian Nalin Mehta notes, "Television grew in India only because the astonishing growth in advertising that fueled the post-reform period. Between 1990–91 and 2014, Indian advertising grew by almost forty times," from INR 9.3 billion to INR 371 billion.[42] The obvious effect of both liberalizations, over time, would be to connect Indian citizens in real time with family, friends, and colleagues anywhere in the world.

India's 1991 deregulation created the entry for private companies to provide services in television broadcasting and in telecommunications. While India's state-run Doordarshan controlled the terrestrial broadcast nodes, satellite transponders provided an alternative means of transmission. Rupert Murdoch's Star TV was the first foreign company to launch a slate of satellite-broadcast channels targeting the Indian audience in 1991. Cable providers created the "last mile" link to homes. The first private Indian network, Zee TV, began airing soap operas and game shows in Hindi in 1992.

Soon international media descended on India in droves, outpaced only by the growth in domestic channels. According to scholar Daya Kishan Thussu's research, "by 1998 nearly 70 cable and satellite channels were operating in India . . . notably STAR, BBC, Discovery, MTV, Sony, CNN, Disney, CNBC, and scores of Indian companies."[43] Today, according to the official Ministry of Information and Broadcasting, India houses 888 "permitted private channels."[44] Indian languages other than English now account for much of the growth in news channels, as Star TV Chairman and CEO Uday Shankar told me when I paid a call on him at his Urmi Estate office in Mumbai. "Vernacular language growth is what is keeping the newspaper alive, and ditto for vernacular language television news channels."[45]

Foreign visitors can turn on CNN and BBC for the news, and watch Homeland or Game of Thrones for entertainment. Just as significant, Indian channels such as Star, Sun, and Zee have developed a global footprint. Members of the great Indian diaspora never have to go long without Bollywood or cricket, now carried not only by satellite or cable providers, but also through Internet apps like Willow (an American venture and the official partner of various cricket boards) or Star India's Hotstar. Times Now launched in the United Kingdom in November 2015, and cable providers across Europe, the United States, and Africa have carried Zee TV from the mid-1990s. Star's Hotstar app, launched in 2015, has done so well domestically that the channel now plans to take it global.[46]

In a new twist during 2016, Zee launched a global English news channel, WION ("World Is One News," a play on *vasudhaiva kutumbakam*) intended to provide a "South Asian perspective" as an alternative to CNN or BBC. Also in 2016, top news anchor Arnab Goswami resigned from Times Now and by 2017 had launched a new channel named Republic TV. Republic TV's global footprint remained unclear at the time of this writing, but Goswami had previously spoken in public forums about the need to end Western "hegemony" over global English news media, and had proposed that India should be the next "media capital of the world."[47]

Technology has transformed India's telecommunications landscape even more dramatically. In 2016, the country where a solitary landline was once a cherished luxury became the world's second largest smartphone market after China. As it has throughout the world, the explosive growth of mobile phones has democratized access to information and is transforming the fabric of daily life. In today's India, a farmer on a cell phone can check crop prices, receive a government subsidy, and stay up to date on the triumphs and triubulations of the Indian cricket team. Indian mobile companies have honed their technology and now deliver service at some of the lowest rates in the world. The Modi government, in particular, has placed mobile banking, in combination with individual national identification numbers, at the core of an ambitious plan to better target government subsidies at their intended beneficiaries. Firms such as Reliance and Bharti are betting big that smartphones will fundamentally change how Indians work, entertain themselves, and stay connected with their families.

Telecom and television—both powered by the private sector—have enabled much deeper Indian connection with the global flow of ideas. Top Indian TV anchors like Goswami or Barkha Dutt keep track of everything from the U.S. presidential campaign to the French economist Thomas Piketty's views on inequality. Some Indian channels have attained global reach, and in the case of cricket India has become the singular global market-maker because of the importance of its home market. These transformations reflect a true opening up of two-way flows in how India thinks about and interacts with the world.

INDIAN BUSINESS GOES GLOBAL

Over the past fifteen years, while India carefully calibrated its opening to the world, its own major businesses have boldly gone global. Once the licensing regime was rolled back, and earlier limits on company size were lifted, Indian businesses found themselves with room to grow. Needless to say, this did not happen all at once. Not all businesses welcomed liberalization in 1991; the slashing of tariffs meant that domestic industry would suddenly face competition from abroad. A group of Indian business leaders, colloquially called the "Bombay Club," became a byword for domestic interests that feared foreign competition battling to keep tariffs and other protections in place.[48] But over time, some of India's more adaptable companies seized the opportunity to become globally competitive. IT entrepreneur Nandan Nilekani has called the changing attitudes toward competition a transformation from the "Bombay Club" to "Bombay House"—the latter a reference to the iconic headquarters of Tata Sons, an Indian conglomerate that has become a $108 billion global corporation competing with the best worldwide in such diverse industries as tea, hotels, and luxury automobiles.[49]

Some of India's new global companies began as old family conglomerates before acquiring businesses abroad. Others are newer companies built from scratch. A generation ago, India's IT industry barely existed. Today it stands out for pioneering processes that have changed the way the world does business. Either way, over the past decade Indian business has become visible around the world and provides an increasingly prominent form of soft power for their country, one that the government has sought to harness to present a new image of the country internationally. In fact, in 1997, the industrialist Rahul Bajaj—a prominent member of the Bombay Club who had demanded protection for domestic industry only a few years earlier—glimpsed a future when Indian firms would become multinationals. He wrote, "If we follow the right policies and have the right work ethic, I have no doubt that by the year 2020, India will take its rightful place among the leading economic powers of the world."[50] It's no coincidence that here again, this time in the words of a business leader rather than a diplomat or prime minister, we see the familiar notion of India attaining its "rightful place" in the world.

In the early 2000s, the notion of Indian companies becoming global conglomerates was still new. This changed when a series of acquisitions by the storied Tata group—with each business a headliner in its industry—propelled the group to become a global behemoth within less than a decade. The Tatas acquired Tetley Tea from the United Kingdom in 2000, a part of Daewoo Motors in 2004, British steelmaker Corus in a $12 billion acquisition in 2007, and then Jaguar LandRover from Ford Motor Company in 2008, in a $2.3 billion deal that captured substantial international attention. Ford had not managed to turn Jaguar LandRover around, and many doubted that an Indian company, particularly one that had launched the world's cheapest car that year, the ill-fated Tata Nano, would be able to steer the luxury brands to success. Proving skeptics wrong, under Tata management, JaguarLandRover has not just recovered but thrived. In 2016, the brands announced their sixth-straight record year in sales.[51] The company has become more visible outside India: Tata Consultancy Services became the title sponsor of one of the best-known sports events in the United States, the New York City Marathon, in 2014.

Or take the Mahindra and Mahindra group. As chairman and managing director Anand Mahindra told me when I visited him in the company's historic Gateway Building in Mumbai, the company's pedigree goes back to pre-independence India; it was founded as Mahindra and Mohammed in 1945 in Bombay. (When cofounder Ghulam Mohammed left for Pakistan after Partition, the firm "didn't have money to change the stationery that said M&M" so they changed the second M to Mahindra.)[52] Founded as a steel company, it became an automobile and tractor manufacturer, and today has moved into IT services, aerospace and defense, solar energy, real estate, hospitality, and financial services, among others. At the advent of economic reforms in 1991, annual turnover was about $840 million.[53] Today it's a $19 billion company operating in one hundred countries, with more than two hundred thousand employees.[54] It's also the world's largest tractor company: ads for Mahindra tractors and utility vehicles punctuate the Sunday morning television talk shows from time to time, at least in Washington, DC. Internally, the company sees itself as global: they developed the motto "Mahindra Rise" as a "core purpose that was globally intelligible" for a workforce including Chinese, Indian, Korean, and American employees, as Mahindra explained.

The growth of some of India's newer companies has been even more dramatic. Reliance Industries Ltd. has gone from nondescript trading firm to global giant in the space of two generations. Reliance began in 1957 as a textile trading company founded by Dhirubhai Ambani, but gradually integrated backward to move from polyester saris to making the polyester to the entire oil refining and petrochemicals process. By 2000, when the company's Jamnagar refinery was completed, it was at the time the world's largest greenfield refinery and petrochemicals facility. When President Bill Clinton visited India in 2000, the length of his meeting with the Ambanis—reportedly 45 minutes, almost as long as his meeting with India's prime minister—received wide press attention in India.[55] I attended a lecture by Reliance executive Hital Meswani, the Ambani brothers' cousin and a member of the conglomerate's senior management, at the University of Pennsylvania in 2005 in which he described how they were doubling the size of the refinery. By the next year, the Jamnagar complex had become the largest refining hub in the world. The company has numerous other businesses in power, telecom, retail, and other sectors, and according to their own projections, accounts for around 3 percent of India's GDP.[56] In 2010, they acquired interests in U.S. shale gas fields.

And of course the entire information technology industry—Infosys, Wipro, TCS, TechMahindra, and others—exploded into public consciousness by the mid-2000s, a well-known story and the inspiration for Tom Friedman's *The World Is Flat*. As more and more services began to be chopped up into discrete tasks and carried out remotely, Indian companies expanded the range of work they could perform for firms around the world. Indian IT has done so well as a global force that it accounted for nearly 9.5 percent of India's GDP in the 2015–2016 Indian fiscal year, more than long-established industries such as chemicals (around 2.5 percent) or textiles (around 2 percent).[57] Average citizens, officials, and politicians alike feel a sense of pride in an industry, built in India from the ground up, that has created opportunity for so many Indians, and has also transformed the way major modern corporations work.

Indeed, the success of the IT industry has changed the Indian government's trade negotiating priorities, for India now actively advocates for its IT services industry on a range of issues that would not have been on the radar screen twenty years ago. Indian trade negotiators are now among the most forward-leaning in the world on services trade issues that affect IT services work directly, such as immigration policy and related concerns. It's in many ways a dichotomous posture given the still-incremental approach to opening India more completely.

These snapshots illustrate the Indian economy's swift evolution from autarky to global ambition. Too many companies to list have raised the country's international visibility—indeed, former Microsoft India CEO and author of *Conquering the Chaos: Win in India, Win Everywhere* Ravi Venkatesan noted that India's business success "caused the world to even notice us."[58] India's corporate titans have also become philanthropists abroad, such as Ratan Tata's $50 million gift to Cornell to support agriculture and nutrition research as well as fellowships, Anand Mahindra's $10 million gift to Harvard to support the humanities, or Nandan and Rohini Nilekani's $5 million gift to Yale to support the study of India. But it has not always been easy, according to Mahindra, for the Indian government to see business as an asset for India on the global stage. In earlier years, political leaders "didn't want to be driven by the lowly objectives of commerce." Politics was seen as "more pure, more hallowed" than business, and middle-class parents wanted their children to become Indian Administrative Service officers in the government, not go into business.

After 1991 preferences began to change, as the economy began to grow faster, and new employment opportunities emerged in the Indian economy. Today an MBA is a desirable degree for younger people. But from Mahindra's perspective, older bureaucrats continue to view the private sector with some suspicion. "They see businessmen as Venus flytraps, almost," as if they harbor an idea that they'll get "trapped in some kind of corruption" by the private sector. The old suspicion of business may have diminished, but it still has not completely gone away.[59]

As its interests became more global, Indian industry began to play a larger role in global forums focused on the intersection of business and global economic policy issues—including in partnership with the Indian government, which had become more interested in projecting a confident, competitive Indian industry on the world stage. For instance, over the past decade, India has become more active with the World Economic Forum (WEF), though the Swiss organization had been involved with India since 1984, inviting politicians and business executives to the Alpine retreat, and partnering with CII to convene an annual India Economic Summit in India even before the advent of reforms.

At the Davos annual meeting of the World Economic Forum in 2006, Indian industry famously declared "India Everywhere" in an India Brand Equity Foundation (IBEF) campaign targeting the world's economic elite. The IBEF itself was a public-private partnership established between CII and India's Ministry of Commerce and Industry, focused entirely on "branding" the country as a desirable destination. India's 2006 delegation to Davos would be its largest ever—more than one hundred delegates from senior government officials to corporate titans—and the IBEF set about marketing the country, an effort two years in the making with a $4 million budget.[60]

Technology entrepreneur turned author and former government minister Nandan Nilekani led the conceptualization of the campaign back then. During a visit to his Bangalore home, I asked him about the experience. The whole idea, as he explained, was that guests at Davos would encounter India in every part of their lives, from signs upon landing at Zurich airport to gift bags with an iPod preloaded with Indian music, to Indian beer at the bars, kebabs, a cultural "soirée," and contemporary art. In that period, as Nilekani recalled, Indian business felt that the country needed to project its new image of being much more aspirational and business savvy.[61]

I met with Hari Bhartia, the soft-spoken co-chairman and founder of the Jubilant Bhartia group and the 2015 co-chair of the WEF Annual Meeting, to ask him about the role of Indian business in positioning India differently abroad. With his longtime involvement in the WEF and in industry associations, he believes that the Forum has played an important role in marketing India to the world, building on the global growth and transformation of Indian business itself to become more confident and more global. As Bhartia sees it, the combination of confidence, scale, and potential have created a new sense of Indian commercial power: "That does not mean we have sorted out all our internal problems, but the very fact that we are a large economy, we are growing at a sometimes 8 to 9 percent and have the capacity to grow . . . you can imagine how big a market we will be. That itself is a power that you have in the world."[62]

The strong Indian contingent at Davos reflected a larger trend of Indian business chambers becoming more active internationally. In addition to its partnership with the IBEF, the Confederation of Indian Industry pioneered a series of "Track II" discussions—a term to indicate informal diplomacy carried out by citizens outside government—for international relationships of particular importance to India. CII partnered with the Aspen Institute to create the first of these focused on the U.S.-India relationship in 2001, and the dialogue remains active today. I've been participating in the annual discussions since 2010 (with a break during my time in the Obama administration). Each year about forty Americans and Indians meet, either in New Delhi or in Washington, DC, to deliberate over issues ranging from trade to geopolitics to regional security.

Its success spawned strategic dialogues with Japan, Singapore, China, Israel, Turkey, and even Bhutan.[63] CII's longtime director general and later chief mentor Tarun Das has been the driving force in each of these. The Federation of Indian Chambers of Commerce and Industry has similarly convened Track II events, including focused efforts to promote trade between India and Pakistan, to try to create a bridge to better ties. FICCI has also created a BRICS Business Council, and serves as the coordinating organization for the "chamber-to-chamber" initiative launched through the Istanbul Process focused on Afghanistan to promote increased trade among all the countries near Afghanistan. Indian business—not long ago at the mercy of government bureaucrats—now plays a large part defining as well as projecting the country's image and its global interests.

THE BUSINESS OF GOVERNMENT

Over the past quarter-century, and especially over the past decade, India has actively worked to brand itself as a free-market democracy. India's most prominent business leaders now sit at the global commercial high table. But though the government has at times partnered with business, it has often done so with diffidence. This may now be changing. The Modi government places a higher priority on commercial diplomacy than did its predecessors, and doesn't appear to harbor any hangups about commerce being inferior to politics. Soon after taking power,

Modi scrapped the old Planning Commission, a symbol of socialist five-year planning, and in its place created a new institution, NITI Aayog, meant to act as a fount for good economic ideas in coordination with the states of India.[64] Diplomacy also received the commercial treatment. In Modi's view—enunciated frankly in 2014 prior to his election—Indian missions abroad should not just focus on filing "long reports" but instead "be more alive to issues like trade facilitation and promoting Indian business abroad, basically acting as force multipliers for the Indian economy," as the *Times of India* reported.[65]

After coming into office, Modi set the tone for India's new approach to the world with his own active international travel. Foreign policy was not expected to be a preoccupation of the Modi government, but it became his area of strength. Every international visit became a high-profile, leader-level investment pitch. In Silicon Valley, Modi personally visited Facebook and Tesla; in New York, instead of a site visit he met with an assembled roundtable of forty-seven CEOs to offer the same message. What's more, the Ministry of External Affairs created a new directorate charged with coordinating foreign investment into Indian states.[66] As Anand Mahindra put it, Modi's speech at the U.S.-India Business Council in 2014 was a turning point for how India presented itself on the world stage: "He said in Washington, 'business runs in my blood—I'm a Gujarati.' I don't think any Indian prime minister, including the ones who created this country, has ever said that. They always had to hide behind the cloak of socialism, thinking that was the acceptable policy."[67]

Four months into office, Modi unveiled a new national campaign that would become a central feature of his foreign policy: "Make in India." The Make in India campaign, complete with a mascot of an Asiatic lion made of wheels and gears, gussied-up into a brand what the previous UPA government had also attempted through its National Manufacturing Policy. The "Make in India" campaign actively seeks global investment to drive a domestic economic transformation via manufacturing sector growth. Since the launch of the campaign, Modi's foreign trips have showcased meetings with major investors—such as with the CEOs of Boeing and Lockheed Martin, and many others—urging them to come manufacture in India. In February 2016, an entire Make in India week took place in Mumbai, like a larger and national version of the state-level Vibrant Gujarat investor summits Modi used to convene as chief minister.

The long road from Nehru's "socialistic pattern of society" to Modi's "business runs in my blood" captures the epic scale of change in India. This journey affects India's idea of its global economic responsibilities and helps situate New Delhi's conflicting goals in the international area. On the one hand, a latent suspicion of commerce and the overhang of decades of protectionism has structured India's trade and investment postures to see market access conversations as untoward "pressure" instead of a regular part of the give-and-take of trade negotiations. Moving slowly staves off political firestorms, though sometimes at the cost of creating bigger ones down the road. This incremental approach to opening markets has at its core the assumption that going slow will protect vulnerable sections of the economy from harm due to external exposure. By contrast, more outward looking East Asian economies such as South Korea, Singapore, and Shinzo Abe's Japan tend to view reform more as an opportunity than a threat.

Looking ahead, the reforms India needs to fully free up its economy are precisely those that remain the most politically sensitive. Indian politicians will have to grapple with how to continue raising FDI limits, cutting red tape, and ending suspicion of foreign capital to become a more open and welcoming destination for foreign investment. They also have to tackle domestic reforms that are often much harder to do. While the GST constitutional amendment and a new bankruptcy law show that Indian politics can at times accomplish difficult things, privatizing state-owned enterprises—even those that lose money— remains a political third rail, creating an unnecessary drain on the public exchequer. Welfare programs like loan forgiveness for farmers remain popular, but do nothing to address the structural reform needs. And two of the major structural reforms the Modi government attempted during its first year and a half—labor law reform and land acquisition—have been devolved to the state level after proving intractable nationally. Both these reforms matter profoundly if India is to attain the aim of generating jobs by expanding manufacturing and increasing exports.

A plethora of Indian labor laws have disincentivized company growth, particular for labor-intensive industries, as Jagdish Bhagwati and Arvind Panagariya persuasively argue. (It's also a reason the Indian economy remains overwhelmingly in the informal sector.) Bhagwati and Panagariya point to the socialist-era Industrial Disputes Act as the law in "most urgent need of reform." The act requires any company larger than one hundred employees to seek government permission in order to shut down, even if it is unprofitable—a constraint "stacked too heavily against the employers to leave sufficient incentive for a massive expansion of employment-intensive sectors."[68]

Unable to grow to scale, Indian companies have not emerged as global leaders in the entry-level manufacturing industry in which low-cost labor should be a decisive asset: ready-made garments. Instead, it's Bangladesh, not India, that became the world's second-largest garment exporter after China. Bangladesh, with a population of around 160 million, is a little more than one-seventh India's size, yet it exports almost 50 percent more garments each year—around $25 billion to India's $17 billion.[69] In 2016, the relaxation of labor laws in the textile industry (permitting seasonal employment, for example) attempted to spur growth in this important sector; at the time of this writing, the results of the changes were unknown.

India's political environment makes this challenging. Indian unions protest anything that may weaken lifelong job security—even if the tradeoff could be greater job creation. In September 2015, some 150 million workers went on strike nationwide against the Modi government's proposed labor law reforms.[70] A consortium of India's labor unions, including the Bharatiya Mazdoor Sangh affiliated with the RSS, called the strike, illustrating that the range of opinion about economic matters does not map evenly across a "right-left" binary. After intensive talks with the government, the Bharatiya Mazdoor Sangh withdrew from plans for the labor strike, but other unions went ahead. One year later, ten Indian labor unions called another national strike to protest economic reforms generally, including plans to close loss-making state-owned enterprises. Some 180 million workers stayed away from the workplace on September 2, 2016, in one of the largest labor strikes in history. This time, however, the Bharatiya Mazdoor Sangh stayed out of the striking consortium entirely.[71]

In response to the pushback on labor reforms, the federal government has devolved labor reform to the states by allowing them to change the size of company requiring government approval to close. Rajasthan has been the first to amend this provision, increasing the cap to three hundred workers from one hundred. A similar dynamic has marked efforts to push through a new land acquisition law to make it easier for the government to purchase land for industry and infrastructure. The government has not been able to secure the votes to get it passed by both houses despite issuing stopgap ordinances in the interim. This tough decision, too, has been pushed to the state level.

As the Indian government looks to spur the kind of economic growth that will lift more citizens out of poverty and transform India's economy, it has bumped up against the limits of the country's complex politics. The UPA government was hamstrung by its obligations to coalition partners who saw the world differently. Many expected the Modi government, with its once-in-a-generation simple majority in the lower house, to reform more quickly given its political strength. Yet it has had a tougher go in the upper house, where Congress remains dominant. It is as if an inherent systemic caution structures the Indian political system by virtue of its complexity and the obligations to so many different political interests.

As far as India has come in its journey shaking off the socialist past, a tough road still lies ahead.

PART TWO

Transition

4

Seeking India's Rightful Place

FORMER INDIAN AMBASSADOR TO the United States and to China Dr. S. Jaishankar is widely regarded as one of the country's sharpest strategic minds. In 2015, Prime Minister Modi appointed him as foreign secretary, the head of India's career foreign service; within months Jaishankar began laying out a new roadmap for Indian power following a vision articulated by the prime minister.[1]

Delivering the Fullerton Lecture at the International Institute of Strategic Studies-Asia in Singapore, Jaishankar charted out the contours of India's new foreign policy: "You would have already noted more energetic diplomacy that seeks a larger and deeper footprint in the world, supported by soft-power initiatives like the International Day of Yoga. The transition in India is an expression of greater self-confidence. Its foreign policy dimension is to aspire to be a *leading* power, rather than just a *balancing* power" (emphasis mine).[2] In remarks just days before the Fullerton Lecture, Jaishankar had posed these rhetorical questions to a Delhi audience: "It is, therefore, time to ask ourselves whether India should raise its level of ambitions. Are we content to react to events or should we be shaping them more, on occasion even driving them? Should we remain a balancing power or aspire to be a leading one?"[3] These speeches marked a more extensive elaboration on the new term, "leading power," that Jaishankar had discussed publicly a few months earlier in New Delhi—following the guidance Modi had laid out in a presentation to India's foreign service "heads of mission" (all the ambassadors and high commissioners serving in Indian embassies worldwide) in February 2015.[4]

For decades, officials and foreign policy leaders have talked about India's desire to claim its "rightful place" in the world. Stepped up efforts to secure—or resecure—for itself its "due" as a *leading power* suggest a far more active sensibility than that of earlier vocabularies. India as a leading power, in other words, would be prepared to *act*—to take part in fashioning the global world it is a part of, and would even at times be at the forefront. Notably, Jaishankar also spoke of self-confidence as a force propelling India's new goal. This, though, is not new.

As Indian citizens seek a larger global role for their country, "confidence" is a quality people nearly always invoke. Vajpayee spoke of a "renewed sense of national pride and self-confidence" following the 1998 nuclear tests.[5] His successor Manmohan Singh spoke of the "renewed self-confidence of a new India" early in his first term, but by the middle of his second term, in reality if not in rhetoric, "confidence" was on the wane. In one of his rare televised press conferences, Singh attempted to battle a growing narrative that India was a cesspool of corruption. Excessive attention to unfolding corruption scandals, said Singh, was "weakening the self-confidence of the people of India."[6] By the time Indians elected Modi to power, confidence—both within the country and among its foreign partners—had shifted to the deficit side of the ledger, and needed urgent restoration.

Modi and his government are focused on presenting that self-confidence, through unleashing India's economic growth, strengthening India's international standing, and raising its profile globally through cultural initiatives. In each case, a strong sense of national pride shapes how a rising India sees its proper role and pursues what it perceives as its due. This sense exists broadly across parties. As discussed in previous chapters, Indians often portray their country and its civilizational heritage in terms of power and strength eroded by successive Muslim invasions beginning in the 8th century CE and followed by the humiliation of two hundred-plus years of British rule. The work to reinstate their country to where it belongs draws upon these ideas as the backdrop. Present-day India may struggle with poverty, sanitation, poor infrastructure, and social problems, but those challenges exist alongside the conviction that India once offered much to the world, and rightly deserves to play that role again. This is exactly the framing Modi used in that speech in Silicon Valley—that until recently "the world saw India at the margins, but is now seeing it at the center."[7] While some outside India might disagree with this characterization, it is certainly the case that Indian leaders are pressing more forcefully to secure for their country a more central place in the world.

PRIDE OF PLACE

India's quest to secure greater representation for itself in global institutions to better reflect the changing balance of power and economic might in the world today is not new. But as sustained high growth rates raise India's profile, the gap between where it sits and where it would like to sit, has never been more apparent. In India's search for a seat at the head table of global politics, we see great continuity in the approaches successive Indian governments have taken.

Permanent membership in the UN Security Council remains a primary focus for India's expectation that institutions of global governance should reform to reflect the world more equally. Ironically—and a point of partisan criticism today—during the 1950s then Prime Minister Nehru turned down offers first from the United States (1950) and then from the Soviet Union (1955) to support a permanent seat for India on the Security Council. According to new archival research drawing upon the correspondence between Nehru and his sister Vijaya Lakshmi Pandit—who led India's delegation to the United Nations and served as ambassador to the United States in the late 1940s and early 1950s—the United States proposed that India take the permanent seat held by China in the Security Council. (This was during a period of struggle within the United Nations for recognition of the People's Republic of China as the legitimate government to replace the Republic of China Nationalists in Taiwan.) Nehru felt strongly that "we are not going to countenance it. . . . India, because of many factors, is certainly entitled to a permanent seat in the security council. But we are not going in at the cost of China."[8]

Indian governments have repeatedly pressed for a larger UN role befitting India's size, its democracy, and what they see as its special moral role in the world. The case India makes for why it should occupy a permanent seat in a reformed Security Council rests on both the recognition of significant change in world politics over the past sixty years, coupled with India's sense of its own important contributions to the functions of the United Nations. For example, in a 2014 presentation compiled by the Ministry of External Affairs, India's "eminently suited" qualifications for a permanent seat included: "population, territorial size, GDP, economic potential, civilizational legacy, cultural diversity, political system and past and on-going contributions to the activities of the UN—especially to UN peacekeeping operations. . . ."[9]

In the early 2000s, the Manmohan Singh government, along with three other countries that felt their country's absence from the Security Council did not reflect their global weight, forged the "Group of Four" (G4) partnership to urge reform. India, Japan, Germany, and Brazil jointly convened a G4 summit in 2004 to convey their shared frustration with a Security Council that represented what power looked like in the middle of the twentieth century. The G4 collaboration has continued over the past decade, and still presses the case for permanent membership for all four powers.[10]

Virtually every serious observer agrees that the Security Council is overweighted with Europeans while at the same time omitting the largest European economy and arguably the most powerful country in the EU, Germany. It also leaves out Japan, the world's third largest economy, and second largest contributor to the United Nations' budget. The body has no Latin American or African representation; and leaves out India, the world's most populous democracy, and a major peacekeeping contributor that has overtaken permanent members United Kingdom and France in several metrics of power over the past twenty-five years. (Indeed, in one measure, India's GDP in PPP terms surpassed the United Kingdom's back in 1991 and France's in 1994.) Despite a generalized abstract agreement that the Security Council is long overdue for an overhaul, little progress toward reform of any kind has occurred since lack of agreement on the fine print—size of expansion, veto powers, and whom to include—has stymied next steps.

The United States has long backed treaty ally Japan's claim to a permanent seat, particularly given Japan's longtime financial support for the UN budget. But it took years of Indian diplomatic effort for Washington to publicly support India's bid for inclusion. It was not until President Obama's visit to India in November 2010 that the United States declared American support for India as a permanent seatholder in a future reformed and expanded Security Council. Obama made the statement during his address to a joint session of India's parliament.

In September 2015, the G4 decided to meet again at the head-of-government level on the margins of the General Assembly. Prime Minister Modi, Chancellor Angela Merkel, President Dilma Roussef, and Prime Minister Shinzo Abe together issued a joint statement calling for "time-bound" Security Council reform.[11] In a departure from previous years, the General Assembly adopted by consensus a resolution to push for a "text-based" reform process. Amid all this, former Indian diplomats have spoken out publicly to say they feel the United States has done nothing to assist New Delhi in its quest for permanent membership, despite the words of support from Obama back in 2010. More pointedly, as former Indian permanent representative to the United Nations Hardeep Singh Puri put it, "My counterpart on the Security Council, Susan Rice, was my friend. She called me and said 'Hardeep, you and I are related in blood' . . . But when it came down to the processes on the ground, they appeared unhelpful. . . . At no stage did we get strength from the Americans. . . . You need support in the negotiating room."[12]

New Delhi has been frustrated with a global system that has not modified to accommodate its own growing global role. As with Security Council reform in the United Nations, India has been pressing for a larger voice in the World Bank and the International Monetary Fund. The financial institutions, created in the mid-twentieth century, are similarly weighted in representation and authority toward Europe and the United States—but by the turn of the twenty-first century, emerging markets had begun to account for an increasingly larger share of global GDP. As a 2015 working paper on global economic governance authored by India's then executive director at the IMF, Dr. Rakesh Mohan, documented:

the share of EDEs [emerging and developing economies] in global GDP is expected to increase from about 40 percent in 2000 to over 60 percent by 2020 in PPP terms and from 20 to 40 percent in MER [market exchange rate] terms. Similarly the share of G7 countries in

global GDP (PPP) is expected to fall from about 44 percent in 2000
to about 30 percent by 2020, with a corresponding increase in the
share of BRICS from 19 percent in 2000 to 33 percent in 2020.[13]

Mohan and Kapur go on to note that despite the 2010 reforms, the
challenge with representation in the IMF lies in the fact that emerging
economies continue to hold only around 40 percent of quota shares
despite accounting for nearly 60 percent of global GDP (PPP). They
also called for the quota formula itself to more heavily weigh the PPP
measure over market exchange rates as a means to achieve greater representation for developing countries.

What about the World Bank? Similarly, India would like to see more
reform as part of a larger shift toward "shareholder realignment" that
would better account for the growth of developing countries' economies
and their increased contributions. Here, too, complex quota formulas
calculate the voting power within each of the World Bank's constituent
groups. Without getting sidetracked by the complexity of these details,
it's fair to say that India has consistently and recently urged continued rebalancing toward what are termed "developing and transition
countries" (DTC). India has been a major recipient of World Bank
financing over the decades, and continues to be an important recipient
country. But it would like to see the decision-making process within
the institution better reflect its increased global economic weight. In
April 2016, India's finance minister, Arun Jaitley, said: "We must accept
that the time has come for raising partnership of DTCs in the IBRD
[International Bank for Reconstruction and Development] and IFC
[International Finance Corporation] to 50 per cent."[14]

As mentioned earlier, the transition from the G7 as the world's critical economic coordinating group to the larger and more inclusive G20
leaders-level format after the 2008 global financial crisis was helpful
to raising India's profile as a global economic power. New Delhi has
used the platform to raise issues like financial volatility and inclusive
development, "leading the emerging market charge," as the *Globe and
Mail* put it. It has also used the forum to press its case for greater carbon space in the larger global deliberations over climate change.[15] (And
although G7 "rebalancing" has not been a hot topic, at some point soon
it will be hard to justify excluding India, given that the club of large

democratic economies includes two that India has surpassed in economic size. Italy and Canada now bring up the tail end of the world's
ten largest economies while India has moved up to number seven at
market exchange rates.)

India's message on reform of older institutions is clear: New Delhi
will continue to press for representation in institutions that reflect its
population size, economic heft, growing military power, and what it
perceives as its just role in global governance. In addition, India has
another "reform track" under way that parallels this push, one that
actively crafts new regional and global organizations in which it can
have a larger voice. I will discuss India's work creating new institutions
of governance in Chapter 6.

On top of its efforts to shape these older institutions of global governance in a manner that better reflects changes in the world over the
past half-century, India has been working to establish what it sees as
its natural role as the preeminent Indian Ocean power. Here, the pride
of place—the only ocean named after a country, as the oft-heard line
goes—and ideas about India's historic role as a power are shaping its
strategic ambitions.

INDIA AS THE PREEMINENT INDIAN OCEAN POWER

"Here lay buried Vasco da Gama who died on the Christmas Eve of
the Year 1524 AD at Cochin." Vasco da Gama's original grave—marked
by an engraved brass plaque—lies inside St. Francis Church in Kochi,
on India's southwest coast in the state of Kerala. The great Portuguese
explorer was the first to discover the sea route from Europe to India,
making his way due south from Lisbon, circling the Cape of Good
Hope (where a cross in his name still stands), moving up the eastern African coast to Kenya, then riding the monsoon winds across
the Indian Ocean to reach Calicut, India in 1498. He would return
to Portugal, then lead another expedition to India, and return home
again. In 1524 the Portuguese king dispatched him to serve as viceroy of
Portugal's India interests. He would die in India later that year, with his
remains repatriated to Portugal in 1539.

Vasco da Gama's India voyages, spanning the entirety of the Indian
Ocean's western region, illustrate the vastness of maritime South Asia.

India sits in the middle of it all, not just a power within South Asia circumscribed by continental geography, but one with the expanse of the Indian Ocean linking it to Africa, the Middle East, Southeast Asia, and ultimately all the way to Europe. During British rule, Lord Curzon of Kedleston—a former viceroy of India—envisioned India at the center of a strategic landscape spanning "Persia and Afghanistan," Tibet and China, Siam, and the "routes to Australia and to the China Seas."[16] As strategist C. Raja Mohan puts it, Indians have more recently rediscovered this expansive, Curzonian sense of their geography—after the trauma of Partition had clipped back India's land borders and reduced its sense of frontier. For Raja Mohan, the Indian rediscovery of Curzon's view has helped shape ambitions for a "forward policy" to extend the country's strategic reach. India can see itself not as on the margins of the Middle East or East Asia, but rather at the strategic center of an underappreciated maritime space. This shift from seeing itself as a continental to a maritime power is under way right now in India.

As Raja Mohan notes, the shift coincided with an unleashed Indian economy after reforms began to bear fruit. An India increasingly more economically connected with the world, rather than inward-looking, would need to protect its commercial interests throughout the sea lanes. An India with energy-intensive economy growth would need linkages from the Gulf through Southeast Asia for its oil and gas supplies. An India that increasingly saw itself as a regional provider of security began to establish stronger, ongoing military ties—especially regional naval ties—with countries throughout South and Southeast Asia, as well as with the world's major powers. In Raja Mohan's words, India's new defense diplomacy "demonstrated a new intent by New Delhi to become an important element in the balance of power in various regions of the Indian Ocean littoral."[17] Indeed, in his remarks at the India Foundation's Indian Ocean Conference held in Singapore in September 2016, Foreign Secretary Jaishankar spoke of "reviving the Indian Ocean as a geopolitical concept."[18]

The Indian Navy began to step up its international port calls, overseas deployments, and joint exercises—and telling the public about it, shaping a new narrative. Photographs of the usual exchanges with neighbors like Sri Lanka, Maldives, and Singapore feature on the Indian Navy's Twitter feed alongside images of naval visits to Kenya,

Tanzania, Madagascar, and beyond. In August 2016, the Indian Navy tweeted an image of a map that showcased the Navy's port calls over the previous year—some forty-one in all, spanning the maritime space all the way from Aalborg (Denmark) to Lisbon to a thicket of ports across the Middle East and Arabian Sea to Southeast Asia, Korea, and as far north as Vladivostok in the Russian Far East.[19] (If you look closely, you can trace the outlines of Vasco da Gama's voyage from Lisbon to India via the African coast.) This expansive global activity contrasts with the Indian Navy's fourteen port calls of 2002–2003, prior to the development of the 2004 naval maritime strategy.[20]

India's extended naval reach and its focus on naval diplomacy have a great deal to do with one other factor, as Raja Mohan notes, spurring India to chart a larger presence throughout the Indian Ocean region: China. China's increasingly deeper ties with the smaller countries of South Asia—especially Bangladesh, Sri Lanka, and Maldives, which ring India's eastern and southern coasts, and of course its "all-weather" friendship with Pakistan—over time began to appear as an encirclement, an effort to strategically eclipse Indian influence in its own neighborhood, especially given Chinese indifference to India's efforts to overcome tensions. China's infrastructure development support, especially for port development in Bangladesh, Sri Lanka, and Pakistan, raised suspicions in New Delhi that the commercial toehold might eventually give way to a military base presence that could limit India's influence.

China's intense involvement developing a deepwater port in Pakistan's town of Gwadar, to eventually link with overland access across Pakistan to western China, has been under way since the early 2000s. But in the latter part of the 2000s, China began more concentrated infrastructure investment in Sri Lanka (especially on major projects like the Colombo and Hambantota ports) and in Bangladesh ($24 billion in proposed loans in 2016, to support railways, a deepwater port, and power plants). China also opened an embassy in Maldives in 2011, making it one of two countries outside of South Asia that year to have a permanent embassy or high commission there. (Saudi Arabia was the other; in 2016, Japan opened an embassy in Malé making it the third outside the region with a full-fledged embassy presence.) Each of these steps began to paint a more strategically competitive picture for New Delhi. Would each of

India's immediate neighbors fall into China's economic embrace, and if so, what might then follow? Two consecutive visits of Chinese military submarines to the Colombo port in 2014 only reaffirmed this suspicion. China's announcement in early 2016 of its plans to build a military base in Djibouti, providing a permanent Indian Ocean defense presence, reinforced the concern.

India's efforts to establish itself as the preeminent Indian Ocean presence has resulted in a clearly articulated maritime defense strategy with an ambitious plan for the Indian Navy, combined with new Indian military diplomacy to extended India's security ties around the region. These efforts build on Indian diplomatic initiatives launched in some cases decades ago to create new institutions for a region that has a deficit of them, and in the process design a central coordinating role for India. (Some of these regional institutions will be considered in greater detail in Chapter 6, along with other institutions of global governance that India has championed as it seeks a bigger voice for itself.)

With respect to India's defense policies, the Navy released India's first maritime doctrine in 2004, with an update in 2009, and a companion maritime military strategy in 2007. In 2015, the Indian Navy revised its maritime security strategy and expanded its scope. As the International Institute for Strategic Studies' Rahul Roy-Chaudhry points out, the transition from India's earlier strategy to its 2015 revision marked a shift from "using" the seas to "securing" the seas. As with Jaishankar's articulation of a foreign policy becoming more active rather than reactive, the shift illustrates a clear decision to shoulder a leadership role in the Indian Ocean.[21] Indeed, by the time the Indian government transitioned from the Singh to the Modi regimes, "the Indian Ocean rose to a level of priority in India foreign policy not seen since Indira Gandhi," in the words of *Hindustan Times* foreign editor Pramit Pal Chaudhuri.[22]

The 2015 strategy explains the new forward-leaning approach as the result of a worldview shifting from the "Euro-Atlantic" to the "Indo-Pacific"; new seaborne security threats, such as the Mumbai attacks of 2008 in which terrorists from Pakistan infiltrated via the sea; and a changed Indian view of its maritime presence as a "vital element of national progress and international engagement." The strategy notes India's increased interactions with all the Indian Ocean states, calls maritime security diplomacy a "cornerstone of her regional foreign policy initiatives," and connects the seas to "India's resurgence in the 21st century."[23] With that, the Indian Navy and the Indian Ocean became linked as a proof-in-progress of India's rise to global power.

India's naval strategy fits within a larger Indian Ocean foreign policy framework that Modi introduced during his visits to the Indian Ocean states of Seychelles and Mauritius in March 2015. While India had maintained ties with these countries over the decades—and both are home to significant Indian diaspora populations (indeed, the majority of Mauritians are of Indian origin)—the Modi framework policy declared India's formal intent to not only protect its own coast and islands in the Indian Ocean, but also to provide assistance to Indian Ocean partner nations, "to deepen our economic and security cooperation," and help them develop their own capabilities. Modi's speech included reference to the importance of collective action in maintaining peace and security, and to the development of a "blue" or maritime economy.[24] And in line with the Vivekananda-style emphasis on cultural diplomacy, Modi has also amped up an initiative through the Ministry of Culture called "Project Mausam," designed to highlight India's historic maritime trade and civilizational links with East Africa, the Gulf countries, and Southeast Asia.[25]

The public rollout of India's new Indian Ocean policy took place during the commissioning of a naval patrol ship, the *Barracuda*, as it was transferred from the Indian Navy to the Mauritian Coast Guard. The *Barracuda* symbolized the new, more active type of maritime security assistance India would undertake: it marked India's first-ever warship export, the first of a planned series of thirteen ships India would supply Mauritius with for coastal and exclusive economic zone surveillance.[26] While not announced during Modi's March 2015 visit to Seychelles, by December 2015 news hit the press that the Seychelles' island of Assumption would play host to India's first-ever naval base on foreign soil.[27] So the Indian Ocean trip of March 2015 ended up signaling a new Indian role as a defense platform exporter, and laid the groundwork for the later announcement of India's first naval base abroad.

India's new maritime ambitions—defending a larger space, projecting power, and being in more places at once—require a larger navy with more platforms to give it greater capabilities. India's earlier naval requirement of 138 submarines and ships was capped by a Cabinet decision in 1964. Defense expert Ajai Shukla notes that a 2012 Cabinet decision raised the ship/submarine requirement to 198, and then a 2016 parliamentary defense committee report projected a requirement of 212 vessels and 458 aircraft looking ahead to 2027.[28] Naval capacity expansion on this scale will require investment of around $61 billion over the coming decade-plus.[29] Shukla further notes, however, that India's defense production and procurement had lagged behind the tempo required to fulfill this goal. The Indian government has opened up defense production to the private sector in a major reform, further eased foreign direct investment (FDI) caps in the sector, and anticipates that between foreign procurement, production from state-owned enterprises, and a spur from new private-sector led initiatives, it will meet its targets. It may not meet this timeline—defense procurement often lags, including in the United States, but the changed scope of ambition is in and of itself a significant change.

India's Indian Ocean framework and maritime strategy illustrate how New Delhi's defense ambitions are supporting its regional leadership efforts, its bid for its rightful place. India has replaced its aging aircraft carrier with a much-delayed delivery from Russia in 2013, and has a second under construction—its first developed and built indigenously. It has a third planned for construction, which will also be indigenously developed. Press reports in early 2016 suggested that India may acquire a fourth from Russia. As part of the U.S.-India Defense Trade and Technology Initiative, aircraft carrier technology features among the subjects of collaboration.[30] Already one of the handful of countries with aircraft carriers, once India has four deployed it will extend its reach across the Indian Ocean. India also plans to add three nuclear-powered submarines to its fleet, and its new maritime surveillance aircraft from the United States (eight Boeing P-8Is, with another four just ordered), provide greater visibility on the seas than it has had in the past. Finally, India plans to emerge as a defense exporter—as with its transfer of the *Barracuda* to Mauritius—and has bid on procurement tenders in the Philippines, and agreed to export patrol boats to Vietnam.[31] These examples illustrate how India has designed naval expansion plans to allow it to project power over the coming decade.

An India more focused on expanding its footprint on the seas has begun to see its interests in different ways, particularly with a much more vocal Indian stance on freedom of navigation concerns, maritime surveilliance, security cooperation, and humanitarian assistance coordination. Indeed, India has repeatedly voiced support for Vietnam in its freedom of navigation dispute with China. India's growing maritime profile and positions have helped accelerate bilateral defense cooperation with the United States, given the increasingly convergent interests New Delhi and Washington share. It is no accident that one specific public announcement during President Obama's Republic Day visit to India in January 2015 was a "U.S.-India Joint Strategic Vision for the Asia-Pacific and Indian Ocean." In a sign of change, in August 2016 (after more than a decade of negotiations delayed over Indian concerns about sovereignty), India and the United States finally reached agreement on a logistics-exchange mechanism that would make reciprocal ship visits and joint exercises far easier to facilitate. (The agreement basically routinizes payments for refueling and services used.) The agreement was a variant of the Logistics Support Agreements the United States concludes with partner countries, but diverted from the template text to respond to India's specific concerns.

The final result, a text known as the LEMOA (Logistics Exchange Memorandum of Agreement) was announced in August 2016 by U.S. Secretary of Defense Ashton Carter and Indian Minister of Defense Manohar Parrikar to a swirl of debate in India about whether it had given up its sovereignty and would be forced to support U.S. basing in India. Parrikar and other senior members of the Modi government went to great lengths to explain to the Indian press and public that the agreement would help India develop its own capabilities as it increasingly sought to extend its reach across the seas. Fears of being subordinated to American "imperialist" military designs have long been a feature of the Indian political landscape, as I will discuss in some detail, so completing the LEMOA showed that the Modi government, in contrast to its predecessor, felt there was more to gain than to lose from the exchange.

Since the Modi government had already laid the groundwork with the public for the idea of a more expeditionary maritime presence, one more involved with other nations around the world and with ambitions to serve as a guarantor of peace and rescuer of first-resort—therefore in need of port stops in friendly places—it was better able to manage the domestic debate over the LEMOA. Fanciful critiques of how Indian national morals might be tarnished by the arrival of lecherous drunk American sailors or how India might be unwittingly forced to support U.S. military interventions elsewhere were quickly dismissed as incorrect understandings of the limited but useful exchanges this agreement would ease.[32]

India still struggles with domestic differences over how it should use its growing global power, but increasingly the emphasis on India's Indian Ocean interests and its desire to ensure its own leadership in the region—what it sees as its rightful place—have overcome some of the country's earlier hesitations and fears. These are consequential developments. In other arenas, the specific concern about sovereignty remains a central factor in how India perceives its interaction with the world. This has been particularly acute for global agreements on nonproliferation and on trade, two cases where India has over the years shown its willingness to walk away from anything it sees as limiting its freedoms, and therefore withholding from India the proper role it believes it should play.

SOVEREIGN RIGHTS, GLOBAL AGREEMENTS, AND GOING IT ALONE

Since independence, successive Indian governments have maintained a consistent posture toward global agreements: if they deem the terms philosophically (as opposed to pragmatically) unfair, denying India its rightful place, India is ready to walk. The nonproliferation regime stands out as the best-known example. For much of the Cold War period, Indian leaders objected to the arbitrary cutoff date of the Nuclear Nonproliferation Treaty, seeing it as discriminatory for designating countries that had tested before 1967 as nuclear weapons states with particular rights, leaving everyone else without them.[33] India, which first tested its own nuclear weapon in 1974, refused to sign the NPT for two reasons: it did not want to foreclose its options, and it objected to being relegated to a second tier of nonnuclear weapons states. At the same time, Indian diplomats argued forcefully, if somewhat impracticably, for total globally "nondiscriminatory" nuclear disarmament.

The decision to stay out of the NPT also left India outside nonproliferation regimes designed to reward treaty signers with technology, and
punish non-signatories by its denial. For three decades, India decided
to furrow a lonely path, despite the costs to its defense programs and
its advanced technology development. In the Clinton administration,
every effort to convince India to sign the Comprehensive Test Ban
Treaty banning further nuclear testing came to naught. In 1996, India
effectively torpedoed the agreement by refusing to sign; the country's
then ambassador to the United Nations in Geneva, the late distinguished diplomat Arundhati Ghose, became something of a national
hero for this defiance. After India's 1998 nuclear tests, extensive negotiations, conducted over "fourteen times at ten locations in seven countries" by then deputy secretary of state Strobe Talbott and then minister
of external affairs Jaswant Singh, couldn't get India to budge.[34] It was
only through the George W. Bush administration's 2005 step of a civil-
nuclear initiative that this impasse finally ended. India still has not
signed the NPT, and it will not, but the world can now work with India
on civilan nuclear energy. India has changed its domestic laws to align
with the four major nonproliferation regimes, as I discuss in Chapter 6,
is pursuing membership in all of them, and is now moving "inside the
tent" despite its anomalous status. But on the fundamental issue of not
signing a treaty India views as discriminatory, successive governments
have not moved an inch.

While nonproliferation no longer represents an unbridgeable gap
between India and much of the world, New Delhi has shown a similar
go-it-alone attitude in multilateral trade, an arena where many countries find it challenging to find common ground with India. Powerful
nationalist ideas of self-reliance and particular views of sovereignty and
sovereign rights—India's pride in its independence—have made economic reforms a particularly contentious arena. As Chapter 3 observed,
room for reforms to open Indian markets further certainly exists.

In places like the United States, and to a lesser degree Europe, few
restrictions prevent the flow of commerce. Despite having slashed tariffs from their 1991 highs, India still has a way to go for others to perceive it as open to trade. In the Heritage Foundation's annual index
of economic freedom, India falls under the "mostly unfree" category
at number 143, below Brazil, Pakistan, and Ethiopia. Heritage notes

India's challenges with corruption, its infrastructure, "uneven" economic reforms, and also states that "Growth is not deeply rooted in policies that preserve economic freedom."[35] Within the Asia-Pacific region, India ranks thirty-third. In another index, the International Chamber of Commerce's Open Markets Index, India ranks "below average" on openness, below Tunisia and above Venezuela.[36] This index compares "observed openness" to trade, trade policy, FDI policy, and trade infrastructure to distill its rankings.

The World Bank's Overall Trade Restrictiveness Index provides a comparative metric based on applied tariffs: India's restrictiveness index using this metric, 14.9 percent, looks high compared with those of China (9.7 percent), Indonesia (4.7 percent), South Korea (9 percent), or Thailand (10 percent). The United States comes in at 5.7 percent. This is a rough gauge, and was last updated in 2012, but aligns with similar research carried out by the Peterson Institute's Zixuan Huang, Nicholas R. Lardy, and Melina Kolb. In a blog post titled, "China is Not the Most Highly Protectionist Big Country," the authors compared weighted average applied tariffs for major world economies. Brazil came in with the highest at 8.3 percent, and India was a close second with 6.3 percent. China, at number three with 3.4 percent was a rather distant third, and the remaining economies all had weighted average applied tariffs of 1.6 percent or lower.[37]

These comparisons illustrate how a real asymmetry has existed when it comes to the kind and number of trade "asks" foreign negotiators may have of Indian counterparts versus those an Indian negotiator would have for their foreign counterpart across the table. Simply put, in trade negotiations with more open countries, India is asked to do more for the very fact that its economy remains less open than those of the countries with which it is negotiating. Press reports indicate a similar dynamic at play with the Asian countries involved in the Regional Comprehensive Economic Partnership talks.

Traditionally, multilateral trade accords allow developing countries longer transition times and at times less stringent obligations. Nonetheless, trade talks have led to some of the biggest flare-ups and disappointments in recent years with India, including the collapse of the Doha round in 2008, from which the WTO has never really recovered.[38] Indian trade negotiators stake out tough positions, framing their priorities on behalf of the country's still-enormous population of the poor. But at the same time, as previous chapters have discussed, the Indian economy is now the world's seventh largest, and Indian companies are becoming ever-more globally competitive in many sectors.

To put it another way, as the aspect of foreign policy that most directly affects citizens, trade holds the possibility of being most disruptive. So despite undeniable gains to most Indians from economic reform and opening to the world over the past two decades, Indian trade negotiators tend not to view further opening as the ticket to further growth. When it comes to trade, many people continue to harbor a vocabulary of fear and suspicion nurtured over decades. Combined with India's willingness to go it alone, this makes the country a challenging negotiating partner. This came to the foreground dramatically in 2014 in the debate over the Bali trade facilitation agreement.[39]

The so-called TFA negotiations represented a global effort to reaffirm that multilateral negotiations still stood a chance of accomplishing something, however minimal, after the collapse of the Doha round negotiations in 2008. Focusing on mundane, and therefore presumably easy to agree upon, issues like how to facilitate customs and coordinate advance notification of goods shipments, the talks were virtually designed to keep the Doha round going. In December 2013, India played a central role developing the terms of the agreement reached in Bali, after plenty of haggling and a dramatic settlement on the final text that that went into "overtime." Part of the agreement included a commitment to continue working toward a solution of thorny issues of food security, stockpiling, and subsidies by 2017. (For example, the base period for calculations on allowable agricultural subsidies remains 1986–1988, which India would like to see updated.) Countries whose current stockpiles of food exceeded WTO guidelines would be protected from any dispute proceedings until 2017, or whenever an agreement was reached, a time-and-process guarantee called the "peace clause."

Indian press reports from early December 2013 highlighted India's concerns about food security—the government had just passed a huge new food security law guaranteeing subsidized grains to nearly 70 percent of the population—as the primary hurdle. When WTO director-general Roberto Azevêdo managed to clear this with the December pact, the *Hindu* illustrated Indian satisfaction at the outcome. "India's Stand Prevails in Bali," declared the newspaper.[40]

Barely six months later, when countries were supposed to go through the formality of signing the agreement protocol to bring it into force, the government of India—by now led by the newly sworn in Modi—abruptly announced that it was backtracking as it believed it had not seen sufficient progress in the intervening months on its food security concerns, and was worried that it would be railroaded into pruning its food security program unless an agreement was reached. Since India had been a central force in crafting the so-called peace clause meant to obviate such fears, its new stance confused many countries. New Delhi's move precipitated an existential crisis within the WTO about its future viability as a negotiating forum, since its consensus procedures made every round vulnerable to individual holdouts (or walkouts).

Perhaps even more strangely, more than a few Indian media reports described New Delhi's stance as a victory for India "against the West." The negotiating mess that unfolded cannot be attributed to simple protectionism, since by all accounts Indian leaders wanted and approved of the actual terms of the trade facilitation deal. Instead, the Indian position was different, more like drawing a line in the sand: that despite the language of the peace clause reprieve to the contrary, Indian leaders would not allow the possibility that international obligations might impinge upon their new food security program, and they were willing to call off the whole thing, never mind the views of the 160 other WTO members, to underscore this point.

India's minister of commerce and industry, in charge of the negotiations, explained her stance to the Lok Sabha, the lower house of Parliament, by framing the concerns as India's "sovereign right" to stockpile food in accordance with its needs for its food security program, without the fear of violating international commitments.[41] (It is another matter that Indian policymakers may very well want to shift away from massive food security stockpiles—given scandals about grain rotting in warehouses and waste inherent to the program—to direct grant support for the poor, or other similar measures.) The commerce minister argued further that sufficient attention to food security matters had not occurred within the WTO in the seven months since December 2013, and that India needed greater assurance this issue would be taken up and not tossed by the wayside once the trade facilitation measures were inked. The timeline for food security negotiations had been agreed upon in Bali, so this objection too surprised many external observers.

The solution, reached via U.S.-India consultations that unfolded over the subsequent four months and included high-level pushes from President Obama and Prime Minister Modi, struck many trade experts outside India as essentially just clarifying the existing commitment. The *Financial Times* world trade editor Shawn Donnan—whose reporting on every twist and turn of the saga was second to none—referred to the eventual solution as one that "hinged on the rewriting of a single sentence and the placing of a comma."[42] All told, the Bali agreement fiasco reaffirmed India's reputation for prickliness, especially when it comes to defending what it sees as rights imperiled by "the West." Yet in this case the language of the offending agreement had been shaped by India itself, albeit by negotiators representing a different government.

THE LEADING EDGE: MOVEMENT OF PERSONS

As the TFA spat shows, India retains a heightened sense of sovereignty when it comes to politically sensitive issues. At the same time, India's emergence as a top global provider of services puts it on the leading edge of an issue sensitive to many Western publics: New Delhi strongly champions the free movement of labor, particularly of skilled workers in such industries as information technology. As Indian IT and IT-enabled services companies have grown increasingly skilled across a growing number of specializations, they have begun to support their global clients not just from a distance (offshore), but also by sending their employees to work in North American and Western Europe (onsite). A firm such as TCS or Infosys, for instance, sends thousands of computer programmers to work on everything from accounting software to cloud computing to Internet of things design (such as home appliances connected to the Internet) at companies as diverse as GE, Amazon Web Services, or Harley-Davidson, to take three examples. Provision of services via the "movement of natural persons" is called "Mode 4" services in the WTO, and India is the world's leading power in terms of the number of mobile highly skilled professionals.

Its entwinement with immigration policies, unique to each country, makes Mode 4 particularly contentious. Crossing borders to work in another country generally requires a visa, and worker visa programs typically have limits on the number that can be issued each year, or in some cases minimum salary requirements to prevent misuse of such programs to undercut market wages. In the United States, highly skilled foreign workers can be employed through the H-1B visa program (and a lesser known but similar visa, the L-1, for intra-company transfers of employees with specialized skills). The H-1B system has a fixed cap on the number of visas that can be issued every year, and contains prevailing wage requirements.

For a brief period spanning the tail end of the Clinton administration and the first years of the Bush administration, Congress raised the cap on annual H-1B visas from 65,000 to 195,000 in response to tech industry demands. But since a 2004 reform to the law, the maximum number of new H-1B slots annually has stood at 65,000, plus an additional 20,000 visas for new advanced degree recipients from U.S. universities.[43] Demand for these visas far outstrips supply. In recent years, the program hit this annual limit in less than a week—in 2016, 236,000 applications came in, reaching the mandated cap within five days.[44] Because demand so outstrips supply, the actual visas are awarded through a lottery of those applications, or "petitions," approved.

Remarkably, according to historical Department of Homeland Security (DHS) data on visas, Indian nationals have been the recipients of an increasing number of work visas each year, and now overwhelmingly dominate this category. In 2003, Indian citizens received around a third of all H-1B visa petition approvals; by 2014 this figure had more than doubled to nearly 70 percent (Table 4.1).[45]

India's closest competitor when it comes to these highly sought after visas is China, which lags with less than 9 percent of annual petition approvals. Canada and the Philippines, both countries with which the United States has deep historical ties, trail even further behind. DHS data include many more countries—a "long tail" of places that receive a tiny percentage of H-1Bs—but the four countries in the table above illustrate the most important trend.

Despite India's successes as measured by the surge in the proportion of skilled-worker visas granted to Indian citizens, U.S. policy

TABLE 4.1 H-1B Petitions Approved by Country of Birth, Percent (% all beneficiaries)

	FY03	FY04	FY05	FY06	FY07	FY08	FY09	FY10	FY11	FY12	FY13	FY14
India	36.5	43.0	44.4	49.9	52.4	54.2	48.1	53.3	58.0	64.1	65.3	69.7
China	9.2	9.1	9.2	8.7	8.7	8.8	9.7	8.9	8.8	7.6	8.2	8.4
Canada	5.1	4.7	4.4	4.1	3.9	3.9	4.5	3.8	3.5	3.0	2.8	2.2
Philippines	4.8	3.9	3.7	3.3	3.3	3.5	4.1	3.2	2.8	2.0	2.2	1.6

Data compiled from U.S. Citizenship and Immigration Services annual H-1B reports to Congress

in this area has become a source of friction in bilateral ties. Instead of viewing these numbers as evidence of a strong economic relationship, and deep people-to-people linkages, Indian officials and media reports often frame the issue in terms of alleged U.S. unfairness to India. This has been particularly true since 2010, when the U.S. Congress passed the Zadroga Act, which applied higher visa fees to companies with more than fifty employees when more than 50 percent of those employees were on an H-1B (or L-1A or L-1B) temporary work visa—meaning that they were "H-1B-dependent" companies. Indian companies began to complain that they were being unfairly targeted. A rash of media reports in India suggested that the Indian government might file a dispute in the WTO, but for years no such filing occured.[46]

After the December 2015 renewal of the Zadroga Act doubled visa fees once again, the Indian government officially began the process of bringing dispute proceedings against the United States in the WTO by filing a formal request in March 2016 for consultations on visas. Officially titled "Measures Concerning Non-Immigrant Visas," the complaint focused on higher fees as inconsistent with U.S. commitments under the General Agreement on Trade in Services (GATS). India contends that higher fees put Indian workers at a disadvantage. The complaint also noted that commitments made in free trade agreements with Singapore and Chile to allot up to 5,400 and 1,400 high-skilled worker visas annually (to citizens of each country, respectively) raised barriers to Indian providers as these allotments would be subtracted from the overall number of available visas.[47]

At the time of this writing, the process of consultations in Geneva was still under way. But experts already see its consequences as potentially far-reaching. My Council on Foreign Relations colleague Edward Alden, a trade and immigration expert, described India's WTO filing as "landmark," for it marks the very first time "that a country's immigration laws have been challenged using the rules of a trade agreement."[48]

From an Indian perspective, New Delhi's proactive approach to this visa issue makes sense. Since India's IT services trade delivers annual revenues of about $108 billion, more than 60 percent of that from the United States, Indian officials naturally seek greater market access for their companies.[49] But arguably India's zeal is driven by more than the bottom line. As discussed earlier, the IT sector has put India on the global map, generating high-quality jobs and creating a new young urban middle class. This makes it a source of deep national pride. As Modi said in his 2014 speech at Madison Square Garden, "Our forefathers played with snakes, but we play with [a] mouse. Our youth push a mouse, and make the whole world shake."[50] Simply put, the IT services sector carries a symbolic weight that most other industries do not.

India's forward-leaning positions on labor mobility sometimes put it on a collision course with developed economies such as the United States. For the most part, this reflects the evolution of global services and patterns of travel that could not have been contemplated fifty years ago. Indian companies have pioneered an entirely new model of services trade, one in which ideas about trade collide with generally accepted principles of national sovereignty in immigration matters, such as participation in a domestic labor market. The H-1B program hits a nerve in the United States, however, when from time to time reports surface about American workers replaced by outside contractors at lower wages, such as the *New York Times* investigative reports during 2015. One story chronicled layoffs at Disney in Orlando, in which workers said they were forced to train their replacements employed by an IT consulting firm from India.[51]

The Trump administration's expressed interest in reforming the program to ensure that it does not create incentives to hire foreign workers over Americans simply due to wages suggests further changes yet to come. A few months into office, the Trump administration announced a review of the H-1B program, and took some minor steps in early 2017 such as the suspension of fast-tracked (or "premium") application processing and a change to a nearly twenty-year old rule to clarify that two-year degrees would not qualify for the "highly-skilled" category. In addition, several U.S. members of Congress from both parties introduced immigration reform bills to reconfigure the H-1B visa program. (At the time of this writing, none of the legislation had advanced.) This all resulted in intense scrutiny in India about growing American protectionism.

Suffice it to say that any time the perception of a direct threat to jobs exists, the proximate cause of that threat will receive scrutiny—as would be the case in any country. What marks India's position on this as more unusual is that India generally frames worker mobility not as an immigration issue—which touches upon national sovereignty—but instead as a trade issue. The world has not fully worked out how to align the two concepts, and the outcome of India's WTO complaint will provide a global legal precedent for these particularly complex international trade and immigration matters.

That said, New Delhi will find it challenging to attain hoped-for openings for its services professionals abroad, if it continues to be perceived by its major trading partners as resistant to offering greater market access in return. In public remarks at a New Delhi think tank in 2016, Commerce Minister Nirmala Sitharaman unwittingly offered a good example. Sitharaman said that blame for delays in completing trade pacts with the EU, Australia, and the Regional Comprehensive Economic Partnership grouping should not fall on India, and other countries' attempts to cast India as "obstructionist" was like trash-talk in sports. To the contrary, she said, India's negotiating partners had rejected its "ambitious" proposals to ease restrictions on movement of persons. She added, apparently without irony, that trading partners sought for India to reduce tariffs on goods like wheat and autos—but that "India will not yield" to pressure.[52] Indian officials will need to strategize for an economic world in which their concerns for market access abroad align with what they permit at home. As the saying goes, you can't have it both ways.

STRATEGIC COOPERATION AND INDIAN SOVEREIGNTY

When it comes to strategic cooperation, India has maintained a proud focus on defending what it sees as its sovereign interests—especially

preserving its freedom of future choice. As India shifts from its long tradition of nonalignment to a strategy of multiple alignments across the
entire "world family," its intellectuals and officials continue to debate
how new partnerships will either enable India's ascent, or potentially
constrain its options down the road.

Take the U.S.-India civil-nuclear cooperation agreement. As alluded
to briefly in Chapter 2, during 2006 to 2008 the Congress-led UPA government, supported from the outside by communist parties, found itself
under constant suspicion from its own coalition partners, who feared
that the civil-nuclear deal would somehow undermine India's interests.
Then Communist Party of India (Marxist) General Secretary Prakash
Karat exemplified the lens through which India's political left viewed
strategic cooperation with the United States. In Karat's view, "forging a
strategic alliance with the United States is a major step toward aligning
India with U.S. imperialism." The CPI(M) would "struggle against the
growing influence of U.S. imperialism in the country and the task of
the Party and the working class [would be] to unite all anti-imperialist
and progressive forces to fight back this trend." They saw their goal as
the "defence of national sovereignty." [53] While the UPA government
eventually won a parliamentary vote of confidence in 2008, it did so
in the face of tough opposition using the familiar language of national
interest and sovereignty.

The difference in perception was stark. Washington viewed the
civil-nuclear agreement as an unprecedented gesture to overcome the
most enduring difference in U.S.-India ties over three decades, one
that would open up the prospect of far greater cooperation across the
board. In contrast, many Indian political and intellectual elites, among
the leftists as well as the BJP, saw proof of insidious American designs.
The BJP, which supported the idea of a civil-nuclear deal and had laid
its early groundwork, opposed its form and saw it as "play[ing] havoc
with the nation's honour." Then leader of the opposition L. K. Advani
charged that the terms would render India a "subservient partner."[54]

Another aspect of strategic cooperation has continually become the
subject of passionate debate in Indian politics: defense agreements
especially with the United States. The long gestation of the LEMOA
agreement attests to the painstaking requirements of negotiating both
across India's domestic political landscape alongside the international

text negotiation. Prior to the 2016 conclusion of the LEMOA, another defense agreement had been at the forefront of Indian public objections.

The story of India's blowup over the end-use monitoring agreement (a provision under the U.S. Arms Export Control Act that provides for follow-up monitoring of sensitive technologies transferred outside the United States), now a quiet matter of the past, illustrates how questions of national sovereignty can spark political firestorms. Take for example a 2009 debate in the Lok Sabha. Then U.S. Secretary of State Hillary Clinton had recently traveled to India and concluded several agreements with her then counterpart, India's External Affairs Minister S. M. Krishna. The publicly released joint statement contained a sentence at the end of the section on defense cooperation that said, "both sides had reached agreement on End Use Monitoring for U.S. defense articles."

Senior BJP leader (and former external affairs as well as finance minister) Yashwant Sinha took up his concerns over this statement in parliament. He spoke at length about his fear that such an agreement would create a situation in which India had suddenly made itself vulnerable to allowing U.S. inspectors access to sensitive military facilities and equipment, including potentially that purchased from other countries: "My question is whether a factory, a fixed asset that you cannot take from one place to another, how will there be verification? There can be on the spot inspection. The most worrisome matter is whether the equipment we have procured from third countries—Russia, Brazil, France—in which American dual-use items have been installed; does America hold the right to inspect those and say whether the use is correct or not?"[55]

A long roster of senior politicians from assorted parties all piled on with similar questions about what such an agreement might imply for India's national sovereignty, and its authority over its own territory and equipment. That several dozen other countries had signed similar agreements with the United States, including its closest allies, did not matter a whit.[56] Bellowed CPI member Gurudas Dasgupta: "[I]t is unbelievable that a great country like India should bow down to the pressure of America. It is incredible; it is outrageous and it is a surrender of Indian sovereignty."[57] The leader of the opposition at the time, Sushma Swaraj—now the minister of external affairs—warned against "servitude."[58] Later that day, parties walked out of parliament to protest what they saw as an insufficient explanation for this agreement.

In the end, this particular storm blew over. But the precise terms of the debate as categories of argument recur over and over again. Across parties, Indian leaders do not necessarily welcome every overture for cooperation from the United States, even when the United States sees itself as bending over backward to help India. Even the overtures that some see as opportunities attract criticism from others. Fiercely protective of the idea of national autonomy, at times to the point of seeing slights where none are intended, political leaders are focused on ensuring that their country's future choices will not be constrained, that foreigners will not step across the veil of sensitivity surrounding India's defense and strategic facilities, and that international interactions will be honed very specifically on Indian terms.

That's why the set of defense "foundational agreements" have been under discussion between India and the United States for so many years, ever the subject of reports in Indian media that depict this as something Washington is "pushing," rather than a regular part of working through the terms of high-end defense cooperation and technology sharing in a world in which the technology edge matters strategically.[59] When Secretary Carter and Minister Parrikar convened their joint press conference in August 2016 to formally announce the conclusion of the LEMOA agreement, a journalist in the briefing room asked about the prospects for other foundational agreements still pending. Parrikar parried the question by remarking upon the "12–13 years" the LEMOA had taken, and then said: "So let me get this logistic agreement in the public domain properly and explain to the people. Then we will eventually go into the other aspects."[60]

Similarly, although India now exercises more with the U.S. military than with any other country, Indian leaders remain circumspect about creating frameworks or formats that might appear to position the country as supporting priorities determined by the United States. While Indian leaders have gone on the record supporting freedom of navigation in the South China Sea, for example, and have taken public positions in support of Vietnam on this front, a suggestion in 2016 by Admiral Harry Harris, commander in chief of U.S. Pacific Command, that India and the United States might undertake joint patrols in the Indo-Pacific prompted a public disavowal from Defense Minister Parrikar: "As of now India has not taken part in joint patrols but we do participate in joint exercises. So the issue of joint patrols at this time does not arise."[61] Shortly afterward, his spokesperson reiterated that Indian forces participate in joint operations only under a UN flag.[62] It is hard to see this firmly held belief changing for the forseeable future absent a dramatic geopolitical realignment of some sort. More likely, India will continue on its path of increasing joint exercises with regional and global powers around the world, reserving any joint military operations for the UN flag.

VIVEKANANDA FOR THE NEW CENTURY

As Chapter 2 discussed in some detail, Swami Vivekananda's American travels not only introduced Indian religion to Americans in a popular sense, but also presented Hinduism as a scientific and more "muscular" faith, a faith without fear. Modi has repeatedly emphasized—through tweets, speeches, and pilgrimages to the late monk's room at a monastery in Bengal—his admiration for Vivekananda and the inspiration the swami provided to his own life as a messenger for India. While Indian diplomacy has explicitly and indeed institutionally promoted culture as part of its international strategy since the early years of independence, with Modi we see a concerted effort to move this to the heart of Indian diplomacy. As a leading power, India looks to define itself in its own terms, and a large part of this involves showcasing its civilizational heritage to the world.

A subtle shift noticed in India, but little remarked upon abroad, has been Modi's frequent use of the Hindi language when abroad. The prime minister speaks English, but often prefers to deliver remarks in Hindi and field questions through a translator. This marks a change from his predecessors. (Within India, where language politics was once a source of bitter conflict but differences have long been managed through the coexistence of great linguistic diversity, a push to increase the use of Hindi in government offices and on government social media met with resentment in states where Hindi is not a first language.)[63] In Modi's first international forays, Indian press accounts remarked upon how his emphasis on using Hindi differed from past prime ministers, and was more akin to the Chinese or Russian practice of speaking one's own language abroad.[64]

Doing so stakes a proud claim for Hindi as a global language, and simultaneously signals a rupture with older elite social hierarchies that idealized English. Traditionally, Indian elites disdained non-English speakers as unsophisticated—and English skills were often a signal of class status, however unfair. Modi's choice of language echoes Indian journalist Shekhar Gupta's observation that "Hindi Medium Types"— ambitious, "tough as nails," small-town strivers—are now taking their place where only elites once trod.[65] In 2014, Modi addressed the UN General Assembly in Hindi, harking back to then foreign minister Vajpayee's 1977 speech at the United Nations, the first-ever General Assembly speech in the language, and one that many Indians still recall fondly.

Modi has also delivered all his speeches to the Indian diaspora gatherings abroad in Hindi. His September 2014 speech at the Council on Foreign Relations—which I attended in person—employed Hindi with simultaneous translation into English. When Modi visited Facebook headquarters in Silicon Valley, Mark Zuckerberg conducted a televised town hall where he asked Modi questions in English but received responses in Hindi. Two joint "vision" government statements crafted in partnership with the United States appeared for the first time with both English and Hindi titles.[66] It is a bid for recognition of Hindi as a language—an *Indian* language—just as deserving of visibility as one of the world's major languages alongside English, French, Russian, Chinese, or any other.

More Hindi is only one aspect of India's stepped-up focus on promoting India's culture and traditions abroad. Where previous Indian governments ensured that Indian musicians, dance troupes, and poets had the opportunity to perform internationally to convey the country's rich cultural heritage, one of the first Modi initiatives kicked this idea up a notch and roped in multilateral diplomacy and the UN system to secure a formal worldwide "International Yoga Day" commemorated each year to coincide with the summer solstice on June 21. In his speech to the General Assembly, Modi called yoga "a precious gift of our ancient traditions." Perhaps to the surprise of some listeners (certainly mine) he went on to list it as a lifestyle option the world could use to tackle climate change.[67] As the *Times of India* astutely noted, despite yoga's popularity in the West, and indeed its emergence as a multi-billion dollar business, its "link to India is often understated."[68]

This emphasis on yoga, as it turns out, is not just a minor detour from usual diplomacy. It represents a core example of how the Indian government wants to claim ownership of its cultural heritage and boost its recognition as Indian abroad. Indeed, yoga made it to the short list of diplomatic priorities Modi outlined to a gathering of India's ambassadors in February 2015, in which he urged them to project yoga "as a possible solution to common everyday problems of people across the world, including stress management."[69]

Indian diplomats secured a formal General Assembly resolution on yoga, passed on December 11, 2014, marking June 21 as the International Day of Yoga.[70] For the inaugural international observance the following year, Modi himself led some thirty-five thousand people in a group yoga session in New Delhi. Indian embassies and consulates in 191 countries convened yoga day gatherings to launch this new civilizational commemoration. In the United States, Indian embassy- or consulate-sponsored events took place in Washington, DC, on the National Mall, and in Atlanta, Chicago, Houston, New York, and San Francisco. The governors of Maryland, Virginia, Texas, Massachusetts, and Illinois, and the mayors of San Francisco, San Jose, Irvine, and Cambridge all sent greetings or issued proclamations about the day. Along with eight cosponsors, Congresswoman Tulsi Gabbard, the only Hindu member of Congress, introduced a resolution in the House focused on how yoga "will help promote better health" and encourage healthier lifestyles.[71] In sum, the International Yoga Day initiative managed to shift a seemingly personal, and certainly apolitical, pursuit to the world of high politics, even if only for a day. In doing so, it reinforced yoga's origins, planting the Indian flag squarely on every mat worldwide.

Previous Indian governments have emphasized India's composite culture, and reserved an important role for India's Islamic heritage in its international profile. The BJP-led government, not surprisingly, has placed great emphasis on projecting India's Hindu traditions as can be seen with the International Day of Yoga. In March 2016, however, Modi highlighted another international cultural initiative frankly unexpected for a leader coming from an RSS background. He spoke at the inauguration of the first-ever "World Sufi Forum" in New Delhi. An Indian Muslim organization, the All-India Ulama and Mashaikha Board, sponsored the undertaking to offer an alternative narrative of Islam, one that works against terrorism and radical interpretations of the faith. At a time when many fear that more hardline interpretations of Islam, such as that represented by the Islamic State, are taking root in the Subcontinent, the Sufi Forum highlighted India's traditions of religious syncretism. The founder-president of the Ulama and Mashaikha Board told an Indian paper that "Sufism stands for peace, tolerance, and unconditional love . . . . we intend to make India the global center for moderate ideology in Islam."[72]

Modi's inaugural speech at the Sufi Forum, before Islamic scholars from some twenty countries, emphasized India's diversity, its pluralism, and the peaceful form of Sufi worship that took hold in India. He also spoke of India as a spiritual center of Sufism, bearing a message that should be nurtured, revived, and spread throughout the world: "Just as it once came to India, today Sufism from India has spread across the world. . . . That is why I urge others in the region to nurture and revive this glorious heritage of ours."[73] He cited the "distinct Islamic heritage of India" along with Muslim poets such as Baba Farid, Bulleh Shah, and Amir Khusrau. (Khusrau in particular is credited with some uniquely Indo-Muslim musical traditions.) He also drew on the "priceless" culture of Sufism in a speech in Udhampur, Jammu and Kashmir in March 2017—at a time when tensions between Kashmir and the Indian central government had increased.

But India has not sought previously, even rhetorically, to use the country's status as home to the world's second largest Muslim population after Indonesia, and a population that has not pursued violent extremism, as a pathway to influence the course of Islam worldwide. And so far there has not been a sustained effort to highlight India's Sufi culture abroad. In this context, however, India's ability to showcase the successes of uniquely Indo-Muslim traditions is hurt by episodes of anti-Muslim violence domestically, such as the "cow protection" vigilante mobs of 2016 and 2017. These incidents have brought an exclusivist religious nationalism forward in which Indian Islam has no place. The effort to highlight globally Indian cultural traditions—in all their diversity—rests on its firmest foundation when the country practices inclusiveness.

5

A Cautious Power

TRADITIONALLY, INDIA HAS BEEN a cautious actor on the world stage. Within South Asia, the long-standing collaboration between China and Pakistan has constrained India geopolitically—although as the previous pages explored, China's growing influence in South Asia and the Indian Ocean has spurred India to up its own maritime game. On peace and conflict issues, although India has long been deeply involved with UN peacekeeping as a top troop contributor, New Delhi generally refrains from vocal positions on tough international conflicts such as Iraq or North Korea, holding its counsel for private diplomatic exchange if at all. On trade and economics, India's lack of domestic political consensus about how far and how fast to open the economy has slowed trade and investment liberalization from where it could be. Despite its calling card as the world's most populous democracy, with tremendous experience managing diversity—however fraught over the years—India shies away from pressing other countries on their own internal issues, including on democracy. Moreover, India rejects foreign comment on India's sensitive domestic concerns. These preferences reflect both India's complex politics, discussed in passing in previous chapters, as well as the legacy of nonalignment with its emphasis on nonintervention as a core principle of international relations.

This stylistic preference for caution has already begun to weaken as India becomes more powerful and focused on advancing its own interests rather than viewing them through a defensive prism. But fundamentally, the constraints imposed by geopolitics, India's contentious domestic politics, inherited ways of thinking about the world, and a complex international system mean that even as India joins the front ranks of global powers it will retain some of its habitual caution, except when it feels that its core interests are at stake. This chapter explores that process in greater depth.

GEOPOLITICAL CONSTRAINTS: CHINA AND PAKISTAN

While previous pages examined how China's expanded diplomacy and military activities have pushed India to articulate clearly its ambition to lead as the preeminent Indian Ocean power, the China factor has also created some real constraints for India over the years. The all-weather friendship between China and Pakistan, and its effects on India, deserve separate discussion.

China looms large for India, both globally and in the South Asian region. Although Nehru imagined in the mid-twentieth century that India and China were brothers with shared interests—complete with the slogan "Hindi-Chini bhai bhai" (*bhai* means brother)—China's surprise incursions across their border leading to war in 1962 revealed Beijing's differing view. It created a rift of suspicion that remains to this day. As Nehru wrote in 1963, "China's behavior toward us has shown such utter disregard of the ordinary canons of international behavior that it has shaken severely our confidence in her good faith. We cannot, on the available evidence, look upon her as other than a country with profoundly inimical intentions toward our independence and institutions."[1] The border remains undemarcated, and nineteen rounds of high-level talks have failed to adjudicate differences.

Related to the fact of the undemarcated border dispute, China lays claim to territory India has long considered its own. The McMahon Line agreed to as the boundary between the British and Tibetan governments in 1814 runs along the northern line of India's northeastern state of Arunachal Pradesh. It has served as the effective border between India and China. But China claims a large part of the Indian state of Arunachal Pradesh beyond the McMahon Line, a territory China calls "South Tibet." China became more vocal about its claim to this territory in the mid-2000s, through steps like issuing official maps depicting most of Arunachal Pradesh within Chinese borders, issuing passports with maps of Arunachal Pradesh and a section of Jammu and Kashmir known as Aksai Chin shown inside Chinese borders, and denying visas to Indian citizens from the state of Arunachal Pradesh. The introduction of Internet mapping services like Google Maps exacerbated these mapping claims by extending to the international commercial arena Chinese government territorial claims on Arunachal Pradesh.

In addition, the long-standing presence of the Dalai Lama and a large Tibetan community in India has been a thorn in the side of the India-China relationship since 1959. That year the Dalai Lama fled to India along with thousands of Tibetan refugees, was granted political asylum by Nehru, and established the Tibetan government-in-exile, known as the Central Tibetan Administration (CTA). According to the CTA, some one hundred forty thousand Tibetans live as "exiles" worldwide, with one hundred thousand of them resident in India.[2] Since the Chinese government views the Dalai Lama and the CTA as "splittists" seeking to break up China through calls for Tibetan autonomy, and since the Chinese government defines the Tibet issue as a "core interest," the continued presence in India of the Dalai Lama and the largest population of Tibetan exiles in the world underscores New Delhi's break with Beijing on an issue the latter considers a question of national sovereignty.

It all makes for a rocky relationship. While the South China Sea dispute has preoccupied American news headlines about Chinese territorial claims, India has faced a similar problem with its northern borders in the areas claimed by China. Border "transgressions," called so because the border itself remains undemarcated, and both sides disagree on its actual delineation, take place with some regularity along the 4,057-kilometer front and have required constant vigilance for the Indian armed forces.

A pattern of increased transgressions appeared to take hold from around 2012 to 2014, after which India intensified its focus on border infrastructure. In 2010 and 2011, India's Home Ministry logged 228 and 211 transgressions; by 2012 that number had increased to 426. In 2013, the Home Ministry reported 411 transgressions. Since 2014, comparable Home Ministry statistics have not been published, but press reports citing the Indo-Tibet Border Police indicate that in 2014, transgressions rose to around 500. Notably, the following year they declined to around

350, and down further to around 200 by October 2016.[3] A high-profile transgression unfolded just as Chinese President Xi Jinping visited India in September 2014—embarrassing his host Narendra Modi. It served to reinforce the message from Beijing: China's territorial claims remain live regardless of India-China progress in other areas.

To add to the security concerns from India's perspective, China's long-running, all-weather friendship with Pakistan has enabled the latter to develop its nuclear weapons program and facilitated the continued presence of terrorist groups focused on India as a target. China has supported Pakistan's civil-nuclear energy development outside the scope of the international nonproliferation regime, and a considerable body of declassified U.S. government documents delineate the extent of U.S. concerns about Chinese assistance to Pakistan's nuclear weapons program.[4] With the development of the China-Pakistan Economic Corridor, a $46 billion infrastructure investment project that will link China's west to Pakistani territory and eventually create a freight corridor to the Indian Ocean via the Gwadar port, Indian leaders saw a third country (China) developing major infrastructure projects throughout territory India claims (the Gilgit-Baltistan areas of the former princely state of Jammu and Kashmir). To underscore the point, India declined to attend China's Belt and Road Forum in 2017 in objection to this violation of sovereignty.

China's protection of Pakistan in the UN Security Council, where Beijing has vetoed efforts to designate Pakistan-based terrorists focused on India, deepens the cleavage. Particularly when it comes to security concerns, China has not supported India's bid for a larger global role, such as with its quest for a UN Security Council seat, or even in India's much more limited application for membership in the Nuclear Suppliers Group. (Economic matters, however, have offered opportunities for cooperation, which I discuss in later pages.) As a result, India gauges its military needs and its strategic doctrine with an eye on China, in true Chanakyan fashion.

China began its economic reforms about fifteen years before India, and though the two had reached similar levels of development in the mid-1950s, by 2015 the size of China's economy had leapfrogged India's by a factor of five at market exchange rates.[5] Over the past decade, China began shoring up its economic ties with all the smaller countries of South Asia, using its abundant capital and endless financing to assist with much-desired infrastructure projects in Sri Lanka, Bangladesh, Nepal, and Maldives. This will only increase with the new Belt and Road Initiative investments.

On the other hand, trade and economic ties have rapidly expanded in the last decade and a half, such that China became India's largest trade partner in goods in 2006. That pattern has continued. Indian governments have expressed dissatisfaction with the balance and composition of trade; the balance favors China and the composition consists of Indian raw material exports in exchange for Chinese finished goods. Still, successive Indian governments have used economic ties as a positive offset for unresolved security problems with China. During President Xi Jinping's visit to India in 2014, he promised investments of some $20 billion to India, all geared toward infrastructure development, including a feasibility study for a bullet train line. And as Chapters 4 and 6 discuss, in some multilateral contexts, India has made common cause with China when both have a shared goal of reshaping institutions of global governance. At the same time, however, Indian strategists have put the *Arthashastra's* mandala theory into practice, by dramatically expanding India's ties with Japan, and with the United States.

The disjuncture between these two parallel tracks—unresolved security challenges along one, with rapid progress economically and multilateral cooperation along the other—has become a truism for all analyses of India-China relations. It also illustrates the constraint on India, making New Delhi more likely to scan the broad horizon carefully before taking stances that it knows will displease Beijing. It has a lot to lose on the economic and the strategic front, so it takes care to weigh its options.

At the other end of the spectrum, but similarly representing a constraint on India, lies Pakistan. India and Pakistan have fought four wars, including the Kargil conflict of 1999. They have long-standing disagreements dating back to independence and partition. Both countries have declared nuclear weapons programs. Pakistan has escalated the security problems in the region by using its nuclear weapons as an umbrella under which it continues to harbor terrorists focused on India. As if that weren't bad enough, Pakistan's development of tactical nuclear weapons coupled with its lack of a no-first-use nuclear doctrine regularly earns it the description of "the most dangerous country in the world."[6] Despite its many crippling domestic woes, such as high population growth, sectarian terrorism, and lagging human development indicators, Pakistan continues to focus its strategy on a perceived threat emanating from India.[7]

Pakistan has failed to rein in UN- and U.S.-designated terrorist groups to such an extent that some terrorist leaders, like the individually designated Hafiz Saeed of the group behind the Mumbai attack of 2008, Lashkar-e-Tayyaba, continue to hold large public rallies that attract tens of thousands. In September 2016 Saeed led Eid prayers in a large public stadium in Lahore offering a message about Kashmir, and in late July 2016 he convened a Kashmir caravan that ran all the way from Lahore to the national capital of Islamabad, with a reported thirty thousand attendees. The caravan focused on jihad in Kashmir, and despite the fact that it was led by an internationally proscribed group and individual, Pakistani law enforcement permitted the enormous gatherings.

Cross-border terrorism incubated in Pakistan has exacerbated the tense situation in Jammu and Kashmir since 1989, particularly given fears of a possible escalation to the use of nuclear weapons given the uncertainties about Pakistan's willingness to use them. (India has a declared no-first-use policy and a second-strike capability, and is close to completing a nuclear triad with armed submarines.)[8] Since 2001, terrorists have also struck targets outside the state, such as the Indian parliament in December 2001, Mumbai in 2008, or more recently Gurdaspur (in Punjab) in 2015 and the Pathankot airbase (also in Punjab) in January 2016. The Pakistan problem also creates a constant threat of terror overshadowing every attempt to better ties, for attacks predictably follow new openings, just as Pathankot followed Modi's surprise stop in Lahore to visit Prime Minister Nawaz Sharif on his birthday on December 25, 2015.

One result of Pakistan's lackluster counterterrorism effort has been a shift in the Indian government's strategy in late 2016, marking a step toward a less cautious approach toward Pakistan. This came only after a cumulative sense evolved over years, despite peacemaking efforts led by both Congress and BJP government, that the hand-of-friendship and dialogue approach to the threat of terrorism from Pakistan could no longer stand as India's only diplomatic response, as it had for every major attack from the parliament attack of December 2001 through Mumbai (November 2008) through the series of attacks in Kashmir and in Indian Punjab during 2015 and 2016 (Gurdaspur, Udhampur, Pathankot).

In September 2016 the terrorist attack on an Indian army base in Uri in the state of Jammu and Kashmir precipitated a much sharper Indian response on the diplomatic and military fronts. Whereas previous terrorist attacks had spurred strong words from the Indian government, concerns about Pakistan's possible willingness to use nuclear weapons had meant that Indian leaders opted for de-escalatory tactics in the past—including after the massive attack in Mumbai in 2008. But the Uri attack appeared to cross a line for the Modi government, which despite a reputation for a hard-line approach to Pakistan had spent its first two years in office pursuing diplomacy and outreach instead. The fact that Pakistan had done little to stop terror groups from operating from its territory, and Pakistan's disinclination to pursue the Pathankot airbase attackers after New Delhi had allowed Pakistani investigators access to the airbase targeted in the January 2016 attack, proved to be the final straw.

Uri instead mobilized the Indian government to develop first more coercive diplomatic responses: a coalition of the members of SAARC decided to boycott the summit planned for Islamabad; India announced a review of its water use under the Indus Waters Treaty with Pakistan; and India announced its review of the "most favored nation" trade status it had granted to Pakistan, unreciprocated, back in 1996.

Those steps were shortly followed by the Indian announcement on September 29, 2016, of "surgical strikes" (not airstrikes, but an operation carried out on foot) across the Line of Control to target terrorists about whom the Indian government stated they had "actionable information" regarding their imminent infiltration into India to carry out attacks. The Indian announcement was worded very carefully, and framed India's actions entirely as counterterrorism steps in its own defense. This was the first time India had carried out a declared cross-border pursuit across the Line of Control with Pakistan, and marked a new Indian willingness to call Pakistan's bluff on the threat of nuclear weapons. India's closely calibrated counterterror actions received support from the United States, from Russia, and from other countries around the world. The White House issued a press release summarizing a call between National Security Advisor Susan Rice and her Indian counterpart, Ajit Doval. The release called for Pakistan to do more to combat terrorism from its soil, and lauded U.S.-India counterterrorism cooperation.[9]

The Pakistani government denied that any such strikes had occurred, thus lowering tension in the region. But one thing became clear from the news of the "surgical strikes": India's first response had hewed to caution over the years, but leaders felt it was time to show a stronger hand in dealing with Pakistan and terrorism. The stronger hand proved effective in the Uri case, but against the nuclear backdrop, the situation has become more fragile.

Apart from the constant concern of terrorism, the Pakistan problem has bedeviled South Asia's regional economic development, constrained economic and security linkages between Afghanistan and India, and limited India's geostrategic reach to the northwest. Pakistan sees any sign of Indian involvement with Afghanistan as a threat to its own interests, and as a result has refused to allow India transit access to Afghanistan and beyond—even though connecting Afghans to the region's largest market would help stabilize Afghanistan's economy and bring much-needed economic security to the entire region. The 2011 Afghanistan-Pakistan Transit Trade Agreement has failed to resolve this problem. Afghan trucks are allowed to carry goods to India, but they cannot cross the Pakistan-India border to reach the region's largest market. Indian trucks remain barred from this route. As a result, South Asia remains one of the least economically integrated regions of the world, according to the World Bank, and a major barrier to increased commerce across all of South Asia lies in the still-impassable trade divide between Pakistan and India—discussed in further detail in Chapter 6.

However, India's path has diverged so significantly from Pakistan's that despite their ongoing troubles, the latter does not existentially challenge India's rise. I do not write this lightly. Pakistan as a security threat and economic impediment to greater regional connectivity constrains India by keeping it mired in ongoing problems, but India's larger trajectory has fundamentally shifted out of Pakistan's league. The India of the twenty-first century is a country that prioritizes defense of its territory and protection of its citizens from terrorism, but has an entire agenda of economic growth, social development, and regional and global leadership that represents a much larger ambition and much larger field of vision than Pakistan's narrowly focused concerns. Pakistan-based terrorist groups can do harm, but they cannot alter the fundamental transformation that has now positioned India among the world's largest economies and with a significant contribution to global democracy, peace and security, development, and governance.

Taken together, India finds itself developing its capacities as an Indian Ocean power, preparing for the possibility of an increased Chinese military presence in the Indian Ocean, and remaining ever vigilant about threats to its citizens from terrorists based in Pakistan, even while trying to somehow evolve a better dialogue with Islamabad. But between China, a global giant with increasing reach all across South Asia, and the ever-present threat of terrorism from Pakistan, India's political leaders cautiously watch their own region and gauge their steps carefully.

NONALIGNMENT AND NONINTERVENTION

Chapters 2 and 4 outlined the importance that India has placed on nonalignment for many decades of its independent history. Within the nonaligned world, nonintervention has been a foundational principle, and one that Indian foreign policy tends to emphasize. But a closer look at how India defines its role in matters of peace and conflict reveals that New Delhi does not steer clear of all involvement in other countries' affairs; rather, it follows specific parameters when determining its involvement in conflicts beyond its shores. In a nutshell, India uses its troops abroad only either under a UN mandate or to protect its interests in its immediate neighborhood.

Historically, India has been the world's largest provider of troops for peacekeeping under the UN umbrella, sending nearly 180,000 personnel since the inception of UN peacekeeping in 1948.[10] India has also fielded the first-ever all-female "formed police unit," deployed in Liberia between 2007 and 2016.[11] Ever since it sent a paramedical unit to Korea in 1950, Indian troops and police have taken part in nearly two-thirds of UN peacekeeping missions: forty-four of sixty-nine missions, according to the Indian permanent mission to the United Nations.[12] These include some of the world's most difficult and dangerous missions, including those in South Sudan and the Democratic Republic of the Congo.

Rising casualties—especially in Africa—have led Indian diplomats to become vocal within the United Nations about improving the process for devising peacekeeping mandates. They criticize the Security Council for its "opaque" procedures, which do not generally take into account the views of the troop-contributing countries. As part of India's call for Security Council reform, one can expect continued attention from New Delhi on advancing troop-contributing countries' experience and views into peacekeeping mandates.[13]

In South Asia, India has been more active on a bilateral basis in its deployment of troops. Indian troops assisted the East Pakistani resistance force in 1971, and ultimately provided full-scale support in the liberation of Bangladesh from the abusive Pakistani army—a war known as the "forgotten genocide."[14] In Sri Lanka, Indian troops deployed as peacekeepers in 1987, aiming to secure the restive Jaffna peninsula from the Liberation Tigers of Tamil Eelam. They were not able to keep peace, took heavy casualties, and withdrew two years later. Widely described as a "debacle," the deployment remains a bruise on Indian foreign policy. (Two years after the withdrawal of Indian forces from Jaffna, a female Tamil Tiger suicide bomber assassinated Rajiv Gandhi in India.) In 1988, India airlifted sixteen hundred troops to the Maldives to put down an attempted coup in the tiny island nation, in which the group seeking to overthrow the then Maldivian government was aided by Tamil mercenaries from Sri Lanka.[15] Indian troops have served in Afghanistan in a limited, civilian-force-protection function, guarding Indian diplomatic facilities and the Indian construction workers and engineers who have built crucial highways, hospitals, and the new parliament building for Afghans. India also trains Afghan troops, but only on Indian soil. Beyond that, India has not moved to deploy forces, likely due to a desire to limit already extensive tensions with Pakistan.[16]

On the whole, though, when it comes to military deployment overseas, a bright red line separates these acceptable contexts—under a UN flag or in India's "near abroad"—from others. India has not sought a part in a coalition of the willing in any global conflict, despite the size of its military—the world's third largest—and its peacekeeping expertise. Perhaps most famously, India came closest to breaking out of this pattern in 2003, but eventually a U.S. request to deploy an army division in Iraq ended, after intense debate both within and outside government, with a polite refusal.[17]

At the United Nations, India abstains from voting in the General Assembly more often than other member states. On the one hand, abstention represents a lost opportunity to weigh in on global issues at least ostensibly significant enough to merit a vote. On the other hand, abstention usually ruffles fewer feathers, and helps India avoid choosing among competing interests. Data compiled by the U.S. Department of State provides a comparative window onto countries and their voting patterns. This American data naturally has its ideological center on Washington, and compares countries' votes against how the United States voted, as opposed to the complete universe. Still, it offers helpful comparative insights, especially in situating how India votes relative to other countries on the same questions.

In 2011, looking at eighty-five out of a total of ninety-five General Assembly votes on which the United States took a position, India—with twenty abstentions—ranked as the third most frequent abstainer, behind Cameroon and South Korea. The following year, with a full agenda of difficult global challenges such as Syria and Libya, more countries chose to use their abstention: twenty-seven countries abstained as much or more than India's fourteen times, out of a seventy-eight-vote subset of a total of eighty-nine votes. But in 2013, India once again bounced back to near the top of the list, with twenty-one abstentions in eighty-three votes (a subset of the ninety overall votes), fewer than only Syria and tied with Iran. In 2014, India was in the top ten for abstentions, but in 2015, had more company in the ranks of heavy abstainers, with twenty-one others abstaining as much or more on the same vote set. This snapshot, albeit of a point in time, shows how India's voting choices frequently illustrate a higher propensity to avoid taking a stand than is the case for many other countries.

At the UN Human Rights Council, too, India employs abstention regularly. Human Rights Watch has calculated votes for all the UNHRC members from 2016 going back to 2011. In 2016, India abstained one-third of the time. In 2015, India abstained six times in twelve votes—half the time. By contrast, the United States and China never abstained in 2015; the United Kingdom did so once, and so did France. In 2014, India abstained six times out of fourteen votes, for a 43 percent total. In 2013 and 2012, as HRW puts it, "India abstained on a majority of country resolutions voted at the Council, including all but one of the resolutions on the Syrian crisis. India rejected resolutions on the human rights situation in Belarus and did not support any of the key joint statements delivered on country situations. India was one of only two member states that did not co-sponsor any country resolutions in 2012 and 2013."[18]

A 2014 statement from India's Permanent Mission to the United Nations in Geneva explains this preference:

> The practice of selectively highlighting country situations and finger pointing has never proved to be productive. It will only harden the stance of countries and make them more defensive and drive them away further from the Council. Resolutions by the Council that have been adopted in confrontational manner have not served their intended purpose. . . . India strongly believes that the advancement and realisation of human rights can be achieved only through the cooperation and full participation of the concerned States. It is therefore paramount that this should be done in an atmosphere of mutual trust and cooperation.[19]

The statement succinctly captures India's strong antipathy toward both public criticism of most governments and third-party diplomatic intervention. In this regard, India remains faithful to the Nehruvian foreign policy playbook.

Glimmers of Change

India's two-year rotation on the UN Security Council from January 2011 to the end of 2012 offered a window on how it may approach the types of conflicts deliberated within the body should it achieve a permanent seat. Here, with one notable exception, India maintained its usual habit of abstaining on controversial votes.

India's tenure coincided with the great upheavals of the Arab Spring: political churn and instability in Libya, Egypt, Syria, Yemen, and others. India abstained—along with Brazil, China, Germany, and Russia—from a resolution on Libya in March 2011, in a vote that opened up the schism between Western nations focused on action and others that preferred caution.[20] India's permanent representative to the United Nations during that period, Hardeep Singh Puri, later told the BBC that India saw NATO as an "armed wing" of the Security Council, and thought the West had used the Security Council resolution as a cover to promote regime change.

Reflecting on the turmoil of the early years of the Arab Spring, and India's tenure on the Security Council during 2011 and 2012, Ambassador Puri told me over coffee in his UN Plaza office—he now works at a think tank—that the assumptions Western countries had harbored about the future of transitions in the Middle East was flawed: "The general expectation was that it would resonate on a Western, liberal, democratic template . . . like what happened in Poland, for instance. . . . There was a completely mistaken strategic diagnosis."[21] By contrast, India held a more cautious view about the likelihood of liberal democracy as an outcome, and that drove India's considerations in its Security Council votes and its diplomatic efforts during this period of tumult.

Upheavals in Syria during 2011 began to preoccupy Security Council and UN Human Rights Council deliberations shortly following the Libya crisis. President Bashar al-Assad's crackdown on civilian protestors that year moved Syria to the front burner. With NATO's intervention in Libya as the recent backdrop, India, Brazil, and South Africa coordinated via their "IBSA" formation—a trilateral of emerging-market democracies founded in 2003 during a meeting in Brasilia—to see if their diplomacy could stave off further conflict. Unlike the BRICS, which includes Russia and China, the IBSA trilateral took as a founding precept the importance of democracy, human rights, the rule of law, and multilateralism.[22] Their focus on Syria was likely also spurred by the fact that during 2011, all three countries held nonpermanent seats on the UN Security Council, which helped further their coordination and gave them the highest-profile platform in the world for their efforts.

As the situation in Syria deteriorated, India worked within the UN system to develop a presidential statement during the month it held the Security Council presidency, August 2011. The statement expressed "grave concern" over the deteriorating situation, condemned "widespread" violations of human rights and the use of force, called for an end to violence, and asked the Syrian government to fulfill its previous commitments.[23] Puri noted that this was the one unanimous presidential statement they had gotten. A week later, India, Brazil, and South Africa sent senior representatives from their respective foreign ministries on an "IBSA mission" to Syria, in an attempt to defuse the situation.[24] All three abstained from an October 2011 vote on a condemnatory resolution, which China and Russia vetoed in any case.

The IBSA mission had little effect on Syria's downward spiral. In Feburary 2012, India voted in favor of a Security Council resolution demanding the end of all violence—by the Syrian government as well as armed groups—supported by the Arab League.[25] It was vetoed, however, by China and Russia. In June of that year, India used its Human Rights Council seat—about which I will say more below—to vote uncharacteristically for a single-country condemnatory resolution against Syria and the killings in El-Houleh.[26]

Looking back on that intense two-year period, Puri saw a genuine effort on India's part, acting with Brazil and South Africa, to advocate for a diplomatic solution, one that "with the benefit of hindsight looks good." That Syria to this day remains an international disaster shows the complexity of the situation and the severe limitations on institutions like the Security Council to achieve action. In retrospect, India's 2012 position emphasizing diplomacy (and inherently arguing against regime change as a first approach) appears to be where the United States has ended up after a four-year slow-motion policy mess that has delivered little solace to Syrians and thus far solved nothing. One has to wonder whether a cautious approach like the IBSA plan, supported by more countries, might well have done better.

India's record on Syria—unusual given its more traditional abstentions on significant and controversial votes—holds out the intriguing possibility that an empowered India may step up to greater global responsibilities. A similar indicator emerged in recent Indian humanitarian relief provided in Nepal after the earthquake, or with its evacuation of civilians out of Yemen in the spring of 2015. In the latter operation, the Indian foreign service and military not only evacuated their own fellow citizens, but assisted many foreign nationals as well. The widened reach indicates how the Indian government sees its growing military capabilities as a force for delivering a global public good. In fact, the Indian embassy in Yemen became the point of contact the U.S. Department of State recommended for stranded Americans in April 2015 after the United States suspended its embassy operations there.[27]

That said, these deviations from India's cautious playbook do not yet amount to a clear pattern. New Delhi refrains from speaking out on every issue, much less joining global coalitions on many matters. On two of the hottest-button global security issues in the past few years, India has chosen ambiguity over clarity. When Russia invaded the Crimean peninsula of Ukraine in 2014, the Indian government said very little about this clear violation of sovereignty—despite a reported request from the Ukrainian government.[28] India has long defended the importance of respecting sovereignty, but in this case, apparently weighing its long-standing ties to Russia, the Ministry of External Affairs tweeted an anodyne remark: "We are closely watching fast evolving situation and hope for a peaceful resolution." A few days later, national security advisor Shivshankar Menon referred to Russia's legitimate interests in Crimea.[29]

At the same time, despite India's concerns about global terrorism and the difficulties its own citizens face due to the rise of the Islamic State— in 2014, IS kidnapped thirty-nine Indians in Iraq—India has refrained from signing on to the U.S.-led Global Coalition to Counter ISIL, which currently includes sixty-five countries in addition to the United States, plus the Arab League, the European Union, Interpol, and NATO. Indian foreign policy experts point to New Delhi's careful intention to fly "below the radar" in order to protect its own citizens and possibly avoid retaliation. Indeed, around seven million Indian citizens work in the Middle East, providing enormous remittance flows back home. The World Bank's annual migration and remittance data shows that in 2015 they sent back $36 billion in remittances, more than half of the more than $69 billion India, the world's largest recipient of remittances, received that year. (Comparable full year data on sending countries was not available for 2016 at the time of this writing; India remained the top remittance recipient in 2016). Yet more cause for caution.

THE TOUGH POLITICS OF REFORMS

India's political diversity, its strong civil society, and its independent democratic institutions keep its domestic political debates ever lively and often contentious. On some international economic matters, such as multilateral trade, an element of pride in safeguarding India's autonomy, or sovereignty, helps shape its interactions with the world. Not surprisingly, domestic politics also constrains India's conduct of international diplomacy. A lack of consensus on how open the Indian economy should be limits India's own freedom of action.

In itself, this interplay between domestic politics and foreign policy is hardly unique to India. However, the complex structure of Indian politics makes it that much harder to create constituencies for reform. I earlier described the country's "extreme democracy," with its politics evolving from the one-time single-party dominance of Congress to a system where two major national parties (Congress and BJP) forge alliances with a proliferation of smaller national or state-based parties.

If pride in the notion of India's policy autonomy explains some aspects of India's positions on the global stage, the country's political economy further explains its economic choices. Unlike in the United States, where poorer populations turn out to vote less than wealthier urban citizens, it's the less advantaged rural India that decides elections. While India has become more urban than before, its population remains overwhelmingly rural: according to the World Bank, in 1960, 82.1 percent of India's population was rural. By 2014 that figure had shrunk to a still-high 67.6 percent.[30] By contrast, while a slightly larger proportion of China's population was rural in 1960, 83.8 percent, by 2014 the country was more than 50 percent urban. Only 18.6 percent of Americans are similarly classified as rural. An analysis done by the data journalism website IndiaSpend.com demonstrated the gap in voter turnout for the most rural and the most urban constituencies: India's most rural areas had voter participation rates ranging in percentage terms from the high 60s to the low 80s. The most urban constituencies, by contrast, showed mid-50s to mid-60 percent turnouts.[31]

Higher turnouts precisely among the most populous sections of the country translates to meaningful power at the ballot box. While successive governments have advanced economic reforms, the tough politics of liberalization has limited their scope and pace. Indeed, after the reformist NDA government lost its reelection bid in 2004, despite surging growth, the UPA government that followed took the lesson from the voters that a broader political consensus on reforms would have to be slowly and carefully developed.

Thus, many "next generation" reforms that observers hoped the UPA would undertake ended up facing endless delays, as governing coalition members did not agree on the basic premise that a quicker opening up to the world would benefit the Indian people. Because India's approach to foreign investment reforms typically involve incremental steps—like raising the limit from 26 percent limit to 49 or 51 percent, and then to a 76 or even 100 percent limit—many FDI-related reforms initiatied in the 1990s still remained incomplete when the UPA took office in 2004. Limited progress took place over the following decade.

Bitter political fights erupted even when the stakes were truly low. Pension reform legislation—allowing private management of funds and up to 26 percent FDI—limped along for a decade before finally crossing the finish line in the UPA's final year. In an equally tedious story, an effort to raise the cap on foreign investment in insurance companies from 26 to 49 percent got bogged down for more than a decade in endless parliamentary reviews and standing committee deliberations. During the UPA's tenure, this became a surprisingly high-profile issue for external India watchers, a symbol of how reforms had stalled. As it turned out, insurance reform passed only in the first year of the Modi government. But even the new law that permits foreigners to own up to 49 percent of an insurance firm contains a phrase about the board remaining "Indian owned and controlled." International lawyers are still trying to parse its meaning, but it underscores the continued suspicion over opening India's market further.

Nothing symbolizes this struggle better than the battle over foreign involvement in Indian retail. A mundane commercial matter of little interest in many other countries around the world—take China, Brazil, or Indonesia, for example—its often-touted benefits include supply chain modernization and possibly greater exports. In India, however, opening markets to foreign retailers became an intense, coalition-breaking political dispute. A brief history of the dispute is instructive. Until 2006, India prohibited foreign investment in retailing of any kind. That year, India changed its policies to permit up to 100 percent foreign investment in wholesale trade, and up to 51 percent in what Indians call "single-brand" retail. A separate category known as "multi-brand retail"—basically any kind of store selling anything other than its own products—remained prohibited to foreign investment.[32] Simply put, India allowed foreigners to own more than half of, say, an Ikea or Christian Dior. But Walmart or Carrefour were not allowed to operate as they do around the world. Instead, they could sell to licensed retailers, not ordinary shoppers.

For anyone who has visited the large convenient SOGO or Carrefour stores in Jakarta, or a Walmart in China or Brazil, or a Tesco in Malaysia, the benefits of organized retail to India would seem obvious. A major study authored by the Indian Council for Research in International Economic Relations jettisoned the typology of "foreign" versus "domestic," using instead the distinction of "organized" versus "unorganized" retailing. They found that following the entry of organized retail, lower-income citizens and farmers would benefit, and that there was "no evidence" that overall employment would decline.[33] However, associations of Indian retailers representing smaller-scale neighborhood stores insisted that their businesses would not survive the entry of foreign multi-brand retailers.

In 2011, under pressure for the sluggish pace of reform, the UPA government attempted to open multi-brand retail and allow up to 51 percent foreign direct investment; at the same time it raised the foreign direct investment limit in single-brand retail to 100 percent. Announcement of the multi-brand opening resulted immediately in protests in major cities. Protestors focused on the harm that foreign retailers would bring to Indian shopkeepers and farmers. Mayawati, head of the Bahujan Samaj Party and at the time chief minister of the most populous Indian state, Uttar Pradesh, declared that FDI in retail was a "conspiracy" by Rahul Gandhi and foreigners to bring about the "economic enslavement" of India, and that foreign participation in multi-brand retail would "destroy" small industries, small farmers, and result in unemployment of millions.[34]

BJP leader Uma Bharati, now cabinet minister for water resources, threatened to personally burn down any Walmart store that opened in India.[35] More debilitating for the government, Mamata Banerjee, head of the Trinamool Congress in West Bengal, and a federal coalition partner at the time, publicly refused to support the new policy. Worried about government stability, the UPA decided to put the changes on ice while it consulted its coalition partners. (Oddly enough, as a result of single-brand reform five years earlier, foreign companies such as British clothier Marks & Spencer and luxury goods purveyor Louis Vuitton had already opened stores in India with barely a peep of protest.)

A year later, in 2012, the UPA announced that it would finally go ahead with the multi-brand retail opening, though with many caveats to soften its effect. Individual states would be allowed to decide for themselves whether they would allow it; tough stipulations on investment requirements and on mandatory local sourcing constrained the new policy further. Nonetheless, the announcement still managed to cause another political explosion. Protestors from the Confederation of All-India Traders tied black gags across their mouths, and bound their wrists in heavy chains with padlocks (Figure 5.1). A large poster depicted a giant red Godzilla on the rampage, with the words "FDI in Retail" emblazoned on its chest.

An enraged Banerjee stormed out of the ruling coalition, rendering the UPA a minority government for the remainder of its term. To its credit, the UPA government stuck with the reform, but the fireworks it attracted combined with a rash of corruption scandals plaguing the government made all further economic reform grind to a halt. Later, two states—Delhi and Rajasthan—that had originally opted to permit FDI in retail when governed by Congress, backed out after elections brought new governments to power. In Delhi, the populist rabble-rousing Aam Aadmi Party led the reversal; in Rajasthan a BJP government did the same, even though the party is generally seen as more market-oriented than its rivals. The reversals in these two states marked the first time any major economic reform in India had been walked back.[36]

The war over multi-brand retail illustrates the emotional tenor of some economic policy debates about India's opening to the world. A vocabulary of "enslavement" instead of "opportunity," or proclamations of imminent destruction instead of the possibility of upgrading infrastructure and becoming part of global supply chains, shows a very different view of this matter than has been predominant in countries like Brazil or China. As the World Bank noted in 2007,

FIGURE 5.1 September 27, 2012: A trader with mock chains around his wrists and a gag tied around his mouth attends a protest in New Delhi. *Photo credit*: REUTERS/Adnan Abidi. Used with permission.

India was "among the few in the world" to prohibit foreign participation in retailing.[37] The multi-brand kerfuffle also shows why Indian political leaders prefer piecemeal reform to sweeping and unambiguous changes, as Jagdish Bhagwati has so persuasively recommended.[38] To be sure, many reforms fly under the radar, such as the opening of the courier services or duty-free shops to foreign investment. But those that attract protest, usually any major reform, must be navigated with the skill of a high-wire walker. Former deputy chairman of the planning commission Montek Singh Ahluwalia refers to this as India's "strong consensus for weak reforms."[39] It helps explain why the Indian foreign direct investment manual runs more than one hundred pages, packed with elaborate specifications on which sector is allowable under the "automatic route" versus the "approval route," and within those categories, mind-numbing detail on which FDI cap applies where, to whom, and with what additional constraints. To sum up, when it comes to foreign investment, at times scrutiny and suspicion still influence policy and can even end political alliances. The inevitable result: political caution.

INDIA AND TRADE AGREEMENTS

As India has sought to carve out its own "rightful economic place" through its priorities and demands within the WTO, so too have ideas about the appropriate interaction with the world echoed in India's approach to trade outside the WTO context, particularly in its bilateral trade agreements and its hesitation towards emerging multi-nation (plurilateral) arrangements such as the TPP, the Information Technology Agreement expansion, or the Environmental Goods Agreement. While India has signed many free trade agreements (FTAs) and Comprehensive Economic Partnership Agreements, invariably these tend to be neither as broad nor as deep in their overall coverage as FTAs completed by the United States or the EU.[40]

As of 2016, India has ten FTAs and six preferential trade agreements either with individual countries or with associations such as ASEAN, and it is in the process of negotiating another twenty-two.[41] Negotiations between the EU and India on an FTA have been under way since 2007, with few signs of concluding any time soon. In 2014, Indian minister of commerce Nirmala Sitharaman called for a review of all completed FTAs to see if they have "provided the benefits" intended.[42]

Meanwhile, with prospects for achieving a global agreement under the WTO diminishing, the United States, EU, and many other countries have shifted to pursuing trade liberalization in specific sectors or regions by assembling groupings of the like-minded. Much of the action has focused on four major sectoral agreements: the expansion of the Information Technology Agreement (concluded in 2015); an Agreement on Government Procurement; an international Trade in Services Agreement; and an Environmental Goods Agreement. India has opted to remain outside all four of these negotiations—despite its own strengths in information technology and in services. By contrast, China is a party to two (the information technology and environmental goods agreements). Traditional trading powers such as the United States, Canada, EU, Japan, South Korea, and even smaller countries such as Israel, New Zealand, and Switzerland belong to all four. In March 2017, Indian negotiators presented a proposal for a services agreement to the WTO, notably with an emphasis on movement of persons. At the time of this writing, the Indian proposal had not advanced, nor had India joined the earlier Trade in Services Agreement process.

At the same time, new regional trade groupings are developing with the conclusion of the Trans-Pacific Partnership (TPP) negotiations and the ongoing Trans-Atlantic Trade and Investment Partnership talks. Like China, India is outside both emerging blocs. India is part of the Regional Comprehensive Economic Partnership (RCEP) negotiation, an alternative Asia-based negotiation that includes China. The Peterson Institute's C. Fred Bergsten describes the RCEP as a "low-quality agreement" and one "considerably less ambitious" than the TPP, given the likelihood that it will cover a limited number of sectors and in a shallow way.[43]

One of the central economic challenges India faces is a rapidly changing economic landscape filled with regional preferential trade blocs of which it is not a part. The TPP, of course, has been abandoned by the Donald J. Trump administration, making its future less certain. But Japan has taken up the charge of seeing it through, even without the United States. The very fact that negotiations reached a conclusion among the TPP countries (Australia, Brunei Darussalam, Canada, Chile, Japan, Malaysia, Mexico, New Zealand, Peru, Singapore, the United States, and Vietnam) indicates the potential for a major opening down the line. China has "cautiously welcomed" the TPP, and the Japanese prime minister stated that "Asia-Pacific regional stability" would benefit from China joining the pact.[44] According to a public statement made by then President Obama, China had been "putting out feelers" about joining the TPP in the future.[45]

Indian leaders will eventually need to make a decision about their country's path, which they have so far avoided. They will have to determine whether participation in larger and more extensive trade agreements will deliver benefits to the Indian economy that will be worth the initial pain of domestic reforms. Taking no decision may be politically expedient, but it carries potentially grave economic consequences for India's future. For instance, can the prime minister's "Make in India" program succeed if India remains disadvantaged in global manufacturing supply chains developed among major trading partners across Asia?

To illustrate the possible costs to India of staying out of a major and extensive preferential trade arrangement, Petersen's Bergsten estimated in the case of the TPP that the cost of trade diversion away from India due to terms and new standards set among the members could be significant, and would take an even bigger toll in a scenario in which China either joins the TPP or becomes part of an expanded "Free Trade Area of the Asia Pacific" across the Asia Pacific Economic Cooperation economies. Under those circumstances, according to Bergsten, the direct cost to India of diversion could be as much as "$45 billion in annual exports and $30 billion in national income." On the other hand, should India join a trade bloc encompassing all of APEC, it could realize export gains of as much as $500 billion, and a national income boost of as much as $200 billion per year.[46] These figures suggest an opportunity cost of almost $550 billion in exports from staying outside a larger future bloc.

Bergsten's estimates provide a sobering argument, especially against the backdrop of the government's intention to double India's 2015 exports of $450 billion to $900 billion by 2020.[47] But how India will approach a major binding agreement remains unknown. For now, Indian officials have clearly indicated their interest in joining APEC, a necessary first step, and one that would be possible without requiring extensive domestic economic reforms. On the other hand, the internal reforms needed to position India to join a binding trade agreement— such as lowering tariffs on a whole host of goods, or raising investment limits—would likely provoke domestic fireworks, as seen with even the relatively minor reforms discussed earlier. Even in the lower-standard RCEP negotiations, India's Asian negotiating partners reportedly issued a "shape-up-or-ship-out" ultimatum in April 2016, demanding that India "agree to eliminate tariffs on most products quickly or leave the talks."[48]

To read some of the Indian press and public deliberation about this, one might come away with the impression that trade agreements, and the TPP in particular, were formed to exclude India. Press coverage routinely describes India as not being "invited" to join.[49] Even more surprisingly, some people believe that India was deliberately left out; perhaps it is easier to see the emergence of plurilateral trade formations as something done against India by others, rather than take responsibility for the outcome of successive choices Indian leaders have made about their own economy. As an American think tank scholar, I have fielded questions on multiple occasions in roundtable discussions in India, where people have used the term "anti-India" to describe the

TPP's formation. I am not entirely sure that my startled efforts to refocus those conversations on the pathway defined by India's choices about market opening were persuasive.

To be sure, India's cautious approach to emerging preferential trade arrangements may not last forever. Chandrajit Banerjee, director general of the Confederation of Indian Industry, says his organization has been "trying to see how India can be actually compliant with the type of standards discussions that are going on . . . we are trying to look ahead and don't want to be losing out."[50] The *Economic Survey of India 2015–2016* put it well: "No matter what India ultimately decides, one thing is clear. Analytical and other preparatory work must begin in earnest to prepare India for a mega-regional world."[51] Nonetheless, India's uncertain approach so far toward a rapidly changing global trade landscape underscores how its domestic politics force it to adopt caution overseas.

THE CLOSED DOOR: FOREIGN HANDS, DRAIN INSPECTORS, AND VALUES

India is gaining not only in power on the world stage but also in its visibility. This means that domestic developments, which once might have been limited to Indian shores, now become the subject of international attention—and not all of it laudatory. Like all countries, India has many domestic problems, and in recent years some of these—like rape, violence against women, caste or religious violence, and corruption—have hit the international headlines.

India as a nation-state perceives criticism coming from abroad as out of bounds, and places limits on what subjects it will discuss with foreign governments. As a matter of official government policy, India does not accept criticism from other governments (and very often from foreign organizations or individuals) about internal social issues, seeing such comment as impinging upon its sovereignty. For example, in 2016 India declined to issue visas to a team from the U.S. Commission on International Religious Freedom (USCIRF), a statutory but independent body that investigates religious freedom. It was not the first time; indeed, a similar visa denial took place in 2009. In response to press inquiries over the 2016 denial, the Indian embassy in Washington issued a release stating, "We do not see the locus standi of a foreign entity like USCIRF to pass its judgment and comment on the state of Indian citizens' constitutionally protected rights."[52] That terse statement just about sums up the government's dim view of foreign organizations commenting upon domestic matters.

In a similar vein, in 2015 India quickly banned a documentary film, *India's Daughter*, about the horrific December 2012 gang rape of a young physical therapy student in Delhi. The director, a UK citizen, had taken permission from the Ministry of Information and Broadcasting as well as from the Ministry of Home Affairs (the relevant authority for Delhi's Tihar Jail, where she filmed one of the rapists), but allegedly had not fulfilled all the requirements relating to that permission. When the BBC decided to air the film anyway, India's home minister obtained a court injunction to prevent it from being shown in India.[53]

Once BBC decided to broadcast the film—unviewable in India— furor broke out. Many people in India—officials included—found the idea of the film's interview with one of the rapists offensive. The home minister stated in parliament that the filmmaker had violated a condition that the film not be used for "commercial" purposes. (BBC is run by a public trust.) But the nature of the broadcaster apart, many people were upset that the filmmaker seemed to be gaining professionally from what had been an unspeakable national tragedy. Prime-time news channels took up discussion of the film and the question of censorship. To protest the ban, the news channel NDTV ran a one-hour black screen with an image of only a flickering oil lamp during prime time. India's Editors' Guild spoke out against the ban. The government remained unmoved, despite the fact that rape and other forms of violence against women have become important subjects of public debate in India.

In parliament, two separate comments from political leaders—in each house—got to the crux of why this one particular film had caused so much offense.

In the Lok Sabha, BJP member and parliamentary affairs minister Venkaiah Naidu stated, "we can ban the documentary in India but there is a conspiracy to defame India and the documentary can be telecast outside. We will also be examining what should be done. . . . *India's name should not be sullied outside*."[54] Not to be outdone, in the Rajya Sabha, Congress member of parliament Ambika Soni tried to fault the government: "[W]hy was it necessary to give a foreign channel the permission to interview these people?"[55]

This perspective too has historical roots. Indeed, the most notable defender of India from criticism by outsiders was Mahatma Gandhi himself. After the 1927 publication of Katherine Mayo's *Mother India*, which assiduously catalogued India's social ills such as child marriage, caste, and discrimination against women, Gandhi penned a rejoinder to the tome he saw as an outrageous, untruthful, and biased view of India: "[T]he impression it leaves on my mind is, that it is the report of a drain inspector sent out with the one purpose of opening and examining the drains of the country to be reported upon, or to give a graphic description of the stench exuded by the open drains."[56] To this day, calling something a "drain inspector's report" has continued relevance in India. The country's domestic challenges are daunting, embarrassing, and at times an open wound; many people would like to wall off these subjects from foreigners. Finally unburdened from decades of being seen mainly as a land of poverty, Indian leaders do not want negative images to displace all of India's complexity—where the inspirational and the doleful live side by side—especially outside the country.

This brings us back to Indira Gandhi's infamous foreign hand. While we have seen the slow diminishing of the post-independence suspicion of foreigners and foreign capital in the business world, when it comes to domestic social issues, ideas about the foreign hand remain alive and well. This sentiment has been formalized in national policy through the Foreign Contribution Regulation Act (FCRA), a regulatory regime governing external funding to Indian nongovernmental organizations (NGOs). This act was strengthened by the Congress-led UPA government during its second term, and received parliamentary reauthorization in 2010. The law has affected major global foundations headquartered outside India, including long-standing contributors to India's development such as the Ford Foundation. FCRA guidelines essentially see foreign funding as a category of suspicion.

The FCRA requires NGOs that receive foreign funding to file annual statements of accounts, an unobjectionable feature that encourages good governance and accountability. But the law also allows the government to deny an NGO a license to accept foreign funds if "irregularities" with the organization exist. Indeed, the FCRA's second purpose as outlined on its website states, "to prohibit acceptance and utilization of foreign contribution or foreign hospitality for any activities detrimental to national interest and for matters connected therewith or incidental thereto."[57]

Any government would want the ability to review international financial flows, and the United States certainly pays attention to financial flows related to terrorist financing. But the FCRA as it stands has been used to cancel the license of, for example, Greenpeace India. The Home Ministry's 2015 cancellation order detailed allegations of financial mismanagement (Greenpeace India has contested this charge in court), and more ominously said that the organization had "prejudicially affected the public interest" and the "economic interests of the state."[58] (Greenpeace India activists had protested against nuclear power plants.) The Madras High Court stayed this license cancellation in November 2015, and the matter remains in court for now.[59] During 2015, both the Ford Foundation and the Bill and Melinda Gates Foundation found themselves the subject of Home Ministry inquiries concerning their grant recipients. According to press reports, the issues have since been resolved.[60] In early 2017, the FCRA license of India's Public Health Foundation was cancelled, under the allegation that it had violated the law by lobbying parliament against tobacco use.

The FCRA issue underscores a still-active suspicion that foreign influence may be undermining Indian interests through the backdoor, and therefore needs to be monitored. As Human Rights Watch's director for South Asia Meenakshi Ganguly told me, "Ambitious about its international image, the Indian government has chosen the classic route of shooting the messenger. Instead of addressing problems, activists that highlight concerns in Indian courts, in the media, or through international advocacy, are deemed anti-national, or driven by some subversive agenda. But you cannot immediately assume that the entire civil society is for some reason dancing to the tune of somebody else's idea. That it's a foreign-driven agenda. Which is not fair—countries have strong civil societies that have done a lot to raise peoples' lives, to improve peoples' lives."[61]

Of course, India's stance on these matters has parallels with some other countries. China famously bristles at the annual U.S. Human Rights Reports, and has begun issuing its own assessments of human rights in the United States. (Homelessness, shootings, health insurance problems, and U.S. airstrikes abroad come under fire.) Russia and Brazil, just to name two other large countries, have a strong sense of sovereignty; indeed, the concept of "whataboutism" originated with Russian counterattacks to foreign criticism (i.e., a critique of Russia would be met with "What about the plight of the American manual worker?" or other failings elsewhere).[62] And of course the U.S. Congress places great importance on national sovereignty.

But given the breadth of India's civil society, and its dynamic participation in global conversations about every issue under the sun, it's quite hard to firewall purely Indian interests from global concerns. In addition, at a time when Indian foundations have begun making grants to support issues of their interest outside of India such as climate change or social entrepreneurship, and at a time when India itself has become so global in its economic interactions, the FCRA appears to reintroduce barriers that have been gradually lowered in so many other areas. As India becomes a global leading power, an increasingly visible presence on the world stage, it will at some point confront the fact that ideas and influences cross national borders, exist in ongoing conversations, and embed each others' civil societies in dialogue everywhere.

ON DEMOCRACY

Democracy figures among the most important elements in any American discussion of India. When the two nations' top leaders meet, their "shared values" and experiences managing diversity nearly always receive top billing as the special factor bringing their countries together. As the world's largest democracy, India has been an early and strong supporter of both the UN Democracy Fund (UNDEF) and the Community of Democracies, a grouping of 106 countries dedicated to upholding democratic principles and human rights. India was a founding contributor to the fund and remains its second largest donor after the United States. Between 2005 and 2017, India donated almost $32 million.[63]

India has a remarkable story to tell about its experience with democracy—both its problems as well as its successes—but it chooses not to proselytize. New Delhi generally refrains from comment on problems with the norms of liberal democracy around the world, and does not project itself as an activist for the liberal democratic order. Instead, India quietly offers training and technical assistance on the practical side of running elections—and is doubling down on its capacity to do so.

The Election Commission of India (ECI) leads this training work, and it is widely regarded as one of India's strongest independent institutions. Barely a few months pass without an election in one of India's twenty-nine states, many of which are larger than most European countries. With two hundred million people, Uttar Pradesh alone has more people than Germany, France, and the United Kingdom combined. And, of course, every five years the ECI runs the world's largest election, one that spans several weeks and involves more than nine hundred thousand polling stations and more than eight hundred million eligible voters. Needless to say, unless China becomes a democracy, no other country holds the prospect of elections on this scale.[64]

I visited former chief election commissioner of India, Dr. S. Y. Quraishi, at his home in Gurgaon to learn how the ECI sees India's role in the world. While India is happy to be a cheerleader for democracy, it is unlikely to become a missionary in the American mode. But it is nonetheless quietly building the capacity to share its expertise more widely. During Dr. Quraishi's tenure, the ECI took advantage of its fiftieth anniversary year in 2010–2011 to hold "Diamond Jubilee" celebrations with a major international conference at the beginning and one at the end to mark the year. Inviting election commissioners from some sixty-plus democracies around the world helped raise the ECI's profile.

The ECI also began signing more cooperation memorandums with countries that needed help, like Kenya. Following a presentation Dr. Quraishi gave in Kenya, the assembled attendees told him, "We can't learn from the American model, we can't learn from the European model. They have very highly developed democracies. But the kind of problems you have and we have . . . we need to do more hand-holding. Since India has handled these problems very effectively, Africa can learn a lot from its experience." The ECI took steps to create a training institution focused on providing democracy and election training for international partners. Today, the India International Institute of Democracy and Election Management (IIIDEM) has been established within the ECI and awaits completion of its permanent campus in Dwarka, just outside Delhi.[65] It will be a huge facility with classrooms, a hostel, and an auditorium, all designed to house visiting delegations for focused training sessions. By 2017 it had trained officers from sixty-eight countries, and established partnerships with the International Foundation for Electoral Systems (IFES), International IDEA, the Commonwealth, and the UN Development Programme. India's long-standing technical assistance development program, ITEC (Indian Technical and Economic Cooperation Program, run by the Ministry of External Affairs), provides support to send foreign election officials and administrative officers for training in India, and IFES has worked with the ECI to develop a training curriculum that can be used anywhere.[66] The idea is that countries interested in learning from India's experience can request this technical cooperation, and through the IIIDEM, New Delhi can now respond more expansively than before.

So India has grown its capacity to bring its lessons to others around the world on democracy, showcasing its great soft-power strength in the process. As outlined above, however, this is markedly different from promoting democracy overseas. In keeping with its tradition, India hesitates to publicly criticize democratic lapses elsewhere, and when it does so, it usually marks a severly deteriorated situation, such as in Syria. Nor does India promote democracy the way the United States and European countries do, by presenting a checklist of specific concerns for individual countries to improve upon, a hallmark of U.S.-style annual reports. Nevertheless, in some ways India's quieter approach, as well as the strength of its South-South relationships built over decades, offer it an alternative kind of influence on the occasions it chooses to exercise it.

Recognizing this, Human Rights Watch (HRW) began approaching India as an "influencer" several years ago. As Meenakshi Ganguly, South Asia director for the organization tells it, the idea came about because HRW was finding its own influence limited by focusing solely on Washington, Brussels, or London as targets for advocacy on major human rights issues. "[A]t the Human Rights Council, there were blocs. Countries were voting in blocs. . . . So we realized that a lot of our issues, which are human rights issues, get locked into diplomacy. So that's when we realized that we needed to start talking to other governments, to make alliances with other governments."

With the emergence of IBSA as a more vocal group, Human Rights Watch began to think about talking with diplomats in New Delhi, Brasilia, and Pretoria as well.[67] India, which has served on the UN Human Rights Council from its 2007 inception through today (its current term expires at the end of 2017), has its own approach to human rights in multilateral organizations, as outlined above. New Delhi prefers not to "name and shame" and usually refrains from single-country condemnatory resolutions.

But within South Asia, the past five years have also witnessed a window cracking open on a more active Indian stance in the UNHRC where earlier one might have anticipated abstentions coupled with quiet bilateral diplomacy. Here, Sri Lanka was the headline case. India uncharacteristically supported U.S.-sponsored resolutions during votes in March 2012 and March 2013. The resolutions urged the Sri Lankan government to do more toward fulfilling the recommendations of its own Lessons Learnt and Reconciliation Commission, including investigating human rights abuses at the 2009 end of the country's long-running civil war against the Tamil Tigers.[68]

India's votes were the subject of extensive national press speculation in the weeks leading up to the March sessions of the UNHRC in 2012 and 2013, as there was a domestic political angle: virtually every political party in the state of Tamil Nadu wanted the Sri Lankan government pressed for accountability on the allegations of human rights and humanitarian law violations in 2009. The 2013 vote came at a steep price for the then Indian government, which deliberated over its position long enough that it lost a governing coalition partner, the Tamil Nadu–based Dravida Munnetra Kazhagam (DMK). The DMK accused the UPA of not being firm enough with Sri Lanka in defending ethnic Tamil interests.

As a result of Sri Lankan dithering on the obligations of the 2012 and 2013 resolutions, the resolution in 2014 took a tougher line. It sought an international commission of inquiry to do what the Sri Lankan government had refrained from investigating for years. The international commission of inquiry proved to be too intrusive for the Indian norm of nonintervention, and in 2014 India once again abstained.[69]

With the Modi government, an interesting point of contrast to the refrain-from-criticism, nonintervention norm emerged in its relationship with Nepal in 2015, over a question of democracy and constitutional representation—a core human rights issue. Again uncharacteristically, the Indian government offered a terse statement rather than effusive congratulations on the Nepali assembly drafting a constitution, an effort that had stretched over a decade. The Indian government expressed concern about violence in Nepal, and urged "dialogue" to resolve differences over the constitution that had prompted protests among Nepal's Madhesi population, who live along the areas directly bordering India, and felt that the new constitution limited their political voice.[70] Given that the Madhesi population resides so closely to India's northern border, and given the open border and the strong cross-border linkages between Madhesis and Indians especially in the bordering states of Bihar and Uttar Pradesh, New Delhi was concerned about unrest.

The Madhesi protests continued for months. Cargo trucks stopped entering landlocked Nepal from India, which disrupted delivery of vital supplies. (A Reuters photo captured a chalkboard in a Nepali restaurant that read, "No gas to cook/No menu to look/U can read a book.") Nepalis saw this as a direct economic blockade the Indian government orchestrated to pressure Kathmandu on its constitution. The Indian government said it had not blockaded the border, but that truck drivers feared entering protest areas. By the end of 2015, Nepali politicians announced their decision to amend the new constitution in line with the requests India had made to better accommodate Madhesi demands. Protests ceased, and trucks began to cross the border again.

In the Sri Lanka and Nepal cases, we see a firm side of India, one that sets aside its noninterventionist principles in order to weigh in on domestic problems in its closest neighbors. These two cases illustrate a structural similarity: both countries are small compared to the behemoth Indian state, and both presented domestic implications for India—political pressure in Tamil Nadu, or spillover from the Madhesi protests into north India. These suggest more immediate factors at play than in the more removed situations in Ukraine or with the Islamic State. They also suggest an emphasis similar to the African Union's transition from nonintervention to non-indifference referenced in

Chapter 2. When closer to home, higher stakes make it harder to remain indifferent. But for the most part, when it comes to democracy promotion the world's largest democracy shows no interest in emulating its Western peers.

On the topic of democracy, it's worth reflecting not only on India's strengths with the mechanism of elections—democracy's technical side—but also the way the country upholds its founding ideals for all its citizens. No other country in the world offers the size and diversity—religious, ethnic, linguistic—of India. In this sense, the scale of India's democracy, like nowhere else in the world, stands as an inspiration. But the many social cleavages that still trouble Indian society, and in particular how India chooses to manage these conflicts, can serve to enhance or diminish its global appeal. Whether Hindu-Muslim conflict, caste conflict, violence against women, poverty, or other concerns about rights and inequality, Indian society remains far from perfect and—like the United States and many other countries—will need to continue its work to form a more perfect union. Some of the social conflagrations in recent years have centered on caste and gender-based violence, freedom of expression and charges of "sedition" in political protest, and of course concerns about Hindu-Muslim violence. While the larger narrative of Indian democracy remains a powerful form of soft power, it is also the case that the perception of increased discrimination and even violence against India's large Muslim minority, or the still-troubling problem of violence against women, or indeed the perception that some views are not simply important disagreements, but rather anti-national thoughts, all serves to tarnish the ideal of Indian democracy enshrined in the Indian constitution. In the final analysis, India's great appeal, as messy, raucous, and unrestrained as its democracy can be, rests on a bedrock of inclusivity.

Just as the United States receives criticism for its domestic problems—of violence, of inequality, of race and the criminal justice system, to name only a few—Indian leaders should not expect to be immune, especially given India's rising global visibility, from global criticism of problems that would seem to undermine the values of freedom of expression and of equality before the law of all citizens. In some high-profile cases where freedom of expression has been curbed—such as when a Home Ministry order prevented an environmental activist from leaving the country to provide testimony overseas—courts have upheld the right to expression.[71] The strength of Indian institutions in upholding the country's constitutional protections gives me reason for continued optimism about India's democracy and its future. But the law enforcement actions to curb speech, or charge citizens with sedition, or the development of vigilante "cow protection" mobs, send a signal that conflicts with India's soft power attractiveness and its image as a rambunctious, disputatious, but fundamentally open democracy.

THE "LEADING POWER" PATH

As India grows more prosperous, more capable, and begins to surpass the world's traditional European powers in some metrics of power, its leaders remain conscious of the country's many continued vulnerabilities. As I stated earlier, India's growth coupled with relative transitions across the world will allow India to emerge as one of the world's major powers even before it fully clears its domestic hurdles. The hurdles remain real, and will likely ensure that India acts with a measure of caution for the foreseeable future, but due to new policy emphases and a continuation of previous initiatives, India now actively seeks to surmount its greatest weaknesses and carve for itself a larger global role.

The next section examines India's future trajectory along two lines, looking at the steps India has been taking to create its own world of multilateral institutions where it can have a larger and more vocal role, as well as the changes under way propelling the Indian economy to higher growth. India is not waiting until the major institutions of global governance reform to create the rightful place that New Delhi believes it should occupy. Indian leaders have cooperated with those of other rising powers to create institutions of global governance they see as more representative of their interests, such as the BRICS, its democratic offshoot IBSA discussed in the context of India's term on the UN Security Council, and a number of other organizations including several intended to institutionalize Indian Ocean diplomatic coordination. India has indicated clearly that it will more actively develop alternatives for its voice.

Chapter 7 examines changes in the Indian economy, and especially the matter of India's economic future. The question of whether India can more fully industrialize has long preoccupied analysts. Autos have been a force for transformational development in so many countries: Japan, Korea, China, Thailand, Mexico, to name a few, and the industry has begun to take off much more significantly in India. The Indian government seeks to unburden the textile sector, already accounting for around 2 percent of GDP, from the regulatory burdens that have prevented India from leveraging opportunities in this space. An escalated focus on vocational training has also taken hold in India to fill a long-standing gap and better provide skills for the types of jobs available.

The next section looks at these developments, their prospects for India's future, and then considers how the United States should work with a rising India.

PART THREE
Looking Ahead

6

India's Changing Global Role

INDIA'S APPROACH TO GLOBAL diplomacy is changing. An Indian sensibility exists—across parties—that sees a special role for India to play globally by virtue of its size, its civilizational accomplishments, and its achievements of democracy against the odds. India's UPA government sought to recover India's "rightful place" in the world, to recall former prime minister Manmohan Singh's words regarding the importance of the U.S.-India civil nuclear deal. Or take Modi's veneration of Swami Vivekananda: in a 2012 tribute piece, he wrote that Vivekananda had "visualized India's pre-ordained destiny of taking on the mantle of the world's leadership."[1] These snapshots, especially the choice of words, illustrate India's leadership ambition in the world.

But given Indian sensitivities about sovereignty—a sensitivity baked into much of India's international positions given its role creating and stewarding ideas of nonalignment—it has historically played defense on the global stage more than offense, so to speak. India has also been outside many of the prominent institutions of global governance—certainly the UN Security Council, but also the Group of Seven, and the nonproliferation regimes. A belief that transcends political partisanship in India is that the country deserves a greater say in institutions of global governance as a matter of basic fairness in the international order.

Successive Indian governments have pressed for greater representation in global institutions and demanded a role commensurate with what they see as India's rightful place. Towards that end, India has two parallel tracks under way. India is more actively pursuing leadership in institutions where it has not had a place—with permanent representation on the UN Security Council the most important of these, and with a strong and continued push for reform in the Bretton Woods international financial institutions to better account for the growth of its economy, as discussed previously. India's changed approach to the global nonproliferation regimes has resulted in its pursuit of membership in all four, though it continues to remain outside the NPT. India has also pressed more actively for membership in the Asia Pacific Economic Cooperation forum, but still remains on the outside as APEC has not welcomed any new candidates since a moratorium on membership expired in 2010. And in the context of global climate change, a global concern in which India had previously staked out an oppositional position, India has shifted its approach to present itself as offering an alternate pathway and global leadership on clean energy.

At the same time, New Delhi has expressly worked to develop alternative institutions and "minilateral" groupings that create space for a greater Indian voice, such as with the BRICS, its IBSA subgroup, the Asian Infrastructure Investment Bank (AIIB), and the New Development Bank (NDB, the BRICS bank). Several Asia-focused institutions like the Indian Ocean Rim Association (IORA), the Conference on Interaction and Confidence-Building in Asia (CICA), and the Indian Ocean Naval Symposium (IONS) further indicate an Indian ambition to shape or create organizations that address its needs, and allow it to play a role it does not yet play elsewhere. India was inducted as a full member of the Shanghai Cooperation Organization in 2017, marking another example of an Asia-focused organization in which India seeks a formal role. While some Americans might be unfamiliar with these various groupings, let alone see their benefits, India is dead serious about these emerging institutions and allocates some of its limited diplomatic resources to its ongoing involvement with them.

INDIA AND GLOBAL REGIMES

India's pursuit of a larger voice in the UN Security Council and in the IMF and World Bank has been a feature of Indian diplomacy for some years, as previous pages considered. Other institutions have seen a new and changed Indian approach to membership, especially India's desire for membership in the global nonproliferation order—again, the issue that cleaved India apart from the U.S.-led nonproliferation order for more than three decades. The decision the United States took in 2005 to work with India on a civil-nuclear agreement not only included an agreement of bilateral cooperation, but also involved joint cooperation to bring India "inside the global nonproliferation tent."

Four major export-control organizations have developed standards for how countries handle advanced technology and chemicals; the four are the Nuclear Suppliers Group (NSG), the Missile Technology Control Regime (MTCR), the Wassenaar Arrangement, and the Australia Group. The Nuclear Suppliers Group includes countries that carry out trade in commercial nuclear energy production, and an exemption from this group to allow members to trade with India—a non-signatory of the NPT, so a break from past NSG practice—was an important step in the U.S.-India civil-nuclear agreement in 2008.

While India continues to stand outside the NPT, New Delhi has made changes to its domestic export-control laws to align with the guidelines of these regimes, and is pursuing membership in all four regimes. In June 2016, India became a full member of the MTCR. Membership gives India access to more advanced missile technology, and potentially allows India to export its own, within regime guidelines.

India has also pursued membership in the NSG. This has been a long diplomatic process, and one that has not yet reached its goal. The NSG, a forty-eight-member group that makes decisions by consensus, has not achieved the unanimity needed to induct India. During its June 2016 meeting in Seoul, the failure to welcome India was a disappointment for New Delhi, and a raft of critics cast the Seoul non-decision as a misstep for Indian diplomacy. (Critics accused the Modi government of a judgment error in applying for membership without guaranteed success, and of course accused the United States of failing to deliver.) Despite ongoing U.S. statements that India was "ready for NSG membership,"[2] China has played its geopolitical card here, raising as a preliminary issue the question of how to induct non-NPT signatories as members, which by all press accounts held up acceptance of India as a member. Observers see China's all-weather friendship with Pakistan as a reason for its reticence to support India's bid, and indeed Pakistan submitted an application for NSG membership in 2016 despite its extensive track record of nuclear proliferation with the A. Q. Khan network uncovered in 2004.

India, with strong U.S. support and that of dozens of other countries in the NSG, will continue to push for membership. Without NSG membership, India can still carry out civil-nuclear commerce with all the NSG members since the group passed its exemption for India in 2008. For New Delhi, then, the NSG membership bid is not so much an avenue to open up commerce, which is already open to India, but rather a mark of belonging to the club that sets the rules. It's exactly the impetus for many of India's diplomatic efforts toward greater inclusion in global regimes—becoming a rule-setter, not just a responder to rules set by others. New Delhi is also preparing to apply for membership in the Australia Group and the Wassenaar Arrangment, two other nonproliferation regimes that have created best practice export controls to track chemical and biological materials and equipment, and for dual-use technologies and munitions. During his January 2015 visit to India, President Obama released a joint statement with Prime Minister Modi that declared support for "India's early application and eventual membership in all four regimes."[3] This marks a dramatic change from decades past, when nonproliferation was a single-point focus on the diplomatic agenda, one in which India stood as an outlier.

Global climate change marks another Indian turnaround. In less than a decade, India has moved from a "playing defense" approach on climate change to a new and different leadership role in setting the global agenda in a manner consistent with India's priorities and concerns. Earlier, New Delhi took an oppositional approach to the Conference of Parties talks, casting itself as a developing nation with decades of development still ahead. New Delhi consistently remarked upon the inherent unfairness that far larger carbon emitters on a per capita basis in the West, countries for whom major economic development had already taken place, were not willing to provide sufficient funding or royalty-free technology to ease a transition to a less-carbon intensive growth trajectory. For many in the West, however, despite recognizing India's still-low per capita emissions, the sheer scale of India's population and economic growth trajectory provided all the rationale needed to seek Indian support to combat climate change—for without India, the third largest emitter, a global agreement could not be complete.

India earlier built a stance based on refusal to acquiesce to global proposals, just as with India's positions in multilateral trade. Indian leaders spoke about protecting Indian interests, defined with the highest priority on economic growth, invariably energy-intensive, and a pathway that would include the use of cheap coal as long as necessary. The Copenhagen Conference of Parties meeting of 2009 did not result in a binding agreement, contrary to hopes for the meeting, and in the West many held India and China responsible for their unwillingness to sign on to a global agreement. The "BASIC" group of Brazil, South Africa, India, and China convened its own subconference within the Conference of Parties, and drafted its own outline of voluntary, but not legally binding, commitments. In that case, the importance of finding a way to secure China's and India's cooperation—given their size— became a frontline concern for developed countries, along with the realization that both were willing to stand apart to protect their carbon-intensive growth trajectories in the name of economic development.

The Conference of Parties meeting in Paris in 2015 showed an Indian evolution to a new stance. Instead of an India resisting a perceived agreement imposed by the West, an India actively shaping the global agenda emerged. New Delhi still prioritizes economic growth in the name of development for its huge population, but the Paris agreement showed a different Indian approach to preserving that interest. It's hard to overstate what a difference India's approach to the 2015 Paris talks represented: previously, India had been seen as a climate holdout, and Western press speculation in the run-up to the negotiations fretted that India might scuttle a global deal. Indeed, India's position on climate issues discussed just weeks earlier at the G20 led the *Financial Times* to declare that New Delhi had "blocked" efforts for an ambitious deal.[4]

Indian negotiators arrived in Paris with a positive proposal that leveraged India's domestic emphasis on renewables as a major energy security focus. Prime Minister Modi and then French President François Hollande announced a new international solar alliance, the declaration of which focused on "sustainable development, universal energy access, and energy security," as well availability, making "clean and renewable energy . . . affordable for all." India has great solar energy generation potential, and intends to scale production to one hundred gigawatts by 2022—said to be a $100 billion solar ramp-up, the world's largest—so the solar alliance created a global leadership role for India building on its preexisting national plans.[5]

Indian multilateral leadership in Paris contrasted with the India of the Doha Round in 2008 and of the Copenhagen Conference of Parties in 2009. Instead of emphasizing inequity in the climate negotiations given India's comparatively minuscule historic contribution to the problem of climate change—something still deeply felt across India—Modi and his environment minister stepped forward with a problem-solving disposition. Environment minister Prakash Javadekar stated as much, telling the press that "India will be flexible and show the world that though India is not part of the problem, still is facilitator [sic] for the solution."[6] India has not commited to a date at which it will cap carbon emissions, but the world perceives the country as leading in renewable energy development, a necessary technology shift relevant to the world. In a new regime governing global collective action on climate change, India stepped forward to help craft the outcome.

And indeed, just as U.S. President Trump pulled the United States out of the Paris Agreement, Prime Minister Modi—on a visit to Germany—stood publicly with Chancellor Angela Merkel to declare India's continued commitment to the agreement.

CREATING ALTERNATIVE INSTITUTIONS

The process of reshaping global institutions has not moved fast enough to accommodate the role New Delhi believes India should play—witness the long delays in Security Council reform, and the incremental but insufficient changes in the IMF and World Bank discussed earlier. India is still pushing to open those doors further, but has developed a substantial second-track approach in which it is creating or joining alternative institutions.

India's parallel track focused on alternative institutions of governance has been far more active than many external observers might guess, and in its own way resembles China's efforts to create alternative institutions not dominated by the West. Part a protest vote, part a pursuit of status in other (smaller) arenas, and part a bid to create institutions responsive to India's priorities, New Delhi's attention to new organizations allows it to "forum-shop," as Dan Drezner put it in the context of China. In this space, India sees China as an ally in coordinating a "developing world" set of priorities, despite reservations about China's rise and Beijing's approach to Indian geopolitical concerns bilaterally. New Delhi shows willingness to cooperate with Beijing in return for a role in new, effectively China-led institutions such as the BRICS, the Asian Infrastructure Development Bank, the BRICS New Development Bank, the Conference on Interaction and Confidence-Building in Asia, and the Shanghai Cooperation Organization. New Delhi is also doubling down on smaller organizations spanning regions that are inherently under-institutionalized, like the Indian Ocean, and subregions within South Asia.

BRICS and IBSA

That famous Goldman Sachs report from 2003—*Dreaming with BRICs*—took on a life of its own after a meeting on the margins of the St. Petersburg G8 Outreach Summit in 2006: Manmohan Singh, Vladimir Putin, and Hu Jintao came together in a trilateral, according to India's chronicle of its own involvement in the BRICS. A foreign ministers meeting later that same year on the margins of UNGA led to the creation of an ongoing dialogue formation, and the first formal summit took place in Yekaterinburg in 2009.[7] The four invited South Africa to join by the third BRICS summit in China in 2011.

I can remember when foreign policy pundits in Washington referred to the BRICS as just another mash-up in the alphabet soup of global organizations. The formalization of BRICS over the years, and the expansion of its activity to networks of cooperation and funding to get things done, suggests more than the empty alphabet-soup critique implies. In little more than a decade, and effectively less than a decade if dating this institution by its 2009 formal inaugural summit, it has developed an agenda and an ongoing diplomatic calendar that includes finance, health, trade, science/technology, education, agriculture, environment, population, communication, and labor matters. The joint statements issued by all five goverments after each summit illustrates how the BRICS became a real institution—from a two-and-a-half-page declaration in 2009 to the voluminous, forty-three-page Ufa declaration of 2015, the agenda has grown and so has their actual activity, complete with sherpas and sous-sherpas modeled after the G7.[8] There's even a youth forum.

New Delhi cares a lot about the BRICS, serving as summit host for 2016 in Goa, and using the occasion of the summit to invite a subgrouping of South Asian and Southeast Asian countries in the Bay of Bengal Initiative for Multisectoral Technical and Economic Cooperation grouping (or BIMSTEC for short, which includes Bangladesh, India, Myanmar, Sri Lanka, Thailand, Bhutan, and Nepal) to meet on the margins. And it was in New Delhi that the fourth BRICS summit of 2012 took place, in which the most significant action thus far from the BRICS emerged with the creation of a development bank.

The BRICS as a coordinated group has maintained a consistent critique of unrepresentative global institutions, calling for UN, World Bank, and IMF reform, but in 2012 they decided to explore setting up their own development bank that they could fund and therefore control. This sensibility of righting a global institutional wrong carries through in the consistent references throughout India's BRICS-related pronouncements, be it speeches, joint statements, or websites, to the BRICS as a collective that represents "43% of the world's population." Representation comprises an ongoing concern in BRICS joint statements, such as welcoming developing world candidates for the IMF and World Bank leadership positions.

By 2014 the BRICS Bank, later named the New Development Bank, had come into being with articles of agreement signed in Brazil, as well as a Contingent Reserves Arrangement. By the 2015 Ufa summit, the BRICS leaders "mark[ed] their entry into force." The New Development Bank describes itself as "an alternative to the existing US-dominated World Bank and International Monetary Fund."[9] With Shanghai selected for the NDB's headquarters, India pushed for and succeeded in securing the founding presidency for a five-year term. Former top Mumbai banker K. V. Kamath was appointed president of the NDB and the bank formally launched in July 2015.

Each of the five BRICS countries has an equal vote in the NDB's governance. When the Indian government announced that the Union Cabinet approved of the NDB and the Contingent Reserves articles, thus bringing India's participation into force, the press statement contained these three sentences: "Besides, the governance structure and decision making in the Bank will be equitable unlike the existing multi-lateral development banks" and "Pending the IMF governance reforms, India does not have much say in the IMF decisions. The proposed CRA will provide an alternative approach."[10] The statement says a lot about why New Delhi has championed BRICS and these new financial institutions.

Similarly, but with far less effect on global diplomacy, the India–Brazil–South Africa subgroup within the BRICS has its own trilateral gathering. As three major democracies, the IBSA focus has been acti-vated more occasionally to weigh in on matters of international peace and security, as chronicled earlier with respect to the year all three countries served on the UN Security Council, and a nominal commit-ment to increase trade. IBSA lacks the intensified diplomatic calendar and expansive agenda of the larger BRICS format, and appears to have had some trouble in recent years with summit postponements, braking the development of this forum. That said, as discussed in earlier pages, the cooperation of Brazil, India, and South Africa within the Security Council on the deterioration of the situation in Syria points to a pos-sible diplomatic tool that India could use further. It has not acquired the momentum of many other alternative institutions, however, despite its advocacy in 2011.[11]

The AIIB

India hasn't limited its alternative financial institution focus to the BRICS. While much has been written about China's role in creating the Asian Infrastructure Investment Bank (AIIB), India too has fol-lowed a similar path and put at least some of its eggs in this China-led basket.[12] The stall in reforming the World Bank and IMF, related to U.S. domestic politics, played a catalytic role in the creation of the NDB as well as the AIIB.

Though China and India grew to become global bilateral donors in their own right, their capital contributions and voting shares in these two global institutions, formed at the end of World War Two, remained stuck in the past. The United States agreed to IMF efforts to revise internal governance in 2010, reforms that increased overall quotas while rebalancing their distribution to increase the voting power of the BRICS and developing countries. China would become the third-largest "member country," and Brazil, India, and Russia would move into the top ten.[13] In order for Washington to officially approve the reforms, the U.S. Congress had to put its seal of approval on the plans first. Congress then failed to pass measures authorizing changes for more than five years—in fact, not until December 2015. Inaction hastened the process of China and India looking to devise alternative institutions that would better reflect their growing economic weight.

It was during the five years that IMF reforms dragged on, that the NDB and the AIIB were conceptualized, founded, and capitalized. Notably, neither of them involve the United States, and both explicitly describe themselves as vehicles to reflect rising power priorities. India's involvement has been largely overlooked by the international media, but New Delhi has ensured that India plays a leadership role in both organizations.

The better-known AIIB, a China-led institution, quickly acquired support from other Asian countries and eventually from many European countries as well, despite U.S. efforts to discourage allies such as Britain from joining, a great error in diplomacy. India came on board the AIIB early on, even hosting the second negotiating meeting for its articles of association in Mumbai. India is also the second largest capital contributor, ensuring for itself a role as a major stakeholder. A former career member of the Indian Administrative Service serves as an AIIB vice president and chief investment officer. The AIIB will be able to draw upon $100 billion in authorized capital, while the NDB can eventually draw upon $50 billion of capital, and $100 billion of contingency reserves. By comparison, the Asian Development Bank has a $160 billion capital base, and the World Bank some $223 billion.[14] So while these newer financial institutions will not rival the existing development bank mechanisms, they will serve as a supplement—and most important, set their own agenda without the shadow of the United States and Europe.

India in Asia

India has been taking steps to become a much more visible player across the entire Indo-Pacific region, extending from the maritime space to the west all the way to the east, across Southeast Asia and East Asia, both through its involvement in Asia's most central regional institutions and through deepened ties with Japan as a core Asian market economy partner. India's "Look East" policy of the 1990s declared a priority to strengthen ties with Southeast and East Asia. India has been a member of the ASEAN Regional Forum since 1994, and became a founding member of the East Asia Summit (EAS) in 2005. In 2014, the Indian government amped up that policy to "Act East," in a shift announced by Modi in remarks during the East Asia Summit held in Nay Pi Daw. The shift from "look" to "act" signals a larger ambition and desire for greater prominence across the larger Asia-Pacific space—surely in the context of India's expanding trade across the Asia-Pacific, but also with a view toward establishing itself as a more visible presence at a time when China has accelerated its own visibility in South Asia.[15] India's stretched diplomatic service appointed a full-time ambassador to ASEAN in 2014 to represent itself more vigorously. Former Singaporean Prime Minister Goh Chok Tong spoke of India as one of "two wings" on a jumbo jet (the other being China), in a vivid metaphor illustrating how ASEAN viewed the quest for regional balance and India's importance to it.

With its ASEAN ties as one pole, India has assiduously worked to strengthen its relationship with Japan—a Chanakyan move, given the complex ties New Delhi and Toyko face with Beijing. In 2000, India and Japan declared a "Global Partnership" to represent their relationship, which expanded in 2006 to a "Strategic and Global Partnership." In 2014, the term for their bilateral ties received a further filip, becoming a "Special Strategic and Global Partnership" during Modi's visit to Tokyo. Japan is a major development partner for India, using the strength of its development agencies and state-owned enterprises to pledge a $35 billion investment in projects in India over five years. Japanese companies have long been involved in India—very successfully, with examples like Suzuki that led the way in subcompact auto production in the 1980s. India has ongoing defense consultations with Japan, and Japan has joined the MALABAR naval joint exercise between India and the United States. A U.S.-Japan-India trilateral consultation began in 2011. With Japan as its special partner in the pursuit of a Security Council seat, in economic development, and in rethinking the space of strategic and global action across all of Asia, India signals its ambitions to rise as a peer, as among the world's top economies and one committed to democracy.

India was a core member of the Asia-wide Conference on Interaction and Confidence Building Measures in Asia (CICA) upon its founding in 1992, an organization first proposed by Kazakhstan. CICA encompasses multiple regions that otherwise have not had a consolidated regional platform. CICA members span Central Asia, Russia, the Gulf, China, Mongolia, and Korea in East Asia; Cambodia, Thailand, Vietnam; and also include Turkey, Iran, Israel, and Azerbaijan. India leads two of CICA's confidence-building measures, those focused on transport and energy security, and seconded a diplomat to the CICA secretariat beginning in 2007.[16] With the Chinese government's assumption of the chair in 2014, Beijing declared its desire for CICA to serve as a "security governance model with Asian features."[17] Here we see an example, like the AIIB and NDB, where India has made common cause with China and other regional partners to create alternative institutions. Expect to hear more about this organization in the coming years.

So, too, with the Shanghai Cooperation Organization (SCO), founded in 1996. The SCO comprises China, Russia, Kazakhstan, Kyrgyzstan, Tajikistan, and Uzbekistan. As a geographic grouping focused on Eurasia, it has emphasized security, counterterrorism, counternarcotics, and economic cooperation. India became an observer in 2005, and in 2015 it—along with Pakistan—received the nod for membership.[18] Formal induction took place in 2017. The CICA and SCO involvement place India within groups that have a more security-focused agenda than ASEAN provides, not to mention a geographic span that includes Central Asia (a region that India sees as part of its historic sphere of connectivity) to India's northwest. The extent to which CICA and SCO provide for coordination or collective action is not yet clear—they may fail to ever do much—but the BRICS example suggests that they are worth tracking. India certainly is.

Of course, the quickened tempo of Indian involvement in the Asia-Pacific has dovetailed nicely with U.S. interests in Asia, particularly Washington's preference to see a stable balance of power across the region. A more active and involved India has more to say about developments across the whole geography, and has strengthened its consultations with the United States, with Japan as noted, and with Australia on Asia-wide matters.

Creating Indian Ocean Institutions

Unlike the several regional institutions that have structured a solid diplomatic calendar for governance across the eastern part of the Asia-Pacific, a look to the west across the Indian Ocean region reveals very thin institutionalization. India has taken steps to support or create new organizations to redress this, like the Indian Ocean Rim Association, or IORA (formerly, and clumsily, called the Indian Ocean Rim Association for Regional Cooperation). India cofounded IORA after Nelson Mandela visited New Delhi in 1995 and spoke about the need for "the concept of an Indian Ocean Rim" as a special platform. Two years later, a formal organization emerged, formed by member countries across the African Indian Ocean littoral (like Kenya, Tanzania, and South Africa); countries in the Gulf (Iran, Oman, United Arab Emirates, Yemen); Indian Ocean island states like Madagascar, Mauritius, and Comoros; and countries like Australia, Indonesia, Malaysia, and Singapore. The sleepy grouping focused on trade questions—including maritime security, fisheries, and tourism. When India held the chair from 2011 to 2013, it contributed a fresh $1 million to the institution to help boost its activity—not much, especially compared with New Delhi's contributions to other new organizations, but more than nothing.[19]

Coinciding with increased attention to the Indian Ocean on matters like piracy, maritime security, and energy trade, IORA members—especially Australia, India, and Indonesia—sought to raise the visbility of the organization. A 2013 op-ed by the foreign ministers of these three countries—Salman Khurshid, Julie Bishop, and Marty Natalegawa—made the case for greater Indian Ocean cooperation, noting that half of all global container traffic and two-thirds of all the oil shipped by sea moves through its waters, and its ports process 30 percent of all global trade. They called for "a new vision" of what Indian Ocean Rim countries could do together across these increasingly strategic waters.[20] At the Perth summit in 2014, members issued an economic declaration. IORA has crafted a new "Blue Economy" initiative centered on maritime trade, sustainability, and climate change to guide its future work.

The Indian Ocean and Asia-Pacific region had no security-focused institution to coordinate approaches to maritime defense questions. So the Indian navy created one. The Indian Ocean Naval Symposium, or IONS, first convened in New Delhi in 2008 looking to create for the Indian Ocean what the Western Pacific Naval Symposium platform had done for the Asia-Pacific. Since then, annual symposia have brought together navies from South Asia, the Middle East, East Africa, Australia, and Southeast Asia, now involving thirty-five countries.[21] IONS aims to enhance interoperability among the navies of all these Indian Ocean countries to better facilitate collaboration on economic zone surveillance, humanitarian assistance, and disaster response. The symposium meets annually, hosted by different Indian Ocean navies such as Sri Lanka, Kenya, South Africa, the UAE, Bangladesh, Indonesia, and Australia.

India's ties with Africa can also be seen as part of its Indian Ocean efforts. The Congress-led UPA government began an India-Africa Forum Summit in 2008, with fourteen African heads of government, for example, and convened another in 2011. The India-Africa Forum obviously draws upon China's Africa Cooperation Forum model, begun nearly a decade earlier. The Modi government has continued the uptempo pace, and expanded the India-Africa Forum Summit to include all fifty-four African countries. India has stepped up its development assistance to Africa as well, with a $10 billion line of credit announced in 2015, on top of the $5 billion line of credit that former Prime Minister Singh had offered in 2011.[22] It can't hurt, either, to strengthen ties with fifty-four countries, because in the quest for a UN Security Council seat, every General Assembly vote counts.

THE REGIONAL IMPERATIVE

As discussed earlier, an Indian focus on economic growth as the linchpin of its rise to power has guided Indian diplomacy over the past fifteen years. The Modi government has built on this foundation, and added a more visible commercial diplomacy element to the strategy. An emphasis on campaigns like Make in India, Start-Up India, and other economic development programs offers an explicit pitch for foreign investment. This face of Indian diplomacy looks much more like the commercial diplomacy of the West.

But the global economic focus also has a regional imperative. The South Asian region, as the World Bank has noted, is one of the least integrated regions of the world.[23] Cementing strong economic ties and linkages—connectivity—among the countries that compose the South Asian Association for Regional Cooperation (SAARC) has a ways to go. South Asian regional trade is under 5 percent of total trade, contrasted with ASEAN's 25 percent—and the Indian government has long sought to overcome some of the differences India has had with its smaller neighbors. The "Gujral Doctrine" of former Prime Minister I. K. Gujral of the late 1990s advocated magnanimity with the neighbors. Former Prime Minister Vajpayee, followed by Prime Minister Singh, attempted peace with Pakistan. The UPA government made great strides with Bangladesh, and nearly managed to resolve a border dispute dating back to 1947. (In a great irony of history, the BJP prevented the UPA government from completing this agreement, only to champion it once elected to power in 2014.)

Early steps like an inauguration invitation to all seven heads of government from the SAARC countries indicated an intensified priority on regional economic integration has emerged. As prime minister, Modi's first visit abroad was to tiny Bhutan, which also receives the bulk of India's development assistance funding, and happens to be sandwiched between India and China. Early visits to Nepal appeared to cement a strong tie with the Hindu-majority country, but a bitter dispute over Nepal's constitution strained ties badly. Ties with Sri Lanka are on the upswing, enabled largely by new leadership in Colombo, and India has at long last resolved the world's most complicated boundary with the regularization of the land border with Bangladesh. The opening to Bangladesh creates opportunities for trade and connectivity toward the entirety of India's east, as it finally offers contiguous land linkages all the way through to Southeast Asia.[24] Some of the intra-regional successes in building trade and infrastructural links have occurred with cooperation among India, Bangladesh, Nepal, Bhutan, and Myanmar. A motor vehicle agreement among India, Bangladesh, Bhutan, and Nepal allows vehicles to cross borders with cargo. A project that also includes China will create an economic corridor linking Bangladesh, China, India, and Myanmar, if realized. The BIMSTEC grouping, receiving a fresh infusion of enthusiasm, offers deepened economic linkages from India to its east, including Thailand and Myanmar.

Pakistan presents the greatest challenge for economic connectivity across South Asia, given the India-Pakistan acrimony discussed previously and the perennial security threat of Pakistan-based terrorists. Trade has for long promised to be the leading edge of India-Pakistan normalization—if only it could be attained, like some distant dream. One estimate suggests that regularizing trade between the two countries could lift bilateral annual trade from $3 billion to $40 billion.[25] To that end, India gave Pakistan "most favored nation" status, using the WTO term, in 1996. Unfortunately, Pakistan has failed to reciprocate and offer India what it prefers to call "non-discriminatory market access," despite coming close to doing so in 2012 when its government declared it was ready to do so but did not follow through.[26] Opening trade ties could also position Pakistan as a link between Afghanistan and Central Asia to India. At present, even without direct land access to Afghanistan, Indian private companies have invested in mining, taken trade delegations, developed infrastructure, and promoted economic ties between regional chambers of commerce. Transit access across the region would benefit all, most especially Pakistan. By September 2016, however, following the terrorist attack in Uri, New Delhi was reportedly reviewing whether it was time to rescind its MFN recognition to Pakistan. For the moment, the energy on economic integration appears achievable within South Asia minus Pakistan.

Of course, India's pursuit of closer integration with the countries of South Asia has an obvious *mandala*-theory objective, given the increased economic and strategic presence of China in the region. India remains a larger trading partner for Afghanistan, Bhutan, Maldives, and Sri Lanka, but China overtook India as the largest trading partner of Bangladesh by 2004, and has for long managed a special economic relationship with Pakistan. Remittances back to Bangladesh, Nepal, Pakistan, and Sri Lanka from India dwarf those from China.[27] So Indian influence has been far from eclipsed in the region (apart from with Pakistan)—but China does keep New Delhi focused on its economic integration goals region-wide. It's Chanakya-style realism on display.

WHERE INDIA COMMANDS DOMINANCE

India's accelerated involvement and investment in a range of alternative global and regional institutions show its pursuit of arenas where it can more definitively shape the rules. As a means of thinking about how a far more powerful India might act in the future, we could briefly consider the case of cricket governance, where I believe the sounds of a less cautious India echo loudly.[28] Like FIFA or the International Olympic Committee, the International Cricket Council (ICC) is a global organization with participants composed of national member associations. And not surprisingly, the England and Wales Cricket Board and Cricket Australia were dominant for most of ICC history. But in 2005, the ICC moved its headquarters from Lord's, the famous London cricket grounds, to Dubai.[29] Press accounts described the decision as financial, but as the BBC observed, cricket's "power base has now moved to the east," in which the Indian market is the big daddy. As Russell Wolff, ESPN's executive vice president and managing director for international, put it, "There probably isn't another market in the world where one sport matters so much disproportionately to everything else."[30]

With India's economic growth, its booming advertising industry, and proliferation of media, cricket became a great beneficiary of corporates' desire to reach more Indian consumers, and television deregulation unshackled India's cricket board, the Board of Control for Cricket in India (BCCI) from the state-controlled television monopoly.[31] Broadcast rights, according to former BCCI president and BJP member of parliament Anurag Thakur, "changed the fate of Indian cricket."[32] As longtime observer and editor-in-chief of ESPNcricinfo Sambit Bal explained, India emerged as the primary profitable country for cricket tours: "An Indian tour on any board's cricket calendar is the most lucrative part of their cricket year."[33] With the rise of the cash-flush and television-friendly Indian Premier League (IPL), suddenly global cricketers could earn, in the seven-week IPL season, more than they might make in a year on their home national team.

These trends resulted in a controversial 2014 ICC restructuring, pushed by India. On the basis of an estimate that India's "value contribution" to ICC earnings went as high as 80 percent, India proposed a change in revenue sharing to send back more to those generating it, a plan that would benefit India above all others—instead of the even split among the ten full ICC members that had prevailed for decades.[34] The BCCI threatened to walk out and create an alternative council entirely should the proposal fail.[35] The brinkmanship worked, and the ICC approved a plan that funneled more like 22 percent of revenue back to

India, instead of the 3 to 4 percent of the past, according to *Mint*, an Indian business daily.[36] As Star TV chairman and CEO Uday Shankar, the man betting big on cricket broadcasting, describes it: "Today the power of cricket comes from the subcontinent, and within the subcontinent both the power of consumption and power of commerce . . . is provided by India. India has become the nucleus."[37]

But three years later, the ICC full members voted for another restructuring. In April 2017, the model that allocated a much larger revenue share to India was voted down in favor of a broader distribution of the pie. Virtually all the other ICC members voted against India's lone objection to return to a more equitable revenue-sharing model. The backlash episode provides in microcosm the cricketing-world version of problems the United States faces when trying to create a global coalition for some particular action. Even the world's biggest power cannot always prevail. Indeed, in 2014 an anonymous BCCI official said, "We enjoy a similar clout in the ICC as the United States of America does in the United Nations."[38] Often such clout is persuasive . . . but at times, despite all efforts, not as much.

Of course, the parallel between India and the cricket economy and India's rise on the world stage is not exact. Specifically, India is not yet singularly vital to the rest of the world in the way that it is in the cricket economy and in cricket governance. There is no prospect that India will become 80 percent of global GDP, since no economy commands that share in our global world. But India's present trajectory, which IMF projections suggest will continue, show a country becoming a more significant share of global GDP with each passing year. If India were to become an engine of growth necessary for everyone else—such as with the potential to become another $10 trillion economy, for example, as the CFR Independent Task Force found—the transformation would deliver another kind of diplomatic heft, just as it has for China.

The political strength India's economic power delivered—and most especially, the manner in which the BCCI chose to wield it in 2014—is why the new cricket world order also tells us something about the *attitude* a wealthier and more powerful India might bring to its international approach in the future. The cricket case shows a side of India to the world that actively demands change and works to create it. Is this a fully generalizable case? Of course not—but as an anecdote, it offers a window into how some see the possibilities of Indian power. Indian politicians can envision a future for the country of influence and power, today more than ever in the past.

That future, in which India is seen as among the handful of global powers in a multipolar world, in which it has the wherewithal to defend itself, serve as a net security provider for the Indian ocean region, and play a leading role shaping multilateral outcomes, all depends on its continued economic growth. As the following pages discuss, India's leaders have accelerated efforts to redress long-delayed next-generation reforms in order to allow their economy to deliver on its huge growth potential.

7

A Changing Economic Future?

MY COLLEGE SEMESTER IN India back in 1990 included a week-long family homestay program. Mine took me to the Gujarati port of Surat, an industrial center on India's western coast, renowned for its diamond and textiles industries. My host family worked in textiles—manufacturing polyester saris, to be precise—and they had other friends in business as well, including one who manufactured gold decorative edging ribbon trim. I had visited factories in the United States before, grew up in an auto industry family, and had worked one summer for General Motors Truck and Bus in Pontiac, Michigan. But state-of-the-art manufacturing in the American auto industry was a world away from pre-liberalization Surat.

The power looms in the gold trim factory we visited were enormous hulks of iron machinery, appearing to my untrained eye like industrial age pipe organs. In another factory, rail-thin men clad in undershirts and *lungi*s—some with the sarong-like garment hitched above their knees—worked barefoot. A few had even abandoned their undershirts, pushing piles of cloth into huge bins half-naked. My black and white photos of those visits look nothing so much as Dickensian. That first encounter with Indian manufacturing left me with a vision that over the decades would prove to be misleading.

While India's world-class IT sector put the country on every global boardroom's agenda, Indian manufacturing has not made a global splash in comparison to the East Asian manufacturing booms, but also alongside countries like Vietnam, or even Bangladesh. India missed the great manufacturing-driven economic transformations of the 1970s, 1980s, and 1990s elsewhere, with challenges running all the way from creaky infrastructure to onerous independence-era laws and regulations that artificially capped the size of its factories. Not long ago, Indian manufacturing's limitations could be symbolized by its severely limited automobile industry: for decades, two Indian companies offered the primary cars available, the Ambassador and the Padmini, produced respectively by Kolkata-based Hindustan Motors and Mumbai-based Premier. The boxy Ambassador, modeled on a 1956 Morris Oxford, came to symbolize India's stagnant economy, rather like the Lada and Trabant did for Russia and East Germany (Figure 7.1).

Ironically, pre-independence India boasted a promising auto industry, with global links. In 1928, General Motors established an assembly plant in Bombay (now Mumbai); Ford Motor Company followed with a plant in Madras (now Chennai) in 1930 and another in Calcutta (Kolkata) the following year. But after independence, a 1953 government directive required cars sold in India to be manufactured within the country, rather than assembled from imported kits. Both American makers exited India.[1] Like so many well-intentioned government

FIGURE 7.1 Ambassador cars outside the Ministry of Finance, 2009

Photo credit: Flickr user Bernard Oh, used under a Creative Commons license (CC-by-ND 2.0). Photo retouched to remove watermark. License: https://creativecommons.org/licenses/by-nd/2.0/

directives, it ended up stunting the very industry it was meant to grow. This left the Ambassador and the Padmini to become the iconic cars during India's decades of autarky. In a world of choice, Indian autos simply didn't offer it for a very long time, and those that were available felt a little like a ride into a time warp.

MAKING INDIAN MANUFACTURING COMPETITIVE

Manufacturing has long been the Indian economy's Achilles heel. Explosive growth in IT-enabled services in the early 2000s contributed much to GDP growth but soon revealed its inability to generate large-scale employment. India's IT and IT-enabled services industries contribute 9.3 percent of GDP (2016), but they employ only 3.7 million people.[2] A traditional manufacturing sector like textiles contributes 2 percent of GDP but employs more than 45 million.[3] As a matter of domestic economic policy, Indian officials have long been concerned about developing a broader manufacturing base for the country.

In part, dating back to before independence, this urge to industrialize reflects India's ambition to join the front ranks of the world's powers. But it also reflects a more pressing concern: about 50 percent of India's employed depend on agriculture for a living, but the country's small and unproductive farms contribute only 17.4 percent of GDP (2015).[4] With 10 to 12 million Indians entering the work force each year, the country needs jobs to ensure that its demographic dividend does not implode. This means creating employment opportunities across a wider range of occuptions, including unshackling manufacturing from artificial constraints that have limited its growth as a sector, and also developing skills training to create pathways for employment attuned to the emerging opportunities available.

The need to make Indian manufacturing more competitive caught the attention of the UPA government early on in its tenure. They created a national manufacturing policy and set up a National Manufacturing Competitiveness Council in 2004. Two years later, the council released a proposal for a national manufacturing policy. In 2011, following stakeholder consultations, the government formally released a national manufacturing strategy. The goal: raise manufacturing as a percentage of GDP from 18 percent to 25 percent, and create 100 million jobs within a decade. To put this in perspective, manufacturing accounts for 30 percent of economic output in China, 31 percent in South Korea, and almost 28 percent in Thailand, according to World Bank data (2013).

Of course, China's industrial miracle took place on the public exchequer, with labor-intensive state-owned enterprises subsidized by the state, and while the Indian government continues to operate enterprises, it's the private sector businesses, not Chinese-style state-run behemoths, that have proven to be India's competitive players, even within the country's legal and regulatory constraints. The UPA government outlined policies to boost manufacturing, including the creation of a national goods and services tax to stitch India's states into a single market, better infrastructure, a more conducive regulatory environment, and skills training to prepare people for employment. None of these, except perhaps the GST given that it would require amending the constitution, was particularly controversial.

By the end of the second UPA term in 2014, the policy goals to deliver manufacturing growth had not been met. Manufacturing as a percentage of GDP remained at 18 percent, not much higher than the 15 percent level back in 1991. The global growth downturn that began in 2007 affected India, but at the same time the slow pace of reform as well as counterproductive policies—including high-profile surprise retroactive tax assessments on offshore mergers—gave global manufacturers little reason to flock to India over more appealing locations such as China, Vietnam, Thailand, or Bangladesh closer to home. The kind of supply chains that developed among China with the countries of East and Southeast Asia, characterized by deep integration across borders, simply do not exist for India. Reasons include infrastructure hurdles such as clogged roads and inefficient ports, a slow-moving bureaucracy that delays export and import procedures, burdensome labor laws that make it difficult to lay off workers even if a company faces insolvency, and constraints on land acquisition for industry, as discussed in Chapter 3.

Add to this the challenges of doing business so endemic in India, such as convoluted customs procedures, overly enthusiastic tax inspectors, and unending permitting and paperwork requirements. India ranks in the bottom third of the World Bank's Doing Business index, now at 130 out of 189 countries.[5] India's rank at 130 held steady from the

2016 to 2017 assessments, after a jump up from 2015 to 2016.[6] (While India improved on individual metrics that comprise the index, other countries improved more.) The Modi government has set a top-down goal of vaulting into the top 50 in this index within three years. They do not yet appear positioned to meet their own target, but they are seized with creating a better business environment, and the World Bank lauded the government's "ambitious reform path" in its latest report. Perhaps the World Economic Forum's Global Competitiveness Report offers more solace; there, India ranked as number 39 for 2016-2017, just shy of the top quartile and a leap up from number 55 the previous year. The Forum noted India's "across the board" improvements including in infrastructure and institutions.[7]

The larger future consideration for Indian leaders lies in how the national quest to boost manufacturing, even assuming that long-overdue further reforms advance expeditiously, will intersect with global technological and economic trends. Changes have been unfolding worldwide—independent of whatever choices India may make in the coming years—that raise questions about the viability of the industrial-led development path to prosperity. Around the world, the rise of automation has raised quality standards and productivity, but at the cost of jobs. The rise of additive manufacturing (3D printing) has only just begun, and could affect supply chain considerations to an as-yet-unknown extent. These two trends alone are just in their infancy, and have already spurred policy debate in the United States about their impact on our own economy.

For the developing world, concerns have already emerged about the concept of "premature deindustrialization," to cite Harvard economist Dani Rodrik's work.[8] The problem of premature deindustrialization describes a downturn in the share of manufacturing in developing economies well before they are able to reach developed-economy prosperity levels. Rodrik attributes this in the developing world in part to the effects of trade and globalization—competition from China and other major manufacturers on the global market. Combined, these trends suggest that India (and sub-Saharan Africa for that matter) faces a steeper climb to follow China down the traditional labor-intensive pathway to prosperity. These changing circumstances affect not just India but the entire world in one way or another, and will likely become even more visible as policy discussions surface in an attempt to find solutions.

The changes that technology will bring to manufacturing, while potentially destabilizing, are no reason for Indian officials to stop trying to unleash the sector. Morgan Stanley's Ruchir Sharma, reflecting on the implications of this technological change, notes that the robotics revolution "is likely to be gradual enough to complement rather than destroy the human workforce." He ventures that "new jobs we can't yet imagine" will help fill the gap.[9] Development institutions like the World Bank, right alongside management consultancies like McKinsey, continue to see opportunity for India to do more to reform laws and policies that inhibit manufacturing's growth, whether for the domestic market or for export. In mid-2016, the World Bank released a report recommending policy changes to help the countries of South Asia, with India a notable focus, benefit from rising wages in China that result in the relocation of apparel sourcing and the potential for job growth.[10] The McKinsey Global Institute issued a set of recommendations in late 2016 that included "Manufacturing for India, in India" in its top five "opportunities for growth and transformation."

McKinsey believes that the technological impact on India may take some time to be fully felt. They cite scenarios in which it could take "two decades or more" for automation to hit more than half of work in some countries, and note that India's "relatively low level of wages . . . and the cost of automation" makes the "business case for adopting and implementing automation technologies . . . less compelling in many sectors, and that adoption in aggregate could take longer."[11] In plain terms, this means India has a window in which to ramp up its manufacturing sector as a job-creating vehicle before automation becomes a more widespread phenomenon.

The passage of the GST amendment makes a down payment toward freeing up manufacturing by creating a national common market that will make it much easier to transport goods within the country. A focus on doubling port capacity by 2025, improving roads and building more of them, and expanding and upgrading the rail system (with an estimated $130 billion investment through 2020, including in freight capacity) will all ease the infrastructure capacity problems bedeviling India.[12] The politically challenging reforms long overdue, however, in land acquisition and in rationalizing the country's labor laws have proven too tough to crack nationally so far.

It's not for want of trying, and here I would disagree with those who say the Modi government has done little on land and labor reform. To the contrary, it has exerted itself in efforts to reform both, and bumped up against political constraints. To ease land acquisition, the government issued ordinances three times between late 2014 and mid-2015. (Ordinances are like an executive order, but lapse if parliament fails to pass it during the subsequent session.) Each time the relevant legislation failed to gain sufficient parliamentary support to pass into law.[13] In the case of labor law reform, referenced previously, a bill to allow employers more flexibility in layoffs met intense and widespread labor opposition in India. The government backed off in order to focus on myriad other priorities, including GST, and moved instead to change what they could in regulation. Reform steps included simplifying inspection-related requirements and bringing them under one "window" to limit opportunities for inspectors to harass businesses, a condition wryly called "inspector raj."[14]

The federal government also signaled its support for state-level experiments as a way of advancing reform it could not accomplish nationally via parliament. During late 2014, the government of Rajasthan decided to implement labor reforms at the state level—which it is empowered to do with the concurrence of the federal government, as labor falls under both as defined by India's constitution. The federal government concurred. Rajasthan thus became the first Indian state to amend its laws to allow employers leeway to lay off up to three hundred employees if needed without government permission, and to raise the threshold for the application of the factories law to twenty employees (up from ten).[15] It's hard to overstate what a departure this represented. As the *Washington Post* put it, "Rajasthan became India's first state to alter the archaic system of overlapping laws that have led more than 98 percent of businesses in India to deliberately avoid expanding beyond nine employees to skirt strict labor regulations."[16] Rajasthan hopes to serve as a model that other states might emulate. (At the time of this writing, the most recently available state-level statistics were from the 2014-15 fiscal year, which did not permit any evaluation of whether Rajasthan's labor reforms had spurred industrial growth.)

In June 2016, another set of reforms came from the central government, targeted specifically at the important, labor-intensive, and large-scale textile industry. Textiles in general have a high proportion of women on the payroll. (In the garment industry, for example, women are almost 70 percent of employees.)[17] The new textile reforms permitted an increase in the number of overtime hours, and allowed for "fixed-term" employment, meaning that companies could bring on new workers to meet increased demand for a short period, without being locked into providing lifetime jobs.[18] Along with tax and production incentives, the textile reforms aim to capture some of the global production demand shifting out of China as wages rise there, and from which Bangladesh and Vietnam have benefited—exactly what the World Bank recommended. The Japanese government has begun work with India's textiles ministry on quality control standards to help boost exports.

The textile reform package is anticipated to create ten million jobs over three years, and help spur an export increase of around $30 billion, a timely potential shot in the arm.[19] At the time of this writing, data had not been released to indicate how well these reforms had incentivized export increases and job creation. A lone press report cited a Textiles Ministry official stating that garment and textile exports went up seven percent from July 2016 to April 2017, offering one possible data point. In this context, it's instructive to remember that India's domestic constraints have left it behind Bangladesh in the ready-made garment industry, despite the latter's problems with factory safety illustrated by the world's largest garment industry disaster, the Rana Plaza collapse of 2013. With one-seventh of India's population, hard-working Bangladesh exports 50 percent more garments, $25 billion compared to $17 billion annually.[20]

Press reports as of early 2017 indicate that more comprehensive and national labor reform might be on the offing, especially with a view to job creation, since the passage of GST has freed up the government to pursue further reforms. That would be a crucial next step, albeit undoubtedly politically fraught, as previous attempts have shown. But it will be vital for India to to tackle if it is to achieve the sustainable growth and job creation needed. Moving ahead on these critical environment-enabling reforms will be all the more important in the aftermath of the 2016 demonetization of Indian currency notes, which at the time of this writing had certainly dampened economic growth, with its medium-term impact and duration unclear. (Moody's, in a late May 2017 report, assessed the shock as a temporary destabilization, and found that the effort would have a longer-term positive effect on "reduc[ing] tax avoidance and corruption."[21]

Despite the political hurdles, it's worth examining a sector where India has quietly built capacity in spite of its many challenges—to gauge where the country could go if fully unleashed. India's auto industry, that one-time stodgy sector, offers a case study of private sector manufacturing success both domestically and for global export—and it has taken off.

THE AUTO INDUSTRY

The story of India's reconnection with the global auto industry holds lessons for how a once-closed sector gradually—and below the radar screen—became one of the world's top auto manufacturers. Though "India" does not bring to mind auto production, it's well past time that it should, as it has become a peer of Mexico and Korea, inching closer to Germany every year in terms of volume. If my father, a thirty-year General Motors "lifer" were still alive, he would have been surprised to hear that in the first half of 2016 (in part due to a major Hyundai labor strike) Indian automobile production overtook South Korea's—making it briefly the fifth-largest auto producer in the world.[22]

Before India's economic opening in 1991, a state-led experiment spurred change in India's auto sector. In 1981, state-owned enterprise Maruti Udyog sought an international partner to manufacture sub-compact cars for India's growing middle class through a government-licensed joint venture. Suzuki was selected the next year, and the partnership flourished. The first car, a boxy white 800cc knock-off of the Suzuki Fronte in Japan, rolled off a factory floor outside Delhi in 1983.[23] The Maruti Suzuki brand remains India's top seller; even the tiny Maruti 800 still lives on in the restyled Alto 800. But it was not until the mid-1990s, after liberalization, that India opened the automobile industry to major investment by foreign manufacturers.[24] The growth of India's automobile market since then represents gradualism more than a boom. Nonetheless, the industry may be poised for growth in a way that could be transformative for India given the expansive economic ripple effects this industry typically produces.

By the mid-2000s, Indian automakers—as part of the globalization of Indian business discussed in Chapter 3—began to look abroad. Tata Motors acquired Jaguar Land Rover from Ford in 2008, and by 2012 had turned the loss-making company around. Mahindra and Mahindra took a majority stake in Korea's Ssangyong Motor in 2011, and in Italian design house Pininfarina SpA in 2015. As a showcase for the industry, India's own Auto Expo (the Delhi Auto Show) took off internationally in 2008, receiving accreditation from the Organisation Internationale des Constructeurs d'Automobiles. I attended in 2010, and was blown away by the scale and variety on display: from the micro-sized Tata Nano to sleek Audi sedans to Mahindra and Mahindra SUVs to motorcycles of every variety.

By the early 2000s, supplying to global car manufacturers for their local as well as global supply chains had helped India emerge as a high-quality global manufacturer for auto components. (Think radiator caps and the like.) Chennai-based Sundram Fasteners won Japanese quality awards, and became the first Indian company to supply General Motors. But India had not yet emerged as a global auto hub in the way that Thailand and South Korea had become, and lagged far behind China.[25] In 2004, India produced a little under 1.18 million cars compared to 3.12 million in South Korea. China's production had not yet taken off; that year the industry produced 2.48 million cars. By the end of 2016 India's 3.68 million produced had nearly caught up with South Korea's 3.86 million and China had roared ahead with more than 24 million produced. (For perspective, Japan produced 7.9 million cars, Germany 5.75, and the United States 3.9 million, all excluding the "light commercial vehicle" category of SUVs, van, and light trucks.)[26] Indian automobile manufacturing may be at a further inflection point. In 2011, Ford Motor Company—already with a major plant in Chennai—announced a $1 billion investment in a new manufacturing plant in Sanand, Gujarat, that would more than double Ford India's production capacity, and would create five thousand jobs. It opened in June 2015. Other global auto majors have followed suit, betting on both India's market and its manufacturing future.

India's promising automobile sector offers clues to India's prospects for further industrialization. While no one was looking, between 2006 and 2016 the Indian automobile industry became a global center for small car manufacturing; India made 31 percent of small cars sold globally in 2015.[27] Anand Mahindra, with a vantage point at one of India's top manufacturers, strikes an optimistic note about where India is headed in autos. He sees India as "well poised" toward auto manufacturing's next generation—one in which IT will play a large role, marking another kind of manufacturing linkage:

> IT was not the sole solution to our problems of employment, but having done the leapfrogging in IT, we are the first [in India] to create the fit between IT and manufacturing. If you look at our cars, the XUV500, we provide as much telematics in that car as cars that are three times the cost. From a touch screen to navigation to talking back voice controls to . . . anything you name. . . .The fact is, India does have the ability to provide very frugally intelligent products.[28]

In his optimistic vision, technological change may end up playing to India's strengths by marrying frugal innovation with world-class IT and autos.

And the industry created 25 million jobs during the 2006–2016 decade, as volumes grew from 1.26 million passenger vehicles in 2005 to 3.38 million by 2015. Room for huge future domestic market expansion is a major reason for anticipated growth. The Automotive Mission Plan 2026, a joint vision document produced by the Society for Indian Automotive Manufacturers and the government of India, aims for the auto industry to become one of the world's top three, contribute 12 percent of India's GDP, become 40 percent of India's manufacturing sector, and generate 65 million jobs by 2026. The Mission Plan projects that the auto industry will serve as an "engine" for India's Make in India plan, and become one of the "largest job creating engines in the Indian economy."[29] The prior decade's Automotive Mission Plan 2006–2016 accomplished its employment goals, exceeded its investment targets, and hit the mark on India's emergence as a small car hub, so unlike many mission plans, this one comes with a solid track record.

The Road Ahead: Sanand

Gujarat, the westernmost state of India, is a high-growth economic success story. It accounts for only about 5 percent of India's population, but contributes about 16 percent of its manufacturing.[30] Sanand sits just twenty-five kilometers from Ahmedabad, and it takes around an hour to get there by road. Along the way, the bustle and construction of fast-growing Ahmedabad slows traffic. When I visited, in May 2015, the names on half-built Ahmedabad buildings signaled the ambition and aspiration of one of India's most prosperous states: one site would soon house "Empire," an office complex, alongside a residence christened "Eternia."

Once you exit the city, traffic picks up speed and the forest of buildings shrinks. Soon enough the Sanand Industrial Estate—a 2,000-hectare industrial park administered by the Gujarat state government—emerges over the horizon. To me it represents the India of tomorrow. On my left side sat plants already up and running: Hyundai and Tata Motors (cars), BoschRexroth (hydraulic components), Faurecia (auto seating), Hitachi Hi-Rel Power (drives), and Colgate-Palmolive (toothpaste and dental care), among others. To my right stretched empty land as far as the eye could see, hinting at the promise of the future.

Sanand represents one of Modi's highest profile economic development achievements as chief minister of Gujarat between 2001 and 2014. The transformation of the hot, dry Ahmedabad exurb began not with foreign manufacturers but with an iconic Indian firm. The Tata Motors plant in Sanand, which manufactures the $2,500 Nano, the world's cheapest car, was originally intended for the state of West Bengal. But a land acquisition dispute in 2008 sparked widespread protests by farmers who would have been displaced by the proposed factory, leading Tata to pull out. As the story goes, upon hearing the news about Tata's exit from West Bengal, Modi sent Ratan Tata, the Tata Sons chairman at the time, a text message with just one word: *suswagatam*, or "welcome" in Sanskrit.[31]

The Tata Nano plant spurred the creation of the vast Sanand Industrial Estate and became a symbol of Gujarat's ease of doing business, in sharp contrast with most other Indian states. Many other manufacturers, both domestic and foreign, soon chose Sanand for their new facilities. At the time of my visit in May 2015, Ford India had built its plant and was preparing to begin production. A month later, autos and engines began rolling off assembly lines, destined for the domestic market as well as for export.

At 460 acres, the Ford plant at Sanand is large by any standard, on par with some of the largest auto manufacturing plants anywhere in the world. It has the capacity to churn out 240,000 vehicles and 270,000 engines per year. Nineteen suppliers have located next door, creating a just-in-time manufacturing ecosystem that is efficient, allows for customization, and reduces the need for large inventory. The assembly line contacts the colocated suppliers as the vehicle body comes out of the paint shop, giving them three and a half hours to bring parts to finish the interior of the car. Plant manager Kel Kearns, an aeronautics engineer and former Royal Australian Air Force flight lieutenant, said: "This is a highly automated, high-volume facility more like what you'd see in North America or Europe than traditionally in Asia-Pacific."[32] By the end of the construction and installation phase as of November 2014, the Ford India Sanand plant had surpassed forty million working hours with industry-leading safety (including no fatalities)—no bare feet and nothing remotely Dickensian here.

The plant contains every step in the production of a vehicle: sheet metal stamping, body shop, engine assembly, engine machining, and the paint shop—the car just moves from one zone to another. As the newest of seven Ford plants built around the world since 2011, Sanand uses the same advanced technology—including automation—in use elsewhere, giving it the capability to manufacture at the standards required for advanced export markets such as Europe. The Sanand plant builds a compact sedan called the Figo Aspire Job 1. Ford describes the Sanand facility on its corporate website as "strengthening India's credentials as the export hub in the Asia Pacific region."

But India's domestic market is the big bet. Ford estimates that India's compact car segment, which accounts for 45 percent of the passenger vehicle market, will grow 63 percent to 1.8 million vehicles annually by 2018, up from 1.1 million in 2014.[33] This figure still looks small compared to the size of India's population—because passenger vehicles do not yet dominate Indian roads. According to the Society for Indian Automotive Manufacturers, two-wheelers (motorcycles and scooters) made up 80 percent of market share in 2015–2016, with passenger vehicles next, but far behind, at 13 percent. Total sales volume of passenger vehicles in India during that year exceeded 2.7 million, compared to around 16 million two-wheelers (Table 7.1).

By comparison, in 2016 Americans bought 17.55 million passenger vehicles (cars, vans, light trucks, and SUVs); the Chinese bought a little over 28 million.[34] Given the eightfold gap with China, India has room for potentially explosive growth as its middle class expands and seeks to transport families more safely by moving up to a car from a scooter or motorcycle. (A visitor to India often witnesses the common sight of a family—mom, dad, two children, maybe an infant—balanced precariously on a scooter, with mom holding the infant sidesaddle, and usually just dad wearing a helmet.)

While Ford's investment in Sanand marks a significant phase in U.S. automakers' positioning for the long haul in India, it is hardly unique. I have followed Ford's India successes for years because of my interest in India and my Detroit auto industry family background, but U.S. makers are just one thread in the larger canvas. Suzuki, Toyota, Honda, Hyundai, Volkswagen, BMW, General Motors, Mercedes Benz, Mitsubishi, Renault, Audi, Nissan, and Skoda all manufacture in India now. They add to the variety of models available from India's dominant domestic makers: Maruti Suzuki (the special joint venture now majority owned by Suzuki), Tata Motors (which includes Jaguar Land Rover), Mahindra and Mahindra, Hindustan Motors, and Premier Automobile. That list does not include manufacturers focused on the motorcycle and scooter markets that still account for the vast majority of vehicle sales in India.

By 2015, India had become a magnet for the world's major auto manufacturers, and its own domestic manufacturers had gone global—a complete transformation over the quarter century since I first arrived in India. During my visit to Sanand, apart from the heat, I felt like I could have been in an auto plant in Michigan. The scale, the quality, the attention to detail—it all felt world class. There was really just one difference from other manufacturing hubs: not everything in Ford India's automotive universe is sourced from India. The dies—huge two-piece presses that stamp sheet metal into recognizable car parts, like doors, hoods, or trunk lids—come from Japan, China, and Korea. (Indian

TABLE 7.1 Automobile Domestic Sales Trends

Category	2009–2010	2010–2011	2011–2012	2012–2013	2013–2014	2014–2015	2015–2016	2016–2017
Passenger Vehicles	1,951,333	2,501,542	2,629,839	2,665,015	2,503,509	2,601,236	2,789,208	3,046,727
Commercial Vehicles	532,721	684,905	809,499	793,211	632,851	614,948	685,704	714,232
"Three Wheelers"	440,392	526,024	513,281	538,290	480,085	532,626	538,208	511,658
"Two Wheelers"	9,370,951	11,768,910	13,409,150	13,797,185	14,806,778	15,975,561	16,455,851	17,589,511
Grand Total	12,295,397	15,481,381	17,361,769	17,793,701	18,423,223	19,724,371	20,468,971	21,862,128

Source: Society of Indian Automotive Manufacturers, Domestic Sales Trends Statistics, via www.siamindia.com

auto manufacturers are vertically integrated with their own tool and die shops.) Nonetheless, India's auto sector is reaching critical mass, and precision engineering will grow along with it. The Hirotec Group, a leading Japanese manufacturer and precision engineering company, expanded its operations in India from design and engineering to tooling and machining in 2011.[35] It currently makes doors, but plans to branch into machining dies soon as well. According to Kearns, "Ten years from now, with more and more OEM [original equipment manufacturer] capacity in India, suppliers will invest in local capability and it will all be here."[36]

ECONOMIC HISTORY, ECONOMIC FUTURE?

India's auto industry serves as a perfect metaphor for its economic history: early promise, harmful protectionism, managed opening, and, finally, global integration leading to rapid growth. Above all, this story underscores the market power of a growing middle class. The auto story encapsulates the tale of India's economic relationship with the world—in terms of foreign capital and technology coming to India, as well as Indian capital going abroad. But the industry is also important in and of itself, for the larger effects it has had, and will likely have, on India as it seeks to enlarge its manufacturing sector. As a sector currently accounting for 7 percent of GDP and a present direct and indirect employment base of around nineteen million people, the path ahead for the auto industry will help steer India's economic future.[37]

Yes, the auto industry uses robots, but more than most other industries it has the potential to spur more extensive industrialization, just as it has in every major country that has emerged as an auto powerhouse. Think of all the components that go into a finished vehicle: seats, trim, windshields, windows, electronics, and more. The need for all these components requires auto manufacturers to have strong supplier networks for parts made of steel, rubber, glass, leather, plastics, electronics, light bulbs, even batteries. And then there are dealer networks for sales, financial institutions to help with sales, "after market" services like maintenance and repair, and the services that support any industry (marketing, payroll, benefits, legal and accounting, etc.). The deep integration of a finished car with back-end networks of suppliers and

front-end networks of financing, repair, and dealer services makes this
industry capable of creating many more jobs than just the workers in
an assembly plant suggest.

Indeed, the auto industry boasts one of the highest "employment
multipliers" of any industry in the United States, and its employment
effects are not limited solely to manufacturing. While the structure
of the industry in the United States differs significantly from that in
India, it's nonetheless useful as a point of comparison. According to
the Ann Arbor, Michigan–based Center for Automotive Research, each
U.S. vehicle manufacturing job creates nearly seven other jobs across
the U.S. economy (ranging from supply chain manufacturing to deal-
ers to finance to after-market services and others). The industry also
generates substantial tax revenue.[38] Moreover, relatively well-paid auto
industry jobs spur spending that further boosts the economy.[39] This
may not be the same in India, and the Center for Automotive Research
has not calculated employment multipliers for India, but it does provide a guide.

The estimate of nineteen million people presently employed (directly
or indirectly) in the auto industry derives from a study by India's
National Skill Development Corporation (NSDC). The same study
estimated that number to grow to thirty-eight million by 2022.[40] The
Society of Indian Automotive Manufacturers projects that the industry will create sixty-five million jobs in the coming decade to 2026.[41]
Against the ten to twelve million jobs needed annually just to absorb
new labor force entrants, this could make a significant contribution. In
terms of jobs, the multiplier effect of India's auto sector will likely look
rather different from the United States. Former *Business Standard* editor T. N. Ninan cites Maruti Suzuki chairman R. C. Bhargava's observation that "every third car in India is driven by a hired driver." As
Ninan estimates, that would amount to 850,000 positions for drivers
for every 2.6 million cars sold in India.[42] Skills training will be central
to preparing India's workforce for the opportunities, and the NSDC
catalogues numerous training programs that have been launched by
private employers to fill gaps left by India's present education system.

As the Maruti Suzuki case illustrates, the involvement of foreign
manufacturers in both vehicles and components has also provided
technology transfer that has brought Indian parts and vehicles up to

global standards and therefore export-ready, another major benefit.[43] For all these reasons, the auto industry offers a special opportunity within the larger manufacturing space, and one shared with other advanced manufacturing industries such as defense, steel, aircraft, and ship-building. Defense and ship-building have been the targets for recent policy reforms—similarly geared toward spurring growth in large industries with deep backwards and forwards employment linkages. And for aircraft, not India's traditional strength, change may be on the anvil: Lockheed Martin has just proposed to relocate its entire F16 production line to India, now signed up with the Tata group as its partner. Whether the Indian government selects this aircraft is of course another matter.

And what has been the fate of Make in India, the personal pitch for global investment in manufacturing that has animated Narendra Modi's diplomatic strategy around the world? If measured by commitments, the news has been encouraging: foreign investment has ticked upward after a notable downturn. Foreign direct investment into India increased 37 percent in calendar year 2015 to more than $39 billion, according to India's Department of Industrial Policy and Promotion. In calendar year 2016, it increased once more, albeit not by as much over the previous year, for a total of $46.4 billion in inflows.[44] The United Nations Conference on Trade and Development (UNCTAD), using a different measure of global inflows (which includes mergers and acquisitions), estimates that inflows to India in 2015 doubled to $59 billion. UNCTAD's report ranked India's FDI inflows for 2015 at number seven in the world.[45] Counting only pledged "greenfield" capital investment—essentially investment in new factories rather than acquisition of existing ones—the *Financial Times* found that India displaced China as the world's top destination for FDI in 2015, with $63 billion in new investment announced during the year. India remained the top FDI destination in 2016 using this same measure, with $62.3 billion in fresh capital investment.[46]

Pledges have come in from some of the world's best-known manufacturers—with a heavy dose of consumer electronics at the lead. In 2015, Foxconn, the world's largest contract manufacturer, best known for making iPhones, announced plans to invest $5 billion manufacturing electronics and in research and development in

Maharashtra over five years. Separately, Foxconn has teamed up with Xiaomi, which sold $1 billion worth of phones in India during 2016, and will now be manufacturing in India 95 percent of all phones sold in India.[47] Huawei, the largest telecom manufacturer in the world, announced that it would begin manufacturing smartphones with India's Flex in October 2016. Huawei also announced the creation of 200 service centers across India. In January 2016, the Wanda Group of China announced a $10 billion commitment to develop a "Wanda Industrial New City" in Haryana that will house, among others, software firms, auto manufacturers, and healthcare companies. (As of this writing, however, a disagreement with the Haryana state government had thrown a wrench into the project, with its future uncertain.)[48] The following month, Lenovo announced that half of all phones it would sell in India would be manufactured there.[49] A national "Make in India" week in Mumbai in 2016 netted more than $200 billion in similar investment pledges.

Combined with other major investment announcements, such as the 2014 announcement of a Japanese package of $35 billion in government and private investment in India over five years—including a focus on the Delhi-Mumbai Industrial Corridor—or a similar 2014 Chinese commitment of $20 billion over five years, the FDI narrative has turned sharply upward, especially compared with the desultory years of 2013–2014. While only a portion of these pledges will ultimately become solid investment, and it is still too soon to have a good sense of what will fully materialize, the new enthusiasm and the scale mark a change from the immediate past.[50]

The FDI uptick has come at a time when domestic investment, on the other hand, has stagnated. Directly linked to India's lagging state banking sector, lending has dried up after a spate of loans, accounting for perhaps as much as 17 percent of all public-sector bank loans, turned sour.[51] The path to bank restructuring remains uncertain, and a major preoccupation for Indian economic policymakers. A recent Moody's credit opinion on India noted the banking sector problem as a "key source of susceptibility to event risk." That said, the credit opinion offered a positive outlook, anticipating that policy measures will "support a sustainable growth recovery" and also noting India's "rapid increase in foreign direct investment" as a stabilizing factor.[52]

THE WORKFORCE OF THE WORLD?

In a short period between 1999 and 2004, India rapidly emerged as the "back office of the world," changing the way the world does business. As discussed in Chapter 3, the combination of low-cost, high-bandwidth communications and an educated white-collar workforce created in India a whole new model of remote services—not just call centers, but remote accounting, research, data processing, design, and even animation.

The demographic dividend so crucial for India's future, and the spur behind India's focus on manufacturing, has also led Modi to talk about an India of tomorrow in which his country might serve as "the human resources capital of the world"—just as China has been the manufacturing capital of the world—by training nurses, drivers, plumbers, cooks, and, of course, yoga instructors. (He even offered an example of a young plumber who also taught yoga in the morning to supplement his income.)[53] This ambition, like India's manufacturing ambition, requires major changes at home in order to compete at a global level. But there's no denying that as other countries, including China, grow older, India's population will remain young. A Bloomberg analysis showed that by 2050, India's share of the global workforce will grow from today's 17.8 percent to 18.8 percent, while China's will shrink from today's 20.9 percent to 13 percent. This explains growing Indian attention to higher education and skills training.[54]

Despite the measures taken, the Indian economy does not appear to be creating jobs at the pace required to employ its large workforce-age population. This concern has become increasingly urgent for Indian political leaders. India's annual Labour Bureau employment–unemployment surveys have not discerned an upward trend in employment, and in fact the most recent survey released indicates a slight increase in unemployment, to 5.0 percent for the year ending December 2015, up from 4.9 percent in 2013–2014, 4.7 percent in 2012–2013, and 3.8 percent in 2011–2012. (No survey was released for 2014–2015.)[55] To what extent the annual employment survey captures the enormity of the Indian economy—in which some 90 percent of those employed are in the "informal" or "unorganized" sector—remains unclear. It is also true that this data is a lagging indicator, so unlike the monthly jobs report in the United States, cannot provide a real-time snapshot of economic activity.

In fact, data insufficiency impedes any discussion of labor and employment in India. The long gap between household surveys and the publication of results means that as of the time of this writing, the most recent all-India comprehensive unemployment survey data available had been fielded between April and December 2015. McKinsey Global Institute devoted substantial space to data insufficiency questions in their June 2017 discussion paper on India's labour market, noting in particular the lack of data available after 2015. They also noted that aggregate data has masked great structural changes: agriculture jobs shrank by 26 million between 2011 and 2015, while non-farm jobs grew more than 33 million in the same period.[56]

This is all to say that despite discouraging jobs news from India released during 2016, it is still too soon to gauge how well the manufacturing push and Make in India initiative have created jobs. High-profile new investment commitments such as Foxconn's have yet to break ground, let alone generate formal employment that would show up in surveys. But at the very least, the employment survey has raised fears of "jobless growth," and further highlighted India's urgent need to implement policy reforms geared toward job creation. The textiles package announced in mid-2016 should be seen precisely through that lens. Given the uncertainties about how the global economy is changing, the challenge India faces is greater in growing the kinds of labor-intensive industries that helped pull hundreds of millions of Koreans, Chinese, Vietnamese, and Thais out of poverty.

Manish Sabharwal, cofounder and chairman of Teamlease Services— one of India's largest temporary staffing agencies—has thought a lot about human capital and the type of training needed to equip Indians with skills to match the types of jobs available. No one can put India's training challenge into starker relief than Sabharwal given his fifteen years placing job seekers into open positions. Within India, Teamlease sees ten thousand open positions every day that they simply cannot fill. "The demand is there," said Sabharwal, over sandwiches in his Bangalore office. But aligning India's education system with the demand is proving to be more of a challenge.[57]

While India is famously home to some of the world's most competi-tive technology institutions, the Indian Institutes of Technology, whose miserly admission rates can make Ivy League schools look like a walk in the park, it also has many colleges that deliver degrees of limited qual-ity. Sabharwal says 15 percent of the high-end security guards in India actually have college degrees, showing the irrelevance of their degrees for job placement. India needs to catch up most quickly in the voca-tional skills. To support infrastructure development and manufactur-ing, the country needs to train millions of metalworkers, carpenters, electricians, plumbers, and other skilled tradespeople. But India has severely limited programs for the type of on-the-job training typically part of education in the skilled trades.

"If India had the same proportion of the labor force as Germany we would have fifteen million apprentices," but India only has three hundred thousand apprentices compared to Germany's more than three million, according to Sabharwal. For comparison, in Japan and China the figures are ten million and twenty million, respectively. As Sabharwal explains, India's 1961 Apprenticeship Act applied all the labor laws of regular employees equally to apprentices—making them more expensive and harder to let go—so employers were reluctant to hire through an apprenticeship system, permanently constraining the pipeline for this effective vocational training model.[58]

Those enrolled in vocational training may not even acquire the right skills. Outdated training curricula equip learners with the wrong skill set, or as Sabharwal put it, "There's a mismatch between what employers want and what vocational skills are taught. Every electrician learns how to fix a DC fan, but there are no DC fans in India other than on trains."

Finding a way to impart the right education and skills to India's young workforce has been an ongoing focus for recent Indian govern-ments. The Congress-led UPA government identified skill develop-ment as a priority in its twelfth five-year plan, released in 2011. The eleventh five-year plan, released in 2006, did the same. The tenth five-year plan—under a BJP-led government in 2002, called vocational training "a very large unmet need." In other words, successive Indian governments of both major national parties identified vocational skills training as crucial for India's future, but had not been able to realign training institutions to fill the gap.

In 2015, the Modi government elevated its attention to skilling and vocational training by launching a "National Skill India Mission." This campaign built on the 2014 bureaucratic change of creating a new ministry of skill development and entrepreneurship composed of departments and commissions that were previously housed in the labor ministry, and links their missions to India's success on the world stage. Notably, one of the ministry's goals includes certification of "global/common standards" for vocational skills—a sign of intensified attention to positioning India's workforce as globally competitive.

The National Skill Development Corporation serves as a node for private sector partners to team up and create skill training programs. According to a 2017 report published by Ernst & Young, over the two-year period ending in fiscal year 2016, around 10.4 million people received skills training through Indian government programs. The private sector, with acute hiring needs, is creating its own skill training programs to target specific needed competencies. TeamLease University, after years of seeking government approval throughout the UPA government's tenure, received a green light to create a new apprenticeship program, NETAP, or the National Employability Through Apprenticeship Program. The two-year program is a public-private partnership along with the Confederation of Indian Industry and the National Skill Development Corporation. Students receive credit for their learning on the job, and fields of placement include automotive industry, engineering, IT, fast-moving consumer goods, electronics, retail, healthcare, and others. Most important, NETAP intends to take on two hundred thousand apprentices every year for the next decade, which, in its own words, will ultimately make it "the world's largest apprenticeship program." It's just one of many in progress; in an October 2016 interview, the secretary of the skill development ministry told *Business Standard* that the overall numbers of those trained per year could be as high as 12 to 13 million if including private employers' programs as well.[59]

While these programs have a long way to go, and the scale of the need suggests years before these economic weaknesses can be sufficiently overcome, the urgency attached to manufacturing and to skilling present an India preparing to transform itself. India's rising generation will be the beneficiaries of this change as they create the India of tomorrow. An India that finally emerges with a stronger manufacturing sector to complement its global services strength, and one prepared to offer its workforce training opportunities to match needs, begins to look like a different country. This propitious shift is taking place as the rest of the world ages, as wages in other countries rise, and as rising incomes in India create a larger class of consumers. With a longer-term perspective in view, though India still needs to surmount profound challenges, and while no one can predict major external shocks and how they might affect India, the country is chipping away at the many constraints that have held its economy back. If India can at last create the investment environment and build the logistics infrastructure to connect itself more seamlessly with the world, it could be headed down a new, more promising, path.

8

How the United States Should Work
with a Rising India

OVER THE PAST DECADE and a half, the U.S. foreign policy community
has coalesced around the importance of deeper ties with India. On a
bipartisan basis, successive U.S. administrations have seen this as one
of America's great strategic opportunities, a chance to overcome historic
differences and build a relationship with Asia's largest democracy, a fast-
growing market in its own right, a stable pillar in a region of turmoil,
and a large country that seeks a balance of power maintained across
Asia rather than Chinese dominance. Larger geopolitical and economic
trends have thus propelled Washington toward a stronger partnership
with New Delhi, while the appeal of shared values of democracy and
an increasingly stronger Indian American community adds additional
ballast.

India's political leadership broadly shares these interests, which has
made the U.S.-India opening among the few areas of bipartisan agreement for both countries over successive changes in government. It
has become hard to remember that not so long ago New Delhi and
Washington were at loggerheads over nonproliferation, enjoyed little to
no defense cooperation, had thin trade ties, and saw each other as on
different "sides" of the Cold War, given India's NAM-era tilt toward the
Soviet Union and its differences with U.S. positions in global forums.

That's why the end of the Cold War and the gradual development
of a more intensive strategic and defense cooperation—culminating to
date in the 2015 signing of an agreed "joint strategic vision" statement

on the Indian Ocean and the Asia-Pacific—marks a noticeable realignment of the two countries' strategic goals. The rapid development of significant trade ties and increased investment has rounded out what was once a weak link in the relationship and created stronger private sector constituencies for deeper relations. (Though, as with all economic relationships, this one is not free of disagreements.) As earlier chapters have discussed, India's entry into the world's top ten economies, surpassing countries like Italy and Canada, has intensified U.S. companies' interest in India, coupled with Indian companies' global expansions, in turn raising the priority of economic ties for both governments. An explicit American commitment from the George W. Bush administration forward to assist India's rise to global power has enabled both countries to establish more substantial cooperation mechanisms covering virtually every area under the sun, in sharp contrast to the limited conversations of the past. (To illustrate the stark difference, former U.S. Ambassador to India Frank G. Wisner recounted a lunch during the mid-1990s with President Clinton and then Indian Prime Minister P. V. Narasimha Rao: back then, the "only subject of strategic significance discussed was a dispute over almond trade."[1]) How times have changed.

A greater convergence between the United States and India on broad geopolitical and economic ideals, however, does not always mean that in practice U.S.-India cooperation remains free of differences. India's desire to shape its place on the world stage and be seen as well as treated as one among the major global powers, includes an indelible commitment to its own ideas of policy autonomy, and a still-dominant prioritization of sovereignty, as previous chapters discussed. The as-yet undecided sense in New Delhi of what its responsibilities as a major power should be can at times lead to ambivalence or calculated inaction. (Although where India has developed an internal consensus, such as its desire for Indian Ocean primacy, New Delhi has been able to take forward its defense ties with Washington in notable ways.) These broad tendencies create what I have characterized as a cautious approach to the use of power.

Further, Washington's general belief that its close partners and allies should support it across the board can sometimes create American expectations from India that do not cohere with New Delhi's strong sense of independence. New Delhi also often prioritizes tactics different from those employed by Washington *even when both countries broadly share the same goal.* On some tough global issues, a general shared assessment and shared sense of preferred outcomes do not always translate into shared approaches, such as with Russia's annexation of the Crimean peninsula, about which Indian officials offered finely crafted remarks designed to walk a tightrope rather than come out swinging publicly on the core question of sovereignty. Finally, Indian ambivalences about further opening its domestic market to foreign participation—even as it seeks greater market access for its own services workers abroad— marks a space where immediate interests diverge, even if both countries share a declared thirty-thousand-foot-level commitment to deeper economic integration. It's this space of strategic agreement and tactical difference in which India and the United States at times misunderstand each other, and will benefit from altered approaches.

SHARED INTERESTS

The end of the Cold War and India's economic liberalization spurred the major geopolitical and geoeconomic changes that have drawn India and the United States closer together. In the mid-1990s, during the Clinton administration, for the first time India's newly opened economy attracted interest as a "Big Emerging Market." A few years later, differences over nonproliferation policy, heightened by India's 1998 nuclear tests, spurred a long-running strategic conversation between Deputy Secretary of State Strobe Talbott and Minister of External Affairs Jaswant Singh. Though neither convinced the other on the core issue of India's right to possess nuclear weapons, the dialogue in a sense inaugurated a new era in U.S.-India ties. New Delhi's view of Washington as perennially defending Pakistan at India's expense changed in the summer of 1999, when President Clinton pressed Pakistan to retreat from its incursion across the line of control in Kashmir, which caused the Kargil War. Shortly afterward, the March 2000 Clinton visit to India, the first by a U.S. president in twenty-two years, began a new diplomatic chapter.

In the intervening two decades, India's large and growing middle class, and its potential, both as a major market and a location of production and services, created a stronger bridge between the U.S. and

Indian economies. During the George W. Bush administration, attention to the balancing role that democratic, stable India could play in the context of a rising China and a region of turbulence from the Middle East to Afghanistan and Pakistan cemented the strategic rationale for an enhanced U.S. diplomatic opening to India. Most famously, the Bush administration declared that the United States should actively strive: "to help India become a major world power in the 21st century . . . understand[ing] fully the implications, including military implications, of that statement."[2]

These twin economic and strategic bases grew stronger still during both terms of the Obama administration. India became a focus for economic initiatives like the National Export Initiative, and an important collaborator on science and technology initiatives, such as clean energy and space. In the wake of the 2008 global recession, the dialogue between Manmohan Singh and Barack Obama at G20 summits showcased the new importance Washington accorded to New Delhi. The Obama administration's most significant strategic shift, the rebalance to Asia, included deepened ties with India as one of its goals.

Shared interests between India and the United States became more obvious and less theoretical over the course of the Obama administration's second term. China's increasing assertiveness across the Asia-Pacific—on maritime claims, strengthening its ties with India's neighbors, and its own claims to Indian territory—have pushed New Delhi and Washington increasingly closer together given the overlapping interest in an Asian balance of power. A shared commitment to combatting terrorism became more specifically relevant to India after the Mumbai attacks of 2008, raising the visibility of the danger posed by terrorists who continue to enjoy safe haven in Pakistan, a fact reinforced by the troubles the Haqqani network has continued to create in Afghanistan. The United States became increasingly vocal about the terrorist groups that target India. Defense ties have continued to advance, with a firm shared commitment to joint defense technology development, an increasingly larger role for U.S. military acquistions in Indian procurement, and a well-coordinated quickened tempo of joint exercises on land, sea, and air.

Economically, U.S. companies continued to see India as an increasingly important market where they had to be present, not just for its large and growing consumer base but also for its talent pool. At the same time, Indian companies increasingly ramped up their investment in the United States—the ninth fastest-growing source of inbound FDI in 2015, and employing some fifty-two thousand Americans (the most recent data available at the time of this writing).[3] The priority level of the economic relationship along with trade volume rose for both countries—even as frictions continued. Cooperation on global concerns, with climate change an important example, became deeper and less acrimonious, and India's votes in favor of the UN Human Rights Council resolutions on reconciliation in Sri Lanka in 2012 and 2013 marked a new U.S.-India convergence. Deepened consultation has surfaced largely similar perceptions of the world and its challenges, as illustrated by the ever-more-expansive proclamations in White House and State Department joint statements after important bilateral meetings. And as detailed previously, the changed relationship on nonproliferation between both countries has brought India "inside the tent" on a matter that had been the source of acrimony for decades. India and the United States had a limited shared agenda for decades, so the dramatic increase in cooperation should be appreciated for the leap that it represents.

Nonetheless, it was not all smooth sailing. As India's economy slowed during the final years of Singh's government, trade disputes became more bitter, and when the arrest of an Indian consular official in New York led to a rupture in relations that stretched over months in 2014, the underlying condition of U.S.-India relations was revealed to be far more fragile than many of us had realized. Ties went into the deep freeze for several months.

For Washington, this roller coaster raises questions on how best to approach an important relationship that does not follow the familiar alliance template set by our relations with long-standing European and Asian partners. New Delhi, as discussed earlier, sees U.S. alliance relationships as inherently unequal, and does not wish to subordinate itself as a junior partner.

India, the proud and rising power considered in the previous pages, has its own internal dynamics and still-staggering social development needs. Despite its accomplishments in lifting so many out of extreme poverty in the past two decades, domestic priorities require focus at home, as do its complex, multilevel politics. But, as earlier chapters have discussed, this country of vast complexity, home to an ancient civilization, also sees itself as a natural leader of the world, both as a democracy others should want to emulate, and increasingly as a "leading power," to use the Modi government's new concept, helping to set the global agenda. Over its decades of independence, New Delhi has maintained a firm stance that India will never accept anything other than relationships of equality with other countries. Despite serious security challenges, India does not seek alliances to defend itself.

This orientation presents challenges for Washington policymakers. I cannot begin to count the number of times I've heard people refer to India as an ally, a conceptual slip that has real implications for U.S. expectations, because Americans tend to expect allies to support American priorities around the world. This can extend down to the level of tactics, where India and the United States may have differences even for a broader shared strategic goal. (For example, both India and the United States endorse—and have affirmed in joint statements—the importance of maritime freedom of navigation, and both carry out regular joint naval exercises. But India, as documented earlier, does not wish to carry out joint patrols in anything other than under a UN flag.) For all the reasons discussed earlier, a formal alliance is neither a future New Delhi desires nor one it is prepared to entertain, even when Indian politicians use the words "natural allies" as a term of art to signal their interest in a closer relationship with the United States. As my former boss, former under secretary of state for political affairs Nicholas Burns, put it:

> When the Bush Administration made its breakthrough with India in 2005–2006, some in the Administration and many beyond hoped that India might become effectively allied with the U.S. in its foreign and defense policy. That was an illusion. We can now see clearly that India, a great civilization with thousands of years of history and the self-confidence that comes with it, will pursue its own interests as a 21st century great power. We will not become formal treaty allies. We'll align on many issues, but we will not be "aligned."[4]

The gap between American expectations and Indian desires creates inevitable misperceptions even in the face of shared goals and a qualitatively transformed bilateral relationship. To complicate matters further, the United States is far more visible in the Indian imagination than India is for the average American. Raising American awareness of India should be a priority for the United States government to equip young Americans with the global knowledge needed to work successfully with India in global business—in which India's market increasingly matters—as well as to ensure a general situational awareness of India so policymakers in the executive or legislative branch know enough to anticipate likely challenges, rather than remain unaware of issues due to lack of familiarity.

The unfortunate fact remains that Americans do not yet put India on the front burner when they think about foreign policy, national security, or business. In government, South Asia may no longer be a policy "backwater," but it tends to fall between two stools, neither demanding attention like countries in crisis, nor automatically turned to as an ally.

Polling provides insights into how Americans see India.[5] In a survey conducted annually by the Chicago Council on Global Affairs, a "thermometer" rating gauges how respondents feel toward particular countries. Over the past four decades, Americans have slowly warmed toward India. From 1978 onward, India hovered between forty-six and forty-nine on a scale from zero to one hundred, reflecting its status as neither friend nor foe. Only in 2010 did India tip from cold to warm by rising to fifty-three, a place it maintained in 2014. In 2016 India inched up two more degrees, to fifty-five (Figure 8.1). To put this in perspective, neighbor Canada measured a seventy in the 2014 survey and special ally UK came in at seventy-four. Among countries that evoke a less positive response, China scored forty-four and Iran a dismal twenty-seven.[6]

When it comes to "importance" to the United States, India doesn't fare too well. In 2010, only 18 percent of Americans saw India as "very important" to the United States—fewer than those who felt similarly about Pakistan (19 percent) and Afghanistan (21 percent), and well below China (54 percent) and Japan (40 percent). Another 50 percent of Americans saw India as "somewhat" important to American interests.[7] Five years later, only 34 percent of Americans expressed either "a great deal" or "a fair amount" of confidence in India to "deal responsibly with

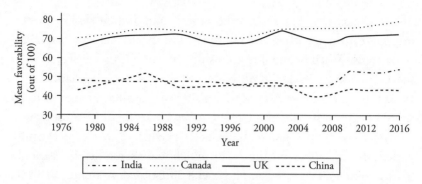

FIGURE 8.1 What Americans Feel about India

Source: The Chicago Council on Global Affairs, *Global Views 2016*. July 11, 2016.

world problems," two points behind South Korea.[8] In sum, Americans are mildly favorable toward India, but they don't see it as mattering very much.

However, polling also suggests an American appetite for a larger Indian role in the world. Nearly two-thirds of respondents would like to see India "exert strong leadership in world affairs." India rated higher on this question than treaty ally South Korea (62 percent), and Permanent Five powers China (51 percent) and Russia (43 percent), but below Japan (73 percent) and the EU (80 percent).[9]

"ALIGN WITHOUT BEING ALIGNED"

Seventeen years after President Clinton's historic visit to India, and a decade after the civil-nuclear deal opened up strategic ties, Washington and New Delhi have overcome many hurdles and crafted a new, wide-ranging partnership. But that process has been challenging on both sides, especially when tactical differences over shared goals emerge. India's long-standing default prioritization of nonintervention, despite a shared view of a situation, can create a difference in approach, such as with the global coalition against the Islamic State, which India has opted not to join.[10]

This has an outsized effect on Indo-U.S. cooperation on the global peace and security questions foremost on the U.S. foreign policy agenda. In short, deeper cooperation has not yet made a difference in any major global crisis. The Council on Foreign Relations (CFR)–sponsored

Independent Task Force on U.S.-India Relations, for which I served as project director, noted in 2015:

> To put it simply, India is not a frontline global partner, not among the top five countries Washington policy officials would call immediately to coordinate on any urgent global issue. India and the United States have not yet collaborated together on any crisis in the United Nations, for example, and on some of the most challenging questions in the Middle East and with Russia, India has been silent. Moreover, U.S. and Indian interests are not fully aligned on these tough questions.[11]

The tough issues on which India and the United States have done little together include those of paramount importance for U.S. foreign policy: Iran, Syria, and Ukraine. While India scaled back its oil and gas purchases from Iran during the most stringent periods of U.S.-led sanctions, and has voted against Iran on the IAEA, it has maintained its own relationship with Tehran (as many European countries have, of course). But India was not among the countries central to negotiating the deal to halt Iran's nuclear program. On Syria, India has pushed for diplomacy and against military action; but most germanely, New Delhi hasn't been seen by Washington experts as a go-to country for advice on developments there. Indeed, on these headline-news concerns, in the American imagination as well as among Washington experts, India is noteworthy for its absence. And taking the final example—Russia's irregular invasion of Crimea—given the priority New Delhi usually attaches to territorial sovereignty matters, especially considering its own concerns about Pakistan's claims to Kashmir, and China's claims to parts of Arunachal Pradesh, India's silence about the invasion baffled many U.S. policy experts—myself included. India put its ties with Moscow above its principle of sovereignty and nonintervention in this instance. And despite its commitment to counterterrorism, India never wanted to join the U.S.-led coalition against the Islamic State, believing that doing so could increase the risk to Indian citizens in the Middle East.

The same, of course, could be said about the United States if examined through Indian eyes. Washington does not always appear so reliable a partner. In particular, the U.S. relationship with Pakistan, and its long-standing sales of defense equipment to the Pakistani military, worries Indian officials that American arms might, as in previous conflicts, be used against them. Continued Pakistani refusal to shut down the terrorist groups that target India has fueled Indian resentment over the years that Washington does not take their concerns about terrorism seriously. These examples show that on issues central to each country—even when there is high-level convergence in the assessment of a situation—some distance still separates Washington and New Delhi.

As a result, the American expectation—so aptly summarized by Nick Burns—that the strength of shared values, increased convergence in a changing world, and ever-increasing business ties will naturally propel India and the United States to a relationship like those with our other democratic allies is one that creates inevitable disappointment. Indian officials do not seek such an outcome because, as discussed in Chapter 2, they believe it would represent an unacceptable constraint on their own policy independence.

India's transition—from nonalignment to a focus on "strategic autonomy" to the current government's creation of a "multialigned" approach to the world—still contains at its core a belief that formal alliances threaten national independence. While many countries see alliance relationships (with the United States or others) as a beneficial security umbrella, a way to protect their own territory, in India the idea spurs anxieties about servitude or subordination. That is India's choice, of course, so looking ahead, the United States will need to adjust its sights on what a partnership with India should entail in order to manage expectations appropriately. The United States will still benefit strategically from a closer relationship with a strong democratic Asian power, even if the relationship does not resemble a traditional alliance, so in that sense U.S. interests are advanced even if not at a pace some in Washington might wish to see. The recommendation developed by the CFR-sponsored Independent Task Force presents an alternative conceptual model for U.S.-India ties as a way of overcoming the hurdle.

Recommendation: Approach India Like a "Joint Venture" Partner, Not an Ally-In-Waiting. Friends and colleagues in India have repeatedly underscored that the model of the U.S.-Japan alliance does not appeal to India's sense of self; many in India see Japan as subordinating its interests to the United States. Instead of subconsciously seeking an alliance, Americans would be better served by explicitly approaching India as a joint venture partner. This business term suggests a partnership between two entities with specific shared objectives, and by its specificity acknowledges that not every undertaking of either entity would be shared. By anticipating cooperation on specific objectives rather than grandly envisioning mutual support on everything, the joint venture framework provides greater room for disagreements without calling into question the basis of the partnership. With a mental model that better captures the type of partnership possible with a proud, powerful India, the United States will increase the odds of success and reduce those of disappointment.

BRINGING INDIA INSIDE THE ECONOMIC TENT: INDIA'S FUTURE, U.S. INTERESTS

The preceding chapters have focused on the ongoing transformation of India's economy for good reason. India's global ambitions rest upon a future of sustained economic growth. The faster pace of reforms put in place by the Modi government has gone beyond the previous UPA government, but ironically has proceeded more slowly than many analysts expected. Sustained major structural reform could place India on a path to sustained high growth.

While only India's own political process can determine its reform trajectory, the United States could do a better job of supporting discussion about how India can attain a more open and faster growing economy, and generate jobs. The U.S.-India economic relationship has without question metamorphosed in the years following the onset of reform, and picked up pace significantly from the mid-2000s forward. The United States is India's top trading partner in goods and services; two-way trade has grown nearly sevenfold from $16 billion in 1999 to more than $114 billion in 2016. But this equals only around one-sixth of U.S.-China trade, and better resembles the scale of U.S. trade with France (population: 66 million), and is about $30 billion shy of two-way trade with South Korea (population: 50 million).[12] In short, U.S.-India trade numbers look good compared to the past, but not when compared with others in the present.

U.S.-India strategic ties have deepened since the 2005 civil-nuclear agreement, but the bilateral economic relationship has not undergone a similar change. The economic dialogue between India and the United States remains fraught—even as both countries declare a shared commitment to increasing trade volumes to $500 billion, for example. In the more technical realms, like space, science, climate, and the environment, strong collaborations have developed that should continue. But, as Chapters 4 and 5 discussed in detail, where the two countries disagree, as they often do about specific details of access to markets or technology worker mobility, we have struggled to find viable solutions.

Strong bilateral relationships are rarely free of economic disputes, as differences between the United States with Canada and Japan illustrate. But the degree to which economic differences have showcased fragility in the U.S.-India relationship points to the need for different strategies. Washington has adopted an all-sticks, no-carrots approach to trade and economic policy issues with India, and it has not borne fruit.[13] Instead, the United States should embark upon a two-track strategy of supporting Indian membership in global economic institutions such as APEC while simultaneously accelerating bilateral consultation toward a more ambitious shared vision for trade and investment. As Indian ambitions for reform of other global institutions illustrates, New Delhi would like a seat at the table of major institutions that more appropriately reflects its larger global role.

Historically, decades of economic autarky and a relatively small economy locked India out of productive economic institutions such as the Asia-Pacific Economic Cooperation forum (APEC), the Organization for Economic Cooperation and Development (OECD), and the International Energy Agency (IEA). By the time the G20 came into being as a financial ministerial in 1999, India had grown large enough to merit membership. New Delhi has long been a part of UN agencies such as UNIDO and UNCTAD, as well as the WTO, IMF, and World Bank. But it remains outside the above-mentioned bodies that play a role in setting norms, pushing new boundaries on standards and openness, and providing a meaningful place for ongoing multilateral conversations on trade and economic policies.

Take APEC. As an Asia-Pacific-wide regime committed to enhancing "free and open trade and investment," it is not a trade *negotiating*

platform, but it does—through its various working groups and full diplomatic calendar of meetings—play a role in setting new non-binding
norms to continually advance economic openness in such traditional
areas as customs and standards, as well as next-generation concerns like
its green goods trade agenda. India has remained outside APEC despite
applying for membership prior to a moratorium on new members put
into place in 1997 and lifted only in 2010. (No new member has been
inducted despite the end of the moratorium.) The Indian economy
has grown fivefold since 1997, and has also become more open even as
much work remains. An APEC missing one of Asia's largest economies
lacks legitimacy and makes little economic sense.

U.S. support for Indian membership in APEC will benefit U.S.-
India ties. Critics worry that India may not be "ready" for membership and specifically may hinder consensus decisions. India's reputation
for disrupting consensus at the WTO, effectively hobbling the Doha
round, precedes it. But this objection is misguided. As a nonbinding
forum, APEC focuses on transparency and peer consultation toward
open trade. Including Indian trade officials in these ongoing conversations in a non-zero-sum environment will expose them to global best
practices.[14] U.S. interests will be better served by allowing successful
Asian countries to explain the benefits of trade and economic openness.

A similar argument holds for easing India into the OECD, founded
in 1948 to run the Marshall Plan. The OECD has over the intervening
decades become an institutionalized place for comparative discussion
on development, anticorruption, corporate governance, poverty, and
many other economic subjects. It has become one of the core global
institutions to discuss aid effectiveness, and compare data and goals
across countries, particularly through its Development Assistance
Committee. India is not an OECD member, but has participated as
an observer in the Development Assistance Committee "High-Level
Meetings" as well as in the Busan Partnership for Effective Development
Cooperation.

India has transitioned from being a recipient of global development assistance to becoming a major donor—or, in Indian words, a
"development partner." India is now the major development partner
to the countries of South Asia, is the fifth largest bilateral donor to
Afghanistan, and over the past decade has emerged as a major donor

to African countries as well. While India still has development needs of its own domestically, for which Western assistance has been shrinking given India's own growing donor profile, that does not detract from the new role it now plays as a donor. It should be a natural step for India to become not just an observer to OECD conversations, but a member. In 2007 the OECD began what it calls "enhanced engagement" with India, China, Brazil, Indonesia, and South Africa, calling them all "key partners." With India now among the world's largest economies, as with the APEC case, it is hard to justify the two-tiered member/observer structure any longer.[15]

Membership in the OECD would open up another opportunity: the IEA. For arcane historical reasons, OECD membership is a requirement for IEA membership. IEA membership also has technical requirements involving a country's level of reserves, its ability to operate what are called "coordinated emergency response measures," and regularly report data on oil companies to the IEA.[16] India has become a "key partner country" for the IEA's outreach to nonmembers, however, and has regular consultations with the IEA secretariat and its staff. In 2015 the IEA worked closely with Indian government officials to put together a special report on India, the *India Energy Outlook*. With India poised to become the world's third largest crude oil importer in 2016, it becomes hard to understand why the country should not be among the core IEA members instead of once again occupying an observer/"partner" position on the outside.[17]

Recommendation: Bring India into Economic Organizations. To better embed India in the institutions of global economic discussion and exchange that help shape international norms, the United States should support Indian candidacy for membership in APEC, the OECD, and, following the OECD, the IEA. Apart from the obvious argument about fairness, including India at the table in each of these institutions will help pull India into a cohort of countries already committed to economic openness and transparency, without the adversarial context that accompanies binding trade negotiations. In and of itself, that would be beneficial. As India becomes a recognized global power, one inside the tent and not held at a distance on the outside, it will be more likely to play a role in setting norms rather than resist the imposition of norms developed by others. Just as the civil-nuclear deal helped pull India inside the global nonproliferation tent, a strategy focused on including India in major economic norm-setting institutions could deliver the same more positive working relationship on these issues central to the global economy.

Recommendation: Develop Stronger Bilateral Trade Ties with India. How will India and the United States reach their shared declared goal of quintupling trade volumes to $500 billion? Despite the shared desire for a much larger trade relationship, it has been challenging for both countries to establish even modest economic agreements (such as a bilateral investment treaty), due to divergences on some of the nuts and bolts inherently part of such negotiations. To achieve the oft-proclaimed shared goal of increasing trade to higher levels, the United States should work closely with India to develop a roadmap for either a free-trade agreement in the longer term, or, depending on the success of a larger Asian trade arrangement to succeed the Trans-Pacific Partnership (TPP), a pathway for Indian membership in a Free Trade Area of the Asia Pacific, should one ever develop.

These types of agreements are not possible in the near term because they are binding negotiations, and at the moment New Delhi and Washington are too far apart on too many trade matters to make this envisionable. Discussions on a bilateral investment treaty, a much less ambitious exercise than an FTA, for example, have taken place sporadically for about a decade, and appear no closer to a conclusion than they were ten years back. But India and the United States should be able to identify a longer-term ambition for their trade and investment relationship. A shared desire to attain a grand ambition yielded the civil-nuclear initiative. By contrast, economically focused conversations have been incremental and highly transactional. Former Vice President Joseph Biden's expressed goal of attaining a $500 billion two-way trade volume serves as an orienting ambition, but it needs concrete and achievable interim steps in order to create a feasible implementation plan.

The United States has embarked upon slow and difficult trade negotiations in the past, and little suggests that an ambitious effort with India will be easy. But deepening economic ties with India, among the world's largest and fastest-growing economies, will be important for the United States in the coming decades. As a CFR-sponsored Task Force on trade noted in 2011, the United States could benefit from "a more flexible and varied" approach to "the sectors and countries that promise the largest economic gains." Instead of waiting for India to be ready for the kind of trade opening we desire, Americans might benefit from a more incremental approach with India to keep things moving, however slowly.[18]

THE MEANING OF STRATEGIC PARTNERSHIP

As I have underscored throughout these pages, over the past decade U.S.-India ties have undergone a dramatic recalibration. Nowhere has this been more manifest than in strategic and defense ties. Where both countries were on opposite sides of the Cold War, now they collaborate in a declared strategic partnership. As mentioned earlier, the civil nuclear deal has turned nonproliferation, once a "cinder in the eye," to use former Ambassador Frank G. Wisner's phrase, into an area of cooperation.[19] China's rise, including its assertiveness in the South China Sea and increasing influence throughout South Asia and the Indian Ocean region, has propelled geopolitical convergence between Washington and New Delhi. They have institutionalized consultation about East Asia, the size and complexity of joint military exercises have increased, the annual "Malabar" naval exercise has become multinational, and in January 2015 the Obama-Modi "Joint Strategic Vision for the Asia Pacific and Indian Ocean" declared the U.S.-India partnership "indispensable to promoting peace, prosperity and stability in those regions."[20]

Geopolitical shifts have enabled the significant development of closer defense ties. For geopolitical experts like former under secretary of state for political affairs Nicholas Burns, this stands among the major strategic developments of the past twenty years:

> Still, India has become a close partner of the U.S. during the past decade. Our trade and investment ties are booming. Our military and political bonds are stronger now than at any time in the past. And we have become close and important security partners in the Indian Ocean and Western Pacific. This is a very positive strategic change for both countries. And, together with other democratic nations such as Japan and Australia, Washington and Delhi should

be strong enough in the next few decades to engage China but also to maintain our military predominance in the Asia-Pacific region in the future. In this sense, the rapid development of the U.S.-India relationship is one of the most important American strategic initiatives of the last two decades. The fact that there is strong bipartisan support for this key relationship is an added source of strength as we look to the future.[21]

In June 2016, during Prime Minister Modi's visit to Washington, the United States declared India a "major defense partner," a term applied to no other partner, and one designed to elevate defense ties with India to those of the closest allies and partners—without begging the debate over an alliance relationship.[22] It was an excellent step, especially in light of India's growing security ambitions across the Indian Ocean discussed earlier, and its increasing defense spending, now the second largest in Asia (after China), and the fifth largest in the world according to the SIPRI data discussed in Chapter 1, placing India behind the United States, China, Saudi Arabia, Russia, and just barely ahead of France and the United Kingdom.[23]

In December 2015, India's defense minister visited the U.S. Pacific Command headquarters in Hawaii for the first time. U.S.-India defense trade has boomed, going from nothing to more than $15 billion in procurements, making the United States one of India's major systems suppliers—a sharp contrast to India's decades of sole reliance on Russian hardware. The sharpest uptick has occurred since 2011; during the years 2011 to 2014, the United States consistently outpaced Russia as a supplier to India when measured by expenditure, according to data released by the Indian Ministry of Defence. In 2011–2012, U.S. arms were almost 28 percent of Indian overall procurement, compared with Russia's nearly 21 percent; in 2012–2013, the United States accounted for 37 percent compared with Russia's 26 percent; and in 2013–2014, U.S. platforms made up 35 percent compared with Russia's 30 percent.[24]

The rising share of U.S. defense equipment in India's overall mix indicates increasing coordination and what defense experts call "interoperability," meaning that Indian and U.S. militaries can better work with each other. India has embarked upon one of the world's largest military modernization efforts, and has already acquired or is adding platforms (such as additional aircraft carriers, maritime surveillance planes, and multi-role combat aircraft) that will allow it to project power across the Indian Ocean region.[25] Both Indian and American officials now comfortably speak of India as a "net provider of security" in the Indian Ocean. The bilateral Defense Trade and Technology Initiative, launched in 2011, focuses on a future of coproduction and codevelopment of defense weapons systems, including a new working group on aircraft carrier technology and another on fighter jet engine technology.[26] This growing defense cooperation should be continued and expanded, and the natural set of shared interests has propelled ties forward.

However, convergence does not mean that Indian policymakers suddenly see themselves in a supporting and instrumental role for American strategic objectives. Understanding this distinction is a fundamental part of appreciating India's approach to its Asia-Pacific goals, which include protecting its own primacy in the Indian Ocean and preserving the principle of freedom of navigation. In the United States, it has become common for foreign policy generalists to see India as the power that can help hedge China's influence. It is certainly true that India's rise in and of itself as a powerful Asian power provides balance within Asia, and serves as an alternative model, one that marries economic growth with a strong democracy. On top of that, New Delhi's increasingly vocal statements about maritime freedom of navigation and the importance of resolving territorial disputes through a rule-based system like the UN Convention on the Law of the Seas align perfectly with U.S. concerns in the Asia-Pacific regarding China's territorial ambitions. But India—in many ways like the United States—does not wish to pit itself as *the* counterbalance against China when it has avenues of cooperation to maintain with Beijing. The creation of the BRICS, the New Development Bank, and the Asian Infrastructure Investment Bank discussed earlier indicate examples where India and China made common cause to create new global institutions that they see as serving their interest in having a larger voice. These do not include American participation, and Washington lobbied actively against the creation of the AIIB. At times the convergence of rising power priorities matters more to New Delhi, especially on matters of representation, status, and the ability to play a larger role in shaping rules of international interaction.

The formal "Joint Strategic Vision for the Asia-Pacific and Indian Ocean Region," with shared principles such as sustainable and inclusive growth, economic connectivity, freedom of navigation, and a shared opposition to terrorism, piracy, and proliferation of weapons of mass destruction, has led to greatly expanded diplomatic and military cooperation across the entire Asia-Pacific region. But when it comes to Pakistan, India's most troubled relationship, Indian officials remain disappointed by continued U.S. support for the Pakistani military despite evidence that at best it does little to rein in terrorist groups operating from its soil, and at worst it actively supports them.

Although Washington has its own concerns with Pakistan—a country that former Secretary of State Madeleine Albright once famously called "an international migraine"—they have not led the United States to limit ties with the Pakistani military, a necessary partner given the U.S. and international presence in Afghanistan since 2001. But Pakistan's terrorism problem shows few signs of abating. With leaders of terrorist groups that attack India (not to mention U.S. troops in Afghanistan) living openly and with impunity in Pakistan, it becomes harder for Washington to maintain a dual-track policy of strong ties with both India and with Pakistan.

For decades, India complained that the United States had "hyphenated" its South Asia policy by seeking to balance every action with New Delhi with a compensating gesture to Islamabad. With the civil-nuclear deal, the Bush administration did away with the hyphenation construct and actively pursued separate and very different policies toward both countries. Former Secretary of State Condoleezza Rice addressed the notion explicitly when she told the press on her way to India in 2005 that "One of the things that we've been able to do is . . . de-hyphenate the relationship with Pakistan because at the same time that our relations with India have been moving forward we have the best relations with Pakistan that perhaps we've ever had as well."[27] In those remarks, Rice pointed to the positive U.S. agenda with Pakistan, including on counterterrorism, the economy, and education.

Events since then have revealed the shallowness of U.S. counterrorism cooperation with Pakistan, rhetoric notwithstanding. Apart from the outrageous discovery that Osama bin Laden had hidden in the Pakistani garrison town of Abbottabad for perhaps a decade, other terrorism-related developments continue to underscore Indian concerns about Pakistan. In recent years, the Pakistani military has shown more willingness than before to crack down against terrorists who threaten Pakistan—and it is certainly true that Pakistani citizens too suffer greatly from the terrorism menace in their country—but Pakistani authorities have failed to move against those that target India (or Afghanistan for that matter). The 2008 Mumbai attacks, in which six Americans were killed along with 160 Indian citizens, escalated U.S. attention to the menace of the Lashkar-e-Taiba, a long-sanctioned UN- and U.S.-designated terrorist group.[28]

The United States has sought to apply additional pressure to Pakistan to rein in terrorist groups, including through mechanisms like a $10 million reward offered in 2012 for information leading to the arrest of the Lashkar's head, Hafiz Saeed. The reward has had little effect, and more than five years on, Saeed remains free. The "suspected mastermind" of Mumbai, Lashkar-e-Taiba terrorist Zakiur Rehman Lakhvi, was released on bail in April 2015 (after fathering a child in prison). Other terrorist groups too, including the Jaish-e-Muhammad and the Haqqani Network, have faced little Pakistani pressure. U.S. officials have publicly accused the Haqqani Network of attacks on U.S. troops and facilities in Afghanistan, as well as some of the bloodiest violence against Afghan civilians. Indian officials have accused Jaish-e-Muhammad of responsibility for a series of terrorist attacks including the October 2001 attack on the Jammu and Kashmir assembly, the December 2001 attack on the Indian parliament, the January 2016 attack on an Indian air force base in Pathankot, and potentially the September 2016 Uri attack as well.

In the long run, the United States cannot sustain policies toward India without regard to its Pakistan policy if the latter continues to harbor terrorists—in violation of all Islamabad's international commitments—who target India. Continued U.S. support for the Pakistani military, despite its refusal to tackle terrorist groups that target India, suggests to Indian officials that Washington does not support New Delhi on its most sensitive national security concern. Indian officials and analysts increasingly emphasize that it will be hard for India to continue cooperating with the United States toward the east if the cooperation India seeks to the west fails to materialize. Washington's moment of choice in South Asia has nearly arrived.

Recommendation: Keep the Focus on Ties with India—the Long Game.
The United States should continue to pursue stronger security cooperation with India. While Washington should maintain its separate
relationship with Pakistan, American officials should insist much more
forcefully—as some members of Congress have begun to do—that
Pakistan take action against terrorists who are destroying its own society
and damaging its relations with its neighbors.[29] Should Pakistan refuse
to take action against all terror groups—not just those that threaten the
Pakistani state—Washington should prepare to reevaluate its relations
with Pakistan. The most important step would be to decisively shift
the balance in the U.S.-Pakistan relationship to favor Pakistani civilians. Policy options include ending U.S. taxpayer-financed support for
defense sales, potentially ending defense sales for all but a limited range
of explicitly counterterrorism-focused platforms, de-notifying Pakistan
as a "Major Non-NATO Ally," scoping U.S. assistance to Pakistan to
favor democracy and governance development over military reimburse-
ments, and working closely with Central Asian partners to maintain
alternate supply lines into Afghanistan. Coalition support funds reim-
bursements should be conditioned on positive action against international terrorism of all kinds. Of course, we should not end potentially
beneficial military cooperation like enhanced International Military
Education and Training, which gives Pakistani officers exposure to best
practices including on human rights.[30]

This shift will be difficult and will likely disrupt U.S. ties with
Pakistan, which since the latter half of the twentieth century have been
dominated by the military. But by recalibrating the Pakistan relationship to tilt toward civilians—where it should have been in the first
place—Washington would preserve its ties with a rising India, and better advance strategic cooperation with New Delhi in the wider Asia-
Pacific. That is the strategic goal on which the United States should be
focused.

THE WORLD'S TWO LARGEST DEMOCRACIES

One of the most obvious and desirable areas for U.S.-India cooperation
has long been democracy. In India's national election of 2014, citizens
cast more than half a billion ballots at more than nine hundred thousand

polling stations—an awe-inspiring exercise of democratic franchise. It was reportedly his admiration for the scale of India's democracy that led former President George W. Bush to prioritize deepening ties. Like Americans, Indian citizens are proud of their democracy, one seen in the early years of Indian independence as improbable given the great poverty and illiteracy in the country. Every election serves to cement the vision of India's founders and their belief in universal adult franchise, against the odds.

But Americans sometimes mistakenly expect to see their own ideas of democracy promotion and interest in championing the liberal world order mirrored in India, anticipating that both countries see their political systems and its traditions in the same way. This misrecognition can lead, as with the misplaced assumptions of an alliance-type of relationship as the desired endpoint, to confusion and disappointment. India guards against perceived intrusions of sovereignty, stemming from its colonial experience. Nonintervention became a bedrock principle Nehru worked to codify internationally through the Non-Aligned Movement. As explained in Chapter 5, India sees active approaches toward democracy promotion, if not at the explicit request of the host country, as an intrusion on sovereignty.[31]

Indeed, to generalize, India sees the United States as too quick to "meddle" elsewhere in the name of democracy—as in Iraq, Libya, Egypt, and Syria. Indian officials remain deeply wary of international action aimed at ensuring transitions to democracy, which often appear to Indian eyes as hasty and without thought for what forces might fill a resulting void. India found little reason to support the United States during the Arab Spring, as former Indian permanent representative to the United Nations Hardeep Singh Puri had explained. (On the other hand, India welcomed the U.S. role in Afghanistan, where it sees the U.S. and international troop presence as having staved off the far worse alternative of rule by the Pakistan-backed Taliban.)

If the limits to collaboration on democracy promotion in other countries stem from India's sovereignty concerns, those concerns become even more pronounced when it comes to many of the liberal democratic norms that U.S. foreign policy holds a special interest in upholding worldwide: freedom of expression, religious freedom, space for civil society, rule of law, human rights, supporting women's empowerment, and many others. These emphases stem from an American focus on universal human rights, and a belief that U.S. policy tools can and should make a positive difference around the world. The American focus on human rights also serves as a symbol of "the values and principles on which the U.S. stands."[32] These concerns are embedded into U.S. foreign policy formulation in the executive branch and in Congressional oversight of the administration. Indeed, in the United States Congress requires as a matter of law annual reports from the State Departmant on human rights around the world, trafficking in persons, and religious freedom. Congress also requires from the U.S. Department of Labor a separate report on child labor around the world. A congressionally mandated but independent U.S. Commission on International Religious Freedom releases its own annual study on religious freedom worldwide.

For the Indian government, these are matters of exclusive domestic jurisdiction; bringing them up impinges on national sovereignty. The Indian constitution enshrines human rights, women's equality, freedom of religion, protection against discrimination, and others—but the Indian government sees these as purely domestic matters. With rare exceptions in the neighborhood, usually linked to a domestic voting group, India generally does not champion human rights outside its borders. Nor does it usually support single-country resolutions in the UN Human Rights Council. Human Rights Watch recently assessed India's voting record on the Human Rights Council as "one of the states least supportive of the Council's mandate to address country situations."[33] And that is for a UN agency of which India has been a member since its creation in 2007.

India sees the United States, or any outside country, as lacking the legitimacy to pass judgment on the conditions within other countries' borders. A statement from the Ministry of External Affairs in 2015 upon the release of a U.S. Commission on International Religious Freedom captures this perspective well: "We take no cognizance of this report."[34]

At the same time, India's experience managing elections on a near-constant basis offers great potential for further partnership. Internationally, India champions democracy, as discussed earlier, stands ready to provide advice if requested, and has eagerly supported the UN Democracy Fund and the Community of Democracies. With an eye toward this reality, the United States should partner with India to do more together on the electoral aspects of democracy, maintaining a focus on the elements that lie within New Delhi's comfort zone.

Finally, finding a way to collaborate more with India on democracy, in India's comfort zone, does not mean abandoning a focus on the values so central to American foreign policy, including in bilateral discussions of concerns. But our approach should adapt, to acknowledge the struggles we continue to have domestically, and to offer ourselves and what best practices we have learned—including the mistakes we have made—as part of an open conversation. This may prove challenging, particularly if a more nationalistic India becomes even more allergic to outside criticism. But we should not stop trying.

Recommendation: Expand Technical Partnership with India on Democracy. Consultation between the U.S. Federal Election Commission and the Election Commission of India (ECI) should be institutionalized.[35] The United States could set aside funds to support training for officials from third countries with the ECI, just as the United States provided funding for agriculture officials from Kenya, Liberia, and Malawi to receive training in Indian agriculture extension schools.[36] Dialogue and support for the Community of Democracies and the UN Democracy Fund should continue, and both have proven to be areas of solid bilateral cooperation. Further emphasizing work with international organizations like International Foundation for Electoral Systems offers another technical avenue to develop programs that could be used anywhere in the world. Above all, the United States should shift to seeing India as a priority partner for advice and consultation on the mechanics of democracy around the world, and work within India's comfort zone to identify additional capacity-building initiatives drawing on the strengths and expertise of India's unparalleled technical experience with elections.

Recommendation: Frame Bilateral Conversations about Rights Broadly to Include Challenges in the United States.

Especially in light of the increasing global visibility of criminal justice and civil rights problems within the United States itself, U.S. officials should lead with a frank recognition of the hurdles we still struggle to overcome, and offer an ongoing discussion as a basis for an open exchange of views—for example on criminal justice reform, or our challenges stopping human trafficking within our own borders, to name just two examples. In the case of India, the violent attacks on Indian citizens in the United States in February 2017 heightened concern in New Delhi for how American race relations affected Indian citizens. This should be part of any discussion agenda. The United States is not perfect, and as we work to tackle our own failings, we ought see our own problems as part of a larger canvas for discussion when designing an agenda to include as well concerns U.S. officials will undoubtedly wish to raise with Indian counterparts. India's growing power and growing prosperity has not ended its many problems, as earlier discussed, and I anticipate that India's many cleavages will continue to roil society. A more extremist, exclusionary Hindu nationalism, most worrisome given episodes of violence, creates challenges for India's self-presentation on the world stage as a champion of multiethnic, multireligious, multilingual diversity. Management of diversity too can and should be one among the many areas of conversation between Washington and New Delhi. But a hectoring checklist of failures and public shaming outside of a comprehensive diplomatic dialogue will shut down conversation and will not advance U.S. interests in strengthening democratic institutions.

TENDING THE DIPLOMATIC GARDEN

In New Delhi, President Obama shared his vision of India becoming an "indispensable" partner for Washington, but historically this has not been the case. For statistical evidence, we need not look further than votes in the United Nations that Washington deems important. In 2015, India voted with the United States only 33.3 percent of the time on "important votes" in the General Assembly. That's the same as the U.S. voting coincidence with China, and the same as with Uzbekistan, a dictatorship that has boiled dissidents alive. It's also worse than with Russia (28.6 percent), not exactly the closest U.S. partner. Going further back to the turbulent years of 2011 and 2012 shows even wider cracks between India and the United States. In 2012, India's voting coincidence with the United States on "important" votes was just 14.3 percent, and in 2011, it had been exactly zero.[37]

Against this backdrop, it's no wonder that the habits of cooperation between both countries do not resemble those the United States has with other major powers. Moreover, because India is not a permanent member of the UN Security Council, U.S. officials do not automatically seek New Delhi's views as they do with other members of the Permanent Five or with long-standing allies like Japan or Germany. India's own ambivalence about working with the United States on global crises has forestalled any opportunity to create a new narrative. At times, working with India has resulted in a negative impression with some American officials. Then U.S. permanent representative to the United Nations Susan Rice's remarks on simultaneous Indian, Brazilian, and South African tenures on the Security Council, sums it up: "This has been an opportunity for them to demonstrate how they might act if they were to obtain permanent membership, and for us to assess our level of enthusiasm about that. . . . Let me just say we've learned a lot, and not all of it, frankly, encouraging."[38]

From an Indian vantage point, that disagreements with the United States might call into question its commitment to support India's quest for a permanent seat on the Security Council seems unfair. Ambassador Rice made her remarks to NPR in late 2011, at a time when Syria topped the U.S. agenda at the Security Council, while India had been working closely with Brazil and South Africa in their own "democracies of the global South" effort to negotiate with the Assad government. The IBSA effort at least attempted something rather than just blocking other proposals. In hindsight, the IBSA plan might well have worked better than the path the world took. Nonetheless, the perception gap illustrates how divergent expectations can strain bilateral ties.

Given New Delhi's long-standing policy preferences of independent decision-making and caution on most issues, discussed in Chapters 4 and 5, India's actions on the Security Council would not have surprised anyone with a longer-term perspective on India's foreign policy. Instead, with India expertise comparatively limited in the U.S. government, these types of disappointments recur.

In an effort to institutionalize annual consultation at the cabinet level, Secretary of State Hillary Clinton crafted, with her counterpart S. M. Krishna, a new annual "U.S.-India Strategic Dialogue." The first one took place in Washington in June 2010. As deputy assistant secretary of state for South Asia during late 2010 to 2013, I staffed and attended the dialogues that took place in Washington. Given the sparse U.S.-India diplomatic calendar—in contrast to the ongoing summits, ministerials, and working groups the United States has with its European and East Asian partners—the strategic dialogue boosted momentum by creating an annual meeting that both countries had to prepare for throughout the year. In 2015 this dialogue formally expanded to become the U.S.-India Strategic and Commercial Dialogue, giving the commercial consultation equally important, cabinet secretary billing, in the manner of the U.S.-China Strategic and Economic Dialogue.

The strategic dialogue concept created an umbrella under which various other consultations within the State Department (space, peacekeeping, global issues, strategic security, education, and many others) as well those across other agencies could "roll up" and frame the year's progress and future priorities in one meeting. Other cabinet-level consultations—such as the Homeland Security Dialogue, the Energy Dialogue dating back to the Bush administration, the Trade Policy Forum, and the Economic and Financial Partnership dialogue—also built frameworks for ongoing consultation.

At the under secretary and assistant secretary levels, new consultations with India (like the East Asia Consultations, and a trilateral consultation with Japan) added to those that had been ongoing (such as the Defense Policy Group and the High Technology Cooperation Group). All of these enhanced the ability to compare views in a formal way on developments in each of the major regions of the world, or on specialized issues.

From my perspective, the Strategic Dialogue and the other cabinet-level annual meetings successfully institutionalized high-level dialogue, a vital spur to bureaucracies on both sides. However, these structures do not necessarily create the thick connectivity, meaning frequent *and ongoing* high-level consultation, that exists with the closest U.S. partners. They are calendar-driven, which ensures that they occur and create action-forcing events, but due to the calendar obligation they are inherently sporadic. In former secretary of state George Shultz's vivid metaphor, the United States needs to tend the diplomatic garden with India a little more.[39]

Recommendation: Build Habits of Cooperation. To enhance consultation with India, U.S. officials should prioritize building "habits of cooperation" that will enable the bilateral relationship to accomplish more. The creation of standing dialogues has redressed one long-standing deficiency in the relationship—the lack of a robust diplomatic calendar. To develop the ongoing, routinized type of cooperation that occurs with the closest U.S. partners, Washington should seek deeper and less formal consultation with New Delhi. American officials should see India as a first-round country to consult on almost any issue, with the purpose of hearing how New Delhi views the stakes in particular global challenges on a regular (even weekly) basis. U.S. cabinet-level officials and their deputies should speak habitually with Indian counterparts, instead of "teeing up" calls only for a last-minute bid to convince New Delhi of a particular policy that has already been decided in consultation with others.

To that end—and I write this knowing full well there will be many in my own country who disagree—Washington should do a better, more proactive job on UN Security Council reform to make good on the promise of seeing permanent membership for India "in a reformed and expanded" Security Council. Other countries, including U.S. allies Japan and Germany, also seek permanent UNSC membership, and the United States needs to develop a slate that it is ready to use its diplomatic heft to support. India should be on that slate of candidates. I have no doubts that India as a permanent Security Council member would present challenges to many U.S. positions, but the perspective Indian diplomats bring to bear on some of the world's most intractable matters of peace and security should be, and deserve to be, heard in the same room as those of China, Russia, France, and the United Kingdom. The realities of sharing the same set of preoccupations at the global high table will require more intensive, ongoing communication about the central peace and security matters confronting the world.

In terms of navigating multiple bureaucracies, it would also help to have a senior person inside the U.S. executive branch with a long-term view and responsibility for advancing ties with India beyond whatever immediate vote or issue might be at stake. As the CFR-sponsored Independent Task Force recommended, someone subcabinet or higher could be a designated "interagency India person" known across the U.S. government as holding this charge.[40] During the Bush administration, by virtue of his intensive involvement in the civil-nuclear negotiation, Nicholas Burns informally emerged as such a person.

As he wrote in *Foreign Affairs*, he traveled to India eight times in two years—and was on the phone very regularly with his counterparts.[41] In late 2015, the State Department and India's Ministry of External Affairs announced a new foreign policy consultation at the deputy secretary-foreign secretary level designed to build more regular high-level conversation. Should it continue, it could fill the role well.

THE ENABLING ENVIRONMENT: SADLY IN THE DARK

Despite India's rising power, and a growing appreciation of the country's importance in the United States, Americans have done little to gain serious familiarity with India—most especially in comparison with other countries and regions. There are opportunity costs to developing expertise in a country or region, undoubtedly, and unfortunately the consistent pattern with India has been a level of attention far below what a rising global power should merit, and well below that of Russia, China, Brazil, and others.

In *Foreign Affairs*, Georgetown professor Charles King made a compelling case for keeping language and area education a high national priority for the United States, arguing that "flying blind is dangerous."[42] He focused on Russia and the former Soviet Union, a region that has received much higher levels of U.S. funding over the years than India and South Asia. As a point of comparison, seven times more American students study Russian than all the Indian languages combined. If we are flying blind on Russia, we must be blind, deaf, and mute on India.

A quarter-century after India embarked on economic reforms, and eighteen years after its nuclear tests, comparatively few Americans study abroad in India, and fewer still enroll in an Indian language in U.S. colleges or universities. While language enrollments do not capture the full universe of courses a student might take on India, they are a good comparative metric against other regions, especially in the absence of much other comparative data. Study of India compares unfavorably with China in virtually every higher education metric, but more surprisingly, also fares poorly compared with much smaller countries such as South Korea or Costa Rica.[43]

During the 1995–1996 school year, for example, only 470 U.S. students studied in India. A decade later, the number had more than quadrupled to 2,115. By 2014–2015, the most recently available year for which data exist, the number had more than doubled again to 4,438 (Table 8.1).[44] This increase, as with so much else in the U.S.-India context, represents a handsome improvement from previous years, but when put in comparative context looks a lot less impressive.

To put it starkly, India fares worse than Ireland, Costa Rica, and South Africa as a study abroad destination. Obviously, students do not necessarily select a study abroad destination on the basis of its rising power in the world—hence Italy as the second most popular destination—but something is wrong when a country of more than one billion people, a top ten global economy, and one with a wealth of cultural heritage to offer attracts fewer American students than tiny Costa Rica. Nascent efforts to try to encourage more American students to study in India—notably the "Passport to India" initiative partnership between the State Department and Ohio State University—have not yet moved the needle significantly. Unfortunately, the initiative has not garnered the high-profile support that a similar China-focused effort—100,000 Strong—has received from the U.S. government, the Chinese government, and the Ford Foundation.[45]

The same pattern shows up in an even more pronounced fashion in language enrollment data.[46] Students in U.S. colleges and universities do not sign up for Indian languages in remotely the same numbers as for languages like Arabic, Chinese, Korean, or even Biblical Hebrew. Of course, India is home to many languages—fifteen on each currency

TABLE 8.1 Leading Destinations of U.S. Study Abroad Students, 2014–2015

Country	U.S. Students	Country	U.S. Students
United Kingdom	38,189	Costa Rica	9,305
Italy	33,768	Australia	8,810
Spain	28,325	Japan	6,053
France	18,198	South Africa	5,249
China	12,790	Mexico	4,712
Germany	11,010	India	4,438
Ireland	10,230		

Open Doors data, International Institute of Education, 2016.

bill, and those do not exhaust the official list—but even aggregating all Indian language enrollments in the United States the total stays below four thousand. Worse, in 2013, Indian language enrollments *dropped* to 3,090 from the 3,924 of 2009 (Table 8.2).[47]

In short, the total enrollments in all Indian languages combined account for *less than one-quarter* those of Korean, and a mere fraction of more commonly taught languages (14 percent of Russian, 9.5 percent of Arabic, or 5 percent of Chinese). It has been like this as long as I've been watching, a situation far more dire if considering the Indian languages individually. No single Indian language crossed a two thousand enrollment threshold in 2013; Hindi saw enrollments of 1,800, but every other language was either in the mid- to low hundreds or in double digits.[48]

English is an official language of India, along with Hindi, and is widely used in international business, so the issue is not narrowly one of ability to communicate. Rather, it is a comparative barometer of the low priority Americans place on developing deeper and more place-specific knowledge of India. Furthermore, despite the widespread use of English in India, the major growth in print and electronic media at huge scale is taking place in languages other than English. It is difficult

TABLE 8.2 Enrollments of Selected Foreign Languages in U.S. Higher Education, 2013

Language	Enrollments	Language	Enrollments
Spanish	790,756	Latin	27,192
French	197,757	Russian	21,962
American Sign Language	109,577	Ancient Greek	12,917
German	86,700	Biblical Hebrew	12,551
Italian	71,285	Portuguese	12,415
Japanese	66,740	Korean	12,229
Chinese	61,055	Modern Hebrew	6,698
Arabic	32,286	*All Indian languages combined*	3,090

Enrollments in Languages Other than English in United States Institutions of Higher Education, Modern Language Association, 2013.

to access these worlds without any language skills other than English. And indeed, a 2012 bipartisan Independent Task Force sponsored by the Council on Foreign Relations expressly recommended increasing opportunities for foreign language study to better enhance U.S. national security preparedness.[49]

While counterfactual evidence does not exist to suggest that more extensive Russian- or Chinese-language capabilities have led to better policy outcomes, the assumption behind federal incentives for these language and other coursework programs prioritizes area knowledge as a core component of national preparedness. Following that assumption to its logical conclusion, it is hard to see why India and South Asia fare so pooly compared with other regions. If anything, it should be near-par with East Asia, instead of receiving only around half the funding levels. These types of discrepancies can and should be remedied. The sources of U.S. federal funding to support area-focused courses and fellowships for language study on U.S. campuses or abroad simply do not elevate India and South Asia to a priority—it is in the lower half. A snapshot of the funding levels for various regions of the world under Title VI of the Higher Education Act, which includes the Foreign Language and Area Studies fellowships and the National Resource Centers, tells the story plainly (Tables 8.3 and 8.4):

TABLE 8.3 Foreign Language and Area Studies Funding by World Area in FY 2015

East Asia	$5,409,000
Latin America	$4,462,738
Russia/East Europe/Eurasia	$3,583,500
Middle East	$3,526,500
Africa	$3,357,000
South Asia	$2,713,500
Southeast Asia	$2,449,500
Western Europe/Europe	$2,034,000
Canada	$349,500

Source: Foreign Language and Area Studies Fellowships Program, Department of Education, FY 2014–2017.

TABLE 8.4 National Resource Centers Funding
by World Area in FY 2015

Latin America	$3,482,017
East Asia	$3,467,200
Middle East	$3,375,000
Africa	$2,370,700
Russia/East Europe/Eurasia	$2,605,000
South Asia	$1,906,340
Southeast Asia	$1,898,850
Western Europe/Europe	$1,558,000
Canada	$425,000

Source: Foreign Language and Area Studies Fellowships
Program, Department of Education, FY 2014–2017.

In addition, private philanthropy, which over the twentieth century played an indispensable role creating international studies in the United States, has moved away from supporting international studies at all, let alone India studies.[50] That is a great pity, because the best American programs on India came into being not only through the post-Sputnik National Defense Education Act of 1958, but also through the contributions of the Ford and Rockefeller Foundations, and the Carnegie Corporation (a foundation, despite the name). Their role in creating South Asian studies at the University of Chicago in the middle of the twentieth century, for example, has been well documented, and predated the National Defense Education Act by nearly a decade.[51] I am a direct beneficiary of this foresight and generosity.

Today, the Ford Foundation has shifted its India focus to supporting institutions in India. The Rockefeller Foundation has moved toward thematic priorities like resilience and food security. The Carnegie Corporation has limited its regional priorities in international peace and security to Russia, China, and the Arab world, although in the past it had supported the study of India. And the MacArthur Foundation recently ended its Asian Security Initiative. Newer philanthropy in the United States with an India focus displays a pronounced preference for development and health-focused NGOs in India, skills development, impact investing, and environmental sustainability, to name the most prominent. All of these are without doubt important. But the few private mechanisms that used to encourage deeper expertise on India— expertise that goes beyond an initial familiarity gained through tourism, for example—within the United States have shifted their gaze.

Finally, the dynamic and increasingly prominent role that Indian Americans play in U.S. business and political life is a development to celebrate, one that has begun to raise the prominence of India on the U.S. national agenda. This should help to further emphasize the study of India within the United States writ large. The networks and linkages to India that Indian Americans have are shaping bilateral ties for the better, playing the role of a "living bridge" between both countries.[52] Many of the language enrollments likely come from Indian American students eager to gain reading and writing skills in a language their parents might speak. According to the president of the Institute for International Education, Allen Goodman, many of the students studying abroad in India are likely Indian American.[53] But three million Indian Americans should not be expected to carry the entire weight of American knowledge of India. On the contrary, it should be a national priority to ensure that millions of other Americans know much more about India as well. More routine acquaintance with India, along the lines that American students have with France, Germany, or Japan, would significantly expand American familiarity in the aggregate of this complex country and society, and give the United States a much deeper bench of expertise to draw upon in every field.

Recommendation: Increase funding for India studies. The U.S. executive branch and Congress should work together to reassess federal support for international studies, and increase funding for India studies. In an ideal world, the overall pie should grow larger to ensure more support for international studies generally, which would increase language courses, other courses about India, and fellowship support for study abroad and language training in India. As King noted, Title VI appropriations have not kept up with their levels during the Johnson administration; if they had, they might have totaled "almost half a billion dollars" (inflation-adjusted) instead of just about $64 million in fiscal year 2014.[54]

As a second option, if the overall Title VI allocation for international studies cannot gain political support for additional funding, then the U.S. executive branch should work with Congress to enlarge the proportion for India and South Asia within the Title VI appropriations. Doing so will mean paring back from other regions, and no one ever wants to cut. But should it come to such a choice, support for Latin America, Russia, and Western Europe should be reduced and the savings should be reallocated to India and South Asia. This is not a comment on the importance of the three regions, but a recognition that neither Latin America nor Western Europe in particular need any incentive to encourage language study or study abroad programs, given the enrollment and study abroad data. With nearly eight hundred thousand enrollments in Spanish—more than all other foreign languages combined—the market mechanism appears to be providing sufficient incentives. Title VI support for Russian language study and Russia/Eastern Europe National Resource Centers exceeded that for South Asia by $800,000 and $700,000 in fiscal year 2015, respectively. Calibrating these funding levels to become more even with South Asia makes better sense; assistance would be better targeted to incentivize students to gain meaningful knowledge of India and South Asia given the persistent disparities discussed above.

Finally, the 1983 Act that created a separate funding stream to support Eastern European and Eurasian studies in the United States, known as "Title VIII," offers a model that the U.S. Congress could similarly employ to create a focused program on India and South Asia to augment the Title VI funding.[55]

Why do I worry about language and study abroad as part of an enabling environment for better understanding India? As I hope the preceding pages have shown, the trajectory of India's rise indicates a country that has already become increasingly important to the global economy, to global peace and security, and to global governance. We are also witnessing the rise of a country interested in defining itself in its own terms, and in seeing its own traditions gain respect and visibility alongside those of the West, including in disciplines of management and leadership. It is a place where regional language media continues to grow by leaps and bounds, and where English no longer dominates corridors of power in the way it once did. I now consider the years

I spent studying French during high school of far less utility than my college and graduate school years with Hindi and Urdu. Even the year I struggled with Tamil came in handy fifteen years later on visits to Tamil Nadu and to Sri Lanka's north and east. I hope the opportunity to study Indian languages becomes more frequent and widespread throughout the United States to give future generations more familiarity with this complex country.

FAMILIAR PARTNERS

The recommendations outlined here all stem from my conviction that the United States needs to do a better job "normalizing," in a sense, the reality of India's importance to our national interests and to the world, just as we assume the importance of so many European countries, Japan, China, Russia, Brazil, and others. The economic opportunity before India is also an opportunity for the United States and its companies, and U.S. companies and business schools have already begun to elevate their attention to this major emerging market. As chronicled throughout these pages, the strategic opportunity lies in further expansion of the growing partnership with a stable democratic India as it increasingly seeks to put its stamp on the world around it and shape global developments. India, as a major rising power of Asia, should be better understood and better appreciated in its own terms—as a competitiveness issue for U.S. economic and business interests, and as a matter of the demands of the new global diplomacy in which all of Asia plays a much more pivotal role.

Epilogue

AS HE SPOKE BEFORE a joint meeting of the U.S. Congress in June 2016, Prime Minister Narendra Modi ventured that the United States and India had together "overcome the hesitations of history."[1] He might well have been talking about India's own transformation.

More than at any time over the past quarter-century, India is well on its way to global power. As I hope the preceding pages have shown, in so many ways India has inched its way already into the top tiers of global economic relevance. It is rapidly becoming one of the world's major military forces, with ambitions to be the Indian Ocean's pre-eminent power. It still faces the national priority to tackle poverty, but systemic changes being put into place through ongoing reforms stand to deliver further economic growth. India continues to harbor some of its long-standing ambivalences about how it should exercise power on the world stage, but the inclination for diffidence is changing. We are witnessing a country chart its course to power, and explicitly seeking not to displace others but to be recognized among the club of world powers, one in which it believes its membership is long overdue.

For decades, a lagging economy and policy of autarky kept prosperity out of reach for Indian citizens, and held the world at arm's length. That has changed, and further change is under way. Indian leaders have set their sights on establishing (or re-establishing) a central place for India on the world stage. Successive governments have undertaken military modernization, and aim explicitly for Indian primacy in the Indian Ocean region. Diplomatic initiatives press for twentieth-century institutions to reform and recognize India's growing clout—in tandem with an entire alternate universe of diplomatic initiatives, often in concert with China, to craft multilateral institutions not led by the West in which India can have that larger voice.

By 2040, fifty years after I first touched down in Delhi during that autumn of discontent, India's transformation may very well have become part of what Larry Summers called the "biggest story of our era." If India plays its cards right, as I believe it will albeit with bumps along the way, the next twenty-five years could be even more transformative than the previous. A $10 trillion economy would place India just behind China and the United States. By 2040, the world's third largest military would have modernized its platforms, become a major naval power in the Indian Ocean, and cemented its role as a net provider of regional security. By then India will have the world's largest population, the world's largest workforce, and, if not the largest, one of the world's largest middle classes. India's advanced technology services economy has already positioned it as an innovation power, though employing a relatively small percentage of its population. If India at last does away with the constraints that have hobbled its manufacturing sector—and the country has begun to tackle its toughest, long-overdue reforms on this front—and succeeds in the quest for matching skills to the jobs available, major weaknesses that have limited opportunity for decades could be finally overcome.

This is no longer some far-off conjecture. Recalling the IMF projections, as soon as 2020 India will account for 8.4 percent of global GDP in purchasing parity terms. If it maintains high growth, imagine how it would look another twenty years out. Even at present, India's 7 percent share of global GDP (PPP) looks much like Japan of 1995 (7.8 percent) or China of 2000 (7.4 percent). As Nandan Nilekani put it, in the context of China's slowdown: "India has another twenty, twenty-five years of demographic dividend. So if it gets its act together in terms of job creation, entrepreneurship, ease of doing business, infrastructure, economic growth, it has the potential to deliver much higher growth than anyone else for a long period. That's strategic. If that happens, everything else falls into place."[2]

The shift within India to seeing itself as a "leading power" in the world, provides to my mind reason to anticipate further steps in that direction. An India that plays a critical role powering the global economy and provides a much-desired market for global companies will see its influence continue to rise in the international commercial world. An India that further sheds its hesitations and that confidently pursues an active role shaping regional and global outcomes, more willing to weigh in on global concerns in its neighborhood, in the Indian Ocean region, and at times beyond, will see its voice carry ever greater heft. Coupled with the long-standing national self-conception of India as a country destined for global leadership, and the public opinion data that show how India's youth feel proud of their country and want it to take on greater global prominence, we can see signs of India's transformation into a country that increasingly sees itself in global rather than regional terms and one deserving a much more significant place on the world stage. The India of tomorrow will expect the world to "give India its due" even more so than today.

Of course, no guarantees exist, and as the preceeding pages have also discussed, India faces many challenges. Its vulnerabilities by this point are well known, and due to sheer scale, are unlikely to be completely surmounted by the time the country becomes one of the world's top three economies. How India handles its multiethnic, multireligious diversity also affects India's soft power, its appeal on the world stage as a model for democracy.

The duality discussed earlier—growing external power coupled with glaring internal weaknesses—will continue to imbue Indian objectives on the world stage with caution. So will its historical preference for nonintervention in global peace and security questions. Few indicators suggest that Indian politics will become simpler in the coming decades; internal fault lines will likely perdure to some extent even if they diminish. So as Indian leaders continue to advance economic liberalization, military modernization, and diplomatic augmentation, they will most likely be forced to manage similar domestic debates over these issues as those that confronted their predecessors.

Our relationship with democratic India—going from estrangement of the Cold War decades to partnership in the twenty-first century—as it emerges among the world's great powers will likely stand as a defining policy shift, one that we missed in the twentieth century but have pursued in the twenty-first. A strong, powerful India in the volatile Indian Ocean region presents a model of economic and democratic success that stands in contrast to the example set by China, and also creates an Asian balance of power. An "indispensable" partner, to use former President Obama's term, will be an India with which our economy has strong economic links (even as we sort through some challenging disagreements on that front), with which we collaborate closely on critical Indian Ocean and Asia-Pacific concerns, with which we consult frequently about peace and conflict matters around the world, and with which we look to the future together and attempt to shape it.

From my perspective, this all implies a world in which India will be a regular, visible presence in our global economic pursuits, our diplomacy, and our defense and national security considerations. India will expect the world to understand and appreciate its qualities and contributions, while charting its own course for what the exercise of global power should entail. Accommodating India's rise and its desire for a voice in major global institutions that better tracks with its bigger economic and political role will require at times tough diplomacy. It will mean understanding that New Delhi will often prefer a more cautious approach to domestic market opening, to the appropriate diplomatic response to democratic failings in third countries, and to the use of force internationally.

The United States should expect that its playbook for bilateral relationships will require adjustments at every turn when it comes to working with India, as New Delhi will seek to set its own terms rather than blankly agree to set Washington templates. New Delhi is not interested in our "advice," but in a conversation of equals, precisely as it sees itself. The United States should, with this in mind, do a better job preparing our own next generation to understand and work with this complex country as it forges its own path to leadership, making its own place in the world.

ACKNOWLEDGEMENTS

This book has incubated over many years, and I am indebted to many people for their ideas, critiques, hints, tangential asides, and assistance over the duration of its development.

The Council on Foreign Relations is the perfect home to write a book. I would like to thank CFR President Richard N. Haass and Senior Vice President and Director of Studies James M. Lindsay for believing in the ideas contained here, supporting the project all along the way, and asking tough questions that helped me revise for a broader readership. My colleagues in the CFR Asia Program have been great interlocutors: Elizabeth Economy, Sheila Smith, Adam Segal, Josh Kurlantzick, Scott Snyder, Yanzhong Huang, Ely Ratner, and Dan Markey, who is now at Johns Hopkins SAIS. I have also learned much from conversations about trade and immigration with my colleague Ted Alden, and on women and foreign policy from Rachel Vogelstein. Columbia University's Jagdish Bhagwati was a CFR senior fellow when I first arrived at the institution, and I thank him for many conversations over the years about India and its economic growth and challenges. Thanks as well go to CFR Publications Director Patricia Dorff for her interest in and support of the manuscript, and her unfailingly good advice on all matters involving publishing.

About halfway through my work on this book, I had the good fortune to serve as the project director for a timely CFR-sponsored Independent Task Force on U.S. relations with India. I thank the chairmen of the Task Force, Charles R. Kaye and Joseph S. Nye, as well as former CFR Washington program director Chris Tuttle, for helping me to see new angles in the U.S.-India relationship. Feedback and discussions with so many CFR members helped me refine some of these thoughts. I would like especially to thank Ralph Buultjens for his serendipitous gift of all five volumes of the Nehru letters to his chief ministers. Two terrific research associates, Ashlyn Anderson and Samir Kumar, supported my work on this book, helped with background research, and read the manuscript closely over a period of three years.

My agent Lisa Adams at the Garamond Agency saw promise in an earlier proposal for this book, and helped shape it to make it a reality. I am in debt to Oxford University Press's David McBride for thinking the idea had a potential market, and for welcoming the title to OUP. Thank you as well to Jeremy Toynbee of NewGen Publishing, who took the manuscript through production.

Thank you to everyone in India and the United States who has been willing to talk with me about these issues over the years. My original plan included a number of topics that for reasons of space and scope I decided to postpone for a future project. I am grateful to a wide range of thinkers for sharing their views: Reuben Abraham, Sambit Bal, Chandrajit Banerjee, Sanjaya Baru, Hari Bhartia, Shobhana Bhartia, William Bissell, Nicholas Burns, Gurcharan Das, Tarun Das, Swapan Dasgupta, Neelam Deo, Shaurya Doval, Chandraprakash Dwivedi, Meenakshi Ganguly, Anant Goenka, Arnab Goswami, Shekhar Gupta, Manjeet Kripalani, Radha Kumar, Ram Madhav, Anand Mahindra, Ashok Malik, Shivshankar Menon, Sunita Narain, Sevanti Ninan, T.N. Ninan, Nandan Nilekani, Baijayant "Jay" Panda, Kiran Pasricha, Devdutt Pattanaik, Hardeep Singh Puri, S.Y. Quraishi, C. Raja Mohan, Swati Ramanathan, Jairam Ramesh, Nirupama Rao, Manish Sabharwal, Shyam Saran, Sandhya Satwadi, Uday Shankar, Tavleen Singh, Ajay Singha, Sean Sovak, Kumud Srinivasan, Anurag Thakur, Ravi Venkatesan, and Richard Wolff. Needless to say, the pages here reflect only my conclusions, not necessarily any of theirs.

Over the many years I have been involved with U.S. foreign policy toward India, two people have been unfailingly thoughtful guides, sounding boards, and partners in advocating for the importance of strong U.S.-India ties. I would like to thank former ambassador to India Frank G. Wisner, and president *emeritus* of the Chicago Council on Global Affairs Marshall M. Bouton, for their guidance these past two decades. I was lucky enough to stumble into a job at the Asia Society in New York nearly twenty years ago, which allowed me to work for Marshall—at the time the executive vice president of the Society—and staff a newly-formed U.S.-India Roundtable group, which has continued to influence my thinking all these years later. So have many of the people involved in that early endeavor.

Finally, I would like to thank my mother, Linda Ayres, and my husband, Sadanand Dhume, for their love and support throughout the intensive years of research and writing this book. During 2014 I experienced serious health problems, which made everything seem all the more difficult, and I would not have recovered were it not for them.

My father passed away before work on this book began. There are sections of it that would have surprised and interested him. Much of India is so different now from the place he saw when I took him to Delhi, Mumbai, and Bhuj in the summer of 1997. Then again, so is Detroit and the entire auto industry. Maybe he knows all of this, wherever he is.

NOTES

Prologue

1. Jairam Ramesh, *To the Brink and Back: India's 1991 Story* (New Delhi: Rupa, 2015), Kindle ed., loc 826.
2. For historical data, see Subhash Bhatnagar, "India's Software Industry," in *Technology, Adaptation, and Exports: How Some Developing Countries Got It Right* (Washington, DC: World Bank, 2006), 51, http://siteresources. worldbank.org/INTEXPCOMNET/Resources/Chandra_2006.pdf. For the most recent data, see the NASSCOM website, www.nasscom.in
3. International Comparison Program, "Purchasing Power Parities and Real Expenditures of World Economies" (Washington, DC: World Bank, 2014), 81, http://siteresources.worldbank.org/ICPINT/Resources/270056-1183395201801/Summary-of-Results-and-Findings-of-the-2011-International-Comparison-Program.pdf.
4. In 2004–2005, 426 million lived on less than $1.90 per day. By 2011–2012, that figure was 262 million. Figures adjusted using 2011 World Bank poverty line. Poverty data from World Bank Poverty and Equity database; data represents 2002–2012 calculations. See also Ambar Narayan and Rinku Murgai, "Looking Back on Two Decades of Poverty and Well-Being in India," Policy Research Working Paper (Washington, DC: World Bank, April 2016), 16, http://documents.worldbank.org/curated/en/841931468196177423/pdf/WPS7626.pdf.
5. Nirupama Rao, interview with the author, in person, June 26, 2015.
6. Baijayant Panda, interview with the author, in person, August 12, 2015.
7. See Fareed Zakaria, *The Post-American World: Release 2.0* (New York and London: W. W. Norton & Company, 2012), 23.

8. See Narendra Modi, "PM at ASEAN Business and Investment Summit" (Speech, Kuala Lumpur, November 21, 2015), http://www.narendramodi. in/text-of-prime-minister-s-address-at-asean-business-and-investment-summit-376148. See also Manmohan Singh, "PM's Address at McKinsey Meet" (New Delhi, October 23, 2007), http://archivepmo.nic.in/ drmanmohansingh/speech-details.php?nodeid=581.

Chapter 1

1. R. Nicholas Burns, interview with the author, in person, June 12, 2015.
2. Government of India, Ministry of Defence (Navy), "Ensuring Secure Seas: Indian Maritime Security Strategy," Naval Strategic Publication (NSP) 1.2 (New Delhi: Ministry of Defence, October 2015), i.
3. Data for 1990, 2010, and 2015 drawn from International Monetary Fund, "World Economic Outlook Database," October 2015, http://www.imf.org/ external/pubs/ft/weo/2015/02/weodata/index.aspx.
4. U.S. Department of Agriculture, Economic Research Service, "Real GDP (2010 Dollars) Projections" (U.S. Department of Agriculture, December 18, 2015), http://www.ers.usda.gov/data-products/international-macroeconomic-data-set.aspx.
5. International Monetary Fund, "World Economic Outlook: Subdued Demand, Symptoms and Remedies" (International Monetary Fund, October 2016), 2, http://www.imf.org/external/pubs/ft/weo/2016/02/pdf/ c1.pdf.
6. Times News Network, "IMF Slashes India's Growth Forecast to 6.6% from 7.6%," *Times of India*, January 17, 2017.
7. National Institution for Transforming India Aayog, "Creating a Movement for Change" (Civil Services Day, New Delhi, March 26, 2016), Slide 6, http://niti.gov.in/file/1766/download?token=aKU3rta-.
8. UN News Service, "UN Projects World Population to Reach 8.5 Billion by 2030, Driven by Growth in Developing Countries," *UN News Centre*, July 29, 2015, http://www.un.org/apps/news/story.asp?NewsID=51526#.Vt9PT_ krK70.
9. Data from interactive database, selection on "median age": United Nations Department of Economic and Social Affairs, Population Division, "World Population Prospects: The 2015 Revision" (New York: United Nations, July 2015), http://esa.un.org/unpd/wpp/Graphs/DemographicProfiles/.
10. Ibid.
11. Kochhar, "Despite Poverty's Plunge, Middle-Class Status Remains Out of Reach for Many." Press Trust of India, "India's Middle Class Population to Touch 267 Million in 5 Yrs," *Economic Times*, February 6, 2011. Jonathan Ablett et al., "The 'Bird of Gold': The Rise of India's Consumer Market" (Washington, DC: McKinsey Global Institute, May 2007). See the Center for Global Development technical note on the Indian middle class for more detail: Christian Meyer and Nancy Birdsall, "New Estimates of

India's Middle Class: Technical Note" (Washington, DC: Center for Global Development, October 2012), http://www.cgdev.org/doc/2013_MiddleClassIndia_TechnicalNote_CGDNote.pdf.

12. "India Online: The Battle for India's E-Commerce Market Is about Much More than Retailing," *Economist*, March 5, 2016.

13. International Institute of Strategic Studies, "The Military Balance 2017" (Routledge, 2017), 289.

14. Sanjeev Miglani, "Indian Government Aims to Cut Defence Imports, Hold Spending Steady," *Reuters*, February 29, 2016.

15. Amrita Nair-Ghaswalla, "India Is World's Largest Importer of Arms," *BusinessLine*, March 10, 2016.

16. Nan Tian, Aude Fleurant, Pieter Wezeman, and Siemon T. Wezeman, "Trends in World Military Expenditure, 2016," SIPRI Fact Sheet, April 2017. Ranking graphic available via https://www.sipri.org/research/armament-and-disarmament/arms-transfers-and-military-spending/military-expenditure. See also global military expenditure data from International Institute of Strategic Studies, "The Military Balance 2017." Ranking graphic available via https://www.iiss.org/-/media//images/publications/the%20military%20balance/milbal%202017/final%20free%20graphics/mb2017-top-15-defence-budgets.jpg?la=en.

17. Catherine Mavriplis, "When Was the Last Time You Saw Women Scientists Celebrate a Space Mission? Indian Women Celebrate @MarsOrbiter," *Twitter*, September 25, 2014, https://twitter.com/CWSE_ON/status/515192127924752384.

18. "India was home to the largest number of poor in 2012, but its poverty rate is one of the lowest among those countries with the largest number of poor." See Marcio Cruz et al., "Ending Extreme Poverty and Sharing Prosperity: Progress and Policies," Development Economics, Policy Research Note (Washington, DC: World Bank Group, October 2015), 7, http://pubdocs.worldbank.org/en/109701443800596288/PRN03Oct2015TwinGoals.pdf.

19. Narayan and Murgai, "Looking Back on Two Decades of Poverty and Well-Being in India," 3, 16. Also see World Bank database, poverty and equity: http://povertydata.worldbank.org/poverty/country/IND

20. "India's Urban Awakening: Building Inclusive Cities, Sustaining Economic Growth" (McKinsey Global Institute, April 2010).

21. Jim Yardley and Gardiner Harris, "2nd Day of Power Failures Cripples Wide Swath of India," *New York Times*, July 31, 2012.

22. Government of India, National Sample Survey Office, "Swachhta Status Report 2016" (New Delhi: Government of India, Ministry of Statistics and Programme Implementation, 2016), 5. Rama Lakshmi, "India Is Building Millions of Toilets, but That's the Easy Part," *Washington Post*, June 4, 2015.

23. International Labour Organization, "India: Why Is Women's Labour Force Participation Dropping?," Comment and Analysis (International Labour

Organization, February 13, 2013). "Breaking the Glass Ceiling" (Economist Intelligence Unit, April 17, 2015). "India a 'Bright Spot' on Cloudy Global Horizon—Lagarde," *Reuters*, March 16, 2015.

24. Jonathan Woetzel et al., "The Power of Parity: Advancing Women's Equality in India" (Shanghai, Mumbai, San Francisco, Minneapolis, Gurgaon, Stamford: McKinsey Global Institute, November 2015).

25. My first single-author book explored the conundrum of Pakistan's national identity, one assumed to be a coherent nation at its birth yet riven by ethnic divides from the very start. Alyssa Ayres, *Speaking Like a State: Language and Nationalism in Pakistan* (Cambridge and New York: Cambridge University Press, 2009).

26. C. Raja Mohan, interview with the author, in person, May 22, 2015.

27. Press Trust of India, "India Has Begun to Get Its 'Due' on World Stage," *Economic Times*, November 7, 2014.

28. See Ashutosh Varshney, *Battles Half Won: India's Improbable Democracy* (New Delhi: Penguin Global, 2014).

29. John Echeverri-Gent, "Politics in India's Decentered Polity," in *India Briefing: Quickening the Pace of Change* (Armonk, NY: M. E. Sharpe, 2002), 19–53.

30. See http://www.bjp.org/en/about-the-party/history?u=bjp-history

31. See Election Commission of India, "Notification No.56/2016/ PPS-II," December 13, 2016, http://eci.nic.in/eci_main/ElectoralLaws/ OrdersNotifications/year2016/Notification13.12.2016.pdf.

32. "The Democracy Tax Is Rising," *Economist*, December 11, 2008.

33. Stephen P. Cohen and Richard L. Park, *India: Emergent Power?*, Strategy Paper No. 33 (New York: National Strategy Information Center, Inc., 1978), 5.

34. George K. Tanham, "Indian Strategic Thought: An Interpretive Essay" (Santa Monica: RAND, 1992), vii.

35. Rama Lakshmi and Emily Wax, "India's Government Wins Parliament Confidence Vote," *Washington Post*, July 23, 2008.

36. Shekhar Gupta, interview with the author, in person, May 23, 2015.

37. Sunil Khilnani, "India as a Bridging Power," in *India as a New Global Leader*, FPC Publications (London, UK: Foreign Policy Centre, 2005), 88.

38. Shyam Saran, "Premature Power," *Business Standard*, March 17, 2010.

39. Ramachandra Guha, "Superpower Fantasies: India Should Seek Other Goals than Joining a Global Race," *The Telegraph*, September 12, 2009. Ramachandra Guha, "Will India Become a Superpower?," in *India: The Next Superpower?* (London: London School of Economics, 2012). Guha worried about the Naxalite challenge, the degradation of federal institutions, rising inequality, and the media sensationalism, in addition to the three vulnerabilities listed above (p. 15).

40. Guha, "Will India Become a Superpower?," 15.

41. Amitabh Mattoo, *The Reluctant Superpower: Understanding India and Its Aspirations* (Carlton, VIC: Melbourne University Publishing, 2012).

42. Deepa Ollapally, "India: The Ambivalent Power in Asia," *International Studies* 48, no. 3–4 (2011): 201–22.

43. "Modest India Doesn't Try to Reorder the World: NSA," *Rediff.com*, February 4, 2013. Sandeep Dikshit, "We Would Rather Be Called Re-Emerging Powers, Says NSA," *The Hindu*, February 3, 2013.

44. Shivshankar Menon, interview with the author, in person, August 7, 2015.

45. Jairam Ramesh, interview with the author, in person, August 12, 2015.

46. Swapan Dasgupta, interview with the author, in person, August 7, 2015.

47. Ram Madhav, interview with the author, in person, May 19, 2015.

48. See Asian Development Bank, "People's Republic of China: Economy" online fact sheet of the *Asian Development Outlook 2017* (April 2017), www.adb.org/countries/prc/economy.

49. Charles R. Kaye, Joseph S. Nye, Jr., and Alyssa Ayres, "Working with a Rising India: A Joint Venture for the New Century," Independent Task Force Report No. 73 (New York: Council on Foreign Relations Press, November 2015), 4.

50. See the discussion in Chapter 1 of Government of India, Ministry of Finance, Chief Economic Advisor, "Economic Survey of India," Vol. 2 (New Delhi: Government of India, Ministry of Finance, February 2016), 3.

51. KPMG International, "Now or Never: 2016 Global CEO Outlook" (KPMG, June 2016), 34, https://home.kpmg.com/content/dam/kpmg/pdf/2016/06/2016-global-ceo-outlook.pdf.

52. Jawaharlal Nehru, *Letters to Chief Ministers 1947–64*, vol. 2, 1950–52 (New Delhi: Government of India, 1985), 488.

53. Cohen and Park, *India: Emergent Power?*, xiii.

54. Atal Bihari Vajpayee, "Suo Motu Statement by Prime Minister Shri Atal Bihari Vajpayee in Parliament on 27th May, 1998" (Speech, Lok Sabha, Twelfth Series, Session Two, 1998/1920 (Saka), New Delhi, May 27, 1998), http://parliamentofindia.nic.in/ls/lsdeb/ls12/ses2/04270598.htm.

55. Manmohan Singh, "PM's Statement in the Lok Sabha on Civil Nuclear Energy Cooperation with the United States" (Lok Sabha, New Delhi, August 13, 2007), http://archivepmo.nic.in/drmanmohansingh/speech-details.php?nodeid=550. See also Mohammed Iqbal, "Faster Reforms Will Earn Us Our Rightful Place, Says Manmohan," *The Hindu*, May 24, 2005.

56. Raj Chengappa, "Modi's Global Push," *India Today*, September 30, 2015. Original text: लेकिन पिछले कुछ समय से अब लोग यह नहीं कहते हैं कि 21वीं सदी एशिया की सदी है, अब लोग कह रहे हैं कि वीं सदी हिंदुस्तान की सदी है। यह आज दुनिया मानने लगी है! यह बदलाव क्यों आया? यह बदलाव कैसे आया? (मोदी! मोदी! मोदी!) यह बदलाव मोदी, मोदी, मोदी के कारण नहीं आया है। यह बदलाव सवा सौ करोड़ देशवासियों के संकल्प की शक्ति से आया है। सवा सौ करोड़ देशवासियों ने ठान ली है मन में संकल्प कर लिया है कि अब . . . अब हिंदुस्तान पीछे नहीं रहेगा। और जब जनता जनार्दन संकल्प करती है, तो ईश्वर के भी आशीर्वाद

मिलते हैं। सारा विश्व, जो कल तक हिंदुस्तान को हाशिये पर देखता था आज वो हिंदुस्तान को केंद्र-बिंदु के रूप में देख रहा है। See Narendra Modi, "The World Is Recognizing the Power of India because of the Hard Work Done by You: PM Addresses the Indian Diaspora at SAP Centre" (Speech, SAP Center, San Jose, September 27, 2015), http://www.narendramodi.in/ pm-s-address-to-the-indian-community-at-sap-centre-san-jose-354664.

57. Chris Ogden, *Hindu Nationalism and the Evolution of Contemporary Indian Security; Portents of Power*, Oxford International Relations in South Asia Series (New Delhi: Oxford University Press, 2014), 147.

58. Anand Mahindra, interview with the author, in person, August 3, 2015.

59. Shobhana Bhartia, interview with the author, in person, May 20, 2015.

60. Bruce Stokes, "The Modi Bounce: Indians Give Their Prime Minister and Economy High Marks, Worry about Crime, Jobs, Prices, Corruption" (Washington, DC: Pew Research Center, September 2015), 7.

61. Bruce Stokes, "India and Modi: The Honeymoon Continues" (Pew Research Center, September 19, 2016).

62. Steve Crabtree, "Indians Are Optimistic, but Business Challenges Persist" (Washington, DC: Gallup, July 2015).

63. Stokes, "The Modi Bounce," 18.

64. James Crabtree, "Lunch with the FT: Indian TV News Anchor Arnab Goswami," *Financial Times*, May 1, 2015. Oscar Rickett, " 'The Newshour' with Arnab Goswami Is India's Most Over the Top News Show," *Vice.com*, January 6, 2016. Sandeep Bhushan, "TRP Wars: The Battle between News Anchors on Indian Television for the Most Eyeballs Just Got Personal," *The Caravan*, June 24, 2015.

65. Nalin Mehta, *Behind a Billion Screens: What Television Tells Us about Modern India* (New Delhi: HarperCollinsIndia, 2015), 6.

66. Rickett, " 'The Newshour' with Arnab Goswami Is India's Most Over the Top News Show."

67. Arnab Goswami, interview with the author, in person, May 29, 2015.

Chapter 2

1. Shyam Saran, interview with the author, in person, May 20, 2015.

2. For more on Indian cosmology, see Diana L. Eck, *India: A Sacred Geography* (New York: Three Rivers Press, 2012).

3. Ibid., Kindle ed., loc 2541.

4. A considerable scholarly debate exists concerning the authorship of this text and whether it was written by an individual, or compiled over time by many scribes. That said, in practice references to the text in general use nearly always include mention of "Chanakya" or "Kautilya" to indicate the author.

5. See Max Weber, "Politics as a Vocation," in *From Max Weber: Essays in Sociology* (Oxford: Routledge, 1948).

6. For an overview, see Roger Boesche, *The First Great Political Realist: Kautilya and His Arthashastra* (Lanham: Lexington Books, 2003). For its economic prescriptions, see Thomas R. Trautmann, *Arthashastra: The Science of Wealth*, The Story of Indian Business (New Delhi: Penguin Books India, 2012).

7. See the *Yale Book of Quotations* entry for "The enemy of my enemy is my friend." Accessed via iOS app; entry 86.

8. For an excellent summary of the core concepts, see Michael Liebig, "Kautilya's Relevance for India Today," *India Quarterly* 69, no. 2 (June 2013): 99–116.

9. Boesche, *The First Great Political Realist*, Kindle ed., loc 947.

10. Shivshankar Menon, "Developing Indigenous Concepts and Vocabulary: Kautilya's Arthshastra" (Speech, Institute for Defence Studies and Analyses, New Delhi, October 8, 2013), http://idsa.in/keyspeeches/KautilyasArthashastraAmbShivshankarMenonNSA.

11. Trautmann, *Arthashastra: The Science of Wealth*, Kindle edition, foreword.

12. Amrita Narlikar and Aruna Narlikar, *Bargaining with a Rising India: Lessons from the Mahabharata* (Oxford: Oxford University Press, 2014).

13. Deep K. Datta-Ray, *The Making of Indian Diplomacy: A Critique of Eurocentrism* (New York: Oxford University Press, 2015), 109–135.

14. Devdutt Pattanaik, interview with the author, via telephone, September 1, 2015.

15. Devdutt Pattanaik, *Business Sutra: A Very Indian Approach to Management* (New Delhi: Aleph Book Company, 2013), Kindle edition, loc 198 of 4528.

16. Ibid., Kindle edition, loc 522 of 4528.

17. Manjari Chatterjee Miller, *Wronged by Empire* (Palo Alto: Stanford University Press, 2013).

18. The most widely cited writing on self-reliance would be Mohandas K. Gandhi, *Indian Home Rule*, trans. Mohandas K. Gandhi, Hinda Svarāja, xv, 102 p. (Madras: Ganesh & Co., 1922), http://catalog.hathitrust.org/Record/100329241. An upstart politician and founder of the Aam Aadmi Party (Common Man Party), Arvind Kejriwal, self-consciously borrowed the title for his own book in 2012.

19. Mohandas K. Gandhi and Anthony J. Parel, *Gandhi: "Hind Swaraj" and Other Writings*, Cambridge Texts in Modern Politics (Cambridge: Cambridge University Press, 2009).

20. See Ananya Vajpeyi, *Righteous Republic: The Political Foundations of Modern India* (Cambridge, MA: Harvard University Press, 2012), Kindle edition.

21. See Emma Tarlo, *Clothing Matters: Dress and Identity in India* (Chicago: University of Chicago Press, 1996).

22. Press Trust of India, "World's Largest 'Charkha' to Be on Display at IGI Airport," *Times of India*, April 17, 2016.

23. "Asia 1930: Gandhi, Salt, and Freedom," *Economist*, December 31, 1999.

24. Jawaharlal Nehru, "Changing India," *Foreign Affairs* 41, no. 3 (April 1963): 457.

25. Letter dated July 15, 1948 in Jawaharlal Nehru, *Letters to Chief Ministers 1947–64*, vol. 1, 1947–49 (New Delhi: Government of India, 1985), 163.

26. Letter dated May 24, 1953 in Jawaharlal Nehru, *Letters to Chief Ministers 1947–64*, vol. 3, 1952–54 (New Delhi: Government of India, 1987), 310–11.

27. Government of India, Ministry of External Affairs, "Panchsheel" (Government of India, 2004), http://www.mea.gov.in/Uploads/ PublicationDocs/191_panchsheel.pdf. Also Government of India, Ministry of External Affairs, "History and Evolution of Non-Aligned Movement" (Government of India, August 22, 2012), http://mea.gov.in/in-focus-article. htm?20349/History+and+Evolution+of+NonAligned+Movement.

28. Thank you to Reuben E. Brigety II for pointing me to the African Union example. See Musifiky Mwanasali, "The Era of Non-Indifference," *Mail and Guardian*, September 13, 2005. See also Paul D. Williams, "From Non-Intervention to Non-Indifference: The Origins and Development of the African Union's Security Culture," *African Affairs* 106, no. 423 (March 2007): 253–79.

29. See "Midway Plaisance Park" (Chicago Park District, n.d.), http://www. chicagoparkdistrict.com/parks/Midway-Plaisance-Park/.

30. See Walter R. Houghton, ed., *Neely's History of The Parliament of Religions and Religious Congresses at the World's Columbian Exposition* (Chicago, 1893), 64, https://archive.org/details/cu31924029062664.

31. Ibid., 444.

32. From the *Evanston Index,* October 7, 1893, cited in Marie Louise Burke, *Swami Vivekananda in America: New Discoveries* (San Francisco and Calcutta: Vedanta Society of Northern California and Advaita Ashrama, 1958), 102.

33. The single most comprehensive source of information on his American sojourn is Burke, *Vivekananda in America*.

34. On the V Club, see "Thrives on Mystery and Vegetables: First Dinner of the 'V' Club Results in an Enjoyable Evening," *New York Times*, April 1, 1894. On Vivekananda's encounters, see "Had No Meats at the Dinner," *New York Times*, May 2, 1894. "The Social World," *New York Times*, May 3, 1894. "Vivekananda's Address," *Harvard Crimson*, May 17, 1894. On yoga, see Stephanie Syman, "Boston Brahma," *Boston Globe*, August 24, 2003. "Swami Vivekananda, The Great High Priest of India," *Washington Post*, October 27, 1894, 7.

35. Torkel Brekke, "The Conceptual Foundation of Missionary Hinduism," *Journal of Religious History* 23, no. 2 (June 1999): 213.

36. See Swami Vivekananda and Swami Nikhilananda, *Vivekananda: The Yogas and Other Works, including the Chicago Addresses, Jnāna-Yoga, Bhakti-Yoga, Karma-Yoga, Rāja-Yoga, Inspired Talks, and Lectures, Poems and Letters. Chosen and with a Biography by Swami Nikhilānanda.* (New York: Ramakrishna-Vivekananda Center, 1953), 52.

37. See Narendra Modi, "Swami Vivekananda's Call to the Nation," *NarendraModi.in*, January 12, 2012, http://www.narendramodi.in/ swami-vivekananda's-call-to-the-nation-3052.

38. Menon, "Developing Indigenous Concepts and Vocabulary: Kautilya's *Arthshastra*."

39. Dhruva Jaishankar, "How India Sees the World," *The Diplomat*, April 21, 2016, http://thediplomat.com/2016/04/how-india-sees-the-world/.

40. See platform at http://www.swadeshionline.in/content/introduction.

41. This opinion piece from the then general secretary of the Communist Party of India (Marxist) conveys the Left's views on the nuclear deal: Prakash Karat, "Why the CPI(M) and the Left Oppose the Nuclear Deal," *The Hindu*, August 20, 2007.

42. Ruhi Tewari and Krishnamurthy Ramasubbu, "Left Withdraws Support, but Govt Sanguine," *Mint*, July 8, 2008.

43. Montek S. Ahluwalia, "Economic Reforms in India since 1991: Has Gradualism Worked?," *Journal of Economic Perspectives* 16, no. 3 (Summer 2002): 67–88.

44. World Bank data offer two poverty lines: one, a $3.10 a day threshold using 2011 PPP, corresponds to what had been the $2 per day poverty level in 2005 PPP. The extreme poverty threshold is now $1.90 per day using 2011 PPP.

45. Jagdish N. Bhagwati and Arvind Panagariya, *Why Growth Matters: How Economic Growth in India Reduced Poverty and the Lessons for Other Developing Countries* (New York: PublicAffairs, 2013). See also Jean Drèze and Amartya Sen, *An Uncertain Glory: India and Its Contradictions* (Princeton, NJ: Princeton University Press, 2013).

46. For a sense of how this intellectual debate was covered in India at the time, see Pramit Bhattacharya, "Everything You Wanted to Know about the Sen-Bhagwati Debate," *Mint*, July 20, 2013. See also Gardiner Harris, "Rival Economists in Public Battle over Cure for India's Poverty," *New York Times*, August 21, 2013.

47. Sunil Khilnani et al., "Nonalignment 2.0: A Foreign and Strategic Policy for India in the 21st Century" (New Delhi: Centre for Policy Research, February 2012).

48. Thomas Wright, "Non-Alignment Rises from Dustbin of History," *wsj. com, India Real Time (blog)*, (March 22, 2012), http://blogs.wsj.com/indiarealtime/2012/03/22/non-alignment-rises-from-dustbin-of-history/?mod=google_news_blog.

49. See Atal Bihari Vajpayee, "India, USA and the World: Let Us Work Together to Solve the Political-Economic Y2K Problem" (Speech, Asia Society, New York, NY, September 28, 1998), http://asiasociety.org/india-usa-and-world-let-us-work-together-solve-political-economic-y2k-problem.

50. The complete array of India's strategic partnerships can be found by searching the bilateral documents available on http://www.mea.gov.in.

51. Robert D. Blackwill, "Atmospherics of the U.S.-India Relationship," *Indian Defence News*, January 25, 2015.

52. Letter dated July 15, 1948 in Nehru, *Letters to Chief Ministers 1*, 1, 1947–49:163.

53. Bharatiya Janata Party, "Ek Bharat, Shreshtha Bharat: Sab Ka Saath, Sab Ka Vikas. Election Manifesto 2014," May 2014, 40, http://www.bjp.org/images/pdf_2014/full_manifesto_english_07.04.2014.pdf.

54. Narendra Modi, "Embarking on 'Swami Vivekananda Yuva Vikas Yatra': CM Blogs on 9/11," NarendraModi. in, September 11, 2012, http://www.narendramodi.in/ embarking-on-swami-vivekananda-yuva-vikas-yatra'-cm-blogs-on-911-3076.

55. Jawaharlal Nehru, "Message of Swami Vivekananda to Modern India," *Prabudha Bharata*, January 1964, www.VivekanandaArchive. org, http://vivekanandaarchive.org/admin/sv_teach_image/_file_ 7760b13dc738525ac016af78853b7fc5548bb97f.pdf.

56. For information about the ICCR charter and its current board, see http:// www.iccr.gov.in/content/governing-body

57. Government of India, Ministry of External Affairs, *Annual Report 2015–16* (New Delhi: Government of India, 2016), 240, https://mea.gov.in/Uploads/ PublicationDocs/26525_26525_External_Affairs_English_AR_2015-16_ Final_compressed.pdf. See also the continually-updated list of ICCR chairs, available via http://www.iccr.gov.in/content/iccr-chair-abroad.

58. R. K. Radhakrishnan, "Kapilavastu Relics to Be Displayed in Sri Lanka," *The Hindu*, September 11, 2011.

Chapter 3

1. Lawrence H. Summers, "The US-India Economic Relations in the 21st Century" (US-India Business Council Annual Dinner, Washington, DC, June 2, 2010).

2. Calvin Coolidge, "Address to the American Society of Newspaper Editors" (Washington, DC, January 17, 1925), http://www.presidency.ucsb.edu/ws/ ?pid=24180.

3. Sheldon Pollock, "Cosmopolitan and Vernacular in History," *Public Culture* 12, no. 3 (Fall 2000): 603.

4. Thank you to Gurcharan Das and Reuben Abraham for this point. Gurcharan Das, interview with the author, in person, May 20, 2015. See Gurcharan Das, "All the World's Gold," *The Hindu*, August 27, 2011. See also Jake Halpern, "The Secret of the Temple," *New Yorker*, April 30, 2012.

5. Pliny the Elder, *Natural History*, trans. H. Rackham, Loeb Classical Library, vol. II (Cambridge: Harvard University Press, 1942), 417.

6. Via email from Grant Parker, "Question about Pliny the Elder and Gold in India (email)," August 1, 2016. The earliest similar reference I have found uses the phrase "sink of the precious metals" and dates to an 1856 British report: see Colonel Sykes, "The External Commerce of British India during Two Periods of Years; Namely, the Eight Years (Ended 30th April) 1834–35 to 1841–42, and the Five Years 1849–50 to 1853–54," *Journal of the Statistical Society of London* 19, no. 2 (June 1856): 107. Das, "All the World's Gold."

7. Lokesh Chandra, ed., *India's Contribution to World Thought and Culture* (Madras: Vivekananda Rock Memorial Committee, 1970), 101.

8. See http://www.rockmemorial.org/. The Vivekananda Kendra, now managing the rock memorial, kindly granted permission to reproduce this

map. The rock memorial effort was spearheaded by Eknath Ranade, a life-long RSS worker.

9. Manmohan Singh, "Address by PM at the Joint Session of the Two Houses of the Parliament of Ethiopia" (Speech, Addis Ababa, May 26, 2011), http://pib.nic.in/newsite/PrintRelease.aspx?relid=72327.

10. Brackets inserted for clarity. Bharatiya Janata Party, "BJP Election Manifesto 2014," 1.

11. For a thoughtful and concise essay on the East India Company, see William Dalrymple, "The East India Company: The Original Corporate Raiders," *The Guardian*, March 4, 2015.

12. For a helpful quick summary, see "India and the British," UK National Archives (n.d.), http://www.nationalarchives.gov.uk/pathways/blackhistory/india/india_british.htm.

13. Shashi Tharoor, "Viewpoint: Britain Must Pay Reparations to India," *BBC News*, July 22, 2015.

14. Mahesh Murthy, "Facebook Is Misleading Indians with Its Full-Page Ads about Free Basics," *LinkedIn.com*, December 24, 2015, https://www.linkedin.com/pulse/facebook-misleading-indians-its-full-page-ads-free-basics-murthy.

15. See Daniel Yergin and Joseph Stanislaw, *The Commanding Heights: The Battle between Government and the Marketplace* (New York: Simon & Schuster, 1998).

16. Nehru, *Letters to Chief Ministers 1*, 1, 1947–49:78.

17. Jawaharlal Nehru, *Letters to Chief Ministers 1947–64*, vol. 4, 1954–57 (New Delhi: Government of India, 1988), 99–100.

18. Ibid., 4, 1954–57:112.

19. Ramachandra Guha, *Makers of Modern Asia* (Cambridge, MA: Belknap Press of Harvard University Press, 2014), 132.

20. Nehru, *Letters to Chief Ministers 4*, 4, 1954–57:457–59.

21. See Chapter 2, "Approach to the Second Five Year Plan" in Government of India, Planning Commission, "2nd Five Year Plan" (Government of India, Planning Commission, 1956), http://planningcommission.gov.in/plans/planrel/fiveyr/index2.html.

22. The best and most readable accounting of the experience of doing business under the "license-permit raj" is Gurcharan Das, *India Unbound: A Personal Account of a Social and Economic Revolution from Independence to the Global Information Age* (New York: Knopf, 2001). On the schedule of industries under state control, see the 1956 Industrial Policy included as an appendix to Chapter 2 of Government of India, Planning Commission, "2nd Five Year Plan."

23. Arvind Panagariya, *India: The Emerging Giant* (New York: Oxford University Press, 2010), Kindle ed., loc 1576.

24. Paul H. Kreisberg, "India after Indira," *Foreign Affairs* 63, no. 4 (Spring 1985).

25. Panagariya, *India*, Kindle ed., loc 615.

26. A huge literature exists on India's economic history. Two recent comprehensive books that focus on policies and economic growth include Panagariya, *India,* and Bhagwati and Panagariya, *Why Growth Matters.* A debate exists among academics on the question of whether India's 1991 reforms decisively changed the growth trajectory, or whether higher growth began during the 1980s due to a "pro-business" as opposed to a more "pro-market" orientation. See for example Atul Kohli, *Poverty amid Plenty in the New India* (Cambridge and New York: Cambridge Univeristy Press, 2012).

27. Bharat Wariavwalla, "India: From Nehrus' Rule to Coalitions," *Los Angeles Times,* December 10, 1989.

28. For a day-by-day first-hand account of the June to August 1991 period, see Ramesh, *To the Brink and Back,* Kindle ed., loc 826. Also "20 Tons of Gold Sold by India," *New York Times,* June 7, 1991.

29. Ramesh, *To the Brink and Back,* Kindle ed., loc 826.

30. Ibid., Kindle ed., loc 843.

31. Complete speech available via "JPRS Report, Near East and South Asia, India [JPRS-NEA-91-044]" (Foreign Broadcast Information Service, August 6, 1991), 26–27, http://handle.dtic.mil/100.2/ADA336171.

32. Bernard Weinraub, "Economic Crisis Forcing Once Self-Reliant India to Seek Aid," *New York Times,* June 29, 1991.

33. Ibid.

34. See the entire list at: Government of India, Department of Industrial Policy and Promotion, "Press Note No. 10 (1992 Series), Revised List of Annex III Items" (Government of India, Department of Industrial Policy and Promotion, June 24, 1992), reproduced as pages 11-16 in http://eaindustry. nic.in/industrial_handbook_200809.pdf.

35. See Government of India, Ministry of Commerce and Industry, Department of Industrial Policy and Promotion, Office of the Economic Advisor, "Statement on Industrial Policy, July 24, 1991" in *Handbook of Industrial Policy and Statistics* 2003-2005 (Government of India, Department of Industrial Policy and Promotion, 2005).

36. Panagariya, *India,* Kindle ed., loc 2768.

37. "Rediff.com in Strong Debut," *CNNMoney.com,* June 14, 2000.

38. Tarun Das, "India: The Unfinished Agenda" (Panel discussion, Asia Society, New York, May 21, 1999).

39. The G6 economies: France, Germany, Italy, Japan, United Kingdom, United States. Dominic Wilson and Roopa Purushothaman, "Dreaming with BRICs: The Path to 2050," Global Economics Paper No. 99 (New York: Goldman Sachs, October 2003), http://www.goldmansachs. com/our-thinking/archive/archive-pdfs/brics-dream.pdf.

40. Government of India, Ministry of Commerce and Industry, "India Brand Equity Foundation: About Us," *Commerce.nic.in,* 2016, http:// commerce.gov.in/InnerContent.aspx?Id=248. See also Tarun Das, *Crossing Frontiers: The Journey of Building CII* (New Delhi: Lustra Print, 2015), 82.

41. Telecom Regulatory Authority of India data reported 52 million wireless subscribers in March 2005, and more than one billion by February 2016. See Telecom Regulatory Authority of India, "Annual Report 2005–2006" (Government of India, Telecom Regulatory Authority of India, September 2006), 31, http://www.trai.gov.in/sites/default/files/ar_05_06.pdf. See also Telecom Regulatory Authority of India, "Press Release No. 26/2016, Information Note to the Press," April 26, 2016, http://www.trai.gov.in/sites/default/files/Press_Release_n026_eng_14_26-04-2016.pdf.

42. Indian numbers use crores, a unit of ten million. Mehta puts India's advertising industry at INR 930 crore in 1990–1991 and INR 37,104 crore by 2014. In U.S. dollars, this would be around $516 million in 1991 to $6.08 billion by 2014 using average annual exchange rates. See Mehta, *Behind a Billion Screens*, 73.

43. This paragraph draws from Mehta, *Behind a Billion Screens,* and from Daya Kishan Thussu, "Privatizing the Airwaves: The Impact of Globalization on Broadcasting in India," *Media, Culture & Society* 21, no. 1 (January 1999): 127.

44. "List of Permitted Private Satellite TV Channels as on 31.03.2017" (Government of India, Ministry of Information and Broadcasting, March 31, 2017), http://mib.nic.in/sites/default/files/Master_List_of_Permitted_Private_Sattellite_TV_Channels_as_on_31-03-2017.pdf.

45. Uday Shankar, interview with the author, in person, May 27, 2015.

46. James Crabtree, "India's Times Now News Channel to Launch in UK," *Financial Times*, November 15, 2015. Urvi Malvania, "STAR India to Take Hotstar Global," *Business Standard*, March 31, 2016.

47. On WION, see DNA Webdesk, "Zee Media's New Global English News Channel to Be Called WION," *DNA*, March 15, 2016, http://www.dnaindia.com/money/report-zee-media-s-new-global-english-news-channel-to-be-called-wion-2189476. On Arnab Goswami, see Rajiv Kumar, "When PM Narendra Modi Echoed Arnab Goswami's Vision," *Financial Express*, November 3, 2016.

48. Years later, Rahul Bajaj, long said to be the leader of the "Bombay Club," said that in the early 1990s his concern was not to prevent an influx of foreign imports once tariffs were slashed, but rather that Indian industry— burdened with constraints on labor, high interest, and poor infrastructure— could not be as competitive. See Rahul Bajaj, "Riding Out the Licence Raj," *Business Standard*, October 27, 2014.

49. Nandan Nilekani, *Imagining India* (Toronto: Viking Canada, 2008). iBook edition.

50. Rahul Bajaj, "Creating Indian MNCs: India Must Take Its Rightful Place among the Economic Powers of the World," *Frontline*, August 9, 1997.

51. "Jaguar Land Rover Reports Strong Full Year Global Sales for 2015," *JaguarLandRover.com*, January 8, 2016, http://www.jaguarlandrover.com/gl/en/investor-relations/news/2016/01/08/

jaguar-land-rover-reports-strong-full-year-global-sales-for-2015/. See also Vikas Bajaj, "Tata Motors Finds Success in Jaguar Land Rover," *New York Times*, August 30, 2012.

52. Mahindra, interview with the author. Also see "Certificate of Incorporation" (Mahindra and Mahindra, 1952), http://www.mahindra.com/resources/pdf/history/Certificate-of-Incorporation.pdf.

53. Assuming revenues of Rs. 1,250 crore in 1991, and a 1991 exchange rate of Rs. 18 to $1. See Kushan Mitra, "Top Gun," *Business Today*, October 2, 2011.

54. See http://www.mahindra.com/about-us

55. Amberish K. Diwanji, "Geo-Political Issues Set to Dominate Proposed Gas Pipeline from Iran to India," *Rediff.com*, April 13, 2000.

56. See "The Reliance Story" and "Founder Chairman" via http://www.ril.com/.

57. See Government of India, Ministry of Finance, Chief Economic Advisor, "Economic Survey of India," 166. On the GDP share of textiles, see Government of India, Ministry of Textiles, "Annual Report 2016–2017" (Government of India, 2017), 1. On chemicals, see Government of India, Ministry of Chemicals and Fertilizers, "Annual Report 2014–2015" (Government of India, Ministry of Chemicals and Fertilizers, 2015), 5.

58. Ravi Venkatesan, interview with the author, via telephone, October 1, 2015.

59. Mahindra, interview with the author.

60. "Delhi in Davos: How India Built Its Brand at the World Economic Forum," *Knowledge@Wharton*, February 22, 2006, http://knowledge.wharton.upenn.edu/article/delhi-in-davos-how-india-built-its-brand-at-the-world-economic-forum/.

61. Nandan Nilekani, interview with the author, in person, August 10, 2015.

62. Hari Bhartia, interview with the author, in person, May 21, 2015.

63. Das, *Crossing Frontiers: The Journey of Building CII*, 111–15. See also http://anantaaspencentre.in/track_II_dialogue.aspx.

64. Government of India, "Cabinet Secretariat Resolution No. 511/2/1/2015" (Gazette of India, January 1, 2015), http://niti.gov.in/writereaddata/files/cabinet-resolution_EN.pdf.

65. Indrani Bagchi, "Overseas Missions Need to Boost Trade: Narendra Modi," *Times of India*, March 26, 2014.

66. Suhasini Haidar, "MEA to Oversee Foreign Investments in States," *The Hindu*, October 25, 2014.

67. Mahindra, interview with the author.

68. Bhagwati and Panagariya, *Why Growth Matters*, 109–124.

69. See Bangladesh Garment Manufacturers and Exporters Association, "Trade Information," *BGMEA.com.bd*, 2016, http://bgmea.com.bd/home/pages/TradeInformation. Also see Banikinkar Pattanayak, "India Likely to Miss Its Garment Export Target for Current Fiscal," *Financial Express*, January 21, 2016.

70. Sujoy Dhar, "Millions Strike in India to Protest against Modi's Labor Reforms," *Reuters*, September 2, 2015.

71. "Millions of Workers Strike for Better Wages in India," www.dw.com, *Deutsche Welle*, (September 2, 2016), http://www.dw.com/en/millions-of-workers-strike-for-better-wages-in-india/a-19522682.

Chapter 4

1. Government of India, Prime Minister's Office, "PM to Heads of Indian Missions" (Press Information Bureau, Government of India, February 7, 2015), http://pib.nic.in/newsite/PrintRelease.aspx?relid=115241.

2. S. Jaishankar, "India, the United States, and China" (Speech, International Institute for Strategic Studies, Fullerton Lecture, Singapore, July 20, 2015), http://mea.gov.in/Speeches-Statements.htm?dtl/25493/IISS_Fullerton_Lecture_by_Foreign_Secretary_in_Singapore.

3. S. Jaishankar, "Remarks by Foreign Secretary at the Release of Dr. C. Raja Mohan's Book 'Modi's World: Expanding India's Sphere of Influence'" (Speech, Launch of Modi's World, New Delhi, July 17, 2015), http://mea.gov.in/Speeches-Statements.htm?dtl/25491/Remarks_by_Foreign_Secretary_at_the_release_of_Dr_C_Raja_Mohans_book_Modis_WorldExpanding_Indias_Sphere_of_InfluencequotJuly_17_2015.

4. See minute 18:35 of S. Jaishankar, "India-U.S. 2015: Partnering for Peace and Prosperity" (Speech, Vivekananda International Foundation, March 16, 2015), http://www.vifindia.org/speeches-video/2015/march/19/india-u-s-2015-partnering-for-peace-and-prosperity-2. See a summary of the February 2015 prime ministerial outline: Government of India, Prime Minister's Office, "PM to Heads of Indian Missions."

5. Vajpayee, "Suo Motu Statement by Prime Minister Shri Atal Bihari Vajpayee in Parliament on 27th May, 1998."

6. See Manmohan Singh, "Of Oxford, Economics, Empire, and Freedom," *The Hindu*, July 10, 2005. See also Simon Denyer, "Singh Says He's No Lame Duck and India Is Not a 'Scam-Driven Country,'" *Washington Post*, February 16, 2011.

7. हाशिये पर देखता था आज वो हिंदुस्तान को केंद्र-बिंदु के रूप में देख रहा है। Modi, "PM Addresses the Indian Diaspora."

8. See the fascinating working paper from the Wilson Center's Cold War history project: Anton Harder, "Not at the Cost of China: New Evidence Regarding US Proposals to Nehru for Joining the United Nations Security Council," Cold War International History Project (Washington, DC: Woodrow Wilson International Center for Scholars, March 2015), 5–6.

9. Government of India, Ministry of External Affairs, "Indian Diplomacy at Work: Our View—UN Security Council Reforms" (New Delhi, 2014), 3, https://mea.gov.in/Portal/CountryNews/3018_Indian_Diplomacy_At_Work.pdf.

10. "Four Nations Launch UN Seat Bid," *BBC News*, September 22, 2004.

11. Government of India, Ministry of External Affairs, "Joint Press Statement at the Meeting of Leaders of the G-4 countries—Brazil, Germany, India, and

Japan—on United Nations Security Council Reform," September 26, 2015, http://www.mea.gov.in/bilateral-documents.htm?dtl/25849/Joint_Press_ Statement_at_the_Meeting_of_Leaders_of_the_G4_countries_Brazil_ Germany_India_and_Japan__on_United_Nations_Security_Council_ Reform.

12. Hardeep Singh Puri speaking on Barkha Dutt, "A 'Four'midable Bid for UN Security Council: G4 Gamechanger?," *The Buck Stops Here* (NDTV, September 26, 2015), http://www.ndtv.com/video/player/the-buck-stops-here/a-four-midable-bid-for-un-security-council-g4-gamechanger/ 384508.

13. Rakesh Mohan and Muneesh Kapur, "Emerging Powers and Global Governance: Whither the IMF?," IMF Working Paper (Washington, DC: International Monetary Fund, October 2015), 7–8, http://www.imf. org/external/pubs/ft/wp/2015/wp15219.pdf.

14. Press Trust of India, "Jaitley Seeks Reform in IMF, World Bank," *Business Standard*, April 18, 2016.

15. Bill Curry, Richard Blackwell, and Brian Milner, "India Leads Emerging-Market Charge at G20," *The Globe and Mail*, September 4, 2013. Also Puja Mehra, "India to Hold G20 Chair in 2018, Delhi May Play Host," *The Hindu*, October 1, 2015.

16. Lord Curzon of Kedleston, *The Place of India in the Empire,* cited in C. Raja Mohan, *Crossing the Rubicon: The Shaping of India's New Foreign Policy* (New York: Palgrave Macmillan, 2004), 205.

17. Ibid., 210.

18. S. Jaishankar, "Remarks by Foreign Secretary at Indian Ocean Conference" (Speech, India Foundation Indian Ocean Conference, Singapore, September 1, 2016), http://www.mea.gov.in/Speeches-Statements.htm?dtl/ 27356/Remarks_by_Foreign_Secretary_at_Indian_Ocean_Conference_ September_01_2016.

19. Government of India, Indian Navy, "Ports Visited since Aug 15," Twitter. com, @*IndianNavy*, (September 2, 2016), https://twitter.com/indiannavy/ status/771875619072118785.

20. Government of India, Ministry of Defence, "Annual Report 2002–2003" (New Delhi: Ministry of Defence, 2003), 26–27, https://www.files.ethz.ch/ isn/15049/MOD-English2003.pdf.

21. Rahul Roy-Chaudhry, "India's Official Maritime Strategy," IISS. org, *IISS Voices*, (December 14, 2015), https://www.iiss.org/en/ iiss%20voices/blogsections/iiss-voices-2015-dda3/december-5c5a/ indias-official-maritime-security-strategy-e6a0.

22. Pramit Pal Chaudhuri, "New Delhi at Sea: The China Factor in the Indian Ocean Policy of the Modi and Singh Governments," *Asia Policy*, no. 22 (July 2016): 27–34.

23. Government of India, Ministry of Defence (Navy), "Ensuring Secure Seas: Indian Maritime Security Strategy," ii.

24. Narendra Modi, "Text of the PM's Remarks on the Commissioning of Coast Ship Barracuda" (Speech, Port Louis, Mauritius, March 12, 2015), http://www.narendramodi.in/text-of-the-pms-remarks-on-the-commissioning-of-coast-ship-barracuda-2954.

25. Government of India, Press Information Bureau, "Government to Establish Cross Cultural Linkages with 39 Indian Ocean Countries under Project Mausam," www.indiaculture.nic.in, *Ministry of Culture*, (March 9, 2015), http://www.indiaculture.nic.in/sites/default/files/press_release/Project%20Mausam.pdf.

26. Pranav Kulkarni, "To Counter China, Govt Pushes Naval Exports to Small Indian Ocean Nations," *Indian Express*, March 4, 2015.

27. Kallol Bhattacherjee, "Seychelles Committed to Indian Naval Base," *The Hindu*, December 23, 2015.

28. Ajai Shukla, "New Stealth Destroyer Launched, yet Navy Faces Major Fleet Shortfalls," *Broadsword*, September 18, 2016, http://ajaishukla.blogspot.in/2016/09/new-stealth-destroyer-launched-yet-navy.html.

29. David Tweed and N. C. Bipindra, "Submarine Killers: India's $61 Billion Warning to China," *Bloomberg*, July 28, 2015.

30. Nick Childs, "China and India—Indigenous Carrier Comparison," *IISS.org, Military Balance Blog*, (February 9, 2016), http://www.iiss.org/en/militarybalanceblog/blogsections/2016-629e/february-foed/china-and-india-indigenous-carrier-comparison-562b. Also Jamie Seidel, "India Eyes Russian Aircraft Carrier as Its Fourth Step towards Super Power Status," *News Corp Australia Network*, March 4, 2016. For specifics on U.S.-India carrier cooperation, see Ashley J. Tellis, "Making Waves: Aiding India's Next-Generation Aircraft Carrier," *CarnegieEndowment.org*, April 22, 2015, http://carnegieendowment.org/2015/04/22/making-waves-aiding-india-s-next-generation-aircraft-carrier.

31. Tweed and Bipindra, "Submarine Killers: India's $61 Billion Warning to China."

32. Unfortunately the bogeyman of "lots [of] children fathered by these often unruly high-spirited American soldiers" was a real criticism. See Bharat Karnad, "LEMOA—A Most Serious Strategic Mistake, and Consequences," *Security Wise*, August 30, 2016, https://bharatkarnad.com/2016/08/30/lemoa-a-most-serious-strategic-mistake-and-consequences/.

33. Jaswant Singh, "Against Nuclear Apartheid," *Foreign Affairs* 77, no. 5 (October 1998): 41–52.

34. Strobe Talbott, *Engaging India: Diplomacy, Democracy, and the Bomb* (Washington, DC: Brookings Institution Press, 2004), 3–4.

35. Terry Miller and Anthony B. Kim, "India," in *2017 Index of Economic Freedom* (Heritage Foundation, 2017), http://www.heritage.org/index/country/india.

36. International Chamber of Commerce, *ICC Open Markets Index*, 3rd ed. (Paris: International Chamber of Commerce, 2015).

37. Hiau Looi Kee, Alessandro Nicita, and Marcelo Olarreaga, "Dataset, Trade Restriction Indices 2009" (World Bank, 2012), http://go.worldbank.org/FG1KHXSP30. See also Zixuan Huang, Nicholas R. Lardy, and Melina Kolb, "China is Not the Most Highly Protectionist Big Country," *PIIE.com, PIIE Charts (blog)*, (June 21, 2017), https://piie.com/research/piie-charts/china-not-most-highly-protectionist-big-country

38. Former U.S. trade representative Susan Schwab has written eloquently about the colliding challenges in the multilateral arena. See Susan C. Schwab, "After Doha," *Foreign Affairs* 90, no. 3 (May/June 2011): 104–17.

39. I wrote about this at the time at *Asia Unbound*: Alyssa Ayres, "India: Tough Talk and the Bali Trade Facilitation Agreement," *CFR.org, Asia Unbound (blog)*, (July 29, 2014), http://blogs.cfr.org/asia/2014/07/29/india-tough-talk-and-the-bali-trade-facilitation-agreement/.

40. Puja Mehra, "India's Stand Prevails in Bali," *The Hindu*, December 7, 2013.

41. Nirmala Sitharaman, "Statement by Nirmala Sitharaman in Lok Sabha Regarding 'India's Stand in the WTO'" (Lok Sabha, New Delhi, August 5, 2014), http://pib.nic.in/newsite/PrintRelease.aspx?relid=107999.

42. Shawn Donnan, "Dealmaker in Charge at the WTO Faces Tough Fight," *Financial Times*, December 2, 2014.

43. "USCIS To Implement H-1B Visa Reform Act of 2004" (U.S. Citizenship and Immigration Services, U.S. Department of Homeland Security, December 9, 2004), https://www.uscis.gov/sites/default/files/files/pressrelease/H-1B_12_9_04.pdf.

44. Sarah Ashley O'Brien, "High-Skilled Visa Applications Hit Record High—Again," *CNNMoney.com*, April 12, 2016. Also Miriam Jordan, "Demand for H1-B Skilled-Worker Visas Forces Agency into Lottery," *Wall Street Journal*, April 7, 2016.

45. See reports from 2004, 2006, 2008, 2010, 2012, and 2014, available via www.uscis.gov: U.S. Citizenship and Immigration Services, "Characteristics of H-1B Specialty Occupation Workers," Annual Report to Congress (Washington, DC: U.S. Department of Homeland Security).

46. This illustrative example is just one of dozens from 2010 on: Nayanima Basu, "India to Resume Visa Fee Hike Dispute with US in WTO," *Business Standard*, November 4, 2013.

47. "United States—Measures concerning Non-Immigrant Visas; Request for Consultations by India (S/L/410; WT/DS503/1)" (World Trade Organization, March 8, 2016).

48. Edward Alden, "India's Landmark WTO Challenge to US," *Nikkei Asian Review*, March 15, 2016.

49. Saritha Rai, "The High Stakes of India's Dispute with the U.S. over Visa Fees," *Bloomberg Business*, March 20, 2016.

50. ". . . हमारे पूर्वज तो सांप के साथ खेलते थे, लेकिन हम Mouse के साथ खेलते हैं। हमारे नौजवान Mouse को घुमाते हैं, सारी दुनिया को डुलाते हैं।" Narendra Modi, "Address to Indian Community at Madison Square Garden, New York" (Speech,

New York, NY, September 28, 2014), http://www.narendramodi.in/
text-of-prime-minister-shri-narendra-modi-s-address-to-indian-community-
at-madison-square-garden-new-york-292061.

51. See Julia Preston, "Pink Slips at Disney. But First, Training Foreign
Replacements," *New York Times*, June 3, 2015. Julia Preston, "Large
Companies Game H-1B Visa Program, Costing the U.S. Jobs," *New York
Times*, November 10, 2015. Haeyoun Park, "How Outsourcing Companies
Are Gaming the Visa System," *New York Times*, November 10, 2015.

52. Arun S., "Commerce Minister Complains of 'Sledging' in Trade Talks," *The
Hindu*, May 2, 2016.

53. Prakash Karat, "The Indo-US Nuclear Deal: Struggle to Defend National
Sovereignty," *The Marxist*, September 2007, 5–6.

54. See Bharatiya Janata Party, "Indo-US Nuclear Deal: Why Does BJP Oppose
It?" (Bharatiya Janata Party, 2008), iii, 15, http://www.bjp.org/images/
upload/other_publications/indo_us_deal_e.pdf.

55. मेरा सवाल है कि जो कारखाना बना है, जो फिक्स्ड एसेट है, जिसे आप उठा कर एक स्थान से
दूसरे स्थान नहीं ले जाएंगे, उस पर कैसे वैरीफिकेशन होगा? वहां आन दि स्पाट ही इंस्पेक्शन हो
सकता है। इसमें सबसे चिंता का विषय यह है कि तीसरे मलकों से भी हम जो सामान मंगाते हैं,
उसमें अगर अमरीकी ड्यूअल यूज़ आइटम लगा हुआ है, तो उसका भी इंस्पेक्शन करने का
अधिकार अमरीका ले लेता है कि हमने रूस से मंगाया, हमने ब्राज़ील से मंगाया, फ्रांस से मंगाया। वे
कहेंगे कि हम इनका भी इंस्पेक्शन करेंगे कि इनका सही इस्तेमाल हो रहा है या गलत इस्तेमाल हो
रहा है। Yashwant Sinha intervention (in Hindi): "Lok Sabha, Fifteenth Series,
Vol. III, Second Session, 2009/1931 (Saka)" (Parliament of India, July 21,
2009), 48–49, http://164.100.47.132/debatestext/15/II/2107.pdf.

56. The State Department's most recently available report to the U.S. Congress
on end use monitoring refers to checks conducted in seventy-nine countries.
U.S. Department of State, "End-Use Monitoring of Defense Articles and
Defense Services Commercial Exports FY 2014" (U.S. Department of
State, 2015), 2, http://www.pmddtc.state.gov/reports/documents/End_Use_
FY2014.pdf.

57. "Lok Sabha, Fifteenth Series, Vol. III, Second Session, 2009/1931
(Saka)," 53.

58. अमेरिका के साथ अच्छे रिश्तों के पक्षधर रहे हैं, लेकिन . . . दोस्ती के स्तर पर रिश्ते चाहते हैं,
दासता के स्तर पर नहीं। Sushma Swaraj, Ibid., 147.

59. This article is illustrative of what must be hundreds along similar lines: "US
Pushes India to Ink Contentious Defence Pacts," *Times of India*, February
27, 2015. See the opinion piece arguing against the "American hug" from a
thoughtful nonpartisan policy opinion leader: Pratap Bhanu Mehta, "The
American Hug," *Indian Express*, April 2, 2016.

60. Ashton Carter and Manohar Parrikar, "Joint Press Conference by Secretary
Carter and Minister Parrikar in the Pentagon Briefing Room" (Transcript,
Washington, DC, August 29, 2016), http://www.defense.gov/News/
Transcripts/Transcript-View/Article/929778/joint-press-conference-by-
secretary-carter-and-minister-parrikar-in-the-pentago.

61. Admiral Harry B. Harris, "'Let's Be Ambitious Together'" (Speech, Raisina Dialogue, New Delhi, March 2, 2016). See also Dinakar Peri, "No Scope for India-U.S. Joint Patrols at This Time: Parrikar," *The Hindu*, March 5, 2016.

62. Anjana Pasricha, "India Rejects Joint Naval Patrols with US in South China Sea," *VOA News*, March 11, 2016.

63. Incidentally, Gujarati—not Hindi—is Modi's first language. India has no singular national language. Hindi and English are the two "official" languages of India for central government and link use among the states, and an additional twenty-two languages are recognized in the eighth schedule of the Indian constitution. Aditya Kalra and Shyamantha Asokan, "Modi's Push for Hindi Struggles to Translate in Some States," *Reuters*, June 19, 2014, India edition.

64. Pranab Dhal Samanta, "No More English, Modi Chooses Hindi for Talks with Foreign Leaders," *Indian Express*, June 5, 2014.

65. By now the term "HMT" is fairly widely recognized in India due to this column: Shekhar Gupta, "The HMT Advantage," *Zee News*, February 15, 2003.

66. For example, see: White House, Office of the Press Secretary, "Vision Statement for the U.S.-India Strategic Partnership—'Chalein Saath Saath: Forward Together We Go,'" September 29, 2014, https://www.whitehouse.gov/the-press-office/2014/09/29/vision-statement-us-india-strategic-partnership-chalein-saath-saath-forw. And White House, Office of the Press Secretary, "U.S.-India Joint Statement साँझा प्रयास - सबका विकास"— 'Shared Effort; Progress for All,'" January 25, 2015, https://www.whitehouse.gov/the-press-office/2015/01/25/us-india-joint-statement-shared-effort-progress-all.

67. Original: योग हमारी पुरातन पारम्परिक अमूल्य देन है। Narendra Modi, "Text of the PM's Statement at the United Nations General Assembly" (Speech, UN General Assembly, New York, September 27, 2014), http://www.narendramodi.in/text-of-the-pms-statement-at-the-united-nations-general-assembly-6660.

68. Chidanand Rajghatta, "Narendra Modi Calls for International Yoga Day," *Times of India*, September 28, 2014.

69. Government of India, Prime Minister's Office, "PM to Heads of Indian Missions."

70. Sixty-ninth session United Nations General Assembly, "Resolution Adopted by the General Assembly on 11 December 2014, 69/131. International Day of Yoga," December 11, 2014, http://www.un.org/en/ga/search/view_doc.asp?symbol=A/RES/69/131.

71. Embassy of India, Washington, DC, "Press Release—'First International Day of Yoga Celebrated in the United States,'" June 21, 2015, https://www.indianembassy.org/informations.php?id=427. On the Congressional resolution, see Tulsi Gabbard, *H.Res.328–114th Congress. Commemorating the*

Inaugural "'International Yoga Day'" on June 21, 2015, https://www.gpo.gov/fdsys/pkg/BILLS-114hres328ih/pdf/BILLS-114hres328ih.pdf.

72. "World Sufi Forum to Spread Islamic Message of Peace, PM Modi to Attend Event in Delhi," *Indian Express*, March 1, 2016.

73. Narendra Modi, "Speech at Launch of World Sufi Forum" (Speech, World Sufi Forum, New Delhi, March 17, 2016), http://www.narendramodi.in/pm-modi-at-the-world-islamic-sufi-conference-in-new-delhi-428276.

Chapter 5

1. Nehru, "Changing India," 458.

2. Central Tibetan Administration, "About CTA," *Tibet.net*, accessed October 6, 2016, http://tibet.net/about-cta/.

3. See Alyssa Ayres, "China's Mixed Messages to India," CFR.org, *Asia Unbound (blog)*, (September 17, 2014), http://blogs.cfr.org/asia/2014/09/17/chinas-mixed-messages-to-india/. The post drew upon Indian Home Ministry data released to parliament in response to a question from a member (Unstarred question 3776 submitted August 13, 2014); the data is retrievable through the Rajya Sabha integrated search form at http://164.100.47.5/QSearch/qsearch.aspx. See also Express News Service, "Border Transgressions by China Down: ITBP." *Indian Express*. October 25, 2016, http://indianexpress.com/article/india/india-news-india/border-transgressions-by-china-down-itbp-3101323/.

4. See William Burr, ed., "China, Pakistan, and the Bomb: The Declassified File on U.S. Policy, 1977–1997," March 5, 2004, National Security Archive, http://nsarchive.gwu.edu/NSAEBB/NSAEBB114/.

5. See T. N. Srinivasan, "Economic Reforms and Global Integration," in *The India-China Relationship: What the United States Needs to Know*, ed. Francine R. Frankel and Harry Harding (Washington, DC: Woodrow Wilson Center Press, 2004), 219–66.

6. David Sanger, "U.S. Exploring Deal to Limit Pakistan's Nuclear Arsenal," *New York Times*, October 15, 2015.

7. C. Christine Fair has explored Pakistan's strategic culture in depth. See C. Christine Fair, *Fighting to the End: The Pakistan Army's Way of War* (New York: Oxford University Press, 2014).

8. N. C. Bipindra, "India Nears Completion of Nuclear Triad with Armed Submarine," *Bloomberg*, February 25, 2016.

9. White House, Office of the Press Secretary, "Statement by NSC Spokesperson Ned Price on National Security Advisor Susan E. Rice's Call with National Security Advisor Ajit Doval of India," September 28, 2016, https://www.whitehouse.gov/the-press-office/2016/06/07/joint-statement-united-states-and-india-enduring-global-partners-21st.

10. Government of India, Ministry of External Affairs, "India and United Nations Peacekeeping and Peacebuilding," *Permanent Mission of India to the UN*, n.d., https://www.pminewyork.org/pages.php?id=1985.

11. "Hailed as 'Role Models,' All-Female Indian Police Unit Departs UN Mission in Liberia," *UN News Centre*, February 12, 2016, http://www.un.org/apps/news/story.asp?NewsID=53218#.Vw1oh2OoC-I.

12. *India and United Nations Peacekeeping* (New York: Permanent Mission of India to the United Nations, 2015), https://www.pminewyork.org/slide_book/peace_keeping/#p=10.

13. This is a long-simmering issue for India with the UN Security Council. For a recent example, see Press Trust of India, "India Hits Out at UN Security Council over Lack of Transparency in Peacekeeping Operations," *Indian Express*, October 13, 2015.

14. See Gary J. Bass, *The Blood Telegram: Nixon, Kissinger, and a Forgotten Genocide* (New York: Knopf, 2013).

15. Sanjoy Hazarika, "Indian Troops End Coup in Maldives," *New York Times*, November 5, 1988.

16. Alyssa Ayres, "Why the United States Should Work with India to Stabilize Afghanistan," Policy Innovation Memorandum No. 53 (New York: Council on Foreign Relations Press, April 2015).

17. "India Rejects Iraq Troop Request," *BBC News*, July 14, 2003.

18. UN voting data compiled from annual U.S. Department of State reports to Congress, "Voting Practices in the United Nations"; see years 2011 through 2015, all available via www.state.gov. On the UN Human Rights Council, see the India data page on HRW's Votes Count tool: Human Rights Watch, "Country Datacard, Human Rights Council Voting Record: India," *VotesCount*, 2016, http://votescount.hrw.org/page/India.

19. Permanent Mission of India to the United Nations, Geneva, "Statement on Agenda Item 4 General Debate: Human Rights Situation That Requires the Council's Attention, September 16, 2014" (Government of India, Ministry of External Affairs, September 16, 2014), http://www.pmindiaun.org/pages.php?id=983.

20. Security Council Meetings Coverage, "Security Council Approves 'No-Fly Zone' over Libya, Authorizing 'All Necessary Measures' to Protect Civilians, by Vote of 10 in Favour with 5 Abstentions" (United Nations, March 17, 2011). See also Barbara Platt, "UN Security Council Middle Powers' Arab Spring Dilemma," *BBC News*, November 8, 2011.

21. Hardeep Singh Puri, interview with the author, in person, June 8, 2015.

22. See http://www.ibsa-trilateral.org.

23. "UN Security Council Presidential Statement, S/PRST/2011/16" (United Nations, August 3, 2011), https://documents-dds-ny.un.org/doc/UNDOC/GEN/N11/442/75/PDF/N1144275.pdf?OpenElement.

24. Government of India, Ministry of External Affairs, "IBSA Delegation Calls On President Assad to Discuss Situation" (Government of India, Ministry of External Affairs, August 11, 2011), http://ibsa.nic.in/president_assad.htm.

25. "Security Council Fails to Adopt Draft Resolution on Syria as Russian Federation, China Veto Text Supporting Arab League's Proposed Peace

Plan," *UN Security Council Meetings Coverage*, February 4, 2012, http://
www.un.org/press/en/2012/sc10536.doc.htm.

26. "Resolution Adopted by the Human Rights Council* S-19/1, The
Deteriorating Situation of Human Rights in the Syrian Arab Republic,
and the Recent Killings in El-Houleh" (UN Human Rights Council,
June 4, 2012), http://www.ohchr.org/Documents/HRBodies/HRCouncil/
SpecialSession/Session19/A-HRC-RES-S-19-1_en.pdf.

27. Ishaan Tharoor, "India Leads Rescue of Foreign Nationals, Including
Americans, Trapped in Yemen," *Washington Post*, April 8, 2015. Also
Embassy of the United States, Sana'a, "Emergency Message for U.S.
Citizens—Updated Departure Options" (U.S. Department of State, April 6,
2015), http://yemen.usembassy.gov/messages040615.html.

28. Devirupa Mitra, "Ukraine Requests India to Support New Government in
Kiev," *New Indian Express*, March 4, 2014.

29. Government of India, Ministry of External Affairs, Office of the
Spokesperson, "We Are Closely Watching Fast Evolving Situation and
Hope for a Peaceful Resolution," *Twitter*, March 3, 2014, https://twitter.
com/MEAIndia/status/440712830900137984. "Russian Interests in Crimea
'legitimate': India," *Times of India*, March 7, 2014.

30. World Bank data bank, percent rural population, 1960 to 2014. Via data.
worldbank.org.

31. Saumya Tewari, "Rural India Continues To Outvote Urban India,"
Indiaspend.com, May 30, 2014.

32. I have followed this issue very closely for years, beginning in my role from
2008 to 2010 as founding director of McLarty Associates' India and South
Asia practice, where we advised companies, including Walmart, on the
investment environment in India. For the 2006 opening, see: Government
of India, Ministry of Commerce & Industry, and Department of
Industrial Policy & Promotion, "Press Note No. 4 (2006 Series)
Subject: Rationalisation of the FDI Policy" (Government of India, Ministry
of Commerce and Industry, February 10, 2006), http://dipp.nic.in/sites/
default/files/pn4_2006_0.pdf.

33. Mathew Joseph et al., "Impact of Organized Retailing on the Unorganized
Sector," Working Paper No. 222 (New Delhi: Indian Council for Research
on International Economic Relations, September 2008), http://icrier.org/
pdf/Working_Paper222.pdf.

34. Ashish Tripathi, "Rahul Gandhi Promoting FDI to Benefit
Foreigners: Mayawati," *Times of India*, November 26, 2011.

35. Press Trust of India, "I'll Set Walmart Store Afire: Uma," *The Hindu*,
November 26, 2011.

36. I wrote about the "flip-flops" at the time: Alyssa Ayres, "A Closer Look at
FDI Flip-Flopping in India," CFR.org, *Asia Unbound (blog)*, (February 4,
2014), http://blogs.cfr.org/asia/2014/02/04/a-closer-look-at-fdi-flip-flopping-
in-india/.

37. World Bank, "India: Foreign Trade Policy," *web.worldbank.org* (2007), http://go.worldbank.org/RJEB2JGTC0.

38. Alyssa Ayres, "Five Questions for Professor Jagdish Bhagwati on the Indian Economy and Prime Minister Modi's Next Steps," *CFR.org, Asia Unbound (blog)*, (May 27, 2014), http://blogs.cfr.org/asia/2014/05/27/five-questions-for-professor-jagdish-bhagwati-on-the-indian-economy-and-prime-minister-modis-next-steps/.

39. Anil Padmanabhan, "We Should Have Done What We Have in Half the Time: Montek Singh Ahluwalia," *Mint*, February 5, 2016.

40. For a discussion on the strategic benefits to India from a more extensive economic relationship with the United States, including through deeper trade, see Ashley J. Tellis and C. Raja Mohan, "The Strategic Rationale for Deeper U.S.-Indian Economic Ties" (Washington, DC: Carnegie Endowment for International Peace, 2015).

41. Data on Indian FTAs completed and underway from Government of India, Ministry of Commerce and Industry, email communication of May 15, 2017. For an older but still useful compendium, see Kirtika Suneja, "PMO Push: Commerce Ministry Plans to Set Up Dedicated Team for Trade Talks," *Economic Times*, April 11, 2016, New Delhi edition.

42. Sruthisagar Yamunan, "Centre to Review All FTAs and SEZs," *The Hindu*, June 14, 2014.

43. See C. Fred Bergsten, "India's Rise: A Strategy for Trade-Led Growth," PIIE Briefing (Washington, DC: Peterson Institute for International Economics, September 2015), 4, 18, http://www.iie.com/publications/briefings/piieb15-4.pdf.

44. "China Cautiously Welcomes Trans-Pacific Free Trade Deal," *BBC News*, October 6, 2015.

45. Sarah Wheaton, "Obama: China Might Join Trade Deal—eventually," *Politico*, June 3, 2015.

46. Bergsten, "India's Rise: A Strategy for Trade-Led Growth," 8.

47. "New Foreign Trade Policy: $900 Bn Exports by FY20," *Indian Express*, April 2, 2015.

48. Suhasini Haidar, "Trading Bloc to India: Cut Tariffs or Exit FTA Talks," *The Hindu*, April 20, 2016.

49. For example, this article: Manoj Kumar, "With TPP Advancing, India Pins Hopes on China-Backed Trade Bloc," *Reuters*, February 11, 2016, India edition.

50. Chandrajit Banerjee, interview with the author, in person, May 22, 2015.

51. Government of India, Ministry of Finance, Chief Economic Advisor, "Economic Survey of India," 129.

52. Embassy of India, Washington, DC, "Press Release—In Response to a Media Query on Visa to USCIRF Visit," March 4, 2016, https://www.indianembassy.org/press_detail.php?nid=2338. On the 2009 denial, see Chidanand Rajghatta, "India Denies Visa to U.S. Religious Freedom Watchdogs," *Times of India*, June 17, 2009.

53. Abhinav Bhatt, "Home Ministry Sends Nirbhaya Documentary Ban Order to BBC," *NDTV.com*, March 5, 2015.

54. Emphasis mine; he delivered the last sentence in Hindi: इंडिया का नाम बाहर बदनाम नहीं होना चाहिए। "Lok Sabha, Sixteenth Series, Vol. VII, Fourth Session, 2015/1936 (Saka)" (Parliament of India, March 4, 2015), 62, http://164.100.47.132/debatestext/16/IV/0403.pdf.

55. "Rajya Sabha, Two-Hundred and Thirty-Fourth Session, Uncorrected Verbatim Debate Transcript" (Parliament of India, March 4, 2015), 39, http://164.100.47.5/newdebate/234/04032015/Fullday.pdf.

56. Mohandas K. Gandhi, "Drain Inspector's Report," *The United States of India*, February 1928, reprint of 1927 "Young India" essay edition, South Asian American Digital Archive.

57. See http://fcraonline.nic.in FAQ, Introduction to FCRA, 2010.

58. Government of India, Ministry of Home Affairs, Foreigners Division, "F.No.II/21022/58(0047)/2013-FCRA(MU)-461-1. ORDER" (Government of India, September 2, 2015), https://fcraonline.nic.in/home/PDF_Doc/Greenpaece%20India%20Society2_040915.PDF. See also Rupam Jain Nair and Frank Jack Daniel, "Interview: India Warns Global Charities Not to Work against Government," *Reuters*, October 1, 2015.

59. "Madras High Court Stays Cancellation of Greenpeace India's Registration," *Times of India*, November 21, 2015.

60. Suhasini Haidar, "Crackdown on NGOs Worries US," *The Hindu*, May 7, 2015.

61. Meenakshi Ganguly, interview with the author, in person, May 18, 2015.

62. "Whataboutism," *Economist*, January 31, 2008, http://www.economist.com/node/10598774.

63. "United Nations Democracy Fund, Contribution Table" (United Nations, April 25, 2017), http://www.un.org/democracyfund/contribution-table.

64. "India Election: World's Biggest Voting Event Explained," *BBC News*, April 9, 2014.

65. Election Commission of India, "Press Release No. 491/Media/5/2011: ECI to Set Up Indian Institute of Democracy and Election Management" (Election Commission of India, January 24, 2011), http://eci.nic.in/eci_main1/current/PN24012011.pdf. See also Government of India, Prime Minister's Office, "Inauguration the Construction of IIIDEM New Campus at Dwarka" (Press Information Bureau, Government of India, January 25, 2016), http://pib.nic.in/newsite/PrintRelease.aspx?relid=135786. See also IIIDEM Campus Brochure.

66. S. Y. Quraishi, interview with the author, in person, August 8, 2015. On ITEC, India has provided technical training and assistance to other global South countries since 1964 through this program.

67. Ganguly, interview with the author.

68. "UN Adopts Resolution on Sri Lanka War Crimes Probe," *BBC News*, March 22, 2012. "UN Passes Resolution against Sri Lanka Rights Record," *BBC News*, March 21, 2013.

69. Nick Cumming-Bruce, "UN Approves Investigation of Civil War in Sri Lanka," *New York Times*, March 27, 2014. See also India's explanation of

vote: Permanent Mission of India to the UN, Geneva, "India's Explanation of Vote Before the Vote on the Draft Resolution 'Promoting Reconciliation, Accountability, and Human Rights in Sri Lanka', Agenda Item 2, at the 25th Session of the Human Rights Council" (Government of India, Ministry of External Affairs, March 27, 2014), http://www.pmindiaun.org/pages.php?id=903.

70. Government of India, Ministry of External Affairs, "Statement on the Situation in Nepal" (Government of India, September 20, 2015), http://www.mea.gov.in/press-releases.htm?dtl/25821/Statement+on+the+situation+in+Nepal.

71. S. N. Vijetha, "Court Relief for Greenpeace Activist Priya Pillai," *The Hindu*, March 13, 2015.

Chapter 6

1. Modi, "Swami Vivekananda's Call to the Nation."

2. Indrani Bagchi, "India's NSG Bid Stops at China Wall," *Times of India*, June 24, 2016.

3. See paragraph fifty-one of White House, Office of the Press Secretary, "U.S.-India Joint Statement साँझा प्रयास—सबका विकास"—'Shared Effort; Progress for All.'"

4. Alex Barker and Pilita Clark, "India Slows Progress on Ambitious Climate Change Accord," *Financial Times*, November 18, 2015.

5. See also Alyssa Ayres, "India at Paris—Working with a Rising India," *Energy, Security, and Climate*, December 9, 2015, http://blogs.cfr.org/levi/2015/12/09/alyssa-ayres-india-at-paris-working-with-a-rising-india/.

6. Press Trust of India, "India Hopes for a Climate Deal as High-Stakes Paris Talks Head for Final Phase," *Times of India*, December 6, 2015.

7. Government of India, Ministry of External Affairs, "About BRICS," *BRICSIndia2016*, n.d., http://brics2016.gov.in/content/innerpage/about-usphp.php.

8. BRICS, "Joint Statement of the BRIC Countries Leaders (First BRICS Summit)" (Yekaterinburg, Russia, June 16, 2009), en.kremlin.ru/supplement/209. BRICS, "II BRIC Summit—Joint Statement" (Brasilia, Brasil, April 16, 2010), http://brics.itamaraty.gov.br/category-english/21-documents/66-second-summit. "Sanya Declaration," April 14, 2011. BRICS, "Delhi Declaration and Action Plan (4th BRICS Summit)" (New Delhi, India, March 29, 2012), http://brics.itamaraty.gov.br/category-english/21-documents/68-fourth-summit. BRICS, "BRICS and Africa: Partnership for Development, Integration and Industrialisation (Fifth BRICS Summit)" (Durban, South Africa, March 27, 2013), http://brics5.co.za/fifth-brics-summit-declaration-and-action-plan/. BRICS, "The 6th BRICS Summit: Fortaleza Declaration" (Fortaleza, Brazil, July 5, 2014), http://brics6.itamaraty.gov.br/media2/press-releases. BRICS, "VII

BRICS Summit: 2015 Ufa Declaration" (Ufa, Russia, July 9, 2015), http://
en.brics2015.ru/documents/.

9. "About the NDB," New Development Bank BRICS, *NDBBRICS.org*,
   (n.d.), http://ndbbrics.org.

10. Government of India, Press Information Bureau, "Agreement on the New
    Development Bank and the BRICS Contingent Reserve Agreement,"
    Press Information Bureau, February 25, 2015, http://pib.nic.in/newsite/
    PrintRelease.aspx?relid=115907.

11. Oliver Stuenkel, "The Uncertain Future of IBSA," Rising Democracies
    Network (Washington, DC: Carnegie Endowment for International
    Peace, February 18, 2015), http://carnegieendowment.org/2015/02/18/
    uncertain-future-of-ibsa-pub-59108.

12. On China and the AIIB, see Daniel W. Drezner, "Anatomy of a Whole-
    of-Government Foreign Policy Failure," *WashingtonPost.com, Spoiler Alerts
    (blog)*, (March 27, 2015), https://www.washingtonpost.com/posteverything/
    wp/2015/03/27/anatomy-of-a-whole-of-government-foreign-policy-failure/.

13. "IMF Board Approves Far-Reaching Governance Reforms" (International
    Monetary Fund, November 5, 2010), http://www.imf.org/external/pubs/ft/
    survey/so/2010/NEW110510B.htm.

14. S. R., "Why China Is Creating a New 'World Bank' for Asia," *economist.
    com, The Economist Explains (blog)*, (November 11, 2014), http://www.
    economist.com/blogs/economist-explains/2014/11/economist-explains-6.

15. "English Rendering of Prime Minister Shri Narendra Modi's Remarks at the
    East Asia Summit" (Speech, East Asia Summit, Nay Pyi Taw, November 13,
    2014), http://www.narendramodi.in/english-rendering-of-prime-minister-
    shri-narendra-modis-remarks-at-the-east-asia-summit-nay-pyi-taw-6881.

16. See Government of India, Ministry of External Affairs, "Conference
    on Interaction and Confidence Building Measures in Asia (CICA)"
    (Government of India, Ministry of External Affairs, October 2013), http://
    www.mea.gov.in/Portal/ForeignRelation/Conference_on_Interaction_and_
    Confidence_Building_Measures_in_Asia__1_.pdf.

17. People's Republic of China, Ministry of Foreign Affairs, "The 5th Meeting
    of CICA Ministers of Foreign Affairs Held in Beijing" (People's Republic of
    China, Ministry of Foreign Affairs, April 28, 2016), http://www.fmprc.gov.
    cn/mfa_eng/zxxx_662805/t1360242.shtml.

18. Press Trust of India, "India, Pakistan Become Full SCO Members," *The
    Hindu*, July 11, 2015.

19. See www.iora.net and also Nirupama Subramanian, "Indian Ocean
    Countries Meet to Focus on Trade Ties," *The Hindu*, July 4, 2013.

20. Salman Khurshid, Julie Bishop, and Marty Natalegawa, "Putting Out to Sea
    a New Vision," *The Hindu*, November 2, 2013.

21. See www.ions.gov.in.

22. Jaishankar, "Remarks by Foreign Secretary at Indian Ocean Conference."

23. "Brief: Regional Integration in South Asia," *WorldBank.org* (October 9, 2015), http://www.worldbank.org/en/region/sar/brief/south-asia-regional-integration.

24. See also Alyssa Ayres, "Modi Doubles Down on the Neighborhood," *YaleGlobal*, June 10, 2014, http://yaleglobal.yale.edu/print/9312.

25. "Pak-India Trade Still a Fraction of $40 Billion Potential," *Express Tribune*, March 13, 2012.

26. Mohsin Khan, "Realising the Potential of India-Pakistan Trade," *East Asia Forum*, March 20, 2016, http://www.eastasiaforum.org/2016/03/20/realising-the-potential-of-india-pakistan-trade/.

27. Ashlyn Anderson and Alyssa Ayres, "Economics of Influence: China and India in South Asia," Expert Brief (Washington, DC: Council on Foreign Relations, August 7, 2015), http://www.cfr.org/economics/economics-influence-china-india-south-asia/p36862.

28. My thinking on lessons for the future of Indian power from the cricket world order first appeared in *The Octavian Report,* from which portions are reprinted, with modifications and updates, with permission. See Alyssa Ayres, "How You Play the Game: Cricket, World Order, and India's Rise," *Octavian Report*, August 2015, http://octavianreport.com/article/how-you-play-the-game-cricket-world-order-and-the-rise-of-india/.

29. "ICC Set to Say Goodbye to Lord's," *BBC Sport*, July 28, 2005.

30. Russell Wolff, interview with the author, in person, May 12, 2015.

31. Boria Majumdar, "How Cricket Was Sold in India," *Open Magazine*, April 14, 2012.

32. Anurag Thakur, interview with the author, in person, May 21, 2015.

33. Sambit Bal, interview with the author, in person, May 26, 2015.

34. Jimmy Smallwood, "ICC Meeting in Dubai Discusses Proposed Changes to Test Cricket," *BBC Sport*, January 28, 2014, http://www.bbc.com/sport/cricket/25927581.

35. Press Trust of India, "BCCI Threatened to Form Parallel World Cricket Body," *ESPNCricinfo.com*, June 7, 2014.

36. Venkat Ananth, "How BCCI Became the 800-Pound Gorilla of Cricket," *Mint*, December 9, 2014.

37. Shankar, interview with the author.

38. On the 2017 backlash, see Nagaraj Gollapudi, "BCCI Outvoted in Crucial Vote on ICC Constitution," *ESPNCricinfo.com*, April 26, 2017. See also Ananth, "How BCCI Became the 800-Pound Gorilla of Cricket."

Chapter 7

1. Amar K. J. R. Nayak, "FDI Model in Emerging Economies: Case of Suzuki Motor Corporation in India," *Journal of the American Academy of Business, Cambridge* 6 (March 2005): 239.

2. Data from Government of India, Ministry of Electronics and Information Technology, "Fact Sheet of IT & BPM Industry," April 7, 2017, http:// meity.gov.in/content/fact-sheet-it-bpm-industry.

3. Government of India, Ministry of Textiles, "Annual Report 2016–2017," 1.

4. Employment data from World Bank dataset, percent employment in agriculture (2010) and agriculture value added, percent of GDP (2015), *data. worldbank.org.*

5. World Bank Group, "Economy Rankings," *Doing Business 2017*, October 2016, http://www.doingbusiness.org/Rankings.

6. In a convoluted matter involving World Bank index arcana, India appeared to leapfrog twelve places from the 2015 published ranking (142) to its 130 slot in the 2016 editions, but that bump up also reflected a rebasing of the index in tandem with improvements in India. Under the rebased ranking, India's former 142 slot of the 2015 index rose to 134, although the index was published as 142 and then revised later. So it is also true to say that India improved only four notches between the 2015 and 2016 editions, if using the rebased rank of 134. To complicate matters further, the 2016 ranking of 130 was later revised downward to 131, so India's 2017 ranking of 130 marked either a one-notch gain or a steady state, depending on the version of the index.

7. World Bank, "Doing Business 2017: Equal Opportunity for All" (Washington, DC: World Bank, 2017), 26. See also Klaus Schwab and Xavier Sala-i-Martín, *Global Competitiveness Report* (Geneva: World Economic Forum, 2016), 7, 17.

8. Dani Rodrik, "Premature Deindustrialization," NBER Working Paper Series (Cambridge, MA: National Bureau of Economic Research, February 2015), http://www.nber.org/papers/w20935.pdf.

9. Ruchir Sharma, *The Rise and Fall of Nations: Forces of Change in the Post-Crisis World*, Kindle (New York and London: W. W. Norton & Company, 2016), loc 916, 944.

10. Gladys Lopez-Acevedo and Raymond Robertson, "Stitches to Riches? : Apparel Employment, Trade, and Economic Development in South Asia.," Directions in Development—Poverty (Washington, DC: World Bank, 2016).

11. Noshir Kaka et al., "India's Ascent: Five Opportunities for Growth and Transformation" (Brussels, San Francisco, Shanghai: McKinsey Global Institute, August 2016). "India's Labour Market: A New Emphasis on Gainful Employment," Discussion Paper, McKinsey Global Institute, June 2017, 17.

12. Raymond Zhong, "Fixing Indian Railways, the Not-So-Little Engine That Could," *Wall Street Journal*, October 6, 2016.

13. Manu Balachandran and Itika Sharma Punit, "Timeline: 200 Years of India's Struggle with Land Acquisition Laws," *Quartz India*, August 5, 2015, http:// qz.com/471117/timeline-200-years-of-indias-struggle-with-land-acquisition-laws/.

14. Neha Thirani Bagri, "Narendra Modi, India's Leader, Moves to Reshape Labor Rules," *New York Times*, October 16, 2014.

15. Rama Lakshmi, "India's Rajasthan State Eases Labor Laws to Spur Investment in Manufacturing," *Washington Post*, January 31, 2015.

16. Ibid.

17. Kaka et al., "India's Ascent," 15.

18. Times News Network, "Govt Brings in Labour Reforms via Rs 6,000cr Textile Pkg," *Times of India*, June 23, 2016.

19. Arun S., "Rs. 6,000 Crore Special Package for Textiles," *The Hindu*, June 22, 2016.

20. On growth in textile and garment exports, see Press Trust of India, "Textile Ministry Finalizing Draft Guidelines of National Textiles Policy," *Economic Times*, June 5, 2017. See Bangladesh Garment Manufacturers and Exporters Association, "Trade Information." Also see Pattanayak, "India Likely to Miss Its Garment Export Target for Current Fiscal."

21. Tommy Wilkes and Manoj Kumar, "India to Renew Labor Law Overhaul Drive to Boost Jobs," *Reuters*, September 22, 2016. On demonetization, see "Government of India—Effective Implementation of Key Fiscal and Banking Sector Reforms Would Address Core Credit Challenges," Issuer In-Depth, Moody's Investors Service, May 31, 2017.

22. "India Beats South Korea to Become the World's No. 5 Auto Producer," *The Korea Herald*, September 25, 2016.

23. Anil Sasi, "Maruti Suzuki 800: The Car with No Name," *Financial Express*, February 23, 2014.

24. Nayak, "FDI Model in Emerging Economies: Case of Suzuki Motor Corporation in India," 240.

25. On Sundram, see Sushila Ravindranath, "Quality Matters for Success," *The Hindu*, January 12, 2000. This was the first Indian company to receive the ISO 9000 quality standards certification, in 1990.

26. See the global vehicle production statistics via Organisation Internationale des Constructeurs d'Automobiles (OICA), *www.oica.net/category/production-statistics*. The United States uniquely produces more "light commercial vehicles" than cars, but the comparison is still illustrative.

27. Society of Indian Automobile Manufacturers, "Automotive Mission Plan: 2016–26 (A Curtain Raiser)" (New Delhi: Society of Indian Automobile Manufacturers, September 2015), 5.

28. Mahindra, interview with the author.

29. See Society of Indian Automobile Manufacturers, "AMP 2026," 3–5. All production data via Organisation Internationale des Constructeurs d'Automobiles (OICA), *www.oica.net*.

30. Government of Gujarat, "Business: Major Industries," *Gujarat: Official Gujarat State Portal*, n.d., http://www.gujaratindia.com/business/major-indus.htm.

31. Anand Adhikari, "Supersize Gujarat," *Business Today*, January 23, 2011.

32. Kel Kearns, Discussion with the author, in person, May 28, 2015.

33. "Ford India Celebrates Figo Aspire Job 1 at Ford's Sanand Plant,"
    @FordOnline, June 14, 2015, http://www.at.ford.com/news/cn/Pages/
    Ford%20India%20Celebrates%20Figo%20Aspire%20Job%201%20at%20
    Ford's%20Sanand%20Plant.aspx.

34. Brent Snavely and Greg Gardener, "Automakers Sell Record 17.55 million
    Vehicles in U.S. in 2016," *Detroit Free Press,* January 4, 2017; Phoenix
    Kwong, "China Car Sales Surge at Fastest Rate in Three Years," *South China
    Morning Post*, January 12, 2017.

35. "Hirotec Starts Manufacturing Facility in Coimbatore," *The Hindu*,
    October 20, 2011.

36. Kearns, Discussion with the author.

37. Confederation of Indian Industry and EY, "Making India a World Class
    Automotive Manufacturing Hub" (New Delhi: Confederation of Indian
    Industry and EY, February 6, 2016).

38. Kim Hill et al., "Contribution of the Automotive Industry to the
    Economies of All Fifty States and the United States" (Ann Arbor,
    MI: Center for Automotive Research, January 22, 2015), 1.

39. Josh Bivens, "Updated Employment Multipliers for the U.S. Economy,"
    Working Paper (Washington, DC: Economic Policy Institute, August 2003),
    5, http://www.epi.org/files/page/-/old/workingpapers/epi_wp_268.pdf.

40. Government of India, National Skill Development Corporation, "Human
    Resource and Skill Requirements in the Auto and Auto Components Sector
    (2013–17, 2017–22)" (New Delhi: Government of India, Ministry of Skill
    Development and Entrepreneurship, July 2015), iv, http://www.nsdcindia.
    org/sites/default/files/files/Auto-and-Auto-Components.pdf.

41. Society of Indian Automobile Manufacturers, "AMP 2026."

42. T. N. Ninan, *The Turn of the Tortoise: The Challenge and Promise of India's
    Future* (New Delhi: Allen Lane [Penguin], 2015), 110–111.

43. Nayak, "FDI Model in Emerging Economies: Case of Suzuki Motor
    Corporation in India."

44. Government of India, Department of Industrial Policy and Promotion,
    "Quarterly Fact Sheet: Fact Sheet on Foreign Direct Investment
    (FDI) From April 2000 to December 2016" (Government of India,
    December 2016), 1, http://dipp.gov.in/sites/default/files/FDI_FactSheet_
    OctoberNovemberDecember2016.pdf

45. United Nations Conference on Trade and Development, "Global
    Investment Trends Monitor" (Geneva: UNCTAD, January 20, 2016),
    http://unctad.org/en/PublicationsLibrary/webdiaeia2016d1_en.pdf.

46. Courtney Fingar, "India Knocks China from Top of FDI League Table,"
    FT.com, *EM Squared (blog)*, (April 20, 2016), http://on.ft.com/1QmSaXH.
    See also Courtney Fingar, ed., "The fDi Report 2017: Global Greenfield
    Investment Trends." *fDi Intelligence*, 6. http://forms.fdiintelligence.com/
    report2017/thankyou.php (registration required to access link.)

47. IANS, "Xiaomi Unveils Second Manufacturing Unit in India in Partnership with Foxconn," *News18.com*, March 20, 2017. BI India Bureau, "Nokia's New Phones Will Be Made in India, Thanks to Foxconn's Expansion Plan," *Business Insider*, October 23, 2016, India edition. Huawei, "Huawei Starts Smartphone Manufacturing in India." Huawei India, New Delhi, September 23, 2016.

48. "China's Richest Man Plans $10 Billion India Development Project," *Bloomberg News*, January 22, 2016. See Ruchika Chitravanshi, "Dalian Wanda's $10 billion Haryana Project on the Verge of Being Pulled Out over Equity Share Row." *Economic Times*. April 28, 2017.

49. Press Trust of India, "Lenovo Says Half the Smartphones Sold in India in 2016 Will Be Locally Made," *Gadgets360.NDTV.com*, February 2, 2016.

50. " 'Make in India' Racks up $222 Billion in Pledges," *Times of India*, February 19, 2016.

51. "Reforming Indian Banks: Bureaucrats at the Till," *Economist*, June 4, 2016.

52. "Government of India—Baa3 Positive," Credit Opinion Quarterly Update (New York: Moody's Investors Service, October 7, 2016).

53. Sanjib Kr Baruah, "India Can Become the World's HR Capital: PM Modi at 'Skill India' Launch," *Hindustan Times*, July 16, 2015. For Modi's speech (in Hindi), see Narendra Modi, "Text of PM's Remarks at the Launch of 'Skill India' " (Speech, National Skill Development Mission Launch, New Delhi, July 15, 2015), http://www.narendramodi.in/text-of-pm-s-remarks-at-the-launch-of-skill-india--206108.

54. Sandrine Rastello, "India to Emerge as Winner from Asia's Shrinking Labor Force," *Bloomberg*, November 8, 2015.

55. Press Trust of India, "India's Unemployment Rate Highest in 5 Years in 2015–16," *Indian Express*, September 29, 2016. See Table 14 in Volume 1 of Government of India, Ministry of Labour and Employment, Labour Bureau, *Report on Employment-Unemployment Survey* 2015-16, September 2016. The 5 percent unemployment rate for all of India masks enormous regional, gender, and rural-urban variation. In addition, the results reflect a one-year lag time for publication. The survey fielded for this publication was carried out between April and December 2015.

56. See the long discussion in "India's Labour Market: A New Emphasis on Gainful Employment," 4-10.

57. This discussion and following paragraphs are based on a wide-ranging discussion with Manish Sabharwal, interview with the author, in person, August 10, 2015.

58. Manish Sabharwal, "Making India Job-Friendly," *Mint*, August 1, 2014.

59. Ernst and Young, "India Transforming Through Radical Reforms," (February 2017), 5. On the TeamLease example, see www.netap.in. On overall figures, see Anjuli Bhargava, "We Don't Have a Magic Wand to Create Jobs: Rohit Nandan, Ministry of Skill Development," *Business Standard*, October 24, 2016.

Chapter 8

1. See Frank G. Wisner remarks beginning around minute 11:05, in "The New Geopolitics of China, India, and Pakistan: Keynote Session" (YouTube video, from a symposium streamed live by the Council on Foreign Relations, May 4, 2016), https://www.youtube.com/watch?v=cgcBKFVH85Y.

2. U.S. Department of State Office of the Spokesman, "Background Briefing by Administration Officials on U.S.-South Asia Relations," *U.S. Department of State Archive*, March 25, 2005, http://2001-2009.state.gov/r/pa/prs/ps/2005/43853.htm.

3. SelectUSA, "Foreign Direct Investment (FDI): INDIA" (U.S. Department of Commerce, 2016), https://www.selectusa.gov/servlet/servlet.FileDownload?file=015t0000000LKMV.

4. Burns, interview with the author.

5. See Alyssa Ayres, "How Americans See India as a Power," CFR.org, *Asia Unbound (blog)*, (September 15, 2015), http://blogs.cfr.org/asia/2015/09/15/how-americans-see-india-as-a-power/.

6. See Dina Smeltz, Ivo Daalder, and Craig Kafura, "Foreign Policy in the Age of Retrenchment," Results of the 2014 Chicago Council Survey of American Public Opinion and US Foreign Policy, Chicago Council Surveys (Chicago: Chicago Council on Global Affairs, 2014), 35, http://survey.thechicagocouncil.org/survey/2014/_resources/ChicagoCouncilSurvey.pdf. See also Marshall M. Bouton et al., "Constrained Internationalism: Adapting to New Realities," Results of a 2010 National Survey of American Public Opinion, Chicago Council Surveys (Chicago: Chicago Council on Global Affairs, 2010), 60–61, http://www.thechicagocouncil.org/sites/default/files/Global%20Views%202010.pdf. Data for 2016 and prior to 2008 via personal communication, Chicago Council on Global Affairs.

7. Ibid., 18, 59.

8. Dina Smeltz et al., "America Divided: Political Partisanship and U.S. Foreign Policy," Results of the 2015 Chicago Council Survey of American Public Opinion and U.S. Foreign Policy, Chicago Council Surveys (Chicago: Chicago Council on Global Affairs, September 2015), 47.

9. Ibid., 48.

10. U.S. Department of State, "The Global Coalition to Counter ISIL," n.d., http://www.state.gov/s/seci/.

11. I was honored to serve as project director for this Task Force during 2015. Its findings and recommendations reflect the wisdom of a collective. See Kaye, Nye, Jr., and Ayres, "Working with a Rising India," 28.

12. Alyssa Ayres, "Bringing India Inside the Asian Trade Tent," Policy Innovation Memorandum No. 46 (New York: Council on Foreign Relations Press, June 2014). For trade data, see U.S. Department of Commerce, Bureau of Economic Analysis, "U.S. Trade in Goods and Services by

Selected Countries and Areas, 1999-Present (Excel)" (U.S. Department of Commerce, June 2, 2017), http://www.bea.gov/international/.

13. See also Tellis and Mohan, "The Strategic Rationale for Deeper U.S.-Indian Economic Ties."

14. Ayres, "Bringing India Inside the Asian Trade Tent."

15. See Organization for Economic Cooperation and Development, "Active With India" (Paris: OECD, 2015).

16. See http://www.iea.org/aboutus.

17. See International Energy Agency, "India Energy Outlook" (Paris: OECD/ IEA, November 2015).

18. Andrew H. Card et al., "U.S. Trade and Investment Policy," Independent Task Force Report No. 67 (New York: Council on Foreign Relations Press, 2011).

19. Steven Mufson, "New Energy on India," *Washington Post*, July 18, 2006.

20. White House, Office of the Press Secretary, "U.S.-India Joint Strategic Vision for the Asia-Pacific and Indian Ocean Region," January 25, 2015, https://www.whitehouse.gov/the-press-office/2015/01/25/ us-india-joint-strategic-vision-asia-pacific-and-indian-ocean-region.

21. Burns, interview with the author.

22. White House, Office of the Press Secretary, "Joint Statement: The United States and India: Enduring Global Partners in the 21st Century," June 7, 2016, https://www.whitehouse.gov/the-press-office/2016/06/07/ joint-statement-united-states-and-india-enduring-global-partners-21st.

23. Nan Tian, Aude Fleurant, Pieter Wezemen, and Siemon Wezemen, "Trends in World Military Expenditure, 2016," SIPRI Fact Sheet (Stockholm: SIPRI, April 2017), 2.

24. Government of India, Ministry of Defence, "Appendix II Referred in the Reply Given in Part (C) of Lok Sabha Starred Question 83 for Answer on 28.11.2014" (Parliament of India, November 28, 2014), http://164.100.47.132/ Annexture_New/lsq16/3/as83.htm. SIPRI data use the "trend indicator value," their own assessment of the volume of deliveries of arms. By that metric, Russia remains India's largest supplier over the 2010 to 2015 period. See SIPRI Arms Transfers Database, armstrade.sipri.org.

25. Shashank Joshi, "Indian Power Projection: Ambition, Arms and Influence," Whitehall Paper (London: Royal United Services Institute for Defense and Security Studies, January 2016).

26. See Robert M. Gates, "America's Security Role in the Asia–Pacific" (speech, IISS Shangri-La Dialogue, Singapore, May 30, 2009). And echoed later: Press Trust of India, "India in Position to Be Net Provider of Security: Manmohan Singh," *Mint*, May 23, 2013.

27. Condoleezza Rice, "Remarks En Route to India" (Press briefing, Washington, DC, March 15, 2005), http://2001-2009.state.gov/secretary/rm/ 2005/43465.htm.

28. See the discussion in Daniel S. Markey, *No Exit from Pakistan: America's Tortured Relationship with Islamabad* (Cambridge and New York: Cambridge University Press, 2013). Husain Haqqani, *Magnificent Delusions.* See also Alyssa Ayres, "What Washington Should Do to Help India-Pakistan Ties," *War on the Rocks,* January 7, 2016, http://warontherocks.com/2016/01/looking-back-to-look-ahead-what-washington-should-do-to-help-india-pakistan-ties/.

29. For example, former Senator Carl Levin, a Democrat and long a vocal critic of insufficient Pakistani action against the Haqqani network, inserted a condition on about one-third of U.S. coalition support funds that requires Pakistan to show action against the Haqqanis. This condition cannot be waived. In 2016, Senator Bob Corker, a Republican, put a hold on the use of U.S. taxpayer funds to subsidize sales of F-16s to Pakistan, expressing concerns about lack of action on terrorism. Suffice it to say that Congressional exasperation with Pakistan and terrorism has bipartisan expression.

30. C. Christine Fair and Sumit Ganguly, "An Unworthy Ally: Time for Washington to Cut Pakistan Loose," *Foreign Affairs,* October 2015.

31. International Foundation for Electoral Systems, "IFES, Indian Election Commission Sign Agreement for Increased Global Collaboration," *Www. ifes.org,* May 17, 2012.

32. Tom Malinowski, "Why We Issue the Human Rights Reports," *State.gov, DipNote (blog),* (June 25, 2015), http://blogs.state.gov/stories/2015/06/25/why-we-issue-human-rights-reports.

33. Human Rights Watch, "Country Datacard, Human Rights Council Voting Record: India."

34. Suhasini Haidar, "Govt. Rejects U.S. Panel's Report on Religious Freedom," *The Hindu,* May 1, 2015.

35. The U.S.-India Task Force also recommended a focus on technical-level cooperation. See Kaye, Nye, Jr., and Ayres, "Working with a Rising India," 45–46.

36. Government of India, Ministry of External Affairs, "U.S.-India-Africa Triangular Partnership to Improve Agricultural Productivity and Innovation in African Countries" (New Delhi: Government of India, Ministry of External Affairs, January 16, 2013), http://mea.gov.in/press-releases.htm?dtl/21058/USIndiaAfrica+Triangular+Partnership+to+Improve+Agricultural+Productivity+and+Innovation+in+African+Countries.

37. U.S. Department of State, "Voting Practices in the United Nations 2015," Report to Congress Submitted Pursuant to Public Laws 101-246 and 108-447 (Washington, DC: U.S. Department of State, June 2016), 44-48, http://www.state.gov/documents/organization/260322.pdf. U.S. Department of State, "Voting Practices in the United Nations 2013," Report to Congress Submitted Pursuant to Public Laws 101-246 and 108-447 (Washington,

DC: U.S. Department of State, March 2014), 42, http://www.state.gov/documents/organization/225048.pdf. U.S. Department of State, "Voting Practices in the United Nations 2012," Report to Congress Submitted Pursuant to Public Laws 101-246 and 108-447 (Washington, DC: U.S. Department of State, April 2013), 31, http://www.state.gov/documents/organization/208072.pdf. U.S. Department of State, "Voting Practices in the United Nations 2011," Report to Congress Submitted Pursuant to Public Laws 101-246 and 108-447 (Washington, DC: U.S. Department of State, April 2012), 25, http://www.state.gov/documents/organization/190024.pdf.

38. Michele Kelemen, "U.S. Underwhelmed with Emerging Powers at U.N.," *NPR.org*, September 17, 2011, http://www.npr.org/2011/09/17/140533339/u-s-underwhelmed-with-emerging-powers-at-u-n. Cited in the thoughtful discussion in David M. Malone and Rohan Mukherjee, "Dilemmas of Sovereignty and Order: India and the UN Security Council," in *Shaping the Emerging World: India and the Multilateral Order* (Washington, DC: Brookings Institution Press, 2013).

39. Neil A. Lewis, "A Reporter's Notebook: Shultz in His 'Garden,'" *New York Times*, June 26, 1987.

40. Kaye, Nye, Jr., and Ayres, "Working with a Rising India," 30.

41. R. Nicholas Burns, "America's Strategic Opportunity with India: The New U.S.-India Partnership," *Foreign Affairs*, November/December 2007.

42. See Charles King, "The Decline of International Studies: Why Flying Blind Is Dangerous," *Foreign Affairs* 94, no. 4 (July/August 2015): 88–98.

43. I have been concerned about this problem for nearly fifteen years. Minor improvements have not bridged the huge gap between India studies and almost every other area. See Alyssa Ayres, "Beyond Disciplines: India Studies in the United States," *India Review* 5, no. 1 (January 2006): 14–36. Also Alyssa Ayres, "Disconnected Networks: Notes Toward a Different Approach to Filling the South Asia Expert Gap," *India Review* 2, no. 2 (April 2003): 69–96.

44. Institute of International Education, "Top 25 Destinations of U.S. Study Abroad Students, 2014–2015," Open Doors Report on International Educational Exchange (New York: Institute of International Education, November 2016). Data prior to 2001 via personal communication from IIE.

45. See also Alyssa Ayres, "India and U.S. Higher Education: Strong Indian Presence in the United States, but Americans Studying in India Still Meager," *CFR.org, Asia Unbound (blog)*, (November 18, 2014), http://blogs.cfr.org/asia/2014/11/18/india-and-u-s-higher-education-strong-indian-presence-in-the-united-states-but-americans-studying-in-india-still-meager/.

46. See also Alyssa Ayres, "Few Takers for Hindi," *CFR.org, Asia Unbound (blog)*, (February 19, 2015), http://blogs.cfr.org/asia/2015/02/19/few-takers-for-hindi/.

47. This data comes from the Modern Language Association's enrollments survey database https://apps.mla.org/flsurvey_search. For the most recent MLA survey report, see David Goldberg, Dennis Looney, and Natalia Lusin, "Enrollments in Languages Other than English in United States Institutions of Higher Education, Fall 2013," MLA Quadrennial Language Enrollments Survey (New York: Modern Language Association, February 2015).

48. Hindi: 1800; Hindi-Urdu: 533; Urdu: 349; Punjabi: 124; Tamil: 82; Bengali: 64; Telugu: 51; Malayalam: 44; Nepali: 27; Gujarati: 6; Kannada: 5; Marathi: 5.

49. Joel I. Klein, Condoleezza Rice, and Julia Levy, "U.S. Education Reform and National Security," Independent Task Force Report No. 68 (New York: Council on Foreign Relations Press, March 2012).

50. King, "Decline of International Studies," 94.

51. Ayres, "Beyond Disciplines," 17. For a detailed history, see Richard Davis, "South Asia at Chicago: A History" (Chicago: Committee on Southern Asian Studies, The University of Chicago, 1985).

52. R. Nicholas Burns, "Remarks at the Fifth Annual White House Diwali Celebration" (speech, Washington, DC, November 7, 2007).

53. Allen Goodman, interview with the author, via telephone, November 17, 2014.

54. King, "Decline of International Studies," 94.

55. See "Title VIII Grant Program," U.S. Department of State. http://www.state.gov/s/inr/grants/

Epilogue

1. Narendra Modi, "A Strong India-U.S. Partnership Can Anchor Peace, Prosperity & Stability across the World" (Joint Meeting of the U.S. Congress, Washington, DC, June 8, 2016), http://www.narendramodi.in/prime-minister-narendra-modi-addresses-joint-meeting-of-u-s-congress-in-washington-dc-484217.

2. Nilekani, interview with the author.

BIBLIOGRAPHIC NOTE

While this book has provided reference notes for specific material cited, there are some books that I found influential or provocative in thinking about India's challenges and its rising role on the global stage.

They include:

Katherine Boo, *Behind the Beautiful Forevers;* Stephen P. Cohen, *India: Emerging Power;* Gurcharan Das, *India Grows at Night;* Bibek Debroy, Ashley Tellis, and Reece Trevor, *Getting India Back on Track;* Simon Denyer, *Rogue Elephant;* Sandy Gordon, *India's Rise as an Asian Power;* Patrick French, *India: A Portrait;* Bharat Karnad, *Why India Is Not a Great Power (Yet);* Sunil Khilnani, *The Idea of India;* Edward Luce, *In Spite of the Gods;* David Malone, *Does the Elephant Dance?;* McKinsey & Company, *Reimagining India;* C. Raja Mohan, *Crossing the Rubicon;* C. Raja Mohan, *Samudra Manthan;* T. N. Ninan, *The Turn of the Tortoise;* Joseph S. Nye Jr., *The Future of Power;* Devdutt Pattanaik, *Business Sutra;* Howard B. Schaffer and Teresita C. Schaffer, *India at the Global High Table;* Somini Sengupta, *The End of Karma;* Mihir Sharma, *Restart: The Last Chance for the Indian Economy;* WPS Sidhu, Pratap Bhanu Mehta, and Bruce D. Jones, eds., *Shaping the Emerging World;* George Tanham, *Indian Strategic Thought;* Shashi Tharoor, *Pax Indica;* Ravi Venkatesan, *Conquering the Chaos;* David Shambaugh, *China Goes Global: The Partial Power;* Nandan Nilekani, *Imagining India;* Ashley Tellis and Sean Mirski, *Crux of Asia;* and Fareed Zakaria, *The Post-American World: Release 2.0.*

BIBLIOGRAPHY

"20 Tons of Gold Sold by India." *New York Times*. June 7, 1991.

Ablett, Jonathan, et al. "The 'Bird of Gold': The Rise of India's Consumer Market." Washington, DC: McKinsey Global Institute, May 2007.

"About the NDB." New Development Bank BRICS. *NDBBRICS.org*, n.d. http://ndbbrics.org.

Adhikari, Anand. "Supersize Gujarat." *Business Today*, January 23, 2011.

Ahluwalia, Montek S. "Economic Reforms in India Since 1991: Has Gradualism Worked?" *Journal of Economic Perspectives* 16, no. 3 (Summer 2002): 67–88.

Alden, Edward. "India's Landmark WTO Challenge to US." *Nikkei Asian Review*. March 15, 2016.

Ananth, Venkat. "How BCCI Became the 800-Pound Gorilla of Cricket." *Mint*. December 9, 2014.

Anderson, Ashlyn, and Alyssa Ayres. "Economics of Influence: China and India in South Asia." Expert Brief. Washington, DC: Council on Foreign Relations, August 7, 2015. http://www.cfr.org/economics/economics-influence-china-india-south-asia/p36862.

Arun S. "Commerce Minister Complains of 'Sledging' in Trade Talks." *The Hindu*. May 2, 2016.

———. "Rs. 6,000 Crore Special Package for Textiles." *The Hindu*. June 22, 2016.

"Asia 1930: Gandhi, Salt, and Freedom." *Economist*, December 31, 1999.

Asian Development Bank, "People's Republic of China: Economy" online fact sheet of the *Asian Development Outlook 2017* (April 2017), www.adb.org/countries/prc/economy

Ayres, Alyssa. "Beyond Disciplines: India Studies in the United States." *India Review* 5, no. 1 (January 2006): 14–36.

———. "Bringing India Inside the Asian Trade Tent." Policy Innovation Memorandum No. 46. New York: Council on Foreign Relations Press, June 2014.

———. "China's Mixed Messages to India." CFR.org. *Asia Unbound (blog)*, September 17, 2014. http://blogs.cfr.org/asia/2014/09/17/chinas-mixed-messages-to-india/.

———. "A Closer Look at FDI Flip-Flopping in India." CFR.org. *Asia Unbound (blog)*, February 4, 2014. http://blogs.cfr.org/asia/2014/02/04/a-closer-look-at-fdi-flip-flopping-in-india/.

———. "Disconnected Networks: Notes toward a Different Approach to Filling the South Asia Expert Gap." *India Review* 2, no. 2 (April 2003): 69–96.

———. "Few Takers for Hindi." CFR.org. *Asia Unbound (blog)*, February 19, 2015. http://blogs.cfr.org/asia/2015/02/19/few-takers-for-hindi/.

———. "Five Questions for Professor Jagdish Bhagwati on the Indian Economy and Prime Minister Modi's Next Steps." CFR.org. *Asia Unbound (blog)*, May 27, 2014. http://blogs.cfr.org/asia/2014/05/27/five-questions-for-professor-jagdish-bhagwati-on-the-indian-economy-and-prime-minister-modis-next-steps/.

———. "How Americans See India as a Power." CFR.org. *Asia Unbound (blog)*, September 15, 2015. http://blogs.cfr.org/asia/2015/09/15/how-americans-see-india-as-a-power/.

———. "How You Play the Game: Cricket, World Order, and India's Rise." *Octavian Report*, August 2015. http://octavianreport.com/article/how-you-play-the-game-cricket-world-order-and-the-rise-of-india/.

———. "India: Tough Talk and the Bali Trade Facilitation Agreement." CFR.org. *Asia Unbound (blog)*, July 29, 2014. http://blogs.cfr.org/asia/2014/07/29/india-tough-talk-and-the-bali-trade-facilitation-agreement/.

———. "India and U.S. Higher Education: Strong Indian Presence in the United States, but Americans Studying in India Still Meager." CFR.org. *Asia Unbound (blog)*, November 18, 2014. http://blogs.cfr.org/asia/2014/11/18/india-and-u-s-higher-education-strong-indian-presence-in-the-united-states-but-americans-studying-in-india-still-meager/.

———. "India at Paris—Working with a Rising India." *Energy, Security, and Climate*, December 9, 2015. http://blogs.cfr.org/levi/2015/12/09/alyssa-ayres-india-at-paris-working-with-a-rising-india/.

———. "Modi Doubles Down on the Neighborhood." *YaleGlobal*, June 10, 2014. http://yaleglobal.yale.edu/content/modi-doubles-down-neighborhood.

———. *Speaking Like a State: Language and Nationalism in Pakistan*. Cambridge and New York: Cambridge University Press, 2009.

———. "What Washington Should Do to Help India-Pakistan Ties." *War on the Rocks*, January 7, 2016. http://warontherocks.com/2016/01/looking-back-to-look-ahead-what-washington-should-do-to-help-india-pakistan-ties/.

Bagchi, Indrani. "India's NSG Bid Stops at China Wall." *Times of India*. June 24, 2016.

————. "Overseas Missions Need to Boost Trade: Narendra Modi." *Times of India*. March 26, 2014.

Bagri, Neha Thirani. "Narendra Modi, India's Leader, Moves to Reshape Labor Rules." *New York Times*. October 16, 2014.

Bajaj, Rahul. "Creating Indian MNCs: India Must Take Its Rightful Place among the Economic Powers of the World." *Frontline*, August 9, 1997.

————. "Riding Out the Licence Raj." *Business Standard*. October 27, 2014.

Bajaj, Vikas. "Tata Motors Finds Success in Jaguar Land Rover." *New York Times*, August 30, 2012.

Bal, Sambit. Interview with the author. In person, May 26, 2015.

Balachandran, Manu, and Itika Sharma Punit. "Timeline: 200 Years of India's Struggle with Land Acquisition Laws." *Quartz India*, August 5, 2015. http://qz.com/471117/timeline-200-years-of-indias-struggle-with-land-acquisition-laws/.

Banerjee, Chandrajit. Interview with the author. In person, May 22, 2015.

Bangladesh Garment Manufacturers and Exporters Association. "Trade Information." *BGMEA.com.bd*, 2016. http://bgmea.com.bd/home/pages/TradeInformation.

Barker, Alex, and Pilita Clark. "India Slows Progress on Ambitious Climate Change Accord." *Financial Times*. November 18, 2015.

Baruah, Sanjib Kr. "India Can Become the World's HR Capital: PM Modi at 'Skill India' Launch." *Hindustan Times*, July 16, 2015.

Bass, Gary J. *The Blood Telegram: Nixon, Kissinger, and a Forgotten Genocide*. New York: Knopf, 2013.

Basu, Nayanima. "India to Resume Visa Fee Hike Dispute with US in WTO." *Business Standard*. November 4, 2013.

Bergsten, C. Fred. "India's Rise: A Strategy for Trade-Led Growth." PIIE Briefing. Washington, DC: Peterson Institute for International Economics, September 2015. http://www.iie.com/publications/briefings/piieb15-4.pdf.

Bhagwati, Jagdish N., and Arvind Panagariya. *Why Growth Matters: How Economic Growth in India Reduced Poverty and the Lessons for Other Developing Countries*. New York: PublicAffairs, 2013.

Bharatiya Janata Party. "Ek Bharat, Shreshtha Bharat: Sab Ka Saath, Sab Ka Vikas. Election Manifesto 2014," May 2014. http://www.bjp.org/images/pdf_2014/full_manifesto_english_07.04.2014.pdf.

————. "Indo-US Nuclear Deal: Why Does BJP Oppose It?" Bharatiya Janata Party, 2008. http://www.bjp.org/images/upload/other_publications/indo_us_deal_e.pdf.

Bhargava, Anjuli. "We Don't Have a Magic Wand to Create Jobs: Rohit Nandan, Ministry of Skill Development." *Business Standard*. October 24, 2016.

Bhartia, Hari. Interview with the author. In person, May 21, 2015.

Bhartia, Shobhana. Interview with the author. In person, May 20, 2015.

Bhatnagar, Subhash. "India's Software Industry." In *Technology, Adaptation, and Exports: How Some Developing Countries Got It Right*, 49–82.

Washington, DC: World Bank, 2006. http://siteresources.worldbank.org/
INTEXPCOMNET/Resources/Chandra_2006.pdf.

Bhatt, Abhinav. "Home Ministry Sends Nirbhaya Documentary Ban Order to
BBC." *NDTV.com*. March 5, 2015.

Bhattacharya, Pramit. "Everything You Wanted to Know about the Sen-
Bhagwati Debate." *Mint*, July 20, 2013.

Bhattacherjee, Kallol. "Seychelles Committed to Indian Naval Base." *The Hindu*.
December 23, 2015.

Bhushan, Sandeep. "TRP Wars: The Battle Between News Anchors on Indian
Television for the Most Eyeballs Just Got Personal." *The Caravan*, June
24, 2015.

BI India Bureau. "Nokia's New Phones Will Be Made in India, Thanks to
Foxconn's Expansion Plan." *Business Insider*. October 23, 2016,
India edition.

Bipindra, N. C. "India Nears Completion of Nuclear Triad with Armed
Submarine." *Bloomberg*, February 25, 2016.

Bivens, Josh. "Updated Employment Multipliers for the U.S. Economy."
Working Paper. Washington, DC: Economic Policy Institute, August 2003.
http://www.epi.org/files/page/-/old/workingpapers/epi_wp_268.pdf.

Blackwill, Robert D. "Atmospherics of the U.S.-India Relationship." *Indian
Defence News*, January 25, 2015.

Boesche, Roger. *The First Great Political Realist: Kautilya and His Arthashastra*.
Lanham: Lexington Books, 2003.

Boo, Katherine. *Behind the Beautiful Forevers: Life, Death, and Hope in a
Mumbai Undercity*. New York: Random House Trade Paperbacks, 2014.

Bouton, Marshall M., et al. "Constrained Internationalism: Adapting to New
Realities." Results of a 2010 National Survey of American Public Opinion.
Chicago Council Surveys. Chicago: Chicago Council on Global Affairs, 2010.
http://www.thechicagocouncil.org/sites/default/files/Global%20Views%20
2010.pdf.

"Breaking the Glass Ceiling." Economist Intelligence Unit, April 17, 2015.

Brekke, Torkel. "The Conceptual Foundation of Missionary Hinduism." *Journal
of Religious History* 23, no. 2 (June 1999): 203–14.

BRICS. "BRICS and Africa: Partnership for Development, Integration and
Industrialisation (Fifth BRICS Summit)." Durban, South Africa, March 27,
2013. http://brics5.co.za/fifth-brics-summit-declaration-and-action-plan/.

———. "Delhi Declaration and Action Plan (4th BRICS Summit)." New
Delhi, India, March 29, 2012. http://brics.itamaraty.gov.br/category-english/
21-documents/68-fourth-summit.

———. "II BRIC Summit—Joint Statement." Brasilia, Brasil, April 16,
2010. http://brics.itamaraty.gov.br/category-english/21-documents/
66-second-summit.

———. "Joint Statement of the BRIC Countries Leaders (First BRICS Summit)."
Yekaterinburg, Russia, June 16, 2009. en.kremlin.ru/supplement/209.

———. "The 6th BRICS Summit: Fortaleza Declaration." Fortaleza, Brazil, July 5, 2014. http://brics6.itamaraty.gov.br/media2/press-releases.

———. "VII BRICS Summit: 2015 Ufa Declaration." Ufa, Russia, July 9, 2015. http://en.brics2015.ru/documents/.

"Brief: Regional Integration in South Asia." WorldBank.org, October 9, 2015. http://www.worldbank.org/en/region/sar/brief/south-asia-regional-integration.

Burke, Marie Louise. *Swami Vivekananda in America: New Discoveries*. San Francisco and Calcutta: Vedanta Society of Northern California and Advaita Ashrama, 1958.

Burns, R. Nicholas. "America's Strategic Opportunity with India: The New U.S.-India Partnership." *Foreign Affairs*, December 2007.

———. Interview with the author. In person, June 12, 2015.

———. "Remarks at the Fifth Annual White House Diwali Celebration." Speech, Washington, DC, November 7, 2007.

Burr, William, ed. "China, Pakistan, and the Bomb: The Declassified File on U.S. Policy, 1977–1997," March 5, 2004. National Security Archive. http://nsarchive.gwu.edu/NSAEBB/NSAEBB114/.

Card, Andrew H., Thomas A. Daschle, Edward Alden, and Matthew J. Slaughter. "U.S. Trade and Investment Policy." Independent Task Force Report No. 67. New York: Council on Foreign Relations Press, 2011.

Carter, Ashton, and Manohar Parrikar. "Joint Press Conference by Secretary Carter and Minister Parrikar in the Pentagon Briefing Room." Transcript, Washington, DC, August 29, 2016. http://www.defense.gov/News/Transcripts/Transcript-View/Article/929778/joint-press-conference-by-secretary-carter-and-minister-parrikar-in-the-pentago.

Central Tibetan Administration. "About CTA." *Tibet.net*. Accessed October 6, 2016. http://tibet.net/about-cta/.

"Certificate of Incorporation." Mahindra and Mahindra, 1952. http://www.mahindra.com/resources/pdf/history/Certificate-of-Incorporation.pdf.

Chandler, Clay, Adil Zainulbhai, and McKinsey & Company, eds. *Reimagining India: Unlocking the Potential of Asia's next Superpower*. 1st ed. New York: Simon & Schuster, 2013.

Chandra, Lokesh, ed. *India's Contribution to World Thought and Culture*. Madras: Vivekananda Rock Memorial Committee, 1970.

Chaudhuri, Pramit Pal. "New Delhi at Sea: The China Factor in the Indian Ocean Policy of the Modi and Singh Governments." *Asia Policy*, no. 22 (July 2016): 27–34.

Chengappa, Raj. "Modi's Global Push." *India Today*, September 30, 2015.

Childs, Nick. "China and India—Indigenous Carrier Comparison." IISS.org. *Military Balance Blog*, February 9, 2016. http://www.iiss.org/en/militarybalanceblog/blogsections/2016-629e/february-f0ed/china-and-india-indigenous-carrier-comparison-562b.

"China Cautiously Welcomes Trans-Pacific Free Trade Deal." *BBC News*, October 6, 2015.

"China's Richest Man Plans $10 Billion India Development Project." *Bloomberg News*, January 22, 2016.

Chitravanshi, Ruchika. "Dalian Wanda's $10 billion Haryana Project on the Verge of Being Pulled Out over Equity Share Row." *Economic Times*. April 28, 2017.

Cohen, Stephen P. *India: Emerging Power*. Washington, DC: Brookings Institution Press, 2001.

Cohen, Stephen P., and Richard L. Park. *India: Emergent Power?* Strategy Paper No. 33. New York: National Strategy Information Center, Inc., 1978.

Confederation of Indian Industry, and EY. "Making India a World Class Automotive Manufacturing Hub." New Delhi: Confederation of Indian Industry and EY, February 6, 2016.

Coolidge, Calvin. "Address to the American Society of Newspaper Editors." Washington, DC, January 17, 1925. http://www.presidency.ucsb.edu/ws/?pid=24180.

Crabtree, James. "India's Times Now News Channel to Launch in UK." *Financial Times*. November 15, 2015.

———. "Lunch with the FT: Indian TV News Anchor Arnab Goswami." *Financial Times*, May 1, 2015.

Crabtree, Steve. "Indians Are Optimistic, but Business Challenges Persist." Washington, DC: Gallup, July 2015.

Cruz, Marcio, James Foster, Brian Quillin, and Philip Schellekens. "Ending Extreme Poverty and Sharing Prosperity: Progress and Policies." Development Economics. Policy Research Note. Washington, DC: World Bank Group, October 2015. http://pubdocs.worldbank.org/en/109701443800596288/PRN03Oct2015TwinGoals.pdf.

Cumming-Bruce, Nick. "UN Approves Investigation of Civil War in Sri Lanka." *New York Times*. March 27, 2014.

Curry, Bill, Richard Blackwell, and Brian Milner. "India Leads Emerging-Market Charge at G20." *The Globe and Mail*. September 4, 2013.

Dalrymple, William. "The East India Company: The Original Corporate Raiders." *The Guardian*. March 4, 2015.

Das, Gurcharan. "All the World's Gold." *The Hindu*. August 27, 2011.

———. *India Grows at Night: A Liberal Case for a Strong State*. New Delhi: Allen Lane (Penguin Books India), 2012.

———. *India Unbound: A Personal Account of a Social and Economic Revolution from Independence to the Global Information Age*. New York: Knopf, 2001.

———. Interview with the author. In person, May 20, 2015.

Das, Tarun. *Crossing Frontiers: The Journey of Building CII*. New Delhi: Lustra Print, 2015.

———. "India: The Unfinished Agenda." Panel discussion presented at the Asia Society, New York, May 21, 1999.

———. Interview with the author. In person, August 12, 2015.

Dasgupta, Swapan. Interview with the author. In person, August 7, 2015.

Datta-Ray, Deep K. *The Making of Indian Diplomacy: A Critique of Eurocentrism*. New York: Oxford University Press, 2015.

Davis, Richard. "South Asia at Chicago: A History." Chicago: Committee on Southern Asian Studies, The University of Chicago, 1985.

"Delhi in Davos: How India Built Its Brand at the World Economic Forum." *Knowledge@Wharton*. February 22, 2006. http://knowledge.wharton.upenn.edu/article/delhi-in-davos-how-india-built-its-brand-at-the-world-economic-forum/.

"The Democracy Tax Is Rising." *Economist*, December 11, 2008.

Denyer, Simon. *Rogue Elephant: Harnessing the Power of India's Unruly Democracy*. London: Bloomsbury, 2014.

———. "Singh Says He's No Lame Duck and India Is Not a 'Scam-Driven Country.'" *Washington Post*. February 16, 2011.

Dhar, Sujoy. "Millions Strike in India to Protest against Modi's Labor Reforms." *Reuters*, September 2, 2015.

Dikshit, Sandeep. "We Would Rather Be Called Re-Emerging Powers, Says NSA." *The Hindu*, February 3, 2013.

Diwanji, Amberish K. "Geo-Political Issues Set to Dominate Proposed Gas Pipeline from Iran to India." *Rediff.com*, April 13, 2000.

DNA Webdesk. "Zee Media's New Global English News Channel to Be Called WION." *DNA*. March 15, 2016. http://www.dnaindia.com/money/report-zee-media-s-new-global-english-news-channel-to-be-called-wion-2189476.

Donnan, Shawn. "Dealmaker in Charge at the WTO Faces Tough Fight." *Financial Times*. December 2, 2014.

Drèze, Jean, and Amartya Sen. *An Uncertain Glory: India and Its Contradictions*. Princeton, NJ: Princeton University Press, 2013.

Drezner, Daniel W. "Anatomy of a Whole-of-Government Foreign Policy Failure." WashingtonPost.com. *Spoiler Alerts (blog)*, March 27, 2015. https://www.washingtonpost.com/posteverything/wp/2015/03/27/anatomy-of-a-whole-of-government-foreign-policy-failure/.

Dutt, Barkha. "A 'Four'midable Bid for UN Security Council: G4 Gamechanger?" *The Buck Stops Here*. NDTV, September 26, 2015. http://www.ndtv.com/video/player/the-buck-stops-here/a-four-midable-bid-for-un-security-council-g4-gamechanger/384508.

Echeverri-Gent, John. "Politics in India's Decentered Polity." In *India Briefing: Quickening the Pace of Change*, 19–53. Armonk, NY: M. E. Sharpe, 2002.

Eck, Diana L. *India: A Sacred Geography*. New York: Three Rivers Press, 2012.

Election Commission of India. "Notification No.56/2016/PPS-II," December 13, 2016. http://eci.nic.in/eci_main/ElectoralLaws/OrdersNotifications/year2016/Notification13.12.2016.pdf.

———. "Press Release No. 491/Media/5/2011: ECI to Set Up Indian Institute of Democracy and Election Management." Election Commission of India, January 24, 2011. http://eci.nic.in/eci_main1/current/PN24012011.pdf.

Embassy of India, Washington, DC. "Press Release—'First International Day of Yoga Celebrated in the United States,'" June 21, 2015. https://www.indianembassy.org/informations.php?id=427.

———. "Press Release—In Response to a Media Query on Visa to USCIRF Visit," March 4, 2016. https://www.indianembassy.org/press_detail.php?nid=2338.

Embassy of the United States, Sana'a. "Emergency Message for U.S. Citizens—Updated Departure Options." U.S. Department of State, April 6, 2015. http://yemen.usembassy.gov/messages040615.html.

"English Rendering of Prime Minister Shri Narendra Modi's Remarks at the East Asia Summit." Speech presented at the East Asia Summit, Nay Pyi Taw, November 13, 2014. http://www.narendramodi.in/english-rendering-of-prime-minister-shri-narendra-modis-remarks-at-the-east-asia-summit-nay-pyi-taw-6881.

Ernst and Young, "India Transforming Through Radical Reforms." February 2017.

Express News Service, "Border Transgressions by China Down: ITBP." *Indian Express*. October 25, 2016, http://indianexpress.com/article/india/india-news-india/border-transgressions-by-china-down-itbp-3101323/.

Fair, C. Christine. *Fighting to the End: The Pakistan Army's Way of War*. New York: Oxford University Press, 2014.

Fair, C. Christine, and Sumit Ganguly. "An Unworthy Ally: Time for Washington to Cut Pakistan Loose." *Foreign Affairs*, October 2015.

Fingar, Courtney. "India Knocks China from Top of FDI League Table." FT.com. *EM Squared (blog)*, April 20, 2016. https://www.ft.com/content/94351bda-0620-11e6-a70d-4e39ac32c284.

Fingar, Courtney, ed. "The fDi Report 2017: Global Greenfield Investment Trends." *fDi Intelligence*. 2017. http://forms.fdiintelligence.com/report2017/thankyou.php (registration required to access link.)

"Ford India Celebrates Figo Aspire Job 1 at Ford's Sanand Plant." *@FordOnline*, June 14, 2015. http://www.at.ford.com/news/cn/Pages/Ford%20India%20Celebrates%20Figo%20Aspire%20Job%201%20at%20Ford's%20Sanand%20Plant.aspx.

"Four Nations Launch UN Seat Bid." *BBC News*, September 22, 2004.

French, Patrick. *India: A Portrait*. New York: Knopf, 2011.

Gabbard, Tulsi. H.Res.328–114th Congress. Commemorating the Inaugural "'International Yoga Day'" on June 21, Pub. L. No. H. RES. 328 (2015). https://www.gpo.gov/fdsys/pkg/BILLS-114hres328ih/pdf/BILLS-114hres328ih.pdf.

Gandhi, Mohandas K. "Drain Inspector's Report." *The United States of India*. February 1928, reprint of 1927 "Young India" essay edition. South Asian American Digital Archive.

———. *Indian Home Rule*. Translated by Mohandas K. Gandhi. Hinda Svarāja, xv, 102 p. Madras: Ganesh & Co., 1922. http://catalog.hathitrust.org/Record/100329241.

Gandhi, Mohandas K., and Anthony J. Parel. *Gandhi: "Hind Swaraj" and Other Writings*. Cambridge Texts in Modern Politics. Cambridge: Cambridge University Press, 2009.

Ganguly, Meenakshi. Interview with the author. In person, May 18, 2015.

Gates, Robert M. "America's Security Role in the Asia–Pacific." Speech presented at the IISS Shangri-La Dialogue, Singapore, May 30, 2009.

Gollapudi, Nagaraj. "BCCI Outvoted in Crucial Vote on ICC Constitution," *ESPNCricinfo.com*, April 26, 2017.

Goldberg, David, Dennis Looney, and Natalia Lusin. "Enrollments in Languages Other than English in United States Institutions of Higher Education, Fall 2013." MLA Quadrennial Language Enrollments Survey. New York: Modern Language Association, February 2015.

Goodman, Allen. Interview with the author. Via telephone, November 17, 2014.

Gordon, Sandy. *India's Rise as an Asian Power: Nation, Neighborhood, and Region*. Washington, DC: Georgetown University Press, 2014.

Goswami, Arnab. Interview with the author. In person, May 29, 2015.

Government of Gujarat. "Business: Major Industries." *Gujarat: Official Gujarat State Portal*, n.d. http://www.gujaratindia.com/business/major-indus.htm.

Government of India. "Cabinet Secretariat Resolution No. 511/2/1/2015." Gazette of India, January 1, 2015. http://niti.gov.in/writereaddata/files/cabinet-resolution_EN.pdf.

Government of India, Department of Industrial Policy and Promotion. "Press Note No. 10 (1992 Series), Revised List of Annex III Items." Government of India, Department of Industrial Policy and Promotion, June 24, 1992. Reproduced as pages 11-16 in http://eaindustry.nic.in/industrial_handbook_200809.pdf.

———. "Quarterly Fact Sheet: Fact Sheet on Foreign Direct Investment (FDI) from April 2000 to December 2016." Government of India, December 2016. http://dipp.gov.in/sites/default/files/FDI_FactSheet_OctoberNovemberDecember2016.pdf.

Government of India, Indian Navy. "Ports Visited Since Aug 15." Twitter.com. *@IndianNavy*, September 2, 2016. https://twitter.com/indiannavy/status/771875619072118785.

Government of India, Ministry of Chemicals and Fertilizers. "Annual Report 2014–2015." Government of India, Ministry of Chemicals and Fertilizers, 2015.

Government of India, Ministry of Commerce and Industry. "India Brand Equity Foundation: About Us." *Commerce.nic.in*, 2016. http://commerce.nic.in/aboutus/aboutus_autonomousbodies-9.asp.

Government of India, Ministry of Commerce and Industry, Department of Industrial Policy and Promotion. "Press Note No. 4 (2006 Series) Subject: Rationalisation of the FDI Policy." Government of India, Ministry of Commerce and Industry, February 10, 2006. http://dipp.nic.in/English/policy/changes/pn4_2006.pdf.

Government of India, Ministry of Commerce and Industry, Department of Industrial Policy and Promotion, Office of the Economic Advisor. "Statement on Industrial Policy, July 24, 1991" in *Handbook of Industrial Policy and Statistics 2003-2005* Government of India, Department of Industrial Policy and Promotion, 2005.

Government of India, Ministry of Defence. "Annual Report 2002–2003." New Delhi: Ministry of Defence, 2003. https://www.files.ethz.ch/isn/15049/MOD-English2003.pdf.

———. "Appendix II Referred in the Reply Given in Part (C) of Lok Sabha Starred Question 83 for Answer on 28.11.2014." Parliament of India, November 28, 2014. http://164.100.47.132/Annexture_New/lsq16/3/as83.htm.

Government of India, Ministry of Defence (Navy). "Ensuring Secure Seas: Indian Maritime Security Strategy." Naval Strategic Publication (NSP) 1.2. New Delhi: Ministry of Defence, October 2015.

Government of India, Ministry of Electronics and Information Technology. "Fact Sheet of IT & BPM Industry." New Delhi, April 7, 2017. http://meity.gov.in/content/fact-sheet-it-bpm-industry

Government of India, Ministry of External Affairs. "About BRICS." *BRICSIndia2016*, n.d. http://brics2016.gov.in/content/innerpage/about-usphp.php.

———. *Annual Report 2015–16.* New Delhi: Government of India, 2016. https://mea.gov.in/Uploads/PublicationDocs/26525_26525_External_Affairs_English_AR_2015-16_Final_compressed.pdf.

———. "Conference on Interaction and Confidence Building Measures in Asia (CICA)." Government of India, Ministry of External Affairs, October 2013. http://www.mea.gov.in/Portal/ForeignRelation/Conference_on_Interaction_and_Confidence_Building_Measures_in_Asia__1_.pdf.

———. "History and Evolution of Non-Aligned Movement." Government of India, August 22, 2012. http://mea.gov.in/in-focus-article.htm?20349/History+and+Evolution+of+NonAligned+Movement.

———. "IBSA Delegation Calls on President Assad to Discuss Situation." Government of India, Ministry of External Affairs, August 11, 2011. http://ibsa.nic.in/president_assad.htm.

———. "India and United Nations Peacekeeping and Peacebuilding." *Permanent Mission of India to the UN*, n.d. https://www.pminewyork.org/pages.php?id=1985.

———. "Indian Diplomacy at Work: Our View—UN Security Council Reforms." New Delhi, 2014. https://mea.gov.in/Portal/CountryNews/3018_Indian_Diplomacy_At_Work.pdf.

———. "Joint Press Statement at the Meeting of Leaders of the G-4 countries—Brazil, Germany, India and Japan—on United Nations Security Council Reform," September 26, 2015. http://www.mea.gov.in/bilateral-documents.htm?dtl/25849/Joint_Press_Statement_at_the_Meeting_of_Leaders_of_the_

G4_countries_Brazil_Germany_India_and_Japan__on_United_Nations_
    Security_Council_Reform.
————. "Panchsheel." Government of India, 2004. http://www.mea.gov.in/
    Uploads/PublicationDocs/191_panchsheel.pdf.
————. "Statement on the Situation in Nepal." Government of India,
    September 20, 2015. http://www.mea.gov.in/press-releases.htm?dtl/25821/State
    ment+on+the+situation+in+Nepal.
————. "U.S.-India-Africa Triangular Partnership to Improve Agricultural
    Productivity and Innovation in African Countries." New Delhi: Government
    of India, Ministry of External Affairs, January 16, 2013. http://mea.gov.in/
    press-releases.htm?dtl/21058/USIndiaAfrica+Triangular+Partnership+to+Imp
    rove+Agricultural+Productivity+and+Innovation+in+African+Countries.
Government of India, Ministry of External Affairs, Office of the Spokesperson.
    "We Are Closely Watching Fast Evolving Situation and Hope for a Peaceful
    Resolution." *Twitter*, March 3, 2014. https://twitter.com/MEAIndia/status/
    440712830900137984.
Government of India, Ministry of Finance, Chief Economic Advisor. "Economic
    Survey of India." Vol. 2. New Delhi: Government of India, Ministry of
    Finance, February 2016.
Government of India, Ministry of Home Affairs, Foreigners Division. "F.No.II/
    21022/58(0047)/2013-FCRA(MU)-461-1. ORDER." Government of India,
    September 2, 2015. https://fcraonline.nic.in/home/PDF_Doc/Greenpaece%20
    India%20Society2_040915.PDF.
Government of India, Ministry of Labour and Employment, Labour Bureau,
    Report on Employment-Unemployment Survey 2015-16, September 2016. http://
    labourbureaunew.gov.in/showdetail.aspx?pr_id=CRjYojJiLYo%3d
Government of India, Ministry of Textiles. "Annual Report 2016–2017."
    Government of India, 2017.
Government of India, National Sample Survey Office. "Swachhta Status
    Report 2016." New Delhi: Government of India, Ministry of Statistics and
    Programme Implementation, 2016.
Government of India, National Skill Development Corporation. "Human
    Resource and Skill Requirements in the Auto and Auto Components Sector
    (2013–17, 2017–22)." New Delhi: Government of India, Ministry of Skill
    Development and Entrepreneurship, July 2015. http://www.nsdcindia.org/
    sites/default/files/files/Auto-and-Auto-Components.pdf.
Government of India, Planning Commission. "2nd Five Year Plan." Government
    of India, Planning Commission, 1956. http://planningcommission.gov.in/
    plans/planrel/fiveyr/index2.html.
Government of India, Press Information Bureau. "Agreement on the New
    Development Bank and the BRICS Contingent Reserve Agreement." *Press
    Information Bureau*, February 25, 2015. http://pib.nic.in/newsite/PrintRelease.
    aspx?relid=115907.

————. "Government to Establish Cross Cultural Linkages with 39 Indian Ocean Countries under Project Mausam." www.indiaculture.nic.in. *Ministry of Culture*, March 9, 2015. http://www.indiaculture.nic.in/sites/default/files/press_release/Project%20Mausam.pdf.

Government of India, Prime Minister's Office. "Inauguration the Construction of IIIDEM New Campus at Dwarka." Press Information Bureau, Government of India, January 25, 2016. http://pib.nic.in/newsite/PrintRelease.aspx?relid=135786.

————. "PM to Heads of Indian Missions." Press Information Bureau, Government of India, February 7, 2015. http://pib.nic.in/newsite/PrintRelease.aspx?relid=115241.

"Government of India—Baa3 Positive." Credit Opinion Quarterly Update. New York: Moody's Investors Service, October 7, 2016.

"Government of India—Effective Implementation of Key Fiscal and Banking Sector Reforms Would Address Core Credit Challenges." Issuer In-Depth. New York: Moody's Investors Service, May 31, 2017.

Guha, Ramachandra. *Makers of Modern Asia*. Cambridge, MA: Belknap Press of Harvard University Press, 2014.

————. "Superpower Fantasies: India Should Seek Other Goals than Joining a Global Race." *The Telegraph*. September 12, 2009.

————. "Will India Become a Superpower?" In *India: The Next Superpower?* London: London School of Economics, 2012.

Gupta, Shekhar. Interview with the author. In person, May 23, 2015.

————. "The HMT Advantage." *Zee News*, February 15, 2003.

"Had No Meats at the Dinner." *New York Times*. May 2, 1894.

Haidar, Suhasini. "Crackdown on NGOs Worries US." *The Hindu*. May 7, 2015.

————. "Govt. Rejects U.S. Panel's Report on Religious Freedom." *The Hindu*. May 1, 2015.

————. "MEA to Oversee Foreign Investments in States." *The Hindu*. October 25, 2014.

————. "Trading Bloc to India: Cut Tariffs or Exit FTA Talks." *The Hindu*. April 20, 2016.

"Hailed as 'Role Models,' All-Female Indian Police Unit Departs UN Mission in Liberia." *UN News Centre*. February 12, 2016. http://www.un.org/apps/news/story.asp?NewsID=53218#.Vw1oh2OoC-I.

Halpern, Jake. "The Secret of the Temple." *New Yorker*, April 30, 2012.

Harder, Anton. "Not at the Cost of China: New Evidence Regarding US Proposals to Nehru for Joining the United Nations Security Council." Cold War International History Project. Washington, DC: Woodrow Wilson International Center for Scholars, March 2015.

Harris, Gardiner. "Rival Economists in Public Battle over Cure for India's Poverty." *New York Times*, August 21, 2013.

Harris, Harry B. " 'Let's Be Ambitious Together.' " Speech presented at the Raisina Dialogue, New Delhi, March 2, 2016.

Hazarika, Sanjoy. "Indian Troops End Coup in Maldives." *New York Times*. November 5, 1988.

Hill, Kim, Debra Menk, Joshua Cregger, and Michael Schultz. "Contribution of the Automotive Industry to the Economies of All Fifty States and the United States." Ann Arbor, MI: Center for Automotive Research, January 22, 2015.

"Hirotec Starts Manufacturing Facility in Coimbatore." *The Hindu*, October 20, 2011.

Houghton, Walter R., ed. *Neely's History of The Parliament of Religions and Religious Congresses at the World's Columbian Exposition*. Chicago, 1893. https://archive.org/details/cu31924029062664.

Huang, Zixuan, Nicholas R. Lardy, and Melina Kolb. "China is Not the Most Highly Protectionist Big Country," PIIE.com, *PIIE Charts (blog)*, June 21, 2017. https://piie.com/research/piie-charts/china-not-most-highly-protectionist-big-country

Human Rights Watch. "Country Datacard, Human Rights Council Voting Record: India." *VotesCount*, 2015. http://votescount.hrw.org/page/India.

"ICC Set to Say Goodbye to Lord's." *BBC Sport*, July 28, 2005.

"IMF Board Approves Far-Reaching Governance Reforms." International Monetary Fund, November 5, 2010. http://www.imf.org/external/pubs/ft/survey/so/2010/NEW110510B.htm.

"India a 'Bright Spot' on Cloudy Global Horizon—Lagarde." *Reuters*, March 16, 2015.

"India and the British." UK National Archives, n.d. http://www.nationalarchives.gov.uk/pathways/blackhistory/india/india_british.htm.

India and United Nations Peacekeeping. New York: Permanent Mission of India to the United Nations, 2015. https://www.pminewyork.org/slide_book/peace_keeping/#p=10.

"India Beats South Korea to Become the World's No. 5 Auto Producer." *The Korea Herald*. September 25, 2016.

"India Election: World's Biggest Voting Event Explained." *BBC News*, April 9, 2014.

"India Online: The Battle for India's E-Commerce Market Is about Much More than Retailing." *Economist*, March 5, 2016.

"India Rejects Iraq Troop Request." *BBC News*, July 14, 2003.

"India's Labour Market: A New Emphasis on Gainful Employment." McKinsey Global Institute, June 2017.

"India's Urban Awakening: Building Inclusive Cities, Sustaining Economic Growth." McKinsey Global Institute, April 2010.

Institute of International Education. "Top 25 Destinations of U.S. Study Abroad Students, 2014–2015." Open Doors Report on International Educational Exchange. New York: Institute of International Education, November 2016.

International Chamber of Commerce. *ICC Open Markets Index*. 3rd ed. Paris: International Chamber of Commerce, 2015.

International Comparison Program. "Purchasing Power Parities and Real
    Expenditures of World Economies." Washington, DC: World Bank, 2014.
    http://siteresources.worldbank.org/ICPINT/Resources/270056-1183395201801/
    Summary-of-Results-and-Findings-of-the-2011-International-Comparison-
    Program.pdf.
International Energy Agency. "India Energy Outlook." Paris: OECD/IEA,
    November 2015.
International Foundation for Electoral Systems. "IFES, Indian Election
    Commission Sign Agreement for Increased Global Collaboration." www.ifes.
    org, May 17, 2012.
International Institute of Strategic Studies. "The Military Balance 2017."
    Routledge, 2017.
International Labour Organization. "India: Why Is Women's Labour Force
    Participation Dropping?" Comment and Analysis. International Labour
    Organization, February 13, 2013.
International Monetary Fund. "World Economic Outlook Database," October
    2015. http://www.imf.org/external/pubs/ft/weo/2015/02/weodata/index.aspx.
———. "World Economic Outlook: Subdued Demand, Symptoms, and
    Remedies." International Monetary Fund, October 2016. http://www.imf.
    org/external/pubs/ft/weo/2016/02/pdf/c1.pdf.
Iqbal, Mohammed. "Faster Reforms Will Earn Us Our Rightful Place, Says
    Manmohan." *The Hindu.* May 24, 2005.
"Jaguar Land Rover Reports Strong Full Year Global Sales for 2015."
    JaguarLandRover.com, January 8, 2016. http://www.jaguarlandrover.com/gl/
    en/investor-relations/news/2016/01/08/jaguar-land-rover-reports-strong-full-
    year-global-sales-for-2015/.
Jaishankar, Dhruva. "How India Sees the World." *The Diplomat*, April 21, 2016.
    http://thediplomat.com/2016/04/how-india-sees-the-world/.
Jaishankar, S. "India, the United States, and China." Speech presented at the
    International Institute for Strategic Studies, Fullerton Lecture, Singapore,
    July 20, 2015. http://mea.gov.in/Speeches-Statements.htm?dtl/25493/IISS_
    Fullerton_Lecture_by_Foreign_Secretary_in_Singapore.
———. "India-U.S. 2015: Partnering for Peace and Prosperity."
    Speech, Vivekananda International Foundation, March 16,
    2015. http://www.vifindia.org/speeches-video/2015/march/19/
    india-u-s-2015-partnering-for-peace-and-prosperity-2.
———. "Remarks by Foreign Secretary at Indian Ocean Conference." Speech
    presented at the India Foundation Indian Ocean Conference, Singapore,
    September 1, 2016. http://www.mea.gov.in/Speeches-Statements.htm?dtl/
    27356/Remarks_by_Foreign_Secretary_at_Indian_Ocean_Conference_
    September_01_2016.
———. "Remarks by Foreign Secretary at the Release of Dr. C. Raja
    Mohan's Book 'Modi's World: Expanding India's Sphere of Influence.'"
    Speech presented at the Launch of Modi's World, New Delhi, July 17,

2015. http://mea.gov.in/Speeches-Statements.htm?dtl/25491/Remarks_by_
Foreign_Secretary_at_the_release_of_Dr_C_Raja_Mohans_book_Modis_
WorldExpanding_Indias_Sphere_of_InfluencequotJuly_17_2015.

Jordan, Miriam. "Demand for H1-B Skilled-Worker Visas Forces Agency into
Lottery." *Wall Street Journal*, April 7, 2016.

Joseph, Mathew, Nirupama Soundararajan, Manisha Gupta, and Sanghamitra
Sahu. "Impact of Organized Retailing on the Unorganized Sector." Working
Paper No. 222. New Delhi: Indian Council for Research on International
Economic Relations, September 2008. http://icrier.org/pdf/Working_
Paper222.pdf.

Joshi, Shashank. "Indian Power Projection: Ambition, Arms and Influence."
Whitehall Paper. London: Royal United Services Institute for Defense and
Security Studies, January 2016.

"JPRS Report, Near East and South Asia, India [JPRS-NEA-91-044]." Foreign
Broadcast Information Service, August 6, 1991. http://handle.dtic.mil/100.2/
ADA336171.

Kaka, Noshir, et al. "India's Ascent: Five Opportunities for Growth and
Transformation." Brussels, San Francisco, Shanghai: McKinsey Global
Institute, August 2016.

Kalra, Aditya, and Shyamantha Asokan. "Modi's Push for Hindi Struggles to
Translate in Some States." *Reuters*, June 19, 2014, India edition.

Karat, Prakash. "The Indo-US Nuclear Deal: Struggle to Defend National
Sovereignty." *The Marxist*, September 2007.

———. "Why the CPI(M) and the Left Oppose the Nuclear Deal." *The Hindu*.
August 20, 2007.

Karnad, Bharat. "LEMOA—A Most Serious Strategic Mistake, and
Consequences." *Security Wise*, August 30, 2016. https://bharatkarnad.com/
2016/08/30/lemoa-a-most-serious-strategic-mistake-and-consequences/.

———. *Why India Is Not a Great Power (Yet)*. New Delhi: Oxford University
Press, 2015.

Kaye, Charles R., Joseph S. Nye Jr., and Alyssa Ayres. "Working with a Rising
India: A Joint Venture for the New Century." Independent Task Force Report
No. 73. New York: Council on Foreign Relations Press, November 2015.

Kearns, Kel. Discussion with the author. In person, May 28, 2015.

Kee, Hiau Looi, Alessandro Nicita, and Marcelo Olarreaga. "Dataset, Trade
Restriction Indices 2009." World Bank, 2012. http://go.worldbank.org/
FG1KHXSP30.

Kelemen, Michele. "U.S. Underwhelmed with Emerging Powers At U.N."
NPR.org, September 17, 2011. http://www.npr.org/2011/09/17/140533339/
u-s-underwhelmed-with-emerging-powers-at-u-n.

Khan, Mohsin. "Realising the Potential of India–Pakistan Trade." *East Asia
Forum*, March 20, 2016. http://www.eastasiaforum.org/2016/03/20/realising-
the-potential-of-india-pakistan-trade/.

Khilnani, Sunil. *The Idea of India*. New York: Farrar Straus & Giroux, 1999.

———. "India as a Bridging Power." In *India as a New Global Leader*, 88. FPC Publications. London: Foreign Policy Centre, 2005.

Khilnani, Sunil, et al. "Nonalignment 2.0: A Foreign and Strategic Policy for India in the 21st Century." New Delhi: Centre for Policy Research, February 2012.

Khurshid, Salman, Julie Bishop, and Marty Natalegawa. "Putting Out to Sea a New Vision." *The Hindu*, November 2, 2013.

King, Charles. "The Decline of International Studies: Why Flying Blind Is Dangerous." *Foreign Affairs* 94, no. 4 (August 2015): 88–98.

Klein, Joel I., Condoleezza Rice, and Julia Levy. "U.S. Education Reform and National Security." Independent Task Force Report No. 68. New York: Council on Foreign Relations Press, March 2012.

Kochhar, Rakesh. "Despite Poverty's Plunge, Middle-Class Status Remains out of Reach for Many." Washington, DC: Pew Research Center, July 8, 2015.

Kohli, Atul. *Poverty amid Plenty in the New India*. Cambridge and New York: Cambridge Univeristy Press, 2012.

KPMG International. "Now or Never: 2016 Global CEO Outlook." KPMG, June 2016. https://home.kpmg.com/content/dam/kpmg/pdf/2016/06/2016-global-ceo-outlook.pdf.

Kreisberg, Paul H. "India after Indira." *Foreign Affairs* 63, no. 4 (Spring 1985).

Kulkarni, Pranav. "To Counter China, Govt Pushes Naval Exports to Small Indian Ocean Nations." *Indian Express*. March 4, 2015.

Kumar, Manoj. "With TPP Advancing, India Pins Hopes on China-Backed Trade Bloc." *Reuters*, February 11, 2016, India edition.

Kumar, Rajiv. "When PM Narendra Modi Echoed Arnab Goswami's Vision." *Financial Express*. November 3, 2016.

Kwong, Phoenix. "China Car Sales Surge at Fastest Rate in Three Years." *South China Morning Post*. January 12, 2017.

Lakshmi, Rama. "India Is Building Millions of Toilets, but That's the Easy Part." *Washington Post*. June 4, 2015.

———. "India's Rajasthan State Eases Labor Laws to Spur Investment in Manufacturing." *Washington Post*. January 31, 2015.

Lakshmi, Rama, and Emily Wax. "India's Government Wins Parliament Confidence Vote." *Washington Post*. July 23, 2008.

Lewis, Neil A. "A Reporter's Notebook: Shultz in His 'Garden.' " *New York Times*. June 26, 1987.

Liebig, Michael. "Kautilya's Relevance for India Today." *India Quarterly* 69, no. 2 (June 2013): 99–116.

"List of Permitted Private Satellite TV Channels as on 31-03-2017." Government of India, Ministry of Information and Broadcasting, March 3, 2017. http://mib.nic.in/sites/default/files/Master_List_of_Permitted_Private_Sattellite_TV_Channels_as_on_31-03-2017.pdf.

"Lok Sabha, Fifteenth Series, Vol. III, Second Session, 2009/1931 (Saka)." Parliament of India, July 21, 2009. http://164.100.47.132/debatestext/15/II/2107.pdf.

"Lok Sabha, Sixteenth Series, Vol. VII, Fourth Session, 2015/1936 (Saka)." Parliament of India, March 4, 2015. http://164.100.47.132/debatestext/16/IV/0403.pdf.

Lopez-Acevedo, Gladys, and Raymond Robertson. "Stitches to Riches? : Apparel Employment, Trade, and Economic Development in South Asia." Directions in Development—Poverty. Washington, DC: World Bank, 2016.

Luce, Edward. *In Spite of the Gods: The Rise of Modern India*. New York: Anchor Books, 2008.

Madhav, Ram. Interview with the author. In person, May 19, 2015.

"Madras High Court Stays Cancellation of Greenpeace India's Registration." *Times of India*. November 21, 2015.

Mahindra, Anand. Interview with the author. In person, August 3, 2015.

Majumdar, Boria. "How Cricket Was Sold in India." *Open Magazine*, April 14, 2012.

"'Make in India' Racks up $222 Billion in Pledges." *Times of India*. February 19, 2016.

Malinowski, Tom. "Why We Issue the Human Rights Reports." State.gov. *DipNote (blog)*, June 25, 2015. http://blogs.state.gov/stories/2015/06/25/why-we-issue-human-rights-reports.

Malone, David M. *Does the Elephant Dance?: Contemporary Indian Foreign Policy*. Oxford and New York: Oxford University Press, 2011.

Malone, David M., and Rohan Mukherjee. "Dilemmas of Sovereignty and Order: India and the UN Security Council." In *Shaping the Emerging World: India and the Multilateral Order*. Washington, DC: Brookings Institution Press, 2013.

Malvania, Urvi. "STAR India to Take Hotstar Global." *Business Standard*. March 31, 2016.

Markey, Daniel S. *No Exit from Pakistan: America's Tortured Relationship with Islamabad*. Cambridge and New York: Cambridge University Press, 2013.

Mattoo, Amitabh. *The Reluctant Superpower: Understanding India and Its Aspirations*. Carlton, VIC: Melbourne University Publishing, 2012.

Mavriplis, Catherine. "When Was the Last Time You Saw Women Scientists Celebrate a Space Mission? Indian Women Celebrate @MarsOrbiter." *Twitter*, September 25, 2014. https://twitter.com/CWSE_ON/status/515192127924752384.

Mehra, Puja. "India to Hold G20 Chair in 2018, Delhi May Play Host." *The Hindu*. October 1, 2015.

———. "India's Stand Prevails in Bali." *The Hindu*. December 7, 2013.

Mehta, Nalin. *Behind a Billion Screens: What Television Tells Us About Modern India*. New Delhi: HarperCollinsIndia, 2015.

Mehta, Pratap Bhanu. "The American Hug." *Indian Express*. April 2, 2016.

Menon, Shivshankar. "Developing Indigenous Concepts and Vocabulary: Kautilya's *Arthshastra*." Speech, Institute for Defence Studies and Analyses, New Delhi, October 8, 2013. http://idsa.in/keyspeeches/KautilyasArthashastraAmbShivshankarMenonNSA.

————. Interview with the author. In person, August 7, 2015.

Meyer, Christian, and Nancy Birdsall. "New Estimates of India's Middle Class: Technical Note." Washington, DC: Center for Global Development, October 2012. http://www.cgdev.org/doc/2013_MiddleClassIndia_TechnicalNote_CGDNote.pdf.

"Midway Plaisance Park." Chicago Park District, n.d. http://www.chicagoparkdistrict.com/parks/Midway-Plaisance-Park/.

Miglani, Sanjeev. "Indian Government Aims to Cut Defence Imports, Hold Spending Steady." *Reuters*. February 29, 2016.

Miller, Manjari Chatterjee. *Wronged by Empire*. Palo Alto: Stanford University Press, 2013.

Miller, Terry, and Anthony B. Kim. "India." In *2017 Index of Economic Freedom*. Heritage Foundation, 2017. http://www.heritage.org/index/country/india.

"Millions of Workers Strike for Better Wages in India." www.dw.com. *Deutsche Welle*, September 2, 2016. http://www.dw.com/en/millions-of-workers-strike-for-better-wages-in-india/a-19522682.

Mitra, Devirupa. "Ukraine Requests India to Support New Government in Kiev." *New Indian Express*. March 4, 2014.

"Modest India Doesn't Try to Reorder the World: NSA." *Rediff.com*, February 4, 2013.

Modi, Narendra. "A Strong India-U.S. Partnership Can Anchor Peace, Prosperity & Stability across the World." Speech presented at the Joint Meeting of the U.S. Congress, Washington, DC, June 8, 2016. http://www.narendramodi.in/prime-minister-narendra-modi-addresses-joint-meeting-of-u-s-congress-in-washington-dc-484217.

————. "Address to Indian Community at Madison Square Garden, New York." Speech, New York, NY, September 28, 2014. http://www.narendramodi.in/text-of-prime-minister-shri-narendra-modi-s-address-to-indian-community-at-madison-square-garden-new-york-292061.

————. "Embarking on 'Swami Vivekananda Yuva Vikas Yatra': CM Blogs on 9/11." *NarendraModi.in,* September 11, 2012. http://www.narendramodi.in/embarking-on-swami-vivekananda-yuva-vikas-yatra'-cm-blogs-on-911-3076.

————. "PM at ASEAN Business and Investment Summit." Speech, Kuala Lumpur, November 21, 2015. http://www.narendramodi.in/text-of-prime-minister-s-address-at-asean-business-and-investment-summit-376148.

————. "Speech at Launch of World Sufi Forum." Speech presented at the World Sufi Forum, New Delhi, March 17, 2016. http://www.narendramodi.in/pm-modi-at-the-world-islamic-sufi-conference-in-new-delhi-428276.

————. "Swami Vivekananda's Call to the Nation." *NarendraModi.in*, January 12, 2012. http://www.narendramodi.in/swami-vivekananda's-call-to-the-nation-3052.

————. "Text of PM's Remarks at the Launch of 'Skill India.'" Speech presented at the National Skill Development Mission

Launch, New Delhi, July 15, 2015. http://www.narendramodi.in/
text-of-pm-s-remarks-at-the-launch-of-skill-india--206108.
———. "Text of the PM's Remarks on the Commissioning
of Coast Ship *Barracuda*." Speech, Port Louis, Mauritius,
March 12, 2015. http://www.narendramodi.in/
text-of-the-pms-remarks-on-the-commissioning-of-coast-ship-barracuda-2954.
———. "Text of the PM's Statement at the United Nations General
Assembly." Speech presented at the UN General Assembly,
New York, September 27, 2014. http://www.narendramodi.in/
text-of-the-pms-statement-at-the-united-nations-general-assembly-6660.
———. "The World Is Recognizing the Power of India
because of the Hard Work Done by You: PM Addresses the
Indian Diaspora at SAP Centre." Speech, SAP Center, San
Jose, September 27, 2015. http://www.narendramodi.in/
pm-s-address-to-the-indian-community-at-sap-centre-san-jose-354664.
Mohan, C. Raja. *Crossing the Rubicon: The Shaping of India's New Foreign Policy*.
New York: Palgrave Macmillan, 2004.
———. Interview with the author. In person, May 22, 2015.
———. *Samudra Manthan: Sino-Indian Rivalry in the Indo-Pacific*. Washington,
DC: Carnegie Endowment for International Peace, 2012.
Mohan, Rakesh, and Muneesh Kapur. "Emerging Powers and Global
Governance: Whither the IMF?" IMF Working Paper. Washington,
DC: International Monetary Fund, October 2015. http://www.imf.org/
external/pubs/ft/wp/2015/wp15219.pdf.
Mufson, Steven. "New Energy on India." *Washington Post*. July 18, 2006.
Murthy, Mahesh. "Facebook Is Misleading Indians with Its Full-Page Ads about
Free Basics." *LinkedIn.com*, December 24, 2015. https://www.linkedin.com/
pulse/facebook-misleading-indians-its-full-page-ads-free-basics-murthy.
Mwanasali, Musifiky. "The Era of Non-Indifference." *Mail and Guardian*.
September 13, 2005.
Nair, Rupam Jain, and Frank Jack Daniel. "Interview: India Warns Global
Charities Not to Work against Government." *Reuters*. October 1, 2015.
Nair-Ghaswalla, Amrita. "India Is World's Largest Importer of Arms."
BusinessLine. March 10, 2016.
Narayan, Ambar, and Rinku Murgai. "Looking Back on Two Decades of Poverty
and Well-Being in India." Policy Research Working Paper. Washington,
DC: World Bank, April 2016. http://documents.worldbank.org/curated/en/
841931468196177423/pdf/WPS7626.pdf.
Narlikar, Amrita, and Aruna Narlikar. *Bargaining with a Rising India: Lessons
from the Mahabharata*. Oxford: Oxford University Press, 2014.
National Institution for Transforming India Aayog. "Creating a Movement for
Change." Speech presented at the Civil Services Day, New Delhi, March
26, 2016. http://niti.gov.in/mgov_file/presentations/Presentation%20for%20
Civil%20Service%20Day%20final.pdf.

Nayak, Amar K. J. R. "FDI Model in Emerging Economies: Case of Suzuki Motor Corporation in India." *Journal of the American Academy of Business, Cambridge* 6 (March 2005): 238–45.

Nehru, Jawaharlal. "Changing India." *Foreign Affairs* 41, no. 3 (April 1963): 453–65.

———. *Letters to Chief Ministers 1947–64*. Vol. 1, 1947–49. 5 vols. New Delhi: Government of India, 1985.

———. *Letters to Chief Ministers 1947–64*. Vol. 2, 1950–52. 5 vols. New Delhi: Government of India, 1985.

———. *Letters to Chief Ministers 1947–64*. Vol. 3, 1952–54. 5 vols. New Delhi: Government of India, 1987.

———. *Letters to Chief Ministers 1947–64*. Vol. 4, 1954–57. 5 vols. New Delhi: Government of India, 1988.

———. "Message of Swami Vivekananda to Modern India." *Prabudha Bharata*. January 1964. www.VivekanandaArchive.org. http://vivekanandaarchive.org/admin/sv_teach_image/_file_7760b13dc738525ac016af78853b7fc5548bb97f.pdf.

"New Foreign Trade Policy: $900 Bn Exports by FY20." *Indian Express*. April 2, 2015.

"The New Geopolitics of China, India, and Pakistan: Keynote Session." YouTube video, from a symposium streamed live by the Council on Foreign Relations, May 4, 2016. https://www.youtube.com/watch?v=cgcBKFVH85Y.

Nilekani, Nandan. *Imagining India*. Toronto: Viking Canada, 2008.

———. Interview with the author. In person, August 10, 2015.

Ninan, T. N. *The Turn of the Tortoise: The Challenge and Promise of India's Future*. New Delhi: Allen Lane (Penguin), 2015.

Nye, Joseph S. *The Future of Power*. New York: PublicAffairs, 2011.

O'Brien, Sarah Ashley. "High-Skilled Visa Applications Hit Record High—Again." *CNNMoney.com*, April 12, 2016.

Ogden, Chris. *Hindu Nationalism and the Evolution of Contemporary Indian Security; Portents of Power*. Oxford International Relations in South Asia Series. New Delhi: Oxford University Press, 2014.

Ollapally, Deepa. "India: The Ambivalent Power in Asia." *International Studies* 48, no. 3–4 (2011): 201–22.

Organisation for Economic Co-Operation and Development. "Active with India." Paris: OECD, 2015.

Padmanabhan, Anil. "We Should Have Done What We Have in Half the Time: Montek Singh Ahluwalia." *Mint*. February 5, 2016.

"Pak-India Trade Still a Fraction of $40 Billion Potential." *Express Tribune*. March 13, 2012.

Panagariya, Arvind. *India: The Emerging Giant*. New York: Oxford University Press, 2010.

Panda, Baijayant. Interview with the author. In person, August 12, 2015.

Park, Haeyoun. "How Outsourcing Companies Are Gaming the Visa System." *New York Times*. November 10, 2015.

Parker, Grant. "Question about Pliny the Elder and Gold in India (email),"
    August 1, 2016.
Pasricha, Anjana. "India Rejects Joint Naval Patrols with US in South China
    Sea." *VOA News*, March 11, 2016.
Pattanaik, Devdutt. *Business Sutra: A Very Indian Approach to Management.* New
    Delhi: Aleph Book Company, 2013.
————. Interview with the author. Via telephone, September 1, 2015.
Pattanayak, Banikinkar. "India Likely to Miss Its Garment Export Target for
    Current Fiscal." *Financial Express.* January 21, 2016.
People's Republic of China, Ministry of Foreign Affairs. "The 5th Meeting of
    CICA Ministers of Foreign Affairs Held in Beijing." People's Republic of
    China, Ministry of Foreign Affairs, April 28, 2016. http://www.fmprc.gov.cn/
    mfa_eng/zxxx_662805/t1360242.shtml.
Peri, Dinakar. "No Scope for India-U.S. Joint Patrols at This Time: Parrikar."
    The Hindu. March 5, 2016.
Permanent Mission of India to the United Nations, Geneva. "India's Explanation
    of Vote Before the Vote on the Draft Resolution 'Promoting Reconciliation,
    Accountability, and Human Rights in Sri Lanka', Agenda Item 2, at the 25th
    Session of the Human Rights Council." Government of India, Ministry of
    External Affairs, March 27, 2014. http://www.pmindiaun.org/pages.php?id=903.
————. "Statement on Agenda Item 4 General Debate: Human Rights
    Situation That Requires the Council's Attention, September 16, 2014."
    Government of India, Ministry of External Affairs, September 16, 2014.
    http://www.pmindiaun.org/pages.php?id=983.
Platt, Barbara. "UN Security Council Middle Powers' Arab Spring Dilemma."
    BBC News, November 8, 2011.
Pliny the Elder. *Natural History.* Translated by H. Rackham. Loeb Classical
    Library. Vol. II. Cambridge: Harvard University Press, 1942.
Pollock, Sheldon. "Cosmopolitan and Vernacular in History." *Public Culture* 12,
    no. 3 (Fall 2000): 591–625.
Press Trust of India. "BCCI Threatened to Form Parallel World Cricket Body."
    ESPNCricinfo.com, June 7, 2014.
————. "I'll Set Walmart Store Afire: Uma." *The Hindu.* November 26, 2011.
————. "India Has Begun to Get Its 'Due' on World Stage." *Economic Times*,
    November 7, 2014.
————. "India Hits Out at UN Security Council over Lack of Transparency in
    Peacekeeping Operations." *Indian Express.* October 13, 2015.
————. "India Hopes for a Climate Deal as High-Stakes Paris Talks Head for
    Final Phase." *Times of India*, December 6, 2015.
————. "India in Position to Be Net Provider of Security: Manmohan Singh."
    Mint. May 23, 2013.
————. "India, Pakistan Become Full SCO Members." *The Hindu*, July 11, 2015.
————. "India's Middle Class Population to Touch 267 Million in 5 Yrs."
    Economic Times. February 6, 2011.

————. "India's Unemployment Rate Highest in 5 Years in 2015–16." *Indian Express*. September 29, 2016.

————. "Jaitley Seeks Reform in IMF, World Bank." *Business Standard*. April 18, 2016.

————. "Lenovo Says Half the Smartphones Sold in India in 2016 Will Be Locally Made." *Gadgets360.NDTV.com*, February 2, 2016.

————. "Textile Ministry Finalizing Draft Guidelines of National Textiles Policy," *Economic Times*. June 5, 2017.

————. "World's Largest 'Charkha' to Be on Display at IGI Airport." *Times of India*. April 17, 2016.

Preston, Julia. "Large Companies Game H-1B Visa Program, Costing the U.S. Jobs." *New York Times*. November 10, 2015.

————. "Pink Slips at Disney. But First, Training Foreign Replacements." *New York Times*. June 3, 2015.

Puri, Hardeep Singh. Interview with the author. In person, June 8, 2015.

Quraishi, S. Y. Interview with the author. In person, August 8, 2015.

Radhakrishnan, R. K. "Kapilavastu Relics to Be Displayed in Sri Lanka." *The Hindu*. September 11, 2011.

Rai, Saritha. "The High Stakes of India's Dispute with the U.S. over Visa Fees." *Bloomberg Business*, March 20, 2016.

Rajghatta, Chidanand. "India Denies Visa to U.S. Religious Freedom Watchdogs," *Times of India*. June 17, 2009.

Rajghatta, Chidanand. "Narendra Modi Calls for International Yoga Day." *Times of India*. September 28, 2014.

"Rajya Sabha, Two-Hundred and Thirty-Fourth Session, Uncorrected Verbatim Debate Transcript." Parliament of India, March 4, 2015. http://164.100.47.5/newdebate/234/04032015/Fullday.pdf.

Ramesh, Jairam. Interview with the author. In person, August 12, 2015.

————. *To the Brink and Back: India's 1991 Story*. New Delhi: Rupa, 2015.

Rao, Nirupama. Interview with the author. In person, June 26, 2015.

Rastello, Sandrine. "India to Emerge as Winner from Asia's Shrinking Labor Force." *Bloomberg*. November 8, 2015.

Ravindranath, Sushila. "Quality Matters for Success." *The Hindu*. January 12, 2000.

"Rediff.com in Strong Debut." *CNNMoney.com*, June 14, 2000.

"Reforming Indian Banks: Bureaucrats at the Till." *Economist*, June 4, 2016.

"Resolution Adopted by the Human Rights Council* S-19/1, The Deteriorating Situation of Human Rights in the Syrian Arab Republic, and the Recent Killings in El-Houleh." UN Human Rights Council, June 4, 2012. http://www.ohchr.org/Documents/HRBodies/HRCouncil/SpecialSession/Session19/A-HRC-RES-S-19-1_en.pdf.

Rice, Condoleezza. "Remarks En Route to India." Press briefing, Washington, DC, March 15, 2005. http://2001-2009.state.gov/secretary/rm/2005/43465.htm.

Rickett, Oscar. "'The Newshour' with Arnab Goswami Is India's Most Over the Top News Show." *Vice.com*, January 6, 2016.

Rodrik, Dani. "Premature Deindustrialization." NBER Working Paper Series. Cambridge, MA: National Bureau of Economic Research, February 2015. http://www.nber.org/papers/w20935.pdf.

Roy-Chaudhry, Rahul. "India's Official Maritime Strategy." IISS. org. *IISS Voices*, December 14, 2015. https://www.iiss.org/en/iiss%20voices/blogsections/iiss-voices-2015-dda3/december-5c5a/indias-official-maritime-security-strategy-e6a0.

"Russian Interests in Crimea 'Legitimate': India." *Times of India*. March 7, 2014.

S. R. "Why China Is Creating a New 'World Bank' for Asia." Economist.com. *The Economist Explains (blog)*, November 11, 2014. http://www.economist.com/blogs/economist-explains/2014/11/economist-explains-6.

Sabharwal, Manish. Interview with the author. In person, August 10, 2015.

———. "Making India Job-Friendly." *Mint*, August 1, 2014.

Samanta, Pranab Dhal. "No More English, Modi Chooses Hindi for Talks with Foreign Leaders." *Indian Express*. June 5, 2014.

Sanger, David. "U.S. Exploring Deal to Limit Pakistan's Nuclear Arsenal." *New York Times*. October 15, 2015.

"Sanya Declaration," April 14, 2011.

Saran, Shyam. Interview with the author. In person, May 20, 2015.

———. "Premature Power." *Business Standard*, March 17, 2010.

Sasi, Anil. "Maruti Suzuki 800: The Car with No Name." *Financial Express*. February 23, 2014.

Schaffer, Howard B., and Teresita C. Schaffer. *India at the Global High Table: The Quest for Regional Primacy and Strategic Autonomy*. Washington, DC: Brookings Institution Press, 2016.

Schwab, Klaus and Xavier Sala-i-Martín. *Global Competitiveness Report*. Geneva: World Economic Forum, 2016.

Schwab, Susan C. "After Doha." *Foreign Affairs* 90, no. 3 (June 2011): 104–17.

"Security Council Fails to Adopt Draft Resolution on Syria as Russian Federation, China Veto Text Supporting Arab League's Proposed Peace Plan." *UN Security Council Meetings Coverage*. February 4, 2012. http://www.un.org/press/en/2012/sc10536.doc.htm.

Security Council Meetings Coverage. "Security Council Approves 'No-Fly Zone' over Libya, Authorizing 'All Necessary Measures' to Protect Civilians, by Vote of 10 in Favour with 5 Abstentions." United Nations, March 17, 2011.

Seidel, Jamie. "India Eyes Russian Aircraft Carrier as Its Fourth Step towards Super Power Status." *News Corp Australia Network*, March 4, 2016.

SelectUSA. "Foreign Direct Investment (FDI): INDIA." U.S. Department of Commerce, 2016. https://www.selectusa.gov/servlet/servlet.FileDownload?file=015t0000000LKMV.

Sengupta, Somini. *The End of Karma: Hope and Fury among India's Young*. New York: W. W. Norton & Company, 2016.

Shambaugh, David. *China Goes Global: The Partial Power*. Reprint edition. Oxford and New York: Oxford University Press, 2014.

Shankar, Uday. Interview with the author. In person, May 27, 2015.

Sharma, Mihir S. *Restart: The Last Chance for the Indian Economy*. Random House India, 2015.

Sharma, Ruchir. *The Rise and Fall of Nations: Forces of Change in the Post-Crisis World*. Kindle. New York and London: W. W. Norton & Company, 2016.

Shukla, Ajai. "New Stealth Destroyer Launched, yet Navy Faces Major Fleet Shortfalls." *Broadsword*, September 18, 2016. http://ajaishukla.blogspot.in/2016/09/new-stealth-destroyer-launched-yet-navy.html.

Sidhu, Waheguru Pal Singh, Pratap Bhanu Mehta, and Bruce Jones, eds. *Shaping the Emerging World: India and the Multilateral Order*. Washington, DC: Brookings Institution Press, 2013.

Singh, Jaswant. "Against Nuclear Apartheid." *Foreign Affairs* 77, no. 5 (October 1998): 41–52.

Singh, Manmohan. "Address by PM at the Joint Session of the Two Houses of the Parliament of Ethiopia." Speech, Addis Ababa, May 26, 2011. http://pib.nic.in/newsite/PrintRelease.aspx?relid=72327.

———. "Of Oxford, Economics, Empire, and Freedom." *The Hindu*. July 10, 2005.

———. "PM's Address at McKinsey Meet." New Delhi, October 23, 2007. http://archivepmo.nic.in/drmanmohansingh/speech-details.php?nodeid=581.

———. "PM's Statement in the Lok Sabha on Civil Nuclear Energy Cooperation with the United States." Presented at the Lok Sabha, New Delhi, August 13, 2007. http://archivepmo.nic.in/drmanmohansingh/speech-details.php?nodeid=550.

Sitharaman, Nirmala. "Statement by Nirmala Sitharaman in Lok Sabha Regarding 'India's Stand in the WTO.'" Presented at the Lok Sabha, New Delhi, August 5, 2014. http://pib.nic.in/newsite/PrintRelease.aspx?relid=107999.

Smallwood, Jimmy. "ICC Meeting in Dubai Discusses Proposed Changes to Test Cricket." *BBC Sport*, January 28, 2014. http://www.bbc.com/sport/cricket/25927581.

Smeltz, Dina, Ivo Daalder, Karl Friedhoff, and Craig Kafura. "America Divided: Political Partisanship and U.S. Foreign Policy." Results of the 2015 Chicago Council Survey of American Public Opinion and U.S. Foreign Policy. Chicago Council Surveys. Chicago: Chicago Council on Global Affairs, September 2015.

Snavely, Brent and Greg Gardener. "Automakers Sell Record 17.55 million Vehicles in U.S. in 2016." *Detroit Free Press*. January 4, 2017.

"The Social World." *New York Times*. May 3, 1894.

Society of Indian Automobile Manufacturers. "Automotive Mission Plan: 2016–26 (A Curtain Raiser)." New Delhi: Society of Indian Automobile Manufacturers, September 2015.

Srinivasan, T. N. "Economic Reforms and Global Integration." In *The India-China Relationship: What the United States Needs to Know*, edited by Francine R. Frankel and Harry Harding, 219–66. Washington, DC: Woodrow Wilson Center Press, 2004.

Stokes, Bruce. "India and Modi: The Honeymoon Continues." Pew Research Center, September 19, 2016.

———. "The Modi Bounce: Indians Give Their Prime Minister and Economy High Marks, Worry about Crime, Jobs, Prices, Corruption." Washington, DC: Pew Research Center, September 2015.

Stuenkel, Oliver. "The Uncertain Future of IBSA." Rising Democracies Network. Washington, DC: Carnegie Endowment for International Peace, February 18, 2015. http://carnegieendowment.org/2015/02/18/uncertain-future-of-ibsa-pub-59108.

Subramanian, Nirupama. "Indian Ocean Countries Meet to Focus on Trade Ties." *The Hindu*, July 4, 2013.

Summers, Lawrence H. "The US-India Economic Relations in the 21st Century." Speech presented at the US-India Business Council Annual Dinner, Washington, DC, June 2, 2010.

Suneja, Kirtika. "PMO Push: Commerce Ministry Plans to Set Up Dedicated Team for Trade Talks." *Economic Times*, April 11, 2016, New Delhi edition.

Swami Vivekananda, and Swami Nikhilananda. *Vivekananda: The Yogas and Other Works, Including the Chicago Addresses, Jnāna-Yoga, Bhakti-Yoga, Karma-Yoga, Rāja-Yoga, Inspired Talks, and Lectures, Poems and Letters. Chosen and with a Biography by Swami Nikhilānanda.* New York: Ramakrishna-Vivekananda Center, 1953.

"Swami Vivekananda, The Great High Priest of India." *Washington Post*, October 27, 1894.

Sykes, Colonel. "The External Commerce of British India During Two Periods of Years; Namely, the Eight Years (Ended 30th April) 1834–35 to 1841–42, and the Five Years 1849–50 to 1853–54." *Journal of the Statistical Society of London* 19, no. 2 (June 1856): 107–26.

Syman, Stephanie. "Boston Brahma." *Boston Globe*. August 24, 2003.

Talbott, Strobe. *Engaging India: Diplomacy, Democracy, and the Bomb.* Washington, DC: Brookings Institution Press, 2004.

Tanham, George K. "Indian Strategic Thought: An Interpretive Essay." Santa Monica: RAND, 1992.

Tarlo, Emma. *Clothing Matters: Dress and Identity in India.* Chicago: University of Chicago Press, 1996.

Telecom Regulatory Authority of India. "Annual Report 2005–2006." Government of India, Telecom Regulatory Authority of India, September 2006. http://www.trai.gov.in/WriteReadData/UserFiles/Documents/AnuualReports/ar_05_06.pdf.

————. "Press Release No. 26/2016, Information Note to the Press," April 26, 2016. http://www.trai.gov.in/WriteReadData/PressRealease/Document/Press_Release_no26_eng.pdf.

Tellis, Ashley J. "Making Waves: Aiding India's Next-Generation Aircraft Carrier." *CarnegieEndowment.org*, April 22, 2015. http://carnegieendowment.org/2015/04/22/making-waves-aiding-india-s-next-generation-aircraft-carrier.

Tellis, Ashley J., Bibek Debroy, and Reece Trevor. *Getting India Back on Track: An Action Agenda for Reform*. Washington, D.C.: Carnegie Endowment for International Peace, 2014.

Tellis, Ashley J., and Sean Mirski. *Crux of Asia: China, India, and the Emerging Global Order*. Washington, DC: Carnegie Endowment for International Peace, 2013.

Tellis, Ashley J., and C. Raja Mohan. "The Strategic Rationale for Deeper U.S.-Indian Economic Ties." Washington, DC: Carnegie Endowment for International Peace, 2015.

Tewari, Ruhi, and Krishnamurthy Ramasubbu. "Left Withdraws Support, but Govt Sanguine." *Mint*. July 8, 2008.

Tewari, Saumya. "Rural India Continues to Outvote Urban India." *Indiaspend.com*, May 30, 2014.

Thakur, Anurag. Interview with the author. In person, May 21, 2015.

Tharoor, Ishaan. "India Leads Rescue of Foreign Nationals, including Americans, Trapped in Yemen." *Washington Post*. April 8, 2015.

Tharoor, Shashi. *Pax Indica: India and the World of the Twenty-first Century*. London: Penguin Global, 2012.

————. "Viewpoint: Britain Must Pay Reparations to India." *BBC News*, July 22, 2015.

"Thrives on Mystery and Vegetables: First Dinner of the 'V' Club Results in an Enjoyable Evening." *New York Times*. April 1, 1894.

Thussu, Daya Kishan. "Privatizing the Airwaves: The Impact of Globalization on Broadcasting in India." *Media, Culture & Society* 21, no. 1 (January 1999): 125–31.

Tian, Nan, Aude Fleurant, Pieter Wezemen, and Siemon Wezemen. "Trends in World Military Expenditure, 2016." SIPRI Fact Sheet. Stockholm: SIPRI, April 2017.

Times News Network. "Govt Brings In Labour Reforms via Rs 6,000cr Textile Pkg." *Times of India*. June 23, 2016.

————. "IMF Slashes India's Growth Forecast to 6.6% from 7.6%." *Times of India*. January 17, 2017.

Trautmann, Thomas R. *Arthashastra: The Science of Wealth*. The Story of Indian Business. New Delhi: Penguin Books India, 2012.

Tripathi, Ashish. "Rahul Gandhi Promoting FDI to Benefit Foreigners: Mayawati." *Times of India*. November 26, 2011.

Tweed, David, and N. C. Bipindra. "Submarine Killers: India's $61 Billion Warning to China." *Bloomberg*, July 28, 2015.

"UN Adopts Resolution on Sri Lanka War Crimes Probe." *BBC News*, March 22, 2012.

UN News Service. "UN Projects World Population to Reach 8.5 Billion by 2030, Driven by Growth in Developing Countries." *UN News Centre*, July 29, 2015. http://www.un.org/apps/news/story.asp?NewsID=51526#.Vt9PT_krK7o.

"UN Passes Resolution against Sri Lanka Rights Record." *BBC News*, March 21, 2013.

"UN Security Council Presidential Statement, S/PRST/2011/16." United Nations, August 3, 2011. https://documents-dds-ny.un.org/doc/UNDOC/GEN/N11/442/75/PDF/N1144275.pdf?OpenElement.

United Nations Conference on Trade and Development. "Global Investment Trends Monitor." Geneva: UNCTAD, January 20, 2016. http://unctad.org/en/PublicationsLibrary/webdiaeia2016d1_en.pdf.

"United Nations Democracy Fund, Contribution Table." United Nations, April 25, 2017. http://www.un.org/democracyfund/contribution-table.

United Nations Department of Economic and Social Affairs, Population Division. "World Population Prospects: The 2015 Revision." New York: United Nations, July 2015. http://esa.un.org/unpd/wpp/Graphs/DemographicProfiles/.

United Nations General Assembly, Sixty-ninth Session. "Resolution Adopted by the General Assembly on 11 December 2014, 69/131. International Day of Yoga," December 11, 2014. http://www.un.org/en/ga/search/view_doc.asp?symbol=A/RES/69/131.

U.S. Citizenship and Immigration Services. "Characteristics of H-1B Specialty Occupation Workers." Annual Report to Congress. Fiscal Year 2004 Annual Report to Congress. Washington, DC: U.S. Department of Homeland Security, November 2006. https://www.uscis.gov/sites/default/files/USCIS/Resources/Reports%20and%20Studies/H-1B/h1b_fy04_characteristics.pdf.

————. "Characteristics of H-1B Specialty Occupation Workers." Annual Report to Congress. Fiscal Year 2006 Annual Report to Congress. Washington, DC: U.S. Department of Homeland Security, March 17, 2008. https://www.uscis.gov/sites/default/files/USCIS/New%20Structure/2nd%20Level%20%28Left%20Nav%20Parents%29/Resources%20-%202nd%20Level/h1B_fy06_characteristics_report_17mar09.pdf.

————. "Characteristics of H-1B Specialty Occupation Workers." Annual Report to Congress. Fiscal Year 2008 Annual Report to Congress. Washington, DC: U.S. Department of Homeland Security, May 1, 2009. https://www.uscis.gov/sites/default/files/USCIS/New%20Structure/2nd%20Level%20%28Left%20Nav%20Parents%29/Resources%20-%202nd%20Level/h1b_fy08_characteristics_report_01may09.pdf.

————. "Characteristics of H-1B Specialty Occupation Workers." Annual Report to Congress. Fiscal Year 2010 Annual Report to Congress. Washington, DC: U.S. Department of Homeland Security, August 4, 2011.

https://www.uscis.gov/sites/default/files/USCIS/Resources/Reports%20
and%20Studies/H-1B/FY10H-1BSpecialtyOccupationalWorkers.pdf.
————. "Characteristics of H-1B Specialty Occupation Workers." Annual
Report to Congress. Fiscal Year 2012 Annual Report to Congress.
Washington, DC: Department of Homeland Security, June 26, 2013. https://
www.uscis.gov/sites/default/files/USCIS/Resources/Reports%20and%20
Studies/H-1B/h1b-fy-12-characteristics.pdf.
————. "Characteristics of H-1B Specialty Occupation Workers." Annual
Report to Congress. Fiscal Year 2014 Annual Report to Congress.
Washington, DC: U.S. Department of Homeland Security, February 26,
2015. https://www.uscis.gov/sites/default/files/USCIS/Resources/Reports%20
and%20Studies/H-1B/h-1B-characteristics-report-14.pdf.
U.S. Department of Agriculture, Economic Research Service. "Real GDP (2010
Dollars) Projections." U.S. Department of Agriculture, December 18, 2015.
http://www.ers.usda.gov/data-products/international-macroeconomic-data-
set.aspx.
U.S. Department of Commerce, Bureau of Economic Analysis. "U.S. Trade
in Goods and Services by Selected Countries and Areas, 1999–Present
(Excel)." U.S. Department of Commerce, June 2, 2017. http://www.bea.gov/
international/.
U.S. Department of State. "End-Use Monitoring of Defense Articles and
Defense Services Commercial Exports FY 2014." U.S. Department of State,
2015. http://www.pmddtc.state.gov/reports/documents/End_Use_FY2014.
pdf.
————. "The Global Coalition to Counter ISIL," n.d. http://www.state.gov/s/
seci/.
————. "Voting Practices in the United Nations 2011." Report to Congress
Submitted Pursuant to Public Laws 101-246 and 108-447. Washington,
DC: U.S. Department of State, April 2012. http://www.state.gov/documents/
organization/190024.pdf.
————. "Voting Practices in the United Nations 2012." Report to Congress
Submitted Pursuant to Public Laws 101-246 and 108-447. Washington,
DC: U.S. Department of State, April 2013. http://www.state.gov/documents/
organization/208072.pdf.
————. "Voting Practices in the United Nations 2013." Report to Congress
Submitted Pursuant to Public Laws 101-246 and 108-447. Washington,
DC: U.S. Department of State, March 2014. http://www.state.gov/
documents/organization/225048.pdf.
————. "Voting Practices in the United Nations 2014." Report to Congress
Submitted Pursuant to Public Laws 101-246 and 108-447. Washington,
DC: U.S. Department of State, July 2015. http://www.state.gov/documents/
organization/245163.pdf.
————. "Voting Practices in the United Nations 2015." Report to Congress
Submitted Pursuant to Public Laws 101-246 and 108-447. Washington,

DC: U.S. Department of State, June 2016. http://www.state.gov/documents/organization/260322.pdf.

U.S. Department of State Office of the Spokesman. "Background Briefing by Administration Officials on U.S.-South Asia Relations." *U.S. Department of State Archive*, March 25, 2005. http://2001-2009.state.gov/r/pa/prs/ps/2005/43853.htm.

"United States—Measures Concerning Non-Immigrant Visas; Request for Consultations by India (S/L/410; WT/DS503/1)." World Trade Organization, March 8, 2016.

"US Pushes India to Ink Contentious Defence Pacts." *Times of India*. February 27, 2015.

"USCIS to Implement H-1B Visa Reform Act of 2004." U.S. Citizenship and Immigration Services, U.S. Department of Homeland Security, December 9, 2004. https://www.uscis.gov/sites/default/files/files/pressrelease/H-1B_12_9_04.pdf.

Vajpayee, Atal Bihari. "India, USA and the World: Let Us Work Together to Solve the Political-Economic Y2K Problem." Speech presented at the Asia Society, New York, NY, September 28, 1998. http://asiasociety.org/india-usa-and-world-let-us-work-together-solve-political-economic-y2k-problem.

————. "Suo Motu Statement by Prime Minister Shri Atal Bihari Vajpayee in Parliament on 27th May, 1998." Speech presented at the Lok Sabha, Twelfth Series, Session Two, 1998/1920 (Saka), New Delhi, May 27, 1998. http://parliamentofindia.nic.in/ls/lsdeb/ls12/ses2/04270598.htm.

Vajpeyi, Ananya. *Righteous Republic: The Political Foundations of Modern India*. Cambridge, MA: Harvard University Press, 2012.

Varshney, Ashutosh. *Battles Half Won: India's Improbable Democracy*. New Delhi: Penguin Global, 2014.

Venkatesan, Ravi. *Conquering the Chaos: Win in India, Win Everywhere*. Boston: Harvard Business Review Press, 2013.

————. Interview with the author. Via telephone, October 1, 2015.

Vijetha S. N. "Court Relief for Greenpeace Activist Priya Pillai." *The Hindu*. March 13, 2015.

"Vivekananda's Address." *Harvard Crimson*. May 17, 1894.

Wariavwalla, Bharat. "India: From Nehrus' Rule to Coalitions." *Los Angeles Times*. December 10, 1989.

Weber, Max. "Politics as a Vocation." In *From Max Weber: Essays in Sociology*. Oxford: Routledge, 1948.

Weinraub, Bernard. "Economic Crisis Forcing Once Self-Reliant India to Seek Aid." *New York Times*. June 29, 1991.

"Whataboutism." *Economist*, January 31, 2008. http://www.economist.com/node/10598774.

Wheaton, Sarah. "Obama: China Might Join Trade Deal—Eventually." *Politico*. June 3, 2015.

White House, Office of the Press Secretary. "Joint Statement: The United States and India: Enduring Global Partners in the 21st Century," June 7, 2016. https://www.whitehouse.gov/the-press-office/2016/06/07/joint-statement-united-states-and-india-enduring-global-partners-21st.

———. "Statement by NSC Spokesperson Ned Price on National Security Advisor Susan E. Rice's Call with National Security Advisor Ajit Doval of India," September 28, 2016. https://www.whitehouse.gov/the-press-office/2016/06/07/joint-statement-united-states-and-india-enduring-global-partners-21st.

———. "U.S.-India Joint Statement साँझा प्रयास—सबका विकास"—'Shared Effort; Progress for All,'" January 25, 2015. https://www.whitehouse.gov/the-press-office/2015/01/25/us-india-joint-statement-shared-effort-progress-all.

———. "U.S.-India Joint Strategic Vision for the Asia-Pacific and Indian Ocean Region," January 25, 2015. https://www.whitehouse.gov/the-press-office/2015/01/25/us-india-joint-strategic-vision-asia-pacific-and-indian-ocean-region.

———. "Vision Statement for the U.S.-India Strategic Partnership—'Chalein Saath Saath: Forward Together We Go,'" September 29, 2014. https://www.whitehouse.gov/the-press-office/2014/09/29/vision-statement-us-india-strategic-partnership-chalein-saath-saath-forw.

Wilkes, Tommy, and Manoj Kumar. "India to Renew Labor Law Overhaul Drive to Boost Jobs." *Reuters*. September 22, 2016.

Williams, Paul D. "From Non-Intervention to Non-Indifference: The Origins and Development of the African Union's Security Culture." *African Affairs* 106, no. 423 (March 2007): 253–79.

Wilson, Dominic, and Roopa Purushothaman. "Dreaming With BRICs: The Path to 2050." Global Economics Paper No. 99. New York: Goldman Sachs, October 2003. http://www.goldmansachs.com/our-thinking/archive/archive-pdfs/brics-dream.pdf.

Woetzel, Jonathan, et al. "The Power of Parity: Advancing Women's Equality in India." Shanghai, Mumbai, San Francisco, Minneapolis, Gurgaon, Stamford: McKinsey Global Institute, November 2015.

Wolff, Russell. Interview with the author. In person, May 12, 2015.

World Bank. "Doing Business 2017: Equal Opportunity for All." Washington, DC: World Bank, 2017.

———. "India: Foreign Trade Policy." *web.worldbank.org*, 2007. http://go.worldbank.org/RJEB2JGTC0.

World Bank Group. "Economy Rankings." *Doing Business 2017*, October 2016. http://www.doingbusiness.org/Rankings.

"World Sufi Forum to Spread Islamic Message of Peace, PM Modi to Attend Event in Delhi." *Indian Express*. March 1, 2016.

Wright, Thomas. "Non-Alignment Rises from Dustbin of History." *wsj.com. India Real Time (blog)*, March 22, 2012. http://blogs.wsj.com/indiarealtime/2012/03/22/non-alignment-rises-from-dustbin-of-history/?mod=google_news_blog.

Yamunan, Sruthisagar. "Centre to Review All FTAs and SEZs." *The Hindu*. June 14, 2014.

Yardley, Jim, and Gardiner Harris. "2nd Day of Power Failures Cripples Wide Swath of India." *New York Times*. July 31, 2012.

Yergin, Daniel, and Joseph Stanislaw. *The Commanding Heights: The Battle between Government and the Marketplace*. New York: Simon & Schuster, 1998.

Zakaria, Fareed. *The Post-American World: Release 2.0*. New York and London: W. W. Norton & Company, 2012.

Zhong, Raymond. "Fixing Indian Railways, the Not-So-Little Engine That Could." *Wall Street Journal*. October 6, 2016.

INDEX

Note: Figures and tables are indicated by italic "*f*" and "*t*" following the page number. Endnote material is indicated by italic "*n*" and note number.

Aam Aadmi Party, 143
Abe, Shinzo, 99
Act East policy, 173
Additive
    manufacturing
    (3D printing), 187
Advani, L. K., 118
Advertising revenue,
    79–80, 263*n*42
Affirmative action,
    3–4, 23–24
Afghanistan
    Afghanistan-Pakistan
    Transit Trade
    Agreement
    (2011), 132
    Haqqani Network in,
    210, 226
    India as bilateral
    donor to, 219
    India-Pakistan
    tensions over, 132

U.S. invasion of
    (2001), 225, 227
Africa
    India-Africa Forum
    Summit (2008,
    2011, 2015), 176
    India as bilateral
    donor to,
    219–220
African Union (AU), 48,
    156–157
Agreement on
    Government
    Procurement, 145
Agriculture sector,
    185, 203
Ahluwalia, Montek
    Singh, 57, 144
AIIB. *See* Asian
    Infrastructure
    Investment
    Bank (AIIB)

Aircraft industry, 200
al-Assad, Bashar, 137
Albright,
    Madeleine, 225
Alden, Edward, 116
All-India Ulama
    and Mashaikha
    Board, 124
Amazon Web
    Services, 113
Ambani, Dhirubhai, 84
Ambassador (auto), 184
APEC. *See* Asia
    Pacific Economic
    Cooperation
    (APEC)
Apprenticeship Act
    (1961), 204
Apprenticeships,
    204, 205
Arab League, 138, 139
Arab Spring, 137, 228

Arthashastra (Chanakya)
authorship
debate, 256*n*4
management books
based on, 37–38, 41
mandala theory, 40,
54, 129, 178
Nehru's study
of, 53–54
strategic statecraft
based on, 40–41,
62, 128, 173, 178
Art of War (Sun Tzu), 39
ASEAN Regional
Forum, 173,
174, 177
Asian balance of power,
97, 102, 174–175,
207, 210, 224,
245–246. *See also*
individual countries
Asian Development
Bank, 28–29, 172
Asian Infrastructure
Investment Bank
(AIIB), 164, 169,
171–172, 224
Asia Pacific Economic
Cooperation
(APEC), 147, 164,
218–219, 220
Asia Society, New York,
60, 77–78
Aspen Institute, 87
AU. *See* African
Union (AU)
Australia Group,
165–166
Automation, 187, 188, 195
Automobile industry.
See also individual
companies and
car models

cross-country
comparisons,
159, 191
as employment
multiplier in
U.S., 199
in India, 173, 184–185,
191–200, 197*t*
Automotive Mission
Plan 2026
(India), 193
Autonomy. *See* Strategic
autonomy theory
Azad, Maulana, 63
Azevêdo, Roberto,
111–112

Bajaj, Rahul,
82, 263*n*48
Bal, Sambit, 179
Balakrishnan, Ajit, 78
Bandung Afro-Asian
Conference
(1955), 47
Banerjee, Chandrajit,
148
Banerjee, Mamata,
142–143
Bangladesh, 16, 177
garment industry,
90, 190
as member of
BIMSTEC,
170, 177
relations with China,
103, 178
relations with
India, 16
Bank of England, 76
Barracuda (ship), 105
BASIC group (Brazil-
South Africa-India-
China), 167

Bay of Bengal Initiative
for Multisectoral
Technical and
Economic
Cooperation
(BIMSTEC),
170, 177
BCCI. *See* Board of
Control for Cricket
in India (BCCI)
Beijing Consensus, 68
Bergsten, C. Fred,
146–147
Bhagwati, Jagdish, 58,
89–90, 144
Bharati, Uma, 142
Bharatiya Janata Party
(BJP). *See also*
individual leaders
on ancient Indian
trade, 70, 72
economic reforms
under, 55–56
election results,
16, 78–79
founding of, 20
on India as global
power, 32
influence of indigenous
knowledge
traditions on,
53–54, 62
as leader of
NDA, 77
movement to build
Ram temple,
4, 20–21
platform of, 20–21
promotion of Hindu
identity and
culture, 20, 22,
54, 123
proposes GST bill, 24

views on relations with U.S., 60–61, 118
Bharatiya Mazdoor Sangh, 90
Bhargava, R. C., 199
Bhartia, Hari, 86
Bhartia, Shobhana, 32
Bharti Airtel, 78, 81
Bhutan, as member of BIMSTEC, 170, 177
Biden, Joseph, 221
Bill and Melinda Gates Foundation, 151
BIMSTEC. See Bay of Bengal Initiative for Multisectoral Technical and Economic Cooperation (BIMSTEC)
bin Laden, Osama, 225–226
Bishop, Julie, 175
BJP. See Bharatiya Janata Party (BJP)
Blackwill, Robert D., 61
Board of Control for Cricket in India (BCCI), 179–180
Boeing, 88
Bofors, 75
Bollywood, 80
Bombay Club/Bombay House, 82, 263n48
Border disputes, 126–128
BoschRexroth, 194
Brazil. See also IBSA Dialogue Forum
BASIC group agreements, 167
as member of G4, 98
protectionist rankings, 110
slowed growth in, 29

Brazil-Russia-India-China-South Africa (BRICS), 7, 164. See also New Development Bank (NDB)
BRICS Business Council, 87
coordination of governance, 169–172, 224
"Dreaming with BRICs" report, 26, 78, 169
Buddhism, 38, 51, 64
Burns, Nicholas, 11, 212, 216, 222–223, 234–235
Bush, George W. and administration, 26, 109, 208, 210, 212, 225, 228, 233
Business Sutra (Pattanaik), 42

Canada
H-1B approved petitions, 114, 115t
within top ten economies, 101
Carnegie Corporation, 239
Carter, Ashton, 107, 120
Center for Automotive Research, Michigan, 199
Central Tibetan Administration (CTA), 127
Centre for Policy Research, Non-Alignment 2.0, 59–60

CFR. See Council on Foreign Relations (CFR), Independent Task Force Report on U.S.-India Relations
Chanakya. See Arthashastra (Chanakya)
Chanakya's 7 Secrets of Leadership (book), 37–38
Chaudhuri, Pramit Pal, 104
Chicago Council on Global Affairs survey, 213–214, 214f
Chicago World's Fair (1893), 49
China. See also Brazil-Russia-India-China-South Africa (BRICS); individual agreements
AIIB and, 172
auto industry, 192, 196
BASIC group agreements, 167
Belt and Road Initiative (2017), 128, 129
China-Pakistan Economic Corridor, 128
Confucius Institutes, 63
as constraint on India, 126–133

China (*Cont.*)
  decline of
    workforce, 202
  economic growth, 8,
    128–129
  H-1B approved
    petitions, 114, 115*t*
  history of permanent
    seat on UNSC
    for, 97
  Indian Ocean
    maritime relations
    and development,
    103–104
  manufacturing
    sector, 186
  maps claiming Indian
    territory, 126–127
  Middle Kingdom
    concept, 38–39
  nonsupportive of
    India's bid for NSG
    membership, 128
  panchsheel principles
    agreement with
    India, 47
  projected population
    growth (2015–2050),
    13, 13*t*
  protectionist
    rankings, 110
  reciprocal human
    rights reports,
    151–152
  relations and trade
    with India, 129,
    145, 168–169, 201
  relations with
    Bangladesh,
    103, 178
  relations with
    Pakistan, 165–166
  relations with Sri
    Lanka, 103, 128–129
  rural vs. urban
    population, 140
  skilled trade
    apprentices, 204
  slowed growth
    in, 28–29
  South Asia trading
    partners, 178
  TPP negotiations
    and, 146
  trade with U.S., 217
  UNHRC voting
    comparisons, 136
  World Bank,
    Overall Trade
    Restrictiveness
    Index, 110
"China is Not the
    Most Highly
    Protectionist
    Big Country"
    (Huang, Lardy, and
    Kolb), 110
CICA. *See* Conference
    on Interaction and
    Confidence- Building
    in Asia (CICA)
CII. *See* Confederation
    of Indian Industry
    (CII)
Civil-nuclear agreement
    with U.S. (2008),
    25, 26, 31, 57, 59,
    109, 118, 165
Clean India (Swachh
    Bharat), 15
Climate change
  global collaboration
    on, 211
  India's approach to,
    164, 166–168
  Paris Agreement
    negotiations, 8,
    167–168
Clinton, Bill and
    administration, 60,
    84, 109, 209
Clinton, Hillary, as
    secretary of state,
    119, 232–233
Cohen, Stephen P., 25, 31
Colgate-Palmolive, 194
Commerce and
    Industry, Ministry
    of, 78, 86
Commonwealth, 154
Communist Party of
    India (Marxist)
    (CPI/M), 56,
    57, 118
Community of
    Democracies, 152,
    229, 230
"Company Raj" period,
    72. *See also* East
    India Company
Comprehensive Test Ban
    Treaty, 109
Confederation of
    All-India Traders,
    143, *144*
Confederation of Indian
    Industry (CII), 78,
    86, 87, 148, 205
Conference of
    Parties talks. *See*
    Climate change
Conference on
    Interaction and
    Confidence-
    Building in Asia
    (CICA), 164,
    169, 174
Congress Party. *See*
    Indian National
    Congress
*Conquering the
    Chaos: Win*

*in India, Win
Everywhere*
(Venkatesan), 85
Corporate Chanakya
(book), 37–38
Corruption, reputation
for, 96, 109–110
Corus, 83
Council on Foreign
Relations (CFR),
Independent Task
Force Report
on U.S.-India
Relations, 30, 180,
214–215, 216–217,
220–222, 227,
230–231, 233–235,
238, 240–242
Covey, Stephen, 41
Cow protection vigilante
groups, 21–22,
124, 158
CPI/M. *See* Communist
Party of India
(Marxist) (CPI/M)
Creative incrementalism,
use of term, 57
Cricket, 80, 81, 179–181
Culture, Ministry of,
64, 105
Curzon, George,
Lord Curzon of
Kedleston, 102

Daewoo Motors, 83
Da Gama, Vasco,
101–103
Dalai Lama, 127
Das, Gurcharan,
41, 69–70
Das, Tarun, 78, 87
Dasgupta, Gurudas, 119
Dasgupta, Swapan, 28
Datta-Ray, Deep K., 41

Defense exports, 14,
106, 224
Delhi-Mumbai
Industrial
Corridor, 201
Democracy tax, 25, 254n32
Democratic elections, 140,
227–228, 229–230
*Difficulty of Being Good,
The* (Das), 41
Discovery of India
(Nehru), 53–54
Domestic welfare
policies, 55, 89
Donnan, Shawn, 113
Doordarshan (state-run
tv), 40, 76, 79, 80
Doval, Ajit, 132
Drain inspector's report,
use of term, 150
Dravida Munnetra
Kazhagam (DMK)
(Tamil), 155
Drèze, Jean, 58
Drezner, Daniel,
168–169
Dutch East India
Company, 69
Dutt, Barkha, 81

East Asia Summit
(EAS), 173
East India
Company, 44, 72
Echeverri-Gent, John, 19
ECI. *See* Election
Commission of
India (ECI)
Eck, Diana, 38
Economic
nationalism, 55
Economic openings,
in India,
67–91. *See also*

Manufacturing and
industrialization,
in India
business of
government, 87–91
defense exports, 106
global business
trends, 82–87
history of global
trade, 69–79, 71f
IMF reforms, 76–77
information
technology (IT),
82, 84–85
Make in India
campaign, 88–89
state-controlled
industrial-
ization, 73–75
telecom and television
revolution, 79–81
Economic self-reliance,
history of, 43–46,
52, 54–59, 72–77,
109, 218
*Economic Survey
2015–2016* (India),
30, 148
Editors' Guild, 149
Election Commission
of India (ECI), 23,
153–154, 230
Electricity, 15
End Use Monitoring
agreement (2009)
(U.S.-India),
119–120
English language use, 122
Environmental Goods
Agreement, 145
Ernst & Young, 205
European Union (EU),
FTA negotiations
with India, 145

External Affairs,
     Ministry of, 63, 88,
     98, 139, 229, 235

Fabian socialism, 45, 55
Facebook, 88
     Free Basics offer, 72
Farid, Baba, 124
Faurecia, 194
FCRA. *See* Foreign
     Contribution
     Regulation
     Act (FCRA)
FDI. *See* Foreign direct
     investment (FDI),
     in India
Federation of Indian
     Chambers of
     Commerce and
     Industry (FICCI)
     BRICS Business
     Council, 87
Figo Aspire Job 1
     (auto), 195
Flex Ltd., 201
Food security programs,
     111–113
Ford Foundation, 150,
     151, 236, 239
Ford India, 195–197
Ford Motor Company,
     83, 184, 192
Foreign Contribution
     Regulation Act
     (FCRA), 150–152
Foreign direct
     investment (FDI),
     in India, 55–56,
     57, 141–143, 144,
     200–201
Foreign hand, use of
     term, 74–75, 150
Foreign language and
     area studies, in

U.S., 236–242,
     237–239t
Foxconn, 200–201, 203
Freedom of navigation.
     See Maritime
     freedom of
     navigation
Free Trade Area of
     the Asia Pacific
     potential, 221
Friedman, Tom, 84
Future Group, 42

Gabbard, Tulsi, 123
Gallup World Poll, 33
Gandhi, Indira, 20, 55,
     63, 74–75, 150
Gandhi, Mohandas K.,
     19, 20, 43–45, 53,
     55, 57, 59, 72, 150
Gandhi, Rahul, 142
Gandhi, Rajiv, 4,
     19, 75, 79
Ganguly, Meenakshi,
     151, 154
Garment industry, 90,
     190. *See also* Textile
     industry
General Electric
     (GE), 113
General Motors, 184, 192
Germany
     auto industry, 191, 192
     country
     comparisons to, 17
     as member of G4, 98
     seeks UNSC
     permanent
     seat, 234
     skilled trade
     apprentices, 204
Ghose, Arundhati, 109
Global Coalition to
     Counter ISIL, 139

Goh Chok Tong, 173
Goldman Sachs,
     "Dreaming with
     BRICs" report, 26,
     78, 169
Gold sales, 75–76
Goodman, Allen, 240
Goods and services tax
     (GST), 24–25, 89,
     186, 188, 189, 190
Goswami, Arnab, 34, 81
Gradualism, in
     economic reform,
     57, 89, 141–144,
     191–192. *See
     also* Economic
     openings, in India;
     India's preference
     for caution
Greenpeace India, 151
Group of Eight (G8), 26
Group of Four
     (G4), 98–99
Group of Seven (G7),
     100–101
Group of Twenty (G20),
     6, 26, 100, 218
GST. *See* Goods and
     services tax (GST)
Guha, Ramachandra, 27
Gujral, I. K., 177
Gupta, Shekhar, 26, 122

Haqqani Network,
     210, 226
Harley-Davidson, 113
Harris, Harry, 120–121
Heritage Foundation,
     economic freedom
     index, 109–110
Hindi language use,
     121–122
Hind Swaraj (M.
     Gandhi), 44

Hinduism, cosmology
    of, 38
Hindu-Muslim riots
    Gujarat (2002), 21
    Uttar Pradesh
    (2013), 21
Hindu nationalism, 16,
    43, 54, 231
Hindu rate of growth,
    use of term, 75
Hindustan Motors, 184, 196
Hitachi Hi-Rel
    Power, 194
Hollande, François,
    167–168
Home Ministry, 127, 151,
    157–158
H-1B approved
    petitions,
    113–117, 115*t*
HRW. *See* Human Rights
    Watch (HRW)
Huang, Zixuan, 110
Huawei, 201
Hu Jintao, 169
Human Rights Watch
    (HRW), 135–136,
    151, 154–155, 229
Hyundai, 194

IBEF. *See* India
    Brand Equity
    Foundation (IBEF)
IBSA Dialogue Forum
    (India-Brazil-South
    Africa), 137–138,
    155, 164, 171, 232
IDSA. *See* Institute
    for Defence
    and Strategic
    Analyses (IDSA)
IEA. *See* International
    Energy
    Agency (IEA)

IFES. *See* International
    Foundation
    for Electoral
    Systems (IFES)
IMF. *See* International
    Monetary
    Fund (IMF)
Independence and
    self-rule, 43–45
India-Africa Forum
    Summit (2008,
    2011, 2015), 176
India and the world,
    37–66. *See*
    also Economic
    openings, in
    India; Military
    modernization
    and defense, in
    India; Multilateral
    diplomacy, India's
    approach to
    autonomy,
    sovereignty,
    *nonalign-
    ment*, 59–62
    diverse political
    landscape, 52–53
    emissary, Swami
    Vivekananda and
    soft power, 49–52
    as G20 member, 218
    global strategic
    partnerships, 60–61
    importance of
    self-reliance, 54–59
    indigenous Indian
    knowledge, 53–54
    knowledge traditions
    and, 37–43
    as member of WTO,
    56, 115–117, 145–146
    nonalignment, Nehru
    and autonomy

    in international
    relations, 46–48
    poverty levels and
    reduction, 58–59
    presentation of Indian
    values abroad,
    Vivekananda's
    legacy, 62–65
    self-reliance,
    Gandhi and
    self-rule, 43–46
    summary conclusion,
    243–246
India and trade
    relations. *See*
    also World Trade
    Organization
    (WTO); *individual
    trade agreements
    by name*
    history of global,
    69–79, 71*f*
    multilateral trade
    accords, 110–111
    potential trade in
    Free Trade Area
    of the Asia Pacific
    region, 221
    potential trade with
    Pakistan, 178
    preference for caution
    with, 145–148
    scope of
    agreements, 145
    trade with China, 129,
    145, 168–169
    trade with Japan,
    129, 190
    trade with U.S., 129,
    217–218, 221–222
World Bank,
    Overall Trade
    Restrictiveness
    Index, 110

India Brand Equity
Foundation
(IBEF), 78, 86, 87
India: Emergent Power?
(Cohen and
Park), 25
India International
Institute of
Democracy
and Election
Management
(IIIDEM), 153–154
Indian Americans,
role in politics/
business, 240
Indian Council for
Cultural Relations
(ICCR), 63–64
Indian Council for
Research in
International
Economic
Relations, 142
Indian Home Rule (M.
Gandhi), 44
Indian Institutes of
Technology, 204
Indian National Congress
Avadi Resolution
(1955), 73–74
decline in dominance
of, 19–20, 22
economic reforms
under, 55, 91
Indian Ocean
trade, 70
influence of
indigenous
knowledge
traditions on, 53–54
Nehru's legacy and,
59–60, 73–75
poverty reduction
approach, 58

proposes GST bill, 24
Indian Navy, 102–108
Indian Ocean Naval
Symposium
(IONS), 164, 176
Indian Ocean Rim
Association
(IORA), 164,
175–176
Indian Premier League
(IPL), 179
"Indian Strategic
Thought"
(Tanham), 25
Indian Workers
Union (Bharatiya
Mazdoor
Sangh), 56
India's Daughter (BBC
documentary), 149
IndiaSpend.com, 140
India's preference for
caution, 125–159
China and Pakistan as
constraints, 126–133
leading power path
and, 158–159
nonalignment and
nonintervention,
133–139
politics of domestic
reforms, 140–144
role of democracy
and, 152–158
trade agreements and,
145–148
UNSC deliberation
of conflicts and,
136–139
India's rightful
place, 95–124
H-1B approved
petitions,
113–117, 115t

multilateral trade
accords, 110–111
as preeminent Indian
Ocean power,
101–108
pride of place
and, 97–101
seeks UNSC permanent
seat, 97–99
sovereign rights and
global agreements,
108–113
strategic cooperation
and Indian
sovereignty, 117–121
Vivekananda's legacy,
121–124
India's time has come,
introduction, 3–35
ambition of global
leadership,
11–12, 25–35
domestic
vulnerabilities,
14–15, 17, 27, 28
economic growth,
5–6, 12–13, 15,
18, 20–30
as G20 member, 6
IMF data, 12–13, 12t,
29–30, 29t
maritime security
strategy, 11
as member
of WTO, 6
middle class, 13–14, 26
per capita
income, 15, 16
poverty levels and
reduction, 14–15
space program, 14
Indonesia
World Bank,
Overall Trade

Restrictiveness
    Index, 110
Indo-Tibet Border
    Police, 127–128
Industrial Disputes
    Act, 90
Industrial Policy
    and Promotion
    Department, 200
Indus Waters
    Treaty (India-
    Pakistan), 131
Information and
    Broadcasting,
    Ministry of, 80
Information technology
    (IT), in India, 26
    early support for, 75
    economic impact,
        116, 185
    as global opening,
        82, 84–85
    labor mobility and
        visas, 113–117
    manufacturing and,
        15, 193
Information Technology
    Agreement
    (2015), 145
Infosys, 78, 84, 113
Institute for Defence
    and Strategic
    Analyses (IDSA),
    Ancient Indigenous
    Historical
    Knowledge
    initiative, 40–41
Institute for
    International
    Education, 240
International Chamber
    of Commerce,
    Open Markets
    Index, 110

International Cricket
    Council (ICC),
    179–180
International Day of
    Yoga, 95, 122–123
International Energy
    Agency (IEA), 218
    India Energy Outlook
    report (2015), 220
International
    Foundation for
    Electoral Systems
    (IFES), 154, 230
International IDEA, 154
International Institute
    for Strategic
    Studies, 14
International Labour
    Organization, on
    female labor-force
    participation, 15–16
International Monetary
    Fund (IMF), 4
    BRICS alternative to,
        170, 171–172
    delays in reforms,
        171–172
    India's projected
        percentage of
        global GDP, 244
    need for emerging
        countries'
        representation at,
        6–7, 99–100
    ranking of global
        economies, 12–13,
        12t, 29–30, 29t
    Rao government
        request for
        assistance, 76
IONS. See Indian
    Ocean Naval
    Symposium
    (IONS)

IORA. See Indian
    Ocean Rim
    Association
    (IORA)
Iran, relations with
    India, 215
Islam, 124
Islamic State (IS), 62,
    124, 139, 214, 215
Italy, 101
ITEC (Indian Technical
    and Economic
    Cooperation
    Program), 154

Jaguar Land Rover
    (auto), 83, 192
Jainism, 38
Jaishankar, Dhruva, 54
Jaishankar, S., 95–96,
    102, 104
Jaish-e-Muhammad, 226
Jaitley, Arun, 100
Japan
    joins Malabar (Naval
        Exercise), 173, 222
    as member of G4, 98
    planned investment
        in India, 201
    seeks UNSC
        permanent seat, 98
    skilled trade
        apprentices, 204
    Strategic and Global
        Partnership with
        India, 173
    TPP negotiations
        and, 146
    trade with India,
        129, 190
Javadekar, Prakash, 168
Joint venture partner
    approach (CFR),
    216–217

Jubilant Bhartia
group, 86
Judicial system, of
India, 23

Kamath, K. V., 170
Kapur, Muneesh, 100
Karat, Prakash, 118
Kargil War (1999), 209
Kautilya. *See*
Arthashastra
(Chanakya)
"Kautilya" (Ramesh), 54
Kearns, Kel, 195, 198
Khan, A. Q., 165–166
Khilnani, Sunil, 26
Khurshid, Salman, 175
Khusrau, Amir, 124
King, Charles, 235, 240
King, Martin Luther, Jr., 45
Knowledge economy, 68
Knowledge traditions, in
India, 37–43, 53–54.
*See also individual
leaders, traditions
and texts*
Kolb, Melina, 110
Korean War
mediation, 46–47
KPMG, CEO survey
(2016), 30
Kreisberg, Paul, 75
Krishna, Raj, 75
Krishna, S. M., 232–233

Labor law reform, 24,
89–91, 188–191
Labor unions and
strikes, 90–91
Labour Bureau,
202–203, 282*n*55
Lagarde, Christine, 16
Lakhvi, Zakiur
Rehman, 226

Land acquisition reform,
24, 89, 91, 188–189
Lardy, Nicholas R., 110
Largest economies data,
12*t*, 29*t*
Lashkar-e-Taiba,
130, 226
Leading power, use of
term, 66, 95–96,
121, 158, 212
Left Front, 78–79
Left wing, use of
term, 52
Legislation. *See
individual countries*
LEMOA (Logistics
Exchange
Memorandum of
Agreement) (U.S.-
India), 107–108,
118–119, 120
Lenovo, 201
Liberal democratic
norms, 228–229
Lockheed Martin,
88, 200
Look East policy, 173

MacArthur
Foundation, 239
Machiavelli, 39–40
Madhav, Ram, 28
Mahabharata, 38, 41
Mahindra, Anand, 32,
83, 85, 88, 193
Mahindra and
Mahindra, 32, 83,
192, 196
Make in India
campaign, 88–89,
176, 200, 201, 203
Malabar (Naval
Exercise), 173, 222
Maldives, 103

Mandala theory, 40, 54,
129, 178
Mandela, Nelson, 175
Manufacturing and
industrialization,
in India, 45, 73–74,
183–206
auto industry,
184–185, *184*,
191–200, 197*t*
competitiveness,
185–191
increase in FDI
and, 201
Make in India
campaign, 200,
201, 203
Sanand Industrial
Estate, 194–198
workforce development,
202–206
Maps
Chinese maps
claiming Indian
territory, 126–127
overseas trade of India
(2300 BC-800
AD), 71*f*
Maritime freedom
of navigation,
106–107, 120–121,
212, 224–225
Maruti Suzuki, 14, 191,
196, 199–200
Maruti Udyog, 190–191
Mattoo, Amitabh, 27
Mauritius, 105
Mavriplis, Catherine, 14
Mayawati, Prabhu
Das, 142
Mayo, Katherine, 150
McKinsey Global
Institute, 13–14, 15,
188, 203

McLarty Associates, 67
McMahon Line
    (1814), 126
Mehta, Nalin, 79–80
Menon, Shivshankar, 27,
    54, 59, 139
Merkel, Angela, 99, 168
Meswani, Hital, 84
Military modernization
    and defense, in
    India, 11, 14, 17,
    30, 102, 133–139,
    223–224. *See also*
    Indian Navy
Miller, Manjari
    Chatterjee, 43
Missile Technology
    Control Regime
    (MTCR), 165
Mobile/smartphones,
    81, 201
Modi, Narendra, 6
    on anti-Muslim
        violence, 22
    approval ratings, 33
    as chief minister of
        Gujarat, 51–52, 194
    economic reforms
        under, 21, 69,
        87–91, 105, 202, 217
    election of, 96
    expansion of
        India-Africa Forum
        Summit, 176
    foreign policy of, 35,
        48, 99, 105–108,
        167, 176
    improvements
        to business
        environment,
        187, 189
    mobile banking, 81
    National Skill India
        Mission, 205

Non-Aligned
    Movement
    summit, 48
promotion of India's
    cultural heritage,
    122–124
relations with U.S.,
    60, 223
solar alliance with
    France, 167–168
sovereign rights and
    trade positions of
    Modi government,
    48, 112, 117
speech excerpts, 8–9,
    18, 24, 31–32, 116,
    173, 243, 255n56,
    265n7, 268n50,
    270n67
trade negotiations,
    112, 113, 117
transition to leading
    power, 65–66, 212
use of Hindi
    language, 121–122
on Vivekananda,
    51–52, 62, 121, 163
Mohan, C. Raja, 17–18,
    60, 102, 103
Mohan, Rakesh, 99–100
Moody's, 201
Mother India
    (Mayo), 150
MTCR. *See* Missile
    Technology Control
    Regime (MTCR)
Multilateral diplomacy,
    India's approach to,
    163–181
    AIIB and, 164,
        171–172
    ASEAN and other
        Asian alliances,
        172–175

BRICS and, 164,
        169–171
    creation of alternative
        institutions, 168,
        175–176
    dominant roles,
        178–181
    forum shopping,
        168–169
    global regime
        memberships and,
        164–168
    IBSA Dialogue
        Forum and,
        164, 171
    regional imperative
        and, 176–178
Mumbai attacks (2008),
    104, 130, 131,
    210, 226
Mumbai Consensus,
    proposed, 67–68
Murdoch, Rupert, 80
Myanmar, as member
    of BIMSTEC,
    170, 177

Naidu, N.
    Chandrababu, 78
Naidu, Venkaiah, 149
NAM. *See* Non-Aligned
    Movement (NAM)
Nandy, Ashis, 76
Narlikar, Amrita, 41, 43
Narlikar, Aruna, 41, 43
Natalegawa, Marty, 175
National Association
    of Software
    and Services
    Companies
    (NASSCOM), 5
National Democratic
    Alliance (NDA),
    32, 77, 141

National Employability
  Through
  Apprenticeship
  Program
  (NETAP), 205
National Export
  Initiative, 210
National Institution for
  Transforming India
  Aayog, 13, 58–59, 88
National Manufacturing
  Competitiveness
  Council, 185–186
National Skill
  Development
  Corporation
  (NSDC), 199, 205
National Skill India
  Mission, 205
NATO. *See* North
  Atlantic Treaty
  Organization
  (NATO)
Natural allies, use of
  term, 60, 65, 212
Natural History (Pliny
  the Elder), 70
NDA. *See* National
  Democratic
  Alliance (NDA)
NDB. *See* New
  Development
  Bank (NDB)
NDTV, 149
Nehru, Jawaharlal.
  See also Indian
  National Congress;
  Non-Aligned
  Movement (NAM)
  declines offer of
  UNSC permanent
  seat, 97
  Fabian socialism
  and, 45, 55

grants asylum to
  Dalai Lama, 127
  as leader in Indian
  National
  Congress, 19
  legacy of, 31, 45,
  46–48, 59–60, 61,
  72–75, 228
  on relations with
  China, 126
  study of
  Arthashastra, 53–54
  on Vivekananda,
  62–63
Nehruvian Socialism,
  use of term, 75
Nepal
  Madhesi protests
  and, 156
  as member of
  BIMSTEC, 170, 177
  relations with India,
  156, 177
NETAP. *See* National
  Employability
  Through
  Apprenticeship
  Program (NETAP)
*New Arthashastra:
  A Security Strategy
  for India, The*
  (HarperCollins
  India), 41
New Development
  Bank (NDB), 169,
  170–171, 172, 224
Newshour, The (tv
  show), 34
New York City
  Marathon
  sponsors, 83
Nikhilananda, Swami, 51
Nilekani, Nandan, 82,
  85, 86, 244

Nilekani, Rohini, 85
Ninan, T. N., 199
Non-Aligned Movement
  (NAM), 8, 46–48,
  61, 228
Non-Alignment 2.0
  (Centre for Policy
  Research), 59–60
Nonalignment and
  nonintervention
  legacy, 46–48,
  59–62, 125, 133–139,
  212, 214–217
"Non-Alignment Rises
  from Dustbin of
  History" (*Wall
  Street Journal*), 60
Nongovernmental
  organizations
  (NGOs), and
  FCRA regulation,
  150–152
Nonintervention. *See*
  Nonalignment and
  nonintervention
  legacy
Nonproliferation stance,
  shifts in, 108–109,
  166, 211
Nonviolent civil
  disobedience,
  44–45
North Atlantic Treaty
  Organization
  (NATO), 47–48,
  137, 139
NSDC. *See* National
  Skill Development
  Corporation
  (NSDC)
Nuclear weapons
  capability, of India,
  18, 25, 26, 109,
  129–130, 209

Nuclear
    Non-proliferation
    Treaty (NPT),
    108–109, 164, 165
Nuclear Suppliers
    Group (NSG), 128,
    165–166

Obama, Barack and
    administration,
    107, 113, 146,
    210, 231
    support for Indian
    membership in
    nonproliferation
    regimes, 98–99, 166
OECD. See
    Organization
    for Economic
    Cooperation and
    Development
    (OECD)
Ogden, Chris, 32
Oil imports, to
    India, 220
Ollapally, Deepa, 27
Olmsted and Vaux, 49
100,000 Strong, 236
Organisation
    Internationale des
    Constructeurs
    d'Automobiles, 192
Organization for
    Economic
    Cooperation and
    Development
    (OECD), 218–220

Padmini (auto), 184, 185
Pakistan, 103
    Afghanistan-Pakistan
    Transit Trade
    Agreement
    (2011), 132

China-Pakistan
    Economic
    Corridor, 128
Indus Waters
    Treaty (India-
    Pakistan), 131
as member of
    SCO, 174
nuclear capabilities,
    128, 129, 131–132
potential trade with
    India, 178
relations with
    India, 16–17,
    126–133, 178
relations with U.S.,
    209–210, 215–216,
    225–227
seeks membership in
    NSG, 165–166
terrorist groups in,
    104, 128, 129–133,
    216, 225–226
Panagariya, Arvind,
    58–59, 74, 75,
    77, 89–90
Panchsheel principles
    agreement with
    China, 47
Panda, Baijayant "Jay," 7
Pandit, Vijaya
    Lakshmi, 97
Paris Agreement
    negotiations, 8,
    167–168
Park, Richard, 25
Parrikar, Manohar, 107,
    120–121
Passport to India
    initiative,
    Ohio State
    University, 236
Pattanaik,
    Devdutt, 41–42

Penguin Books India,
    series on history of
    Indian business, 41
Pew Research
    Center, 33
Philanthropy. See
    also individual
    organizations
    by India's corporate
    titans, 85
    shifts in focus in U.S.,
    239–240
Philippines, H-1B
    approved petitions,
    114, 115t
Piecemeal reform. See
    Gradualism, in
    economic reform
Pininfarina SpA, 192
Pliny the Elder, 70
Political parties. See also
    specific parties
    coordination with
    single-state
    parties, 22–23
    plethora of, 19, 23
"Politics as a Vocation"
    (Weber), 40
Population
    demographics, of
    India, 13, 13t, 32
Portugal, 101–102
Poverty reduction,
    14–15, 58–59
PPP. See Purchasing
    power parity
    (PPP), of India
Premature
    deindustrialization
    (Rodrik), 187–188
Premier Automobile,
    184, 196
Print media, 79
Project Mausam, 105

Public Health
Foundation, 151
Public interest
litigation, 23
Purchasing power parity
(PPP), of India,
6, 29–30, 29*t*, 98,
99–100, 244
Puri, Hardeep Singh,
99, 137–138, 228
Putin, Vladimir, 169

Quraishi, S. Y., 153

Ramesh, Jairam,
27–28, 54
Ram temple, in
Ayodhya, 4, 20–21
Rao, Nirupama, 7
Rao, P. V. Narasimha,
4–5, 54, 75–77
Rashtriya Swayamsevak
Sangh (National
Volunteers'
Association) (RSS),
20, 28, 56, 90,
123, 260*n*8
Rediff.com, 78
Regional Comprehensive
Economic
Partnership
(RCEP), 110, 117,
146, 147
Reincarnation belief, 42
Reliance Industries Ltd.,
42, 81, 84
Religions, in India. *See
also individual
religions*
plurality of, 16,
123–124
secular liberalism
vs. Hindu
nationalism, 22

tensions
among, 21–22
Remittances, 139, 178
Remote white-collar
workforce, 202
Republic TV, 34, 81
Retail industry, 141–144
Rice, Condoleezza, 225
Rice, Susan, 99, 132, 232
Right wing, use of
term, 52, 54
Rockefeller
Foundation, 239
Rodrik, Dani, 187–188
Roussef, Dilma, 99
Roy-Chaudhry,
Rahul, 104
RSS. *See* Rashtriya
Swayamsevak
Sangh (National
Volunteers'
Association) (RSS)
Rural poverty, 15
Russia. *See also*
Brazil-Russia-
India-China-South
Africa (BRICS)
annexation of
Crimean peninsula
(2014), 139,
209, 215
slowed growth in, 29

SAARC. *See* South
Asian Association
for Regional
Cooperation
(SAARC)
Sabharwal, Manish,
203–204
Saeed, Hafiz, 130, 226
Salt March (1930), 44–45
Sanand Industrial
Estate, 194–198

Sangh, Jan, 20
Sangh Parivar, 20, 56
Sanskrit language, 53, 69
Saran, Shyam,
26–27, 38–39
SCO. *See* Shanghai
Cooperation
Organization
(SCO)
Self-reliance (*swadeshi*),
43–46, 52, 54–59,
72–77, 109
Self-Reliance Awakening
Forum (Swadeshi
Jagran Manch), 56
Self-rule (*swaraj*), 43–45,
55, 57–58, 72
Sen, Amartya, 58
Seychelles, 105
Shah, Bulleh, 124
Shanghai Cooperation
Organization
(SCO), 7, 164,
169, 174
Shankar, Uday, 80, 180
Sharma, Ruchir, 188
Shastri, Lal Bahadur, 74
Shukla, Ajai, 106
Shultz, George, 233
Singapore, 89
Singh, Jaswant, 109, 209
Singh, Manmohan
during administration
of, 18, 176, 177, 211
on ancient Indian
trade, 70
approval ratings, 33
civil-nuclear
agreement with
U.S. (2008),
25, 31, 59
discussions with
U.S. at G20
summits, 26, 210

as finance minister,
4–6, 75–77, 79
formation of
BRICS, 169
formation of G4, 98
on national pride, 96
speech excerpts, 9, 25,
31, 70, 76, 96
strategic autonomy, 48
Singh, V. P., 3
Sinha, Yashwant, 119
SIPRI. *See* Stockholm
International Peace
Research Institute
(SIPRI)
Sitharaman, Nirmala,
117, 145
Skilled trade
apprentices, 204
Socialist planning,
post-colonial, 73
Society for Indian
Automotive
Manufacturers, 193,
195–196, 197t, 199
Soni, Ambika, 149–150
South Africa. *See also*
Brazil-Russia-
India-China-South
Africa (BRICS);
IBSA Dialogue
Forum
BASIC group
agreements, 167
South Asian Association
for Regional
Cooperation
(SAARC), 131, 177
South China Sea
disputes, 120–121
South Korea, 76, 135
auto industry, 191, 192
manufacturing
output, 186

views reforms as
opportunity, 89
World Bank, Overall
Trade Restrictiveness
Index, 110
Sovereignty
autonomy and
nonalignment,
59–62
liberal democratic
norms seen as
under domestic
jurisdiction,
228–229
Modi government
trade positions
and rights of, 48,
112, 117
sovereign rights and
global agreements,
108–113
strategic cooperation
and, 117–121
Soviet Union, former
supports UNSC
permanent seat for
India, 97
Space program, 14
Sri Lanka
Lessons Learnt and
Reconciliation
Commission,
155, 156
as member of
BIMSTEC, 170, 177
relations with China,
103, 128–129
relations with India,
64, 156, 178
UNHRC resolutions
and, 211
Sri Padmanabhaswamy
temple,
Kerala, 69–70

Ssangyong Motor, 192
Star India's Hotstar
(app), 80–81
Start-Up India
campaign, 176
Star TV, 80
Stockholm International
Peace Research
Institute (SIPRI),
14, 223
Strategic and Global
Partnership
(India-Japan), 173
Strategic autonomy
theory, 48, 61, 216
Student exchange
programs, 227,
235–237, 236t,
240–242
Subramanian,
Arvind, 57
Sufism, 124
Summers, Larry,
67–68, 244
Sundram Fasteners, 192
Sun Tzu, 39
Suzuki, 173, 190–191, 196
Swadeshi (magazine), 56
Swaraj, Sushma, 119–120
Swatantra Party, 55
Syria, and IBSA
diplomatic efforts,
137–138, 171,
215, 232

Tagore,
Rabindranath, 51
Talbott, Strobe, 109, 209
Tamil Tigers, 4, 134
Tanham, George, 25
Tata, Ratan, 85, 194
Tata Consultancy
Services (TCS),
83–84, 113

Tata Motors, 192,
194–195, 196, 200
Tata Nano (auto), 192,
194–195
Tata Sons, 82, 83
TCS. *See* Tata
Consultancy
Services (TCS)
Teamlease Services, 203
TeamLease
University, 205
TechMahindra, 84
Telecom/television
revolutions, 79–81
Terrorism and terrorist
groups. *See also*
Mumbai attacks
(2008); *individual
terrorist groups*
attacks in India,
130–132, 210, 226
China's UNSC
resolution
vetoes, 128
global coalition
against IS, 139,
214, 215
emanating from
Pakistan, 17, 104,
128, 129–133, 216,
225–226
Tesla, 88
Tetley Tea, 83
Textile industry, 44,
90, 159, 183,
185, 190
Thailand
as member of
BIMSTEC,
170, 177
World Bank,
Overall Trade
Restrictiveness
Index, 110

Thakur, Anurag, 179
Tharoor, Shashi,
call for British
reparations, 72
Thussu, Daya
Kishan, 80
Tibet, sovereignty and
border disputes,
126–128
Times Now (tv
channel), 34, 80–81
Title VIII Grant
Program, 241
"To the Fourth of July"
(Vivekananda), 65
TPP. *See* Trans-Pacific
Partnership (TPP)
Trade in Services
Agreement, 145
Trade relations. *See*
India and trade
relations; World
Trade Organization
(WTO)
Trans-Atlantic Trade
and Investment
Partnership, 146
Trans-Pacific Partnership
(TPP), 145,
146–148, 221
Trump, Donald J. and
administration
abandonment of
TPP, 146
proposed reforms to
H-1B visa program,
116–117
withdrawal from Paris
Agreement, 168

Ukraine, Russian
annexation of
Crimean peninsula
(2014), 139, 209, 215

Uncertain Glory, An (Sen
and Drèze), 58
UN Convention on the
Law of the Seas
(UNCLOS), 224
UN Democracy Fund
(UNDEF), 152,
229, 230
UN Development
Program
(UNDP), 154
UN General Assembly
(UNGA)
India's voting pattern,
135, 231
resolution on
International Day
of Yoga, 123
UN Human Rights
Council (UNHRC),
61, 154–155
country comparison
of abstention votes,
135–136
India's support for
reconciliation in
Sri Lanka, 211
India's voting pattern,
135–136, 138,
155–156, 229
UN Security Council
(UNSC), 6–7
China's vetoes on
designation of
Pakistan-based
terrorists, 128
IBSA diplomacy with
Syrian conflict,
137–138, 171, 232
India's abstention
votes, 136–137
India's preference
for caution and,
136–139

permanent
membership,
97–99, 128, 176,
232, 234
resolution demanding
end of violence by
Syria (2012), 138
resolution on
Libya, 137
Union Bank of
Switzerland, 75
United Kingdom (UK)
colonization of
India, 72, 96
India Act (1784), 72
Tharoor, Shashi call
for reparations, 72
UNHRC voting
comparisons, 136
United Nations (UN).
See also individual
UN agencies
Indian Permanent
Mission to the UN
statement (2014), 136
India's contribution
to peacekeeping
operations, 61–62,
125, 133–134
India's preference for
UN vs. "coalition
of the willing,"
61–62, 121
United Nations
Conference
on Trade and
Development
(UNCTAD)
on India's FDI inflows
(2015), 200
United Progressive
Alliance (UPA), 18,
24, 30, 58. See also
individual leaders

FDI-related reforms,
141, 142–143
India-Africa Forum
Summit (2008,
2011), 176
National
Manufacturing
Policy, 88
national
manufacturing
policy, 185–186
skill development
priority, 204
slowed reforms, 78–79
support for U.S.-
India civil-nuclear
deal, 57, 118
United States (U.S.). See
also U.S. relations
with rising India,
recommendations
for; individual
agencies and
presidents;
individual
agreements
auto industry, 196, 199
celebration of
International Day
of Yoga, 123
civil-nuclear agreement
with India (2008),
25, 26, 31, 57, 59,
109, 118, 165
delays to IMF/World
Bank reforms,
171–172
foreign language
and area studies,
236–242, 237–239t
Global Coalition to
Counter ISIL, 139
H-1B visa program,
114–116

Higher Education
Act (1965), Title VI
appropriations, 238,
240–241
India files complaint
with WTO over
U.S. visa fees,
115–117
Indian FDI in, 211
invasion of
Afghanistan (2001),
225, 227
National Defense
Education Act
(1958), 239
perceived as foreign
hand, 74–75
policies on Syria, 136
relations with India,
26, 60–62, 121,
210, 223
relations with
Pakistan, 209–210,
215–216, 225–227
social divide in, 16,
230–231
student exchange
programs, 227,
235–237, 236t,
240–242
supports UNSC
reform and
expansion of
permanent seats,
97, 98–99, 234
Swami Vivekananda's
oratory and visit
to, 49–50
trade with
China, 217
trade with India, 129,
217–218, 221–222
UNHRC voting
comparisons, 136

United States (U.S.)
(*Cont.*)
World Bank,
Overall Trade
Restrictiveness
Index, 110
Zadroga Act (2010), 115
Universal human rights,
228–229
University of
Chicago, 49
Vivekananda Visiting
Professorship, 64
UPA. *See* United
Progressive Alliance
(UPA)
U.S.-China Strategic
and Economic
Dialogue, 233
U.S. Commission on
International
Religious Freedom
(USCIRF),
148–149, 229
U.S. Federal Election
Commission, 230
U.S.-India Business
Council, 67, 88
U.S.-India Defense Trade
and Technology
Initiative (2011),
106, 224
U.S.-India Joint
Strategic Vision for
the Asia-Pacific and
Indian Ocean, 107,
207–208, 222, 225
U.S.-India Strategic
and Commercial
Dialogue (2015),
232–233
U.S. International
Military Education
and Training
program, 227

U.S. Labor
Department, 229
U.S. relations with
rising India,
recommendations
for, 207–242
align without being
aligned, 212,
214–217
American familiarity
with India, 213,
235–242
bilateral economic
relationship,
217–222
Chicago Council
on Global
Affairs survey,
213–214, 214*f*
cooperation on
democracy, 227–231
diplomacy, 231–235
meaning of strategic
partnership,
222–227
shared interests,
209–214
U.S. State Department,
232–233, 235
Passport to India
initiative, with
Ohio State
University, 236
sends Americans to
Indian embassy in
Yemen, 139
on UNGA voting
patterns, 135
U.S. Human
Rights Reports,
151–152, 229

Vajpayee, Atal Bihari
during administration
of, 18, 32, 177

as foreign
minister, 122
India and the United
States as "natural
allies," 60, 65
on national pride, 96
rapprochement with
U.S., 60, 77–78
speech excerpts, 31, 60
on Vivekananda,
62, 65
Vajpeyi, Ananya, 44
Varshney, Ashutosh, 19
Vedanta Society, 50
Venkatesan, Ravi, 85
Vice News, 34
Vietnam, 107
Vigilante
groups, 21–22
Vivekananda, Swami,
49–52, 62–65, 70,
121–124, 163
Vivekananda Rock
Memorial
Committee,
70, 260*n*8
Vocational training,
204–206

Walt Disney
Company, 116
Wanda Group of
China, 201
Warsaw Pact, 47–48
Washington
Consensus, 68
Wassenaar Arrangement,
165, 166
Weber, Max, 40
Why Growth Matters
(Bhagwati and
Panagariya), 58
Willow (app), 80
WION (tv channel), 81
Wipro, 84

Wisner, Frank G., 222
Wolff, Russell, 179
World as a family
    proverb
    (*vasudhaiva
    kutumbakam*),
    48, 61
World Bank
    on apparel sourcing in
        South Asia, 188
    BRICS alternative
        to, 170
    delays in reforms,
        171–172
    Doing Business
        Index,
        186–187, 279n6
    India on need for
        shareholder
        realignment, 6–7,
        99, 100
    Overall Trade
        Restrictiveness
        Index, 110

poverty benchmarks,
    15, 259n44
remittances data
    (2015), 139
on size of
    manufacturing
    sectors, 186
World Economic Forum
    (WEF), 85–87
    Global Competitiveness
        Report, 187
World Is Flat, The
    (Friedman), 84
World's Parliament
    of Religions
    (1893), 49–50
World Sufi Forum,
    123–124
World Trade
    Organization
    (WTO), 6, 56,
    218–219. *See also*
    H-1B approved
    petitions

Bali Trade
    Facilitation
    Agreement, 111–113
Doha Round (2008),
    55, 110–111
Measures Concerning
    Non-Immigrant
    Visas complaint
    by India, 115–117,
    145–146
movement of natural
    persons (Mode 4),
    113–117, 115t
peace clause (Bali
    Agreement), 111–112
Wronged by Empire
    (Miller), 43

Xiaomi, 201
Xi Jinping, 128, 129

Zakaria, Fareed, 8
Zee TV, 80–81
Zuckerberg, Mark, 122